THE
LISTENER'S
COMPANION

THE GREAT COMPOSERS
AND THEIR WORKS

THE
LISTENER'S
COMPANION

THE GREAT COMPOSERS
AND THEIR WORKS

NICOLAS SLONIMSKY

SCHIRMER TRADE BOOKS
NEW YORK/LONDON/PARIS/SYDNEY/COPENHAGEN/MADRID

For permission to reprint some of the material in this collection, the author gratefully acknowledges the Los Angeles Philharmonic Association and *The Christian Science Monitor*.

Cover illustration: SuperStock Inc.

Schirmer Trade Books
an imprint of the Music Sales Publishing Group

Order No. SCH 10116
International Standard Book Number: 0.8256.7278.3

Exclusive Distributors:
Music Sales Corporation
257 Park Avenue South, New York, NY 10010 USA
Music Sales Limited
8/9 Frith Street, London W1D 3JB England
Music Sales Pty. Limited
120 Rothschild Street, Rosebery, Sydney, NSW 2018, Australia

Printed and bound in the United States of America
by Vicks Lithograph and Printing Corporation

CONTENTS

IV   WOLFGANG AMADEUS MOZART (1756–1791): The Supreme 41

FOREWORD

The foundations of my father's legacy are the rock-solid volumes found in every music library, the indispensable *Baker's Biographical Dictionary of Musicians* and *Music Since 1900*. Compiling and updating successive editions of these works occupied much of his later life, along with writing his autobiography, *Perfect Pitch*, and a more idiosyncratic "reading dictionary," the *Lectionary of Music*. The *Lexicon of Musical Invective*, vituperative reviews of composers' works since Beethoven was, and is, a classic; in a very different way, so is the *Thesaurus of Scales and Melodic Patterns*, a dizzying musical sourcebook greatly valued by composers, arrangers, and performers.

In addition to these and other volumes, he produced a huge number of short pieces over his entire adult life in the United States, appearing first in the *Boston Evening Transcript* and in musical publications in the 1920s. In succeeding decades, his short writings appeared as program notes, reviews, record liner notes, and newspaper and magazine articles on every conceivable musical topic, especially composers, performers, individual works, musical form and technique, national styles, as well as innumerable musical oddities, anecdotes, and minihistories. Each was written for a single specific purpose and publication—he never wrote on spec.

The Listener's Companion includes a small portion of these miscellaneous writings. With few exceptions, these entries have not previously appeared in book form. Most of the biographies were written for the *Christian Science Monitor* during the 1950s and 1960s, and a substantial number of the entries on individual pieces were written as program notes for the Los Angeles Philharmonic and the Little Orchestra Society. The rest were culled from accumulated clippings and carbon copies dating from the 1920s into the 1980s. This considerable time span, and the publications' differing readerships, accounts for interesting variations in perspective, writing style, and level of musical analysis.

In selecting these composers and these works, I was obviously constrained first of all by what exists and, within that, by what groupings might constitute a relatively balanced and complete "chapter" on a major composer and his (alas, there are no women covered in this volume) works. Considering that these writings were individual and unrelated in origin, the coverage turns out to be remarkably broad, though regrettably missing important composers and compositions. I hope that readers will find the book no less valuable for not being all-inclusive.

This volume is all Slonimsky. Nothing inauthentic has been added, written, rewritten, inserted, substituted, elongated, or otherwise corrupted. Nevertheless, these materials could not always be presented together in full exactly as they originally appeared in a newspaper, concert program, or record liner. Editing consisted primarily of cutting repetitive biographical or analytic material. Present-tense references to composers alive at the time of writing have been changed to the past tense and mention of contemporaneous events deleted.

Although he was relatively diligent about retaining manuscript copies and clippings, my father never reworked them for later use. Indeed, I doubt he ever looked at them again. Every piece was written afresh. In compiling this volume, I often found myself comparing two or even three articles on the same piece of music, all different, all differently interesting, with not so much as a phrase repeated. In some such instances I retained and inserted valuable or especially well-written segments from versions not selected.

My father took delight in dropping indigestible words into his writings, little verbal nuts that must be cracked before being swallowed. I have been merciless in retaining all that appeared in my selections. Accordingly, you are warned that, if the meaning of, for instance, "colubrine," "gemmation," "purfling," "Canossa," or "fanfaronade" has slipped your mind, a dictionary—the larger the better—should be kept close at hand.

It is not intended that this book or even its chapters be read straight through in their entirety. The book is conceived as an extended set of program notes anchored in a biographical base, a volume to consult in association with listening to a live or recorded performance, a companion and guide to brief you on the event, designed to expand your musical experience. And if you like a guide/raconteur with humorous anecdotes and spicy stories, you've got the right guy—albeit the risqué parts are sometimes a bit quaint.

This book comes into being as, I hope, a credible addition to the Slonimsky "canon." If it is successful in that regard, thanks are due to a number of musical types who provided valuable guidance to this nonmusician editor. Richard Carlin of Schirmer Books showed the first gleam of the eye, spending days with me in the bowels of the Library of Congress digging the raw materials out of acres of boxes housing the then-uncatalogued Slonimsky collection. When I had sorted and created a preliminary assembly, Dr. Malena Kuss provided an incisive qualitative scan that helped me cook the materials down to a provisional table of contents. Robert Beckhard found some additional articles and reviews in his addictive archival pokings. Styra Avins and Terry Eisinger, the ultimate Brahms mavens, reviewed that chapter for factual and linguistic accuracy. Randy Schoenberg and the entire Schoenberg family responded to my request for permission to quote their eminent relative, and Sabine Feisst provided many specifics as well, plus overnight translation service. Finally, Richard Kassel vetted the entire manuscript, plowing undaunted through the words and the works and the centuries. He pointed out issues resolved by subsequent scholarship, advised on the relative importance of musical works, established the order of entries in each chapter, and proposed cuts and revisions.

The project was animated by my belief that musicians and music-lovers would welcome more Slonimsky writings. No longer can there be new ones, but the trove of which this is part enjoyed only ephemeral exposure at publication and deserves to be explored. In a lifetime that actually exceeded a century, my father was witness, participant, and chronicler of the transformation of his art. Educated in the traditional, he championed the revolutionary. In his first career, as a conductor, he challenged a reluctant public to open its ears and reconsider its assumptions. When he took up the cause with words, he found a second and perhaps less risky career as a musicologist, in which his commitment to the new could be expressed alongside his mastery of the great musical tradition.

For me, compiling this volume has, in a way, extended that long life. In the process, I have reexperienced the flavor of the sixty-two years of our joint existence, and tried to assure that he continues to be heard.

Electra Slonimsky Yourke
New York City
September 1999

PRELUDE: Interview with Myself

My visitor came in without ringing the bell—the door was ajar—and surveyed the rows of bookshelves lining the walls and the orchestral scores lying in artistic disarray on top of the piano with an air of intimate acquaintance with every object in the room.

"L. O. Symkins is my name," he declared, and his voice sounded strangely familiar, like a phonograph recording of one's own words. "I came to ask you how you happened to select musicology as your vocation."

"I did not select musicology," I replied. "Musicology selected or, rather, annexed me."

"I am sure," my visitor observed, "that the annexation was not against your will. You've been called the Scourge of Music Dictionaries, and no one becomes a scourge unwillingly."

"Perhaps you are right. Musicology came to me by way of general lexicography," I said. "Ever since childhood I was fascinated by encyclopedias. I memorized the alphabetical indications on the bindings: 'A to Anno'; 'Annu to Balt'; 'Balt to Brai'; 'Brai to Cast'; 'Cast to Cole'; 'Cole to Dama...'"

My visitor nodded: "Yes, yes! The *Encyclopedia Britannica*." He seemed well versed in lexicographical matters.

"My interest in encyclopedias," I continued, "made me aware of their inadequacies. Some information found in these impressive volumes lacked precision. That annoyed me. Particularly unsatisfactory were the articles about music and musicians. And since I am a professional musician, I naturally began to think of ways and means to secure documentary data from unimpeachable sources, such as birth registers, old programs, and similar documents that would confirm or refute the information in music dictionaries."

"So I suppose you were delighted when you found that musicians were born on wrong dates, that opera stars sang Wagner at the putative age of ten, that Lully was appointed court orchestra leader at thirteen. . ."

"How do you know all this?" I exclaimed. "This is exactly the sort of thing I have been extirpating from the dictionaries. Take the Lully case. According to a highly reputable encyclopedia, he was born in 1639 and was appointed music director of the court orchestra in 1652; that is, at the age of thirteen. But he was really born in 1632 and got his job at twenty, which is precocious enough for anybody. Incidentally, Lully's tercentenary was celebrated on the wrong day all over France. He was born on November 28, 1632, and not on November 29, as most music dictionaries say."

"I suppose you have obtained Lully's birth certificate to prove the date. Undoubtedly you got the exact hour of his birth as well."

"Four-thirty in the afternoon," I replied modestly.

My visitor was silent for a moment. "This . . . chronomusicology is not the only thing that interests you in music, I hope," he said.

"Certainly not. Musicology, as I understand it, covers a lot of ground: musical analysis, musical theory, even musical geography."

"By musical geography you probably mean the mapping of musical regions, particularly those yet unexplored," remarked the visitor.

"Quite so. For instance, I became intrigued by the fact that so few Latin American composers were represented in music dictionaries. So I made a grand tour south of the border, and when I returned, I had two hundred and ninety composers in my musicological bag. I figured out that there is one composer per four hundred forty-three thousand square miles of territory in South America, Central America, and the West Indies. I also drew a map of Latin American dances. The national dance of Chile is the *zamacueca*, and the name fitted very nicely into the elongated strip of Chilean territory on the map."

"How about purely theoretical investigations?"

There was a knowing look in my visitor's eyes. I had a definite feeling that he knew the answers to his questions in advance. Still I decided to go along. I admitted that I was the author of a huge book of newfangled melodic patterns, very serpentine in outward appearance on music paper, complete with master chords that would enable anyone to produce as dissonant a harmony as the heart desires.

"One more question," my guest insisted. "Did you ever invent a word that got into a dictionary?"

"Yes, I did. 'Pandiatonicism.'"

"Pan . . . what?"

"'Pandiatonicism,'" I repeated firmly. "It is the modern technique of free combinatory usage, melodically, contrapuntally, and harmonically, of the seven different tones of the diatonic scale." I was convinced that he could readily supply the definition himself. Anticipating his further importunities, I told him that my polysyllabic creation has been duly incorporated into several American and European music dictionaries.

"Didn't you invent 'invecticon,' too?" he asked.

"No," I replied. "I did not. A friend of mine did, but I used the word for the index in my anthology of criticism entitled *Lexicon of Musical Invective*."

I could not bear the knowing look in my visitor's eyes. "It is now my turn to ask you a question," I said. "Is L. O. Symkins your real name?"

"Why, of course! In fact, it is my surreal name. I am your anagram." He quickly looked at his wristwatch, and I noticed that it was not a wristwatch at all, but a word-counter. "I must really be going," he said. "It is already 861 words o'clock."

The word-counter on my own wrist gave the same number of words in our interview.

JOHANN SEBASTIAN BACH
(1685–1750)
Musical Fountainhead

The word Bach means "brook, stream." It is symbolic that the greatest man of music, Johann Sebastian Bach (1685–1750), should bear such a meaningful name. For Johann Sebastian Bach, music is the fountainhead of crystal waters. The stream divides itself into contrapuntal branches; the speed of the stream varies; the tributaries of intricate counterpoint reach a confluence of harmony; but this confluence is often stirred by turbulent undercurrents, creating a suspended dissonance; it is only after further progress that the final equilibrium is reached, resolving into a final chord, serene and triumphant.

Johann Sebastian Bach came from a remarkable family of musicians. Long before his time, musicians named Bach were famous throughout Thuringia as municipal players, the *Stadtpfeifer*, so that even musicians of different names were commonly described as "the Bachs." The family was clan-conscious and often arranged meetings in the towns of Eisenach (where Johann Sebastian was born), Arnstadt, or Erfurt. At one of these meetings, 120 Bachs made their appearance. They amused themselves by performing popular songs with improvised vocal and instrumental parts in a fine polyphonic manner. These Bachs were expert artisans, but they also possessed jollity. Johann Sebastian himself was greatly interested in his family, and in his later years started a detailed genealogy, which is preserved under the title *The Origin of the Family of Musical Bachs*.

With such a musical background, Bach as a boy was destined to become a professional musician. He was lodged with his elder brother, who held him in strict discipline, never allowing him to go beyond prescribed exercises. But Bach's musical curiosity could not be stifled. In a latticed cabinet in his brother's house there was an alluring object; not a sweet pie, not a sugary confection, but something much more precious to young Bach: a volume of pieces for the harpsichord by various German composers. His brother would not permit him to use the music, but Bach managed to extract the rolled sheets through the lattice openings and copy the music at night by moonlight. An old story relates that he completed his task in six months, a few days each month when the moon was shining. This was the only surreptitious act in Bach's entire life, for it is difficult to find in the annals of music a master more forthright and less tempted by guile than Johann Sebastian Bach.

Intellectual curiosity and a reverence for older masters were the great driving forces of Bach's character as a musician. As a boy of fifteen he started out on his life's career, first as a choirboy, then as an organ player. When he served as an apprentice in North Germany, he undertook a walk of thirty miles to Hamburg, to hear the great organist Johann Adam Reinken. He stopped at a roadside inn, and had two small fish for his meal. To his surprise, he found a coin in each and so was able to provide for the next meal.

Bach's first important position was as an organist in Arnstadt. Only eighteen, he was already well qualified to perform, to compose, and to improvise. But his artistry drove him farther than the requirements of this modest post. He let his musical fancy roam, and was strongly reprimanded by his superiors for using "strange variations" in playing the hymns, which in this unusual form confused the congregation. There was another reason for this reprimand; drawn by the fame of the organist Dietrich Buxtehude (1637–1701), Bach took a leave of absence to make a journey to Lübeck, where Buxtehude held his famous evening concerts. Legend has it that Bach made the entire long journey on foot.

There are indications that Bach hoped to inherit Buxtehude's job in Lübeck after his retirement, but encountered an insurmountable obstacle in the person of the eldest of Buxtehude's five daughters, who was offered to him in marriage as a *conditio sine qua non* for getting the job. (Buxtehude himself had to marry his predecessor's daughter to obtain his Lübeck position.) At another time, Handel also made a trip to Lübeck, and he, too, was deterred from seeking the post by the confrontation with Fräulein Buxtehude.

Bach returned to Arnstadt with renewed zeal for music. At the age of twenty-three he went to Weimar, leaving his cousin, one of the innumerable musical Bachs, in charge of his post at Arnstadt. In Weimar, he wrote most of his great organ works, and in his next place of employment, Cöthen, the greatest of his chamber music works. He conducted the orchestra for Prince Leopold, who himself took part as the player on the viola da gamba. It was in Cöthen that Bach wrote his famous Brandenburg concertos, dedicated to Duke Christian Ludwig of Brandenburg.

Bach learned the art of composition through a diligent study of the vocal and instrumental works of German and Italian composers of the seventeenth century. Sometimes he copied works by contemporary masters; manuscripts extant in Bach's own handwriting without further identification have plagued generations of Bach editors and have at times led to the erroneous attribution of these copies to Bach himself. The chronology of his works is not always easy to establish. Not many original manuscripts have come to us, and very few bear the date of composition.

The circumstances of Bach's life and his teaching in Leipzig are well known, and the records of his pedagogic activities are plentiful. The Thomasschule (St. Thomas School) was an ancient and venerable institution founded in the year 1212 "to uphold and expand Christianity and German culture on a pagan frontier." Bach arrived in Leipzig in 1723, with a family of five children. Charles Sanford Terry, in his biography of Bach, gives a complete account, from the archives of the Thomasschule, of the small things in Bach's domestic routine. Thus we know just what repairs were made in Bach's house, the exact dates when the walls were white-washed, and even the name of the scrubwoman. We know that Bach's kitchen got a new oven. From the birth records we also know that children were born into Bach's family annually. The mortality was high. There was a little girl Bach born in 1723, who died shortly thereafter; there was an imbecile child born to the Bachs in 1724. There was another one who died in infancy in 1725. Finally, in 1726, a daughter was born who not only survived infancy, but eventually got married. There were four more children after her.

Bach's appointment at the Thomasschule did not come without difficulties. The senate of Leipzig, in whose hands the appointment of teachers was placed, first turned to Georg Philipp Telemann (1681–1767), then to Christoph Graupner (1683–1760). Telemann had declined the offer, and Graupner could not accept it because his patron, the landgrave of Hesse, would not release him from his con-tract. When finally the senate invited Bach, a member of that august body declared: "Since it is impossible to get the best, we will have to be satisfied with second best."

Bach's duties were manifold. He was a cantor, director of a chorus of fifty-five boys. The school played a great role in the community, and one of its important civic duties was attending the funerals in town. It was also profitable: the school charged a definite fee, so many groschen for attendance by the entire school, corre-spondingly less if only part of the school attended. The cantor was to receive fifteen groschen for each funeral when the entire choir attended. The town authorities cooperated by arranging funerals in the afternoon, so that lessons would not be missed. Weddings were also profitable: Bach's fee as choir director was one thaler for each wedding.

Discipline at the Thomasschule, as in all German schools of the time, was very severe. The scholars were punished both by fines and by whipping. The use of impertinent language, in Latin or German, was punished by a fine of six pfennigs, and vomiting, even if involuntary, and not as a consequence of drinking, called for a fine of two groschen. Musical faults were punishable, too, and a mistake in singing called for the application of the birch. The rods and birches were in the charge of older boys who were called "purgers" (*Purganten*).

Bach was fortunately relieved of some of the duties of a cantor. To escape the association with extramusical tasks, he preferred to be styled *director musices*. The comparative leisure allowed Bach to compose prodigiously, but there is no evidence that Bach himself or his immediate colleagues ever realized the greatness of the music written by the cantor of the Thomasschule. An early French dictionary sets Bach down as a "skillful composer of polyphonic music," nothing more.

Frederick the Great of Prussia, who was a flute player and a composer himself, wished to see Bach at his Potsdam Palace. When Bach was finally able to accept the invitation, Frederick himself led him through the palace. At the king's request, Bach tested the harpsichords and pianofortes installed in the palace rooms, and improvised a fugue in six parts for the king. Frederick then gave him a theme, which Bach elaborated in the form of a trio for flute, violin, and harpsichord. The final version of the work was in the form of a "puzzle canon." Bach presented it to Frederick with a flattering dedication, in conformity with the custom, to "a sovereign admirable in his music as in all other arts of war and peace."

Bach's works were intended in most part for the practical purpose of instructing young musicians. The technical achievement of Bach's forty-eight preludes and fugues is an unexcelled marvel of creative music. Bach's inventions for keyboard instrument are no less wonderful from the structural point of view. And yet these studies, designed to instruct, possess a beauty of expression that is apparent even to the untutored. In some passages of these works, Bach transcends the limits of harmonic combinations permissible in his time; such moments presage the development of modern music.

With the exception of opera, Bach left the mark of his genius in every musical form. For a modern musician, his music is a treasure trove of fantastically bold contrapuntal and melodic devices; his use of unrelated diminished seventh chords and modulating excursions into the tonality of the Neapolitan sixth comes very close to the techniques of atonality and polytonality. It is even possible, by selecting appropriate passages in Bach's works, to find quasi-dodecaphonic usages.

INSTRUMENTAL WORKS

Chaconne in D Minor for Unaccompanied Violin, from Partita No. 2, BWV 1004 (1720)

Bach's sonatas and partitas for unaccompanied violin present an unexampled challenge. In these works Bach achieved the extraordinary feat of writing counterpoint in two, three, and four voices, and even fugues, on a single stringed instrument. This he achieved by double, triple, and arpeggiated quadruple stops; by dint of harmonic and melodic figurations a rich pattern of modulation is contrived, all this without sacrificing the fluency of the melodic line and the clarity of harmonic progressions.

Bach wrote a group of three sonatas and three partitas for unaccompanied violin in the period between 1718 and 1723, when he was in his middle thirties. In Bach's time, the term "sonata" still retained its etymological meaning "sounded"— that is, to be played on an instrument, without further specification as to form, as distinct from a cantata, meaning "sung." An instrumental sonata was usually in the form of a suite in four movements, alternately slow and fast. A partita (*partita* in Italian means "divided") was an instrumental suite of dance forms, known as "classical suite." It includes an allemande (which means "German" in French, but the reason for this attribution is obscure) in fast Y time; courante (literally, "running"), a rapid dance in T time; sarabande (the origin of the word is dubious, but the form developed in Spain), a stately dance in measured triple time; bourrée (French for "brushwood"), a rapid dance in y time; and gigue, a fast movement in V time.

Bach's Second Partita for Unaccompanied Violin includes the most famous movement ever written for violin solo, the D-Minor Chaconne. A mystery surrounds the etymology and the origin of the chaconne. There is a theory that it was imported from Mexico in the sixteenth century and was originally an unrestrained and orgiastic mestizo dance. If so, then the chaconne lost all its wildness during the passage from Mexico to Europe. The Baroque form of the chaconne is one of the

Muſicaliſches
Opfer
Sr. Königlichen Majeſtät in Preußen ꝛc.
allerunterthänigſt gewidmet
von
Johann Sebaſtian Bach.

Allergnädigſter König,

Ew. Majeſtät weyhe hiermit in tiefſter Unterthänigkeit ein Muſicaliſches Opfer, deſſen edelſter Theil von **Deroſelben** hoher Hand ſelbſt herrühret. Mit einem ehrfurchtsvollen Vergnügen erinnere ich mich annoch der ganz beſondern Königlichen Gnade, da vor einiger Zeit, bey meiner Anweſenheit in Potsdam, **Ew. Majeſtät** ſelbſt, ein Thema zu einer Fuge auf dem Clavier mir vorzuſpielen geruheten, und zugleich allergnädigſt auferlegten, ſolches alſobald in **Deroſelben** höchſten Gegenwart auszuführen. **Ew. Majeſtät** Befehl zu gehorſamen, war meine unterthänigſte Schuldigkeit. Ich bemerkte aber gar bald, daß wegen Mangels nöthiger Vorbereitung, die Ausführung nicht alſo gerathen wollte, als es ein ſo treffliches Thema erforderte. Ich faſſete demnach den Entſchluß, und machte mich ſogleich anheiſchig, dieſes recht Königliche Thema vollkommener auszuarbeiten, und ſodann der Welt bekannt zu machen. Dieſer Vorſatz iſt nunmehro nach Vermögen bewerkſtelliget worden, und er hat keine andere als nur dieſe untadelhafte Abſicht, den Ruhm eines Monarchen, ob gleich nur in einem kleinen Puncte, zu verherrlichen, deſſen Größe und Stärke, gleich wie in allen Kriegs- und Friedens-Wiſſenſchaften, alſo auch beſonders in der Muſik, jedermann bewundern und verehren muß. Ich erkühne mich dieſes unterthänigſte Bitten hinzuzufügen: **Ew. Majeſtät** geruhen gegenwärtige wenige Arbeit mit einer gnädigen Aufnahme zu würdigen, und **Deroſelben** allerhöchſte Königliche Gnade noch fernerweit zu gönnen

Ew. Majeſtät

Leipzig den 7. Julii
1747.

allerunterthänigſt gehorſamſten Knechte,
dem Verfaſſer.

Musical
Offering
to His Royal Majesty in Prussia and
most humbly dedicated
by
Johann Sebastian Bach

Most gracious King,

To Your Majesty is dedicated herewith in deepest humility a Musical Offering, whose most excellent part itself proceeds from your own lofty hand. With a respectful delight I remember still the quite singular royal grace when, some time ago, during my stay in Potsdam, Your Majesty condescended to play for me on the clavier a theme for a fugue, and at the same time most graciously obliged me to enlarge on the same forthwith in your own highest presence. To obey Your Majesty's command was my most humble duty. However, I noticed quite soon that, because of the lack of necessary preparation, the performance did not succeed as well as such a superb theme required. I consequently resolved and undertook immediately to work out completely this truly royal theme and then publish it to the world. This project has now been completed to the best of my ability, and it has no other purpose than this sole irreproachable one: to exalt, although only in one small aspect, the glory of a monarch whose greatness and might, just as in all the sciences of peace and war so also especially in music, everyone must admire and venerate. I make bold to add this most humble request: that Your Majesty deign to honor the present small work with a gracious reception, and that you further extend the highest royal favor to

Your Majesty's

Leipzig, 7 July
1747

most humbly obedient servant,
the composer

most concentrated and unified movements, further restrained by a thematic bass line that governs the harmony.

This particular unaccompanied Chaconne is a marvel of melodic, harmonic, and contrapuntal organization. Beginning in deliberate T time, in the key of D minor, it maintains a stately movement with a quarter note as the principal unit. It is then "doubled" twice, and proceeds in animated motion in sixteenth notes, with several passages in thirty-second notes. There follows a section in D major. The illusion of full harmonies is sustained by the rapid alternation of the lower and upper pedal points on the dominant. Then the original statement in D minor returns with ingenious variations in sixteenth notes, thirty-second notes, and triplet passages. The coda simply recapitulates the original statement.

Orchestral Suite No. 3 in D Major, BWV 1068 (c. 1729–31)

The suite is a collection of dances, with a prelude or an overture to open the series. The number of dances and their nature varies. Usually the first dance is in common time (Y), and in quick movement. The second dance is slow and stately. The third dance may be a spirited allegro. Then comes a group known under the comprehensive name "gallant dances." These may include a minuet or a gavotte, or any of the French dances current in the sixteenth and the seventeenth centuries. The concluding movement is usually a gigue. In Bach's time, not much significance was attached to titles. A suite might have been called an overture, a partita, or even a sinfonia. It is only later in history that the titles have assumed the significance of a definite form.

The Overture of Bach's Suite No. 3 in D Major is in common time (Y), which is the usual time signature for the opening movement in most suites. There are three themes in the Overture, and the one in dotted rhythm serves as background for the entire Overture. The counterpoint is not as complex as it is in Bach's fugues, and even the Bachian device of inversion is free, so that only the direction of the melody is reversed. The Overture consists of two contrasting sections. The first is of a symphonic nature; the second section is based on the imitation of a characteristic rhythmic figure.

The melody of the second movement has become popular under the title Air on the G String, in a violin arrangement by the German violinist August Wilhelmj (1845–1908), who transposed Bach's original melody a ninth lower in order to exploit the rich sonorities of the lowest string on the violin. In Bach's original, the violin part does not require the G string at all. The late Donald Francis Tovey called it a "devastating derangement." Derangement or not, it is effective, and the temptation to use it in place of the movement as written by Bach is great.

The third movement of the suite is a twin Gavotte, each gavotte consisting of two sections. The first Gavotte is repeated after the second. A Bourrée follows the Gavotte. Both the gavotte and the bourrée are dances of French peasant origin, but it would be risky to try to establish the etymological derivation of these dances. The final movement of the suite is a Gigue, which is a frenchified version of the old English jig. It is in Z time, and, like all the dances of the suite, is in two sections.

Concerto No. 1 in C Minor for Two Harpsichords, BWV 1060 (1729)

The solo parts in Bach's concertos were often interchangeable. A concerto for harpsichord could have been originally a violin concerto. Double and triple concertos were often arranged by Bach for different groups of solo instruments. The Concerto for Two Harpsichords in C Minor was probably written not for keyboard instruments but for violin and oboe with orchestral accompaniment. At least, traces of typical oboe or violin passages are detectable in the two harpsichord parts.

Concerto for Two Harpsichords in C Minor

BWV 1060

The concerto must have been written in 1729 in Leipzig, at the time when Bach took over the direction of the Collegium Musicum there. The meetings were held weekly, and Bach was expected to provide the music. It is probable that there were good pianists (or rather, harpsichord players) among the members of the Collegium Musicum. It is possible also that Bach had in mind two of his sons as soloists in the concerto.

The C-Minor Concerto is in three movements, Allegro, Adagio, and Allegro. The opening movement, in ɣ time, is distinguished by the characteristically Bachian persistence of musical motion. The solo instruments and the accompanying orchestra echo one another in free imitation. The thematic material is expressive and rhythmic. The succeeding slow movement, Adagio, is in ѵ, in the key of E-flat major. The rhythmic design contributes to a feeling of sustained energy, with even division of twelve or twenty-four notes to a bar. A modulation leads to the dominant (fifth step, G) of the principal key of C minor. The final Allegro, in + time, proceeds along a brisk pattern. The rhythmic drive is determined, leading to a conclusive ending.

Ricercare à Six, from The Musical Offering, BWV 1079 (1747), orchestration by Anton Webern

We hear from Potsdam that last Sunday, May 7, 1747, the famous Kapellmeister from Leipzig, Bach, arrived with the intention of hearing the excellent Royal music. In the evening, at about the time when the regular chamber music in the royal apartments usually begins, His Majesty was informed that Kapellmeister Bach had arrived at Potsdam and was waiting in His Majesty's antechamber for His Majesty's most gracious permission to listen to the music. His August Self immediately gave orders that Bach be admitted, and went, at his entrance to the so-called Forte-and-Piano, condescending also to play, in person and without any preparation, a theme to be executed by Kapellmeister Bach in a fugue. This was done so happily by the aforementioned Kapellmeister, that not only His Majesty was pleased to show his satisfaction, but also all those present were seized with astonishment. Bach has found the subject propounded to him so exceedingly beautiful that he intends to set it down on paper in a regular fugue and have it engraved on copper.

In these words, the *Spenersche Zeitung* of Berlin, in its issue of May 11, 1747, apprised its readers of the visit of Johann Sebastian Bach at the palace of Frederick the Great of Prussia. On that famous occasion the king, who was an excellent musician, played for Bach on the harpsichord a fine tune of his own invention, containing both diatonic and chromatic elements, and asked him to improvise a fugue on it.

Bach's response is history. Upon his return to Leipzig, he expanded his improvisation by writing a magnificent "musical offering" (*Das musikalische Opfer*), a cornucopia of learned devices comprising a mirror canon, imitation in contrary motion, a crab canon (with the royal theme played backward), and culminating in a magnificent "ricercare" in six voices. His offering was entitled "Regis Iussu Cantio Et Reliqua Canonica Arte Resoluta" ("At the King's Command, Theme and Additions Resolved by Canonic Art").

Ricercare.

The term *ricercare* or *ricercar* (literally, "to research") was originally applied to the "searching" of correct intonation on a string instrument, in other words, tuning. By a semantical extension it came to signify the seeking of the tonality of the principal part of the work, a preamble or a prologue. Through further differentiation, the ricercare developed into a full-fledged fugal exposition, and the terms "ricercare" and "fuga" became interchangeable. Bach's *Musical Offering* is indeed a manifestation of the highest art of the fugue.

Bach's marginal remarks in the manuscript are most revealing of the traditional obsequiousness to ruling sovereigns of the time. To illustrate the augmentation, in which the thematic notes assume double value, Bach writes: "As the notes augment, so may the King's fortune grow." At the change of the key, Bach submits, "As the modulation rises, so may rise the glory of the King." There is also a riddle canon, with the Latin motto "Quaerendo invenietis" ("By seeking you shall find out"), in which the performer must find the proper place and form of the entries. The quest is not simple, since the imitation is to be made in inversion.

Anton Webern (1883–1945), who adapted his great polyphonic skill mainly to dodecaphonic techniques, had profound reverence for the great masters of the Baroque art, and particularly for Bach, and approached the task of orchestrating the concluding portion of Bach's ricercare with great fidelity to the spirit of the music. But he believed, as did his revered teacher Arnold Schoenberg, that Classical music must be arranged in terms of modern instrumental ideas. In his orchestration, Webern used a flute, oboe, English horn, clarinet, bass clarinet, bassoon, horn, trumpet, trombone, harp, and string quartet. The opening notes of the "Royal Theme" are given to the muted trombone, and the rest of the subject is allotted to muted horn and muted trumpet. This overlapping of instruments is fashioned after the medieval hocketus (literally, "hiccup"), an effect created by a deliberate discontinuity of a melody. Expression marks and tempo indications in Webern's score are noteworthy: *zart fliessend, fliessender, sehr fliessend, rubato*. Who would think that an ultramodernist like Webern, arranging the music of Bach, would ask the players to perform tenderly, flowingly, more flowingly, and in free measure? In this instance, classicism and modernism suddenly turn romantic.

ORGAN WORKS
Toccata, Adagio, and Fugue in C Major, BWV 564 (c. 1708–17)

In 1703, when Bach was only eighteen years old, he received his first position as organist, at the New Church in Arnstadt. His duties were set forth as follows:

> Whereas our right honorable and gracious Count and Lord, Count of Schwarzburg, has been pleased to appoint you, Johann Sebastian Bach, to be organist of the New Church, you shall in particular be faithful, loyal, and useful to his lordship, and in general show yourself apt and adroit in your calling, eschewing other tasks and occupations, and on Sundays, feast days, and other seasons appointed for public worship in the said New Church, shall attend at the organ committed to you and perform thereon as shall be required of you. In your conduct and behavior you shall be God-fearing, temperate, well disposed to all, shunning ill company, and in every way show yourself an honorable servant and organist before God and your worshipful masters. In return, you shall receive for annual pay and entertainment 50 florins, and for board and lodging 30 thalers, drawn as follows: from the tax on beer taverns, 25 florins, from church funds, 25 florins, and the rest from the hospital.

This was the beginning of Bach's career as a virtuoso of the organ. But apparently his extemporaneous embellishments of church chorales were not always welcomed by the congregation. In the minutes of the New Church of Arnstadt there is found the transcript of Bach's questioning by the Superintendent Olearius, in which the latter admonished Bach to abandon his ways of playing: "Complaints have been made that you accompany the hymns with strange variations, and mix the chorale with many ornaments alien to the melody, which confuses the congregation. If you desire to introduce a counter-theme, you must keep it, and not change it to yet another."

A more serious and less answerable complaint voiced at the same meeting was that Bach took four months for his leave of absence, instead of the allotted time of four weeks. Bach explained, rather weakly, that he thought his assistant could attend to the needs of the congregation during his absence. The true explanation is that Bach used the time for a journey to Lübeck to hear the great Buxtehude play. The pretty story to the effect that he made that journey on foot is not borne out by existing evidence.

The great Toccata, Adagio, and Fugue in C Major must have been written during Bach's Weimar period, between 1708 and 1717. It is not improbable that Bach played this work in the presence of the hereditary prince of Hesse, who was so impressed with Bach's playing that he took a ring off his finger and gave it to Bach as a token of appreciation. Constantin Bellermann, rector of the Minden Lyceum, recorded his impression of Bach's prodigious technique of the pedals: "His feet, flying over the pedals as though they had wings, made the notes reverberate like thunder." Referring to the prince's gift of a ring, Bellermann asks rhetorically: "Now, if Bach's feet deserved so rich a gift, what reward would be worthy of his hands?" There is an extended pedal solo in the Toccata, which requires "flying feet" for adequate performance.

The word "toccata" comes from the Italian *toccare*, "to touch"; it is a piece for a keyboard instrument, in the form of a free fantasia, or a prelude. The first part, a prelude, is essentially in unison structure, in rapid movement, with frequent pauses between well-marked phrases. The second part is an adagio, in which an ornamented melody is projected onto an even-measured bass figure. The third part is a lively fugue, in which the subject has a so-called tonal answer, obtained, as in any fugue, by transposing the subject a fifth higher or a fourth lower, and then replacing the first supertonic to occur in the answer by the tonic.

Passacaglia in C Minor, BWV 582 (c. 1708–17)

The problem of modern arrangements of Baroque music, particularly Bach, is a vexatious one. In their Calvinistic fanaticism, musical fundamentalists regard any attempt to transcribe Bach's music for a medium other than the one Bach intended it for as a cardinal sin. Paraphrasing the Italian dictum "Tradutore—traditore" ("To translate is to betray") they say, in effect, "Trascritore—traditore."

Yet Bach himself was an industrious arranger of instrumental works by his Baroque contemporaries, among them Antonio Vivaldi (1678–1741). The protean capacity of Bach's own arrangements is demonstrated by two of his keyboard concertos which are arrangements of his violin concertos—surely the most extraordinary case of transplantation of unrelated instrumental species. The title of Bach's *Das Wohltemperierte Klavier* (*The Well-Tempered Clavier*) indicates merely that the work (which was written primarily for didactic purposes) is designed for a keyboard instrument.

The piano virtuoso Ferruccio Busoni (1866–1924), who was second to none in his dedication to Bach, did not flinch from his intention of making a piano arrangement of Bach's Chaconne, originally for unaccompanied violin, lavishing on it all the gothic splendor of pianistic sonorities. To purists, Busoni's modus operandi was an abomination of desecration, and they invoked the strongest Baroque anathema on his head. Incidentally, in his own performances of Bach, Busoni allowed himself surprising dynamic and agogic liberties, even to the point of using rubato. It is doubtful that a pianist who today tried to emulate Busoni's free interpretation could pass muster even at a conservatory recital. The musical morality of today is much more severe.

The harpsichordist Wanda Landowska suggested that the proper rule of comportment in playing Bach should be the same as in society: one should feel free, but not to the extent of putting one's feet on the table or trampling the drawing-room carpet in mud-covered boots. Schoenberg stated his own attitude toward modern arrangements of Bach with great definitude in connection with his transcriptions of two organ chorales of Bach for a modern orchestra. "Our present musical concepts," he wrote, "demand clarity in the motivic procedure, in both the horizontal and vertical dimensions. We must achieve this transparency of design in order to build a musical structure in a proper manner. I therefore regard my transcriptions of Bach's works not only as my right, but also as my duty." And Schoenberg did not hesitate to include in his orchestration such un-Bachian instruments as the triangle and the celesta.

Even liberal musicians object to tampering with the actual notes in Bach's music. The German-American composer Lukas Foss (b. 1922) was roundly castigated for his irreverent treatment of Bach's pieces, which he decomposed and reassembled according to the precepts of the stochastic method of composition. And then there is that great Baroque composer P.D.Q. Bach, the author of such works as a Toot Suite for Organ (three grinders), Concerto for Piano vs. Orchestra, and various MADrigals.

Bach's Passacaglia and Fugue in C Minor is peculiarly suitable for orchestral transcriptions. The grand sonorities of the original, written for organ or cembalo, make the transference to string and brass choirs seem natural. The Baroque passacaglia reflects the spirit of *Zopfmusik*—"pigtail," or old-fashioned, music—to perfection. The "pigtail" is the cantus firmus placed in the bass, which determines the harmonic progressions, while the upper voices engage in ornamental variations. Bach took the subject for his C-Minor Passacaglia and Fugue from a Passacaglia by André Raison, a French organist active in Paris early in the eighteenth century. The fugue in this instance is a modern misnomer; Bach indicates his fugal sequel to the passacaglia as "thema fugatum," a canonic development of the theme rather than the classical type of fugal structure. Bach elevates this "fugation" to a glorious edifice of florid counterpoint.

RELIGIOUS VOCAL WORKS
Cantata No. 51, "Jauchzet Gott in allen Landen" (date unknown)

The figure of Bach looms so immense on the musical horizon that we are often reluctant to enter Bach's technical laboratory, to examine his tools and pry into his methods, for fear that by watching his modus operandi we might lose grasp of his inspiration. Yet Bach's own attitude toward his works was that of an expert craftsman who has achieved his mastery over the material by repeated use of well-tried formulas, musical punches, and clichés. Bach took the florid singing line from the Gregorian chant, and developed it into a fine art. There is no essential difference between Bach's use of such florid figures in his vocal and his instrumental pieces, except for the natural limitations of the medium. In his capacity as a practicing church organist, Bach was duty-bound to produce a given number of organ pieces and various arrangements of hymns and other religious songs.

One of the most remarkable practices in Bach's time was the literal illustration of the text. Numerous examples of such illustrations are found in the fascinating book of André Pirro, *L'Esthétique de Jean Sebastien Bach*. In it the author examines the relationship between certain words in the text and certain intervals in Bach's music. The vividness and consistency in the employment of identical intervals for identical concepts are striking. For instance, the word "far" is invariably translated by the interval of a minor ninth; the concept of firmness and steadfastness is illustrated by a repeated note; anguish is expressed by narrow chromatic intervals; upward movement is transcribed in the form of an upward arpeggio; downward movement is depicted by a downward progression along the diminished seventh chord; descent to hell and reference to Satan are also expressed in the intervals of the diminished seventh chord. The opening phrase of the chorale "Oh, Difficult Step" is represented by three whole tones in an ascending row, a usage forbidden in vocal music. The phrase "Lead on" is illustrated by a continuous upward scale covering more than three octaves.

The score of Bach's cantata "Jauchzet Gott" is marked "For the fifteenth Sunday after Trinity and at any other time." Obviously, then, the text and the meaning of the cantata were adaptable for different periods of the church calendar. The feeling of jubilation that pervades the music makes it particularly suitable for a festive occasion, New Year's Day, Michaelmas Day, or an election of the council. There is evidence that the words of several arias were rewritten to suit such diverse occasions. The author of the text may have been Bach himself.

The cantata consists of five sections, aria, recitative, aria, chorale, and alleluja. The music is set in the key of C major, which was often associated with rejoicing and thanksgiving. The form is that of a solo cantata without chorus. The part of the soloist, a soprano voice, abounds in ornamental passages and figurations that require exceptional virtuosity. Various guesses have been made as to the identity of the singer for whom Bach wrote the work. Almost certainly it must have been a boy singing falsetto, possibly Bach's son Philipp Emanuel.

Cantata No. 53, "Schlage doch" (date unknown)

Bach was a composer of "utilitarian" music (*Gebrauchsmusik*), designed for special purposes, church services, weddings, as pedagogical aids. A remarkable feature of Bach's vocal music is its melodic symbolism, the illustrative use of musical phrases. In one extraordinary instance, the words "Lead me" are illustrated by an ascending scale of twenty-four steps, followed by relays from the bass to high soprano. This illustrativeness of the vocal line was highly useful in practice, for it enabled the listener to form an association between the melody and the verbal phrase, and incidentally helped in understanding the words, even in perfect enunciation.

Bach was equally literal whenever the text contained references to sounds and instruments. When the words spoke of "thundering drum rolls," there were drums expressly included in the score. And when the voice invokes "the flutes' melodious choir," three flutes respond in the orchestra. When the voice enjoins the flutes to stop—"Flutes be silent!"—they instantly comply.

Bach's church Cantata No. 53, "Schlage doch," speaks of the last stroke of the clock; the campanella is included in the score to illustrate the clock chime. This cantata was probably written for a funeral service, but the date and the occasion are uncertain. The words may be translated thus:

Strike then, oh desired hour!
Strike, announce the desired day!
Come, ye angels, near to me.
Open to me Heaven's eyes,
That I might see soon my Jesus,
In my soul's serene repose.
I await in my inner heart
Only the last stroke of the clock.
Strike then, oh desired hour,
Strike, announce the desired day!

Cantata No. 158, "Der Friede sei mit Dir" (date unknown)

On June 25, 1708, Bach wrote "a submissive memo to the honorable and distinguished parochial councilors of St. Blaise's, the church at Mühlhausen where he was employed as organist:

> Your Magnificence, noble and learned gentlemen, my gracious patrons and masters, God has been pleased to open to me an unexpected situation, a more adequate subsistence and the opportunity to pursue the object which concerns me most, the betterment of church music…. His serene Highness, the Duke of Saxe-Weimar, has been graciously pleased to give me the entrée to his Capelle as one of his chamber musicians.

His Magnificence, the burgomaster, and the noble gentlemen of the council of St. Blaise's let Bach go not without regret, and Bach became the court organist and *camer musicus* at Weimar, the celebrated town of old German culture, which has been described as "something between a capital and a village," where Goethe and Schiller later lived in greatness, where Liszt shone, and where young Richard Strauss made his spectacular beginning. Goethe apostrophized Weimar in a distich which, freely translated, reads:

> O, Weimar, you have an uncommon fate:
> Like Bethlehem in Israel, little and great!

Among Bach's duties at Weimar, as previously at Mühlhausen, was the composition of "agreeable and harmonious cantatas." He had a very small choir at his disposal, probably not more than twelve singers in all. The number of instrumentalists was also very limited, but by the provisions of the contract every *musicus vocalis*, that is, singer, could be used in the orchestra as *musicus instrumentalis*. The cantatas were to be sung each Sunday, and there were also special festivals, for which special cantatas were to be written. According to Neumeister, a Lutheran clergyman who published a collection of biblical poems in 1700, with which Bach must have been thoroughly familiar, "A cantata seems to be nothing else than a portion of an opera composed of recitativo and aria together." A cantata could be very long or very short, depending upon the number and arrangement of separate parts. It could also be scored for any number of vocalists and instrumentalists, according to needs and available performers. Bach wrote nearly two hundred cantatas in all, but the authorship of some has not been authenticated. The dates of composition of these cantatas are established with great difficulty.

The Passion of Our Lord According to St. Matthew, BWV 244 (1727)

The Bach family represents the most cogent argument in favor of the heredity of acquired characteristics. At least twenty Bachs who were musicians are cited in music dictionaries for their accomplishments. Moreover, Bachs were exceptionally fertile. The greatest Bach of them all, Johann Sebastian, was married twice and had twenty children, four of whom became important musicians in their own right. So many Bachs in the generation preceding Johann Sebastian had been organists, choir masters, vocalists, and town pipers that the name Bach was sometimes used as a synonym for a musician. The very letters of Bach's name, B-A-C-H, in German nomenclature (B flat, A, C, B natural in English usage) form an interesting chromatic theme which has been used as a subject in a number of works by many composers; Bach himself intended to use it in the last fugue of his work *The Art of the Fugue*, but it remained unfinished at his death.

The year of Bach's birth, 1685, was annus mirabilis in music history, for it was also the year of the birth of George Frideric Handel. (Domenico Scarlatti was born in the same year, too.) The birthplaces of the two great German musicians were a short distance from each other, but they never met. Handel went to London, where he rose to fame as a composer of great oratorios. Bach remained a modest organist, music master, and composer of religious music for his church. Another strange coincidence in the lives of Bach and Handel: both were operated on for cataracts by the same English surgeon. Handel's operation was successful, but not Bach's. Mercifully, Bach died before blindness lowered its veil. He was buried in a churchyard in Leipzig, but the location of his grave was not properly marked, and it was not until nearly a century and a half after his death that the coffin with his remains was found and identified. A famous physiologist of the day had a set of striking photographs taken of Bach's skull and bones. The photos were published in a deluxe edition as an awesome souvenir of human greatness.

Bach's life was deficient in spectacular events. After the death of his father, he was trained in music by his older brother, a methodical pedant, who played the same chorales in the same church for forty years. When he allowed himself to add a grace note or a trill, the congregation would comment on it as an extraordinary occasion: "Our Bach got quite excited today!" Johann Sebastian did not follow his brother's example in pedantry. During his employment as organist at the age of nineteen in Arnstadt, he was once summoned to the consistory and reprimanded for "introducing into the music many strange variations, with the admixture of numerous alien tones, thus bringing about confusion in the congregation." An even more serious reprimand was administered to Bach for leaving church during a sermon and going into the wine cellar.

Bach's duties at his posts in the Lutheran churches consisted of composing religious services for performance on holidays and training young scholars in music. His instrumental works were mostly didactic in nature. Even the epoch-making *Well-Tempered Clavier* was designed by Bach, according to the explicit description on the title page, to instruct music lovers in the art of playing on keyboard instruments in all twenty-four major and minor keys, and to enlighten them in the technique of counterpoint. Before Bach, usable keys were limited to those with a few sharps or flats in the key signature. Bach democratized the practice by extending composition to all keys in the circle of scales.

Opening of Bach's *The Passion of Our Lord According to St. Matthew*, BWV 244

From his predecessors, Bach learned to interpret melodic intervals and chords symbolically. Early in the Baroque period, major keys became associated with positive and happy conditions and events, while minor keys were used to express sadness and death. Ascending intervals portrayed the spirit of determination and firm volition; descending progressions reflected indecision and hesitancy. Chromatic convolutions denoted suffering and distress; diatonic and triadic progressions indicated energy and healthy endeavor. Sometimes, intervals illustrated the text literally. The throwing of dice for Christ's garments is represented by trill-like figures; the dividing of the lot among the soldiers, by syncopation; the Cross, by an involuted melisma; and the silence of Christ during the questioning, by rests between chords in the accompaniment. Chords, other than major and minor, possess peculiar connotations in the musical vocabulary of the Baroque period. The most important among them is the chord of the diminished seventh, because of its protean capacity of fitting into any key, major or minor, by enharmonic change. This chord invariably makes its appearance whenever sin, disaster, or hell are mentioned in the text.

The adoption of such associative devices is easily explained. They facilitate the understanding of the text when it is not intelligible in performance, as is often the case. A passage like "In Adam's Fall, sinned we all," illustrated by a series of falling intervals and harmonized by diminished-seventh chords, immediately conveys the substance and the sentiment of the phrase, a feeling of distress, sorrowful realization, and acknowledgement of guilt. This intervallic vocabulary becomes in Baroque music the lingua franca of musical expression.

The foundation of Bach's sacred music is the Lutheran chorale. Heinrich Heine said that Luther's chorale "Ein' feste Burg" is the Marseillaise of the Reformation. The melodic materials of Protestant church music are rooted in German national songs. Bach's contemporary, the Hamburg music critic Johann Mattheson (1681–1764), deplored the "malady of melody" in German music. Bach remedied this condition by bringing the German chorale to the melodic apogee of expressiveness. But Bach also used the accumulated musical experience of other nations. The French writer Romain Rolland said: "Bach absorbed French and Italian art of composition, but his music remains echt deutsch." The peak of German sacred music is reached in Bach's great Passions.

Passion plays, with recitation and singing, date back to the early centuries of Christianity. Gradually, a standard order of scenes was established, and all four Gospels were often performed during Holy Week. The cast included the Evangelist, who narrated the course of events (usually a tenor), Christ (usually a bass), and a chorus representing the crowd. After the Reformation, Passions were performed to German texts in Protestant countries; the Latin text continued to be used in Roman Catholic districts.

The emergence of opera in the seventeenth century influenced the character of Passions, often imparting dramatic characteristics to the performance. As a theatrical spectacle of an operatic nature, Passion plays survive in the open-air productions in Oberammergau, in Bavaria, with a cast recruited among the common people of the countryside. The powerful attraction of the subject, even in modern times, is demonstrated by the extraordinary success of the setting of the St. Luke Passion by the Polish composer Krzysztof Penderecki (b. 1933).

Bach wrote two Passions, one based on the gospel according to St. John and one on the gospel according to St. Matthew. Some portions of Bach's music for the *St. Mark Passion* are also extant. Disparate numbers for the *St. Luke Passion*, in Bach's handwriting, have long been known, but stylistic analysis seems to indicate that the work is by a lesser composer, copied by Bach for use in church services. The text of the *St. Matthew Passion* was supplied to Bach by a local postal official in Leipzig, who had a knack for turning out striking devotional prose. He collaborated with Bach in other works; many of his texts became famous thanks to Bach's music.

The *St. Matthew Passion* is in two parts, containing arias, recitatives, chorales, duets, choruses, and instrumental interludes. Several chorales in the score are derived from secular songs by other composers, among them "Innsbrück, ich muss Dich lassen," in the harmonization of the Flemish composer Heinrich Isaac. As if to prove the unlimited magic of musical transliteration, Bach uses—in place of the genial words of the original, bidding farewell to the gemütlich Alpine town—the tragic query addressed to Christ: "Who has struck you so?" Five chorales in the *St. Matthew Passion* are derived from "Mein Gemuth ist mir verwirret" by Hans Leo Hassler (1564–1612). The music of another chorale comes from a surprising source, a French love song, "Il me suffit de tous mes maux," which Bach found in a sixteenth-century anthology. Such derivations from popular songs by no means degrade the religious sentiment of the music. The practice is not new; the frivolous medieval folk melody, "L'Homme armé," served as the cantus firmus of many sacred works by Renaissance composers.

Bach brought out *The Passion According to St. Matthew* on Good Friday, April 15, 1729, at the Thomaskirche in Leipzig. It is unlikely that the performance was at all adequate. Bach consistently complained about the inferior quality of choristers and instrumentalists at the school. They drank habitually and often begged in the streets. Besides, Bach experienced difficulties with his church superiors. According to his contract, Bach was required "to extend due respect and obedience to the eminent council, sustain its honor and reputation, and obey the inspectors and the rector of the school." Bach also had to sign a pledge to write the kind of music that "would not be too long or operatic in character, and would contribute to the piety of the congregation." On occasion he was reprimanded for contravening these instructions.

Despairing of his prospects in Leipzig, he began looking elsewhere for employment opportunities. In a typically humble letter to a former schoolmate who occupied an influential post at the Russian consulate in Danzig, he asked him for a recommendation to secure another position. He candidly detailed his distressing financial situation at the Thomaskirche, where he had to depend on wedding and funeral services to eke out his meager allowance. "My present employment," he wrote, "pays me about 700 thalers. If there are more funerals than usual, my income increases proportionately; but when the air is salubrious, these extra earnings fall off. For example, I lost more than 100 thalers last year because the number of funerals was only average." The letter was never answered, and Bach remained in Leipzig.

The Passion of Our Lord According to St. Matthew, unquestionably the greatest work of its kind, had to wait a hundred years for another complete performance after its original presentation at the Thomaskirche. On March 11, 1829, the twenty-year-old Felix Mendelssohn conducted it in Berlin. The event was tantamount to a rediscovery of Bach's greatness. Great impetus was given for further performances of Bach's works and to wide publication of his music. In 1850, on the hundredth anniversary of Bach's death, a complete edition of Bach's collected works was undertaken in Germany. By this act Bach had finally received full recognition as the fountainhead of Classical music.

GEORGE FRIDERIC HANDEL
(1685–1759)
The Magnificent

For sheer splendor of sound there is no other composer whose music can match that of George Frideric Handel. It is a flowing river of tones that seems to be following its predestined course without intervention of a human hand. There is in it dignity and beauty and a sort of impersonal greatness that makes the word "genius" least appropriate to Handel. For men of genius are in a constant state of turmoil; they are often victims of moods and passing fancies; they work under an inner compulsion that drives them to accomplishment almost against their will.

Handel was not an ordinary genius. His creative impulse was strong and dependable; he could compose music under any circumstances, and the speed of his production was astounding. He wrote one of his operas in two weeks, and he completed his greatest score, *Messiah*, in twenty-four days.

Handel was a supreme master of the musical craft. His fugal counterpoint is a thing of wonder. Yet despite the greatness of his knowledge, his music is distinguished by a fundamental simplicity of melodic line and harmonic sequence. This simplicity is explained by the fact that to Handel the singing voice was the supreme criterion of natural excellence. His instrumental writing was a reflection of the vocal line. His music breathed at a measured pace; his rhythmic design was steady despite the artful syncopation of his fugues and canons.

Handel was born in Halle, Germany, in 1685—a great year in music, for Bach and Domenico Scarlatti were also born in that year. In seventeenth-century Germany, music was regarded as little more than a menial occupation, and Handel's father had greater ambitions for the boy. But musical talent is a stubborn thing, and early in life Handel found himself irresistibly drawn to keyboard instruments. He taught himself to play the notes on a dumb spinet in which the strings were covered with heavy cloth. Then he met a friendly organist who let him practice on a real instrument. Soon Handel learned the elements of composition. An opportunity was presented to him to go to Hamburg, where he wrote his first opera. Then he traveled in Italy. He became an accomplished professional composer.

That was the time when the English court and English society were eager to secure the services of foreign composers for the London opera houses. Like many other Germans and Italians, Handel found himself in London, with promises of a fine career and rich material rewards.

Handel's first London production was an opera, *Rinaldo*, in Italian, which was sumptuously staged. In the garden scene there were real birds in huge cages, and natural flowers. Handel's music was rewarded by enthusiastic applause. The court looked on him favorably, and he was asked to write music for a grand festival to be held on the Thames. It was an extraordinary spectacle. Handel conducted an orchestra in a large flat barge which followed the king's boat. The suite of instrumental pieces he composed for the occasion came to be known as *Water Music*.

But Handel was not the only lord of music in London. An Italian composer named Giovanni Battista Bononcini (1670–1747) was also writing operas for London's theaters at the time, and he was favored above Handel by the aristocratic Queensberry, Rutland, and Marlborough families. The adherents of the rival factions decided to test the relative merits of the two composers by asking them to contribute one act each to an opera dealing with the Roman hero Muzio Scaevola (the man who put his right arm into the fire to prove his courage).

The combined opera was not a success, but it inspired an epigram by the Lancashire poet John Byrom that created a phrase that became a part of the English language: tweedle-dum and tweedle-dee. Here is the complete text:

> Some say, compar'd to Bononcini
> That Mynheer Handel's but a Ninny;
> Others aver, that he to Handel
> Is scarcely fit to hold a Candle:
> Strange all this Difference should be,
> Twixt Tweedle-dum and Tweedle-dee.

It should be explained that *mynheer* is Dutch for "Mr." or "Sir," and that in eighteenth-century parlance this title was equivalent to "Dutchman," and "Dutchman" was equivalent to "German," the word "Dutch" being a variation of "deutsch," which is the German word meaning German.

History showed that Tweedle-dum Handel proved to be much greater than Tweedle-dee Bononcini. Still, Handel had to face strong competition from the Italian-loving section of the English public. He produced one opera after another, without much success.

Providentially, this failure proved to be a great boon to music. Disillusioned in his career as an opera composer, Handel decided to turn to oratorio, and wrote his greatest masterpieces in this genre, culminating in the *Messiah*. His last oratorio, *The Triumph of Time and Truth*, was given at Covent Garden in London in 1757; as usual, Handel presided at the organ and directed the performance.

A few years before his death, Handel began to lose his eyesight. He had an affliction that was incurable; an operation was attempted but it brought no relief. The news of his illness was even published in a London theatrical journal. But still Handel continued to play in public, performing on the organ. Money was coming in from performances of his old works, and Handel was able to pay off all his debts. He had enough strength to lead a performance of *Messiah* at the keyboard a week before his death. He was buried in Westminster Abbey.

The famous British musical historian Charles Burney (1726–1814) gives his impression of Handel, whom he knew personally, in these words:

> The figure of Handel was large, and he was somewhat unwieldy in his actions; but his countenance was full of fire and dignity. His general look was somewhat heavy and sour, but when he did smile, it was the sun bursting out of a black cloud. There was a sudden flash of intelligence, wit, and good humour, beaming in his countenance which I hardly ever saw in any other.

Handel's greatness lies primarily in his oratorios and operas. His instrumental music, though of very fine quality, does not impose as Bach's instrumental music does. His suites for harpsichord are brilliant without being inspired.

Of much greater importance are his instrumental concertos. Some of his organ concertos may have been composed as interludes for his oratorios. But the most glorious of Handel's instrumental compositions are his twelve grand concertos, written in the style of a concerto grosso. There are usually three instrumentalists forming the section known as concertino, and four sections known as ripieno. *Concertino*, of course, means "little concerto," and *ripieno* is the same word as the English "replenish," so that these string parts are designed to provide the support rather than the essential substance. In all these works there is a part for the figured bass, to be executed on the harpsichord.

Handel cast his mighty shadow on English music for a century after his death. English composers of oratorios were mesmerized by Handel's art so that they could do no more than produce mediocre facsimiles. It was not until the advent of Mendelssohn that a new great influence swung the British nation. In America, too, Handel was the musical god. His works were among the first Classical compositions heard in colonial America. Boston's Handel and Haydn Society has much more Handel than Haydn in it, and *Messiah* still traditionally opens its season. Long before Bach became widely known, Handel was acknowledged as the greatest of the greatest.

Overture to Agrippina *(1709)*

A revival of Handel's operas began to materialize in Germany in the 1920s. It gathered momentum quickly, and soon was followed by a similar revival in England and elsewhere in Europe. A true reconstruction of the ambience of Handel's day in opera appears impossible, however, mainly because of the present unavailability of castrated singers, whose parts have to be replaced by women or countertenors, which latter are also rare. And the wanton supremacy of celebrated singers which allowed them to strut on the stage like so many roosters crowing their cockle-doo-dle-doo's in the high register of their voices in complete disregard of the written notes, could not be tolerated today. In Handel's time, Baroque opera was indeed baroque in the primary sense of the word—bizarre, strange, ungainly.

Although virtually all of Handel's operas were written to Italian librettos, few of them were produced in Italy in Handel's lifetime. A signal exception was *Agrippina*, which was staged in Venice on December 26, 1709, during Handel's stay there. It deals with the murderous mother of Nero, who was herself murdered by Nero's hired killers, after an attempt to scuttle the boat in which she was returning from her visit to her son failed. (She swam ashore.) The scenario, by an Italian nobleman, is much less bloody than the historic events, and includes no murders. In the final chorus, the Emperor Claudius, his wife Agrippina, her son and his step-son Nero, Nero's future successor, the Emperor Otho, Otho's wife Poppaea, who subsequently became the second wife of Nero himself, and for whose sake Nero killed his mother, all sing together in perfect Baroque harmony.

The overture, in G minor, is a typical Italian sinfonia, with thematic materials independent of the contents of the opera itself. The Neapolitan influence, particularly that of Alessandro Scarlatti (1660–1725), is much in evidence in the score, with its da capo arias and formal divisions, but Handel scholars seem to descry in it signs of an incipient dramatic style in the new manner of "the Great Saxon."

The Faithful Shepherd: *Suite (1712; revised 1734)*

Handel was the first of the three great German composers (the other two were Haydn and Mendelssohn) whose second country was England. He was the only one who became naturalized as an English citizen. Perhaps his name should have an umlaut on the *a,* but during his life in England, he signed his name without one. He also changed the German form of his name Georg Friedrich to the half-English, half-Gallic form George Fréderic. But he spoke in a heavy German accent to the end of his days. De Quincey gives a description of Handel in England. "A Polyphemus as to enormity of appetite," he used to order a dinner for seven. "He rang furiously for the dinner to be served, upon which the waiter would timidly suggest that perhaps his honor might choose to wait for the six commensals who had not yet arrived. "De who, de what?" would Handel exclaim. "The company, sir," was the waiter's reply. "De gombany!" ejaculated Handel. "I am de gombany!"

Handel died in England, and was buried in the Westminster Abbey, at the feet of the coffin of the duke of Argyle. One hundred eleven year later, Charles Dickens was to become Handel's "silent neighbor," in the words of Hugo Leichtentritt, in his great Handel biography.

By a curious twist of musical politics the German Handel became the greatest protagonist of Italian opera in England. There was a great deal of struggle between the opera in English and the opera in Italian in the early 1700s. The music critic Charles Burney (1726–1814) sets down the year 1705 as the period when the first real opera on an Italian model, though not in the Italian language, was produced on the English stage. The celebrated essayist, poet, and statesman Joseph Addison (1672–1719) rebelled against "the absurdity of going to an opera without understanding the language in which it is performed." The English singers who felt that they were displaced from the English stage by the Italian invaders, and were further handicapped by the fact that many Italian singers preserved their bel canto by early castration (a practice that the beef-eating Britons never applied to their own opera singers), joined in the campaign. There is a report that a servant of Katharine Tofts, an English singer, "committed a rudeness of the playhouse by throwing of oranges, and hissing when Mrs. L'Epine, the Italian gentlewoman, sung."

When Handel arrived in England in the autumn of 1710, the Italian opera reigned supreme. He was given the collaboration of an Italian poet, and in 1711 his opera *Rinaldo* was produced. Handel composed forty-six operas, all to Italian texts. He wrote with great facility. Thus, *Rinaldo* was written in fourteen days.

Il Pastor fido (*The Faithful Shepherd*) was the second opera written by Handel for the Italian season in London. The story was conventional, abounding in interlocked love triangles. The shepherd Mirtillo is loved by two shepherdesses, Amarillis and Eurilla. Silvio loves Amarillis, but is loved by Dorinda. Mirtillo, "the faithful shepherd," wins Amarillis through the oracular powers of a priestess of Diana, and Dorinda wins Silvio. A contemporary opera-goer noted in his diary after the performance, "The scenery represented merely an Arcadian landscape. The costumes were old. The opera was short." Apparently Handel thought well of *Il Pastor fido*, for many years later he presented a new version "intermix'd with chorus's" with an added prologue entitled "Terpsichore."

Charles Burney in his celebrated *General History of Music* gives a detailed account of the first performance of *The Faithful Shepherd*, its music and its singers, among whom the castrato Valeriano, was the most successful. He calls the overture "one of the most masterly and pleasing of the kind," and comments further, "The first air for a soprano lets us know what kind of voice the Cavalier Valeriano was possessed of; and the pathetic style of the first part of his song, as well as the agility necessary to the execution of the second, seem to imply abilities in that performer of no mean kind."

Burney mentions the "purity and simplicity" of Handel's music, which, "when the melody and the voice are exquisite would be always pleasing to an audience, as a contrast to rich harmony and contrivance." He observes, however, that "some of these airs are now too trivial and far advanced in years to support themselves totally without harmony." Burney notes that the ornamental style of Handel's vocal writing,

> so much admired at the beginning of the century, has, however, been long banished from the opera as undramatic for the voice part is so much overpowered and rendered so insignificant by the complicated business of the accompaniments that she loses her sovereignty. Such ingenious contrivances seem best calculated for instruments where narration and poetry are out of the question; but in a drama where instruments are, or ought to be, the humble attendant on the voice, riot and noise should not be encouraged.... Handel has been accused of crowding some of his songs with too much harmony; but that is so far from being the case in this opera that he not only often leaves the voice without any other accompaniment than a violoncello, but sometimes even silences that.

On the opera in general, Burney says:

> It is inferior in solidity and invention to almost all his other dramatic productions, yet there are in it many proofs of genius and abilities which must strike every real judge of the art, who is acquainted with the state of dramatic music at the time it was composed. In the first place, it was a pastoral drama, in which simplicity was propriety. Besides, Handel had, at

this period, no real great singer to write for. Valeriano was only of the second class.... Nothing but miraculous powers in the performers can long support an opera, be the composition ever so excellent. Plain sense and good poetry are equally injured by singing unless it is so exquisite as to make us forget everything else. If the performer is of the first class, and very miraculous and enchanting, an audience seems to care little about the music or the poetry.

Water Music *(1717)*

The 1880 edition of the *Encyclopedia Britannica* contained the following paragraph in its article on Handel: "The system of wholesale plagiarism carried on by him is perhaps unprecedented in the history of music. He pilfered not only single melodies but frequently entire movements from the work of other masters, with few or no alterations, and without a word of acknowledgment."

This severe judgment ignores the permissive ways of the eighteenth century, when musical larceny was common, as was the purloining of verses and even of scientific discoveries, on a par with respectable adultery, provided it was carried out within one's own class. The only imperative was not to get caught. Handel escaped detection, and as a result scholars are still struggling with the monumental task of segregating the "pilfered" portions in Handel's music from the self-borrowed, revised, renamed, and original creations. Bononcini, Handel's hapless Italian rival in the competition for supremacy on the London opera scene, was not so lucky. He was imprudent enough to submit to a stuffy London academy a madrigal previously published by another Italian composer. When that composer objected, Bononcini was promptly run out of town. He went to Paris, where he unsuccessfully attempted the transmutation of base metals into gold in collaboration with a local alchemist and lost all his savings. He eventually wound up in Vienna, where he died in misery.

Despite the elimination of his Italian rival, Handel failed to achieve success in the field of opera. It was a felicitous failure for music, for it forced Handel to turn to oratorio, in which he attained the summit of glory, culminating in his crowning masterpiece, *Messiah*. It is as the composer of oratorios in the English language that Handel endeared himself to his adoptive country and had the honor of burial in Westminster Abbey. Incidentally, the year of his birth on the marble pedestal is marked 1684 instead of 1685. This is due to the fact that Handel was born in February and the first of the year, according to the Julian calendar in force at the time, was in March. No such calendaric misadventure befell Bach, Handel's great contemporary, who was born a few weeks after Handel, in March, and thus safely within the new year 1685.

The circumstances surrounding the composition of the *Water Music* have been embellished by romantic inventions, but the basic facts seem to be clear. In 1710 Handel was appointed court director of music to the elector of Hannover. While occupying that post he made two visits to England, where he produced some operas. While he was in London, the elector of Hannover became King George I of England, and Handel, with his old patron on the throne, decided to remain in England. In 1727 he became a British subject.

On July 17, 1717, the king arranged a spectacular aquatic festival on the Thames River. The king with his retinue occupied a luxuriously appointed boat, which was followed by a barge with some fifty musicians. Handel was commissioned to write instrumental music to be played on the river, and it was subsequently published under the title *Water Musick*. It is impossible to establish whether this score contained the pieces actually played on the barge.

OVERTURE.

Opening of Handel's *Water Music*

Concerto Grosso No. 12 in G Major (1739)

What the fugue is to Bach, the concerto grosso is to Handel. Just as Bach established the fugal tradition by perfecting an art that had existed before him, so Handel created an architecturally perfect type of the concerto grosso, which was not his invention. In a concerto grosso the "soloist" is not a single instrumentalist assigned a virtuoso role, but a group of instruments bearing the collective name of concertino—"little concert." This concertino group is accompanied, echoed, and generally aided and abetted by a large group of instruments of less pronounced individuality, which group constitutes the concerto grosso—"big concert." It is from the nonsoloist group that the entire composition takes its name.

Handel wrote twelve compositions for strings entitled concerto grosso in one month, October 1739. There was an advertisement in the *London Daily Post* announcing "Twelve Grand Concertos... composed by Mr. Handel." It added that "subscriptions are taken by the author, at his house in Brook Street, Hannover Square." After their publication in April 1740, another advertisement mentioned the fact that the concertos were "played in most public places with the greatest applause."

The Concerto No. 12, Op. 6, is in the key of G major, associated in Handel's music with lively and virile moods. The concertino group consists of two violins and cello. An introductory musical paragraph leads to an Allegro, which opens a characteristic Handelian merry-go-round. The increase in the musical momentum is achieved by sequences rising higher and higher. There is a cadenza for the violin, and the movement slows up to a conclusion. The second movement is an Adagio in a minor key, distinguished by stately eloquence. There follows an Allegro in the form of a full-fledged fugue. The subject of the fugue is based on the three notes of the G-major triad. The first violin of the concertino group opens the fugal festivities. It is fugally imitated by the second violin, and then by the cello, which latter is bolstered up by its colleagues from the nonsoloist group. Another fugal subject, also derived from the G-major triad, is introduced by the cello, and is passed over to the second and the first violin. There is much episodic development, and sequences are rampant. At one point, a melodic figure is repeated eight times on different degrees of a descending scale. The movement comes to a close after every development of the two fugal themes appears exhausted. There is the inevitable cadenza before the slow coda. The last movement is an Allegro in jig time, typical of the Classical instrumental suite. It is a short movement in brisk motion.

FRANZ JOSEPH HAYDN
(1732–1809)
A Genius of Perfection in Music

Franz Joseph Haydn exemplified the spirit of the eighteenth century in the charm, orderliness, and simple poetry that were the virtues of the age. The eighteenth century was the era of mass production in music. A formula was developed, and imitation became easy for minor composers. The sheer quantity of symphonic works of Haydn and Mozart is staggering; in comparison, nineteenth-century symphonists were laggards. The romantic elevation to individual symphonic creation had to wait until the advent of Beethoven. But the level of productivity fell spectacularly in the post-Classical years.

Haydn's life was serene and unperturbed by tragedy. He had a difficult childhood in the little town of Rohrau in Lower Austria, where he was born, but soon he was sent to Vienna, where he applied himself to earnest study under favorable circumstances. Still a young man, he was fortunate in securing a position in 1761 as second Kapellmeister to Prince Paul Anton Esterházy on his estate in Eisenstadt. There he composed some of his greatest symphonies, string quartets, and also a series of pieces for the baryton, a now obsolete bass viol, a string instrument favored by the prince, who played on it himself.

Haydn is popularly known as "the father of the symphony." Cautious musicologists are unwilling to support this designation, for it is seldom possible to establish a priority on any musical form, and there were symphonies written before Haydn. But there is no doubt that Haydn gave the firm outline to the Classical symphony in several movements that became the model for composers of a later day. In chamber music as well, Haydn's historical role is great. He created the string quartet, which has the same formal consistency as a symphony. Haydn's string quartets show an amazing development of counterpoint; like his symphonies, they became the models emulated by his successors.

In 1791 an enterprising German violinist, Johann Peter Salomon, approached Haydn in Vienna to write a group of symphonies for his concerts in London. Salomon himself was to be the "leader," that is, first violinist at the London concerts, and Haydn was to conduct from the pianoforte. Haydn accepted Salomon's persuasive and lucrative offer, and Salomon deposited five thousand gulden in a Vienna bank for Haydn as security. The story is told that before Haydn left Vienna, Mozart asked him how he expected to get along in England without the knowledge of English, and that Haydn replied, "My language is understood all over the world." It was during his first trip to London in 1791 that Haydn learned of Mozart's death.

Salomon was a master of publicity and advertised his concerts in the London newspapers with fine commercial flair. "The celebrated Haydn's arrival was yesterday announced in the musical circles," read the notice in the *London Oracle* of February 6, 1794. "Mr. Salomon most respectfully acquaints the Nobility and Gentry," it continued,

> that his first concert will be on Monday next, the 10th February. Subscriptions are at 5 Guineas for the 12 concerts. The Ladies' Tickets are blue and the Gentlemen's are red. Dr. Haydn will supply the Concerts with New Compositions, and direct the Execution of them at the Piano Forte. Every nerve is to be exerted to leave an impression deeper than ever of this excellent band. The Doctor has been writing with all his original fancy and fertile combination. Some Italians of fine taste have heard him in private, and they express most liberally their astonishment at his science and power.

Haydn did not limit his London activities to music. His personal journal abounds in references to English matrons and widows who showered their attentions upon him. About each one of them he remarked, "The finest woman I ever saw." He carefully saved a batch of letters from a Mrs. Schroeter, breathing womanly passion, and commented with regard to them that the lady, although sixty years of age, was still very beautiful. In the meantime, an Italian singer with whom Haydn had a liaison of long standing expressed her anxiety about Haydn's long absence. As to Haydn's wife, whom he left in Vienna, she was concerned mainly with the purchase of a new house. But when she died, Haydn avoided further matrimony, despite his written promise to the widowed Italian singer to marry her after "the four eyes" (her husband's and his wife's) were closed for eternity.

Haydn was so prolific that he himself could not remember how many symphonies he wrote, and the catalogue that he compiled is very incomplete. As a result, musicologists until this day cannot agree on the authenticity of numerous works attributed to Haydn. One of the items taken off the Haydn list is the celebrated "Toy" Symphony, the score of which includes a trumpet, a drum, a whistle, a triangle, a quail, and a cuckoo. It now seems certain that the work was written by Mozart's father, possibly in collaboration with Haydn's brother, Michael.

Mastery and supreme professionalism combined in Haydn with gentle humor. When Prince Esterházy made up his mind to disband his private orchestra, Haydn accepted the princely decision with regret and, as a final contribution, composed and performed the "Farewell" Symphony. According to the instructions in the score, the musicians left, one by one, after completing their parts, until only the conductor remained on the stage; he blew out the candle and departed. Prince Esterházy was touched by this little spectacle, and decided to retain the orchestra.

Haydn was an eminently practical man. Like most composers of his day, he wrote music to order. Such was the perfection of his technique that he never had to wait for inspiration to come, and the quality of his music was uniformly high. One of Haydn's commissions was the composition of the Austrian national hymn, "Gott erhalte unser Kaiser" ("God Save Our Emperor"), which remained in force until the fall of the Austro-Hungarian Empire.

In the eyes of awed posterity, Haydn appears as a formidable father spirit, the demiurge of the symphony, the progenitor of the string quartet, the presiding officer of musicians' heaven. However, the life of Haydn, abounding in colorful episodes, shows him as a puckish rather than paternal spirit, given to mischievous moods even on solemn occasions. The jocular implications of the "Farewell" Symphony and the "Surprise" Symphony are characteristic manifestations. Haydn could write a perpetual canon on a dog's death. When he himself felt bodily exhaustion, he had a card printed with the first bars from one of his vocal works, "The Old Man": "Gone forever is my strength—l/lOld and weak am I!" It is ironic that even in death Haydn continued to play poor Yorick. His skull was stolen from the coffin by a deranged admirer; it was later returned anonymously to Prince Esterházy, but proved to be spurious. At one time several Haydn skulls were in circulation in Vienna. In 1932, on the Haydn bicentennial, the authenticity of the skull reposing in the Vienna Academy of Music was accepted with seeming finality.

SYMPHONIES
Symphony No. 88 in G Major (1787)

According to a convenient textbook description, Haydn was "the father of the symphony," even though the symphonic form was first developed earlier in Haydn's century by the musicians of the Mannheim School. But Haydn was undoubtedly the "perfecter of the symphony," whose mastery of polyphonic craftsmanship and orchestration enabled him to diversify the symphonic palette with ingenious rhythmic variations and instrumental colors. He added a third dimension to the rather bleak surfaces of the Baroque structures. He became the first Classicist of music, applying the same art of formal excellence in diversity to the composition of string quartets. Here the parental relationship of the creator to the product stands clear. Haydn was certainly the father of the string quartet.

The fanciful nicknames attached to many of Haydn's symphonies—the "Surprise" Symphony, the "Military" Symphony—are inventions by publishers to attract performers. Some are grouped according to the place of their performance—the "London" symphonies, the "Paris" symphonies.

Symphony No. 88 was a commissioned work, written for the violinist Johann Peter Tost, formerly a member of the Esterházy orchestra led by Haydn. In 1788,

Tost went to Paris, carrying with him the scores of two symphonies by Haydn, identifiable as Nos. 88 and 89, which he had arranged to publish in France. For good measure, he also sold for publication a symphony by the young Bohemian composer Adalbert Gyrowetz, and brazenly put Haydn's name on the score. When poor Gyrowetz came to Paris some years later and claimed the symphony as his own, neither publishers nor musicians at large would believe him. Thus another spurious work was added to the Haydn catalogue. Somehow the two genuine symphonies

Sinfonia No. 88

I

found their way to Haydn's Vienna publisher, and Tost accused Haydn of unfair dealing. Distressed by this imbroglio, Haydn wrote to the Paris publisher asking him to straighten out the situation and to find out whether Tost had sold him some other works of Haydn to which he had no right. "Please, write me quite frankly," Haydn begged the Paris publisher, "and tell me how Tost conducted himself in Paris, and particularly whether he engaged in any Amours." In the meantime, the Bastille fell and, in the revolutionary turmoil, Tost apparently escaped from Paris.

The G-Major Symphony is in four movements. An introductory Adagio leads to the main body of the movement, Allegro, a characteristically energetic piece of music progressing on its own momentum once the creative spark is struck. Remarkably enough, the traditional entry of trumpets and drums is deferred to the second movement, Largo, producing a singular impact because of the delay. The next movement, Minuetto, follows the Classical formula. The Finale: Allegro con spirito offers a treat to the musical cognoscenti in a magisterial canon with precise imitation between the upper and the lower strings, a locus Classical of polyphonic studies.

Symphony No. 92 in G Major ("Oxford") (1789)

Of Haydn's 104 symphonies, at least two dozen have acquired descriptive nicknames, most of them unjustified. But the "Oxford" Symphony is quite proper in its designation. Haydn conducted it at the University of Oxford in July 1791, in acknowledgment of an honorary degree of doctor of music conferred on him on that occasion. The work itself was written three years earlier, but the Oxford performance was the first. Haydn received a handsome remuneration for his services, but he had to pay the travel expenses. He noted in his expense book: "One and a half guineas for the bell peals at Oxforth [*sic*]—and half a guinea for the robe." He was greatly pleased with the sumptuous vestment he wore at the ceremony, for according to reports the robe was a resplendent affair of cream-colored silk.

The Oxford doctorate was arranged for Haydn by the famous English music historian Charles Burney. So genuinely elated and patriotically proud was Burney at his part in the undertaking that he burst into verse to celebrate Haydn's landing on the British islands:

> Welcome, great master, to our favorite isle,
> Already partial to thy name and style;
> Long may thy fountain of invention run
> In streams as rapid as it first begun;
> While skill for each fantastic whim provides,
> And certain science ev'ry current guides.

The press reports were as magnificent as any Haydn had received in England. "A more wonderful composition never was heard," wrote the *Morning Chronicle*. "The applause given to Haydn, who conducted this admirable effort of his genius, was enthusiastic; but the merit of the work, in the opinion of all the musicians present, exceeded all praise."

The "Oxford" Symphony is typical of his style, both in form and content. The principal key is G major, and there are few modulatory deviations from it. A brief adagio, in ¾, serves as an introduction to an Allegro spiritoso, with the strings announcing both subjects, the first in the tonic, the second in the dominant, as decreed by sonata form. The development is thorough, and the coda is protracted.

There follows an Adagio in D major, in ⅔ time, written in simple ternary form. The Minuetto, returning to G major, is marked allegretto; it includes a contrasting trio in which the bassoons and the horns create a bucolic atmosphere. The Finale: Presto, in ⅔, is full of kinetic energy.

Sinfonia No. 92
"Oxford"

I

Symphony No. 95 in C Minor (1791)

The task of cataloguing Haydn's symphonies and other instrumental works has been an important branch of musicological industry for some century and a half, and the end is not in sight. In the meantime, bloody polemics rage on the pages of musical periodicals regarding the attribution of this or that Haydn item, with the learned contenders, shoulder deep in the dust of Central European libraries, calling each other names. It has already been proved that the celebrated "Toy" Symphony was not written by Haydn, but by Mozart's father, and that the melody on which Brahms wrote his Variations on a Theme by Haydn was borrowed by Haydn from another source.

Happily, no cloud hangs over the twelve "London" symphonies, which Haydn wrote for the German violinist and manager Johann Peter Salomon, active in England, and which were performed during Haydn's two visits to London, in 1791–92 and 1794–95. The published edition states unequivocally: "Printed for the Proprietor, Mr. Salomon, and to be had at Monzani and Cimador's Music Shop, No. 2 Pall Mall." These "London," or "Salomon," symphonies are Haydn's last, numbering from No. 93 to No. 104. Haydn conducted Symphony No. 95 himself from the pianoforte, with Salomon leading the violin section.

There are four movements. The first, Allegro, opens with a germinal motive that invites fugal development by an artful arrangement of intervals around the strategic dominant of the key. These potentialities are exploited in due time. The subject proper is an ascending figure rich in kinetic energy. The second important theme is in the relative major key. In the recapitulation it appears in the key of C major.

The second movement, Andante cantabile, is in E-flat major, in § time. It is an instrumental aria with variations. An elegiac episode in the homonymous key of E-flat minor occurs before the return of the theme. There follows a Minuet, in C minor, with a trio in C major. It is a typical Classical move-ment, in which Haydn shows himself to be a perfect musical courtier.

The finale, Vivace, is in the form of sonata-rondo, in alla breve (²/²) time. It begins with a lively subject in C major, and develops in the best tradition of Classical musical architecture, of which Haydn was a master.

The symphony is prefixed by the words "In Nomine Domini," and the words "Laus Deo" ("Praise be to God") appear at the end of the manuscript, a lifelong habit. Haydn was deeply religious and believed in the necessity of prayer and gratitude for divine help in his work.

Symphony No. 99 in E-flat Major (1793)

Symphony No. 99 was announced by Salomon in the London program as "New Grand Overture." (No distinction was made in common usage at the time between a symphony and an overture.) "The incomparable Haydn produced an Overture of which it is impossible to speak in common terms. It abounds with ideas as new in music as they are grand and impressive; it rouses and affects every emotion of the soul. It was received with rapturous applause," commented the *Morning Chronicle* on the day after the concert. The symphony was repeated the following week, eliciting further enthusiasm from the *Chronicle*:

> The richest part of the banquet, as usual, was due to the wonderful Haydn. The first movement was encored; the effect of the wind instruments in the second movement was enchanting; the hautboy [oboe] and flute were finely in tune, but the bassoon was in every respect more perfect and delightful than we ever remember to have heard a wind instrument before. But indeed the pleasure the whole gave was continual, and the genius of Haydn, astonishingly inexhaustible, and sublime, was the general theme.

The first of the symphony's four movements, opening with an introduction, adagio, erupts in a brilliant Vivace assai, built in a characteristic binary form, in which the second half is a mirror image of the first. The movement is built in sonata form that is, however, remarkably free of convention, with the melodic material of the whole related in thematic structure to the principal theme.

The second movement, Adagio, in G major, in ⅜ time, introduces a songful subject, which develops in a number of ingenious rhythmic variations. Haydn projects the woodwind instruments to great advantage in a graceful interlude, which so enchanted the reviewer of the *Morning Chronicle* of London at the first performance of the symphony.

The third movement, Allegretto, is a minuet, in E-flat major. It is spaciously designed, with fine contrasts of piano and forte. The trio travels to the remote key of C major, and the modulation to the original tonality is bold. The Finale: Vivace, in ⅜ in E-flat major, is a rondo with ingratiating countersubjects. The whole movement, with its leaping appoggiaturas across large intervals, imparts a rococo sense of coquettish play. After a momentary pause, the principal theme returns in full splendor. The ending is in forte.

Symphony No. 104 in D Major ("London") (1795)

The key of the 104th Symphony is variously designated as D minor, D major, or simply D, which latter designation, although ambiguous, is more rational, seeing that it accounts for the introduction, which is in D minor, and the exposition of the first movement, which is in D major.

The date of the performance would never have been established had Haydn not identified the new symphony, performed in London on May 4, 1795, as "die 12. und letzte der englischen" ("the twelfth and last of the English ones"). The program of the concert listed a "New Overture" and, in parentheses, "Sinfonia"—for in 1795, the concert managers (and composers, for that matter) still allowed the terms "overture" and "sinfonia" to be used interchangeably, although musical science of the period had already differentiated them. The "London" Symphony was given for Haydn's last benefit concert. Haydn wrote in his diary, in his realistic manner: "The hall was filled with a picked audience. The whole company was delighted, and so was I. I took in this evening 4,000 gulden. One can make as much as this only in England." Four thousand gulden was then equivalent to about two thousand dollars.

The introduction, in D minor, has sixteen bars in slow tempo. It opens with a fanfarelike proclamation by full orchestra which, in this symphony as in most Haydn symphonies, includes strings, woodwinds (two of each), two horns, two trumpets, and kettledrums. This fanfare recurs twice, in F, and in D, contrasted with the intervening passages in piano. There is a pause at the end of the introduction. The principal movement, Allegro, opens with a tuneful theme in ⁴⁄₄, in the strings. The key is D major, by which the whole symphony is usually designated. The full orchestra bursts in, with some new material, rhythmic and lively. The music soon heads for the dominant, which course, in the tradition of all Classical forms, is as inevitable as the move of the king's knight in a chess opening. In place of a new second subject, the flute and the first violins take up the first theme in the dominant. This is very unusual in sonata form, and a symphony is nothing more than an orchestral sonata. The exposition ends in the key of the dominant, which is as it should be, according to the Classical formula.

The development of a symphony is like speculation about facts. The facts are the original subjects of the exposition. In the development section, they are pleasantly distorted, repeated in various keys, raised chromatically to shrieking pitch, or lowered into the gloom of the bass register. Indeed, there is often but a reminiscence of a theme left, a reflection of a vision of a dematerialized soul. The development of the first movement contains allusions to the second half of the principal theme, a four times reiterated note, and a plaintive appoggiatura, first in the strings, then in the flute and the oboe, in canonic imitation with the lower strings. The echoing of the reminiscent figure continues until the usual pause on the dominant, leading to the recapitulation, which is, in sonata form, a repetition of the exposition, with such variations as the composer may deem permissible or desirable. The principal theme appears in the strings, as it did in the exposition, and then reappears, obscurely hidden in the second oboe, with contrapuntal figures in the flute and the first oboe. The full orchestra comes in. There are imitations in canon between the woodwinds and the strings. The movement ends brilliantly.

On March 10, 1794, the London journal *The Oracle*, commenting on the second movement of a Haydn symphony, remarked rhetorically: "For Grace and Science, what is like it?" In Symphony No. 104, its science is bold, its modulations whimsical, but the Grace is there, spelled with a capital G. The main theme of the movement appears in variation form, in the original key of G major. Then it modulates upward, in chromatic progression. There is a pause after a string passage, and the flute plays a short cadenza, accompanied by oboes and bassoons. Another chromatic modulation brings in the dominant key. The theme returns fortissimo, embellished with triplet figurations. The flute continues the figure alone. The movement ends pianissimo, with a fine passage in the horns.

The Minuet, in D major, opens with a vigorous upbeat. The initial eight-bar period is then echoed in lighter orchestration. The dynamic contrasts of tutti and lighter scoring continue throughout the Minuet. There is a two-bar rest, and a two-bar trill before the end of the section, which is not repeated. The trio, in B-flat major, follows immediately. Only the first period of the trio is repeated. After the trio, the Minuet is resumed da capo, as all minuets must, to bring them back to the original key.

The fourth movement opens with a spirited dancelike tune, against the background of sustained horns and cellos. The time is alla breve ($\frac{2}{2}$), as in the first movement. The key is D major. The first violins carry the theme, in the low register, then an octave higher, joined by the oboe. The full orchestra is then brought into play, and the theme appears in various guises.

Haydn here uses once more the modification of sonata form that he applied in the first movement, and the principal theme in the dominant key serves in place of a new subject. There is a display of technique in the first and second violins, in converging and diverging scales. A quiet interlude follows with a dreamy melody in the relative minor key. The exposition concludes merrily, and is often not repeated in performance, as strict adherence to sonata form would demand. Few performers, however, follow the tradition of repeating the exposition, for this practice slackens the listener's attention and interest.

The development presents some canonic interplay of themes. The return of the exposition, that is, the recapitulation, enters softly, with the principal theme again in the violins. It then blossoms forth into a brilliant orchestral display. The dreamy melody appears again in the violins, while the flute gently traces an ascending scale. An orchestral outburst follows, but soon yields to a woodwind trio, a flute and two oboes, exhibiting the main theme in rotation. The symphony concludes with a forceful restatement of the theme, in the splendor of full orchestral dress.

CONCERTOS
Concerto for Violoncello in C Major (c. 1765)

A veritable musicological cliff-hanger is the story of Haydn's two concertos for violoncello and orchestra. In the case of the C-Major Concerto, it is listed in all catalogues of Haydn's works accompanied by the forbidding mark "verschollen," irretrievably lost. That the work actually existed is attested by the musical quotation of the opening bars of the cello solo in Haydn's own catalogue, compiled by him toward the end of his life. In November 1961, the electrifying news came of the discovery of an eighteenth-century copy of the "verschollenes Konzert" in the National Museum of Prague. One can well imagine the thrill when the discoverer checked on the theme of the concerto with the Haydn catalogue, and found that the two excerpts were identical. This, of course, established the authenticity of the lost concerto beyond all doubt. Stylistic analysis suggested that the concerto was written about 1765. And so, after two centuries, the concerto received its first performance, on May 19, 1962, at the Prague Spring Festival. The soloist was Miloš Sadlo, with the Czech Radio Symphony Orchestra, conducted by Charles Mackerras.

The concerto is scored for two oboes, two horns, and strings. The wind instruments are engaged mainly in the introduction and the ritornellos, when the soloist participates only by duplicating the corresponding part in the ensemble. This type of reinforcement was necessary in eighteenth- century performances owing to the smallness of the performing groups. In the original score of the Haydn Concerto, the cello part is written in to help out the basses; in twentieth-century practice, with a plentiful supply of instruments, such duplication is unnecessary.

From a formal standpoint, the concerto is entirely orthodox. The first movement, Moderato, in the principal key of C major, in $\frac{4}{4}$ time, is typical of initial movements of most instrumental works of the time, with symmetrical structures determining the progress of the music. The soloist is given a melodious voice; technically brilliant passage work employs familiar Baroque devices. The middle movement, Adagio, is in ternary form in the key of F major, in $\frac{2}{4}$ time; the third and last movement, Allegro di molto in C major and in $\frac{4}{4}$ time, provides a fitting conclusion. There are some interesting modulatory digressions into neighboring keys, before the principal key is asserted with dynamic vigor.

Concerto for Violoncello in D Major (1783)

The problem of authenticity of Haydn's works has been a major concern of music scholars. In his old age Haydn compiled a list of his symphonies, but it proved grossly inaccurate; his memory played him false. But there have also been pleasant reaffirmations of authorship, a notable instance of which is the restoration of Haydn's D-Major Cello Concerto to the Haydn column after it had been credited for many decades to Anton Kraft, Haydn's first cellist in his orchestra at Esterháza, thanks to an assertion in a German musical encyclopedia (1837). Kraft absorbed Haydn's melodic and contrapuntal techniques to perfection; since he wrote a cello concerto of his own, it is not surprising that the great D-Major Concerto was also ascribed to him. Fortunately, Haydn's original manuscript was eventually discovered in Vienna, and a new authentic edition, establishing Haydn's authorship beyond all doubt, was published in Vienna in 1962. The title page, in Haydn's own hand, bears the inscription "Concerto per il Violoncello, di me Giuseppe Haydn 1783." At the end of the manuscript, Haydn appended his customary valediction: "Laus Deo"—Praise be to God.

Kraft's name remains intimately associated with Haydn's concerto, because it was he who gave its first performance. It appears certain that Haydn wrote the concerto for the wedding of Prince Nikolaus Esterházy and Princess Maria Josepha Hermenegild Liechtenstein at the Liechtenstein Palace in Vienna on September 15, 1783. To judge by the almost stenographic rapidity of Haydn's handwriting in the concerto, the commission must have been given to Haydn with considerable urgency. After the discovery of the manuscript, the first performance of the concerto in its definitive form was given by Enrico Mainardi on May 19, 1957. Mainardi also composed the cadenzas for this performance.

The Violoncello Concerto is in three movements: Allegro moderato, Adagio, and Allegro. The writing is of extraordinary lucidity. The principal theme is stated without preliminaries. The violoncello is occupied without respite, either enunciating the subject or providing brilliant figurations, two to a beat, then four to a beat, six to a beat, and finally, eight to a beat. The result of this treatment is an energetic exposition of thematic material, in perfect balance with ornamental sonorities.

The theme of the Adagio is an exact reproduction, melodically and rhythmically, of a fragment of the original subject of the first movement. It progresses by measured accumulation of decorative melismas, concluding on a quiet cadence.

The Finale: Allegro, is set in the rhythmic style of a gigue. The subject is structurally related to the principal themes of both the first and the second movements. This cyclic affinity, rare in eighteenth-century music, provides an extraordinary feeling of musical unity. The concerto ends, as it began, in decisive tonal affirmation.

Symphonie Concertante in B-flat Major (1792)

Multiple concertos for instruments with orchestra, so popular in the eighteenth century, lapsed into innocuous desuetude in the nineteenth. The twentieth century witnessed a revival of these concertos in modern dress. One of the most extraordinary multiple concertos is Haydn's Symphonie Concertante, a quadruple concerto for solo violin, oboe, cello, and bassoon, accompanied by a full symphony orchestra. Haydn wrote it when he was sixty, at the height of his creative strength, for the same organization for which he composed the "London" symphonies. Examination of the score has surprises in store for those who believe in the myth of "Papa Haydn," a benevolent and bewigged gentleman who wrote melodious music for easy listening. For in the Symphonie Concertante we find Haydn, the Musical Scientist, the man Beethoven went to for the study of counterpoint, the intellectual musician who found satisfaction in structural organization as well as in the art of melody.

The selection of two string instruments of high and low range, and two woodwind instruments, also of high and low pitch, as solo instruments in the Symphonie Concertante affords six possibilities for instrumental duets, and four combinations for trios, besides four-part harmony and solo passages for each instrument singly. These combinations are artfully exploited and provide constant variety of timbre and range.

The Symphonie Concertante is in three movements, in the key of B-flat major. It opens with an Allegro in sonata form, $\frac{4}{4}$ time. This first movement is of considerable length, and the exposition of principal subjects is detailed and complete. There is a flowery cadenza in the best rococo manner. The second movement is an Andante, in § time. The solo instruments are given ample opportunity to display both the singing and the technical quality of their genre. The figurations are brilliant and varied.

The last movement, Allegro con spirito, is in the form of a rondo. There is an interesting departure from the instrumental character of a concerto in recitatives for solo violin that follow the melodic and harmonic procedures associated with opera. These recitatives, in adagio, interrupt the spirited progress of the movement at frequent intervals. Other solo instruments contribute their fiorituras and little arias, as well as rapid figurations. There is an effective interplay between the solo instruments and the orchestra. Once more, a recitative of the violin intervenes, and the movement concludes in a brilliant finale.

Concerto for Trumpet in E-flat Major (1796)

Haydn's catalogue is an inchoate body of titles and dates, monstrously overgrown and interspersed with exasperating question marks expressive of the editor's own state of confusion. Not a year passes without a discovery of an unknown Haydn manuscript, or—much worse—the demotion of a consecrated Haydn item to the list of works by a lesser composer, or to the realm of the Great Anon.

It is a relief to note that an overwhelming majority of Haydn's symphonies, concertos, choral works, and various instrumental pieces can be confidently embedded in the authentic division. Among these works is the Trumpet Concerto in E-flat Major, which Haydn wrote in 1796 for Anton Weidinger, the Viennese inventor of the *cornet à pistons* (cornet) capable of playing an entire chromatic scale.

The concerto is in three movements: Allegro, Andante, and Finale: Allegro. The first movement, in ¼ time, in E-flat major, has a lengthy orchestral introduction presenting the principal subjects. The trumpet enters with fine bravado after this exordium. According to the traditions of sonata form, to the perfection of which Haydn contributed so importantly, the theme appears in various related keys. The contrasting section is remarkable because it contains a descending chromatic passage in the solo part to honor Weidinger's invention. There is a long cadenza for the trumpet before a businesslike ending.

The second movement, Andante, in § time, is in the key of A-flat major. It has the rhythmic lilt of a serenade, with a simple melody, which subsequently undergoes a series of amiable variations. The Finale: Allegro, in ⅞ time, returns to the principal key of E-flat major. The statement of the main theme is given to the orchestra, and is reintroduced by the trumpet. A dialogue ensues between the solo instrument and the orchestra. There is a trumpet cadenza, and the concerto comes, to the utmost satisfaction of the musical ear, to an explicit and brilliant close.

VOCAL WORKS
The Seven Last Words of Christ (1795–96)

The story of the composition of *The Seven Last Words of Christ* was told by Haydn himself in one of the few explicit statements he ever made regarding his works: "About fifteen years ago," wrote Haydn in 1801 (so the time referred to must have been about 1786),

> ...I was asked by a clergyman in Cadiz to write instrumental music to the Seven Words of Jesus on the Cross. It was then customary every year, dur-

ing Lent, to perform an oratorio in the Cathedral at Cadiz, the effect of which the following arrangements contributed to heighten. The walls, windows and columns of the Church were hung with black cloth, and only one large lamp, hanging in the center, lighted the solemn and religious gloom. At noon all the doors were closed, and the music began. After a prelude, suited to the occasion, the Bishop ascended the Pulpit and pronounced one of the seven words, which was succeeded by reflections upon it. As soon as these were ended, he descended from the Pulpit and knelt before the Altar. The pause was filled by music. The Bishop ascended and descended again a second, a third time, and so on; and each time the Orchestra filled up the intervals in the discourse.

My Composition must be judged on a consideration of these circumstances. The task of writing seven Adagios, each of which was to last about ten minutes, to preserve a connection between them, without wearying the hearers, was none of the lightest; and I soon found that I could not confine myself within the limits of the time prescribed. The music was originally without text, and was printed in that form. It was only at a later period that I was induced to add the text. The partiality with which this work has been received by scientific Musicians, leads me to hope that it will not be without effect on the public at large.

The "seven last words" refer strictly speaking not to separate words but to seven phrases. They are (1) "Father, forgive them; for they know not what they do." (2) "Verily I say unto thee, this day shalt thou be with Me in Paradise." (3) "Woman, behold thy son; Son, behold thy mother." (4) "Eli, Eli, lama sabacthani?" (5) "I thirst." (6) "It is finished." (7) "Father, into Thy hands I commend my spirit."

The original instrumental form of the oratorio consisted of an introduction, seven pieces in a free sonata form, and a finale. The most unusual part of the music was the final portion of the oratorio describing the earthquake after the death of Christ. The music is marked "presto e con tutta la forza," and contains characteristic chromatic progressions and diminished-seventh chords.

Haydn made an arrangement of *The Seven Last Words of Christ* for voices with instrumental accompaniment under most unusual circumstances. A German musician named Joseph Friebert made use of Haydn's score for a vocal composition. Haydn heard Friebert's version and became interested in the possibilities of expanding the work into a real oratorio. He selected a text and fitted it into the music. Haydn added the voice parts and several instruments to the original score. He also made other additions and emendations. The result was a remarkably homogeneous work that quickly took its place among the most popular religious oratorios of the concert repertoire.

The Seasons *(1799–1801)*

Haydn's last work of large dimensions was *The Seasons*, an oratorio with a German text adapted from the eighteenth- century Classic poem by James Thomson (1700–1748). The project was suggested to Haydn by the Dutch-born nobleman and music patron, Gottfried, Baron van Swieten, who had also translated for Haydn the text of *The Creation*, after Milton's *Paradise Lost*. But whereas Haydn worked on *The Creation* with feverish enthusiasm (he said he had felt "one moment as cold as ice, the next as if on fire"), he hesitated to accept the new commission.

Besides, he objected to van Swieten's treatment of the text, and nearly quarreled with him on that account. But once begun, *The Seasons* progressed quickly to completion. Its first performance took place at the Schwarzenberg Palace in Vienna, on April 24, 1801, a few weeks after Haydn's sixty-ninth birthday, and two years after the first performance in the same palace of *The Creation*. On May 29, 1801, Haydn conducted *The Seasons* at his benefit concert in Vienna. The new oratorio was a success, but Haydn said afterward: "*The Seasons* gave me the finishing blow."

The dramatis personae in *The Seasons* are Simon, a farmer, his daughter Jane, and a young peasant named Lucas. All four seasons are represented in James Thomson's original poem, as well as in Haydn's oratorio. When *The Seasons* became popular in English-speaking countries, the problem of retranslation from the German adaptation back into Thomson's native tongue presented formidable obstacles. There were several versions, each successive effort trying to salvage as many lines from the original as possible while leaving the melodic rhythm of Haydn's music intact.

HOMER'S Hymn on Mercury

WOLFGANG AMADEUS MOZART
(1756–1791)
The Supreme

Wolfgang Amadeus Mozart (1756–1791) was the supreme and prodigious Austrian composer whose works in every genre are unsurpassed in lyric beauty, rhythmic variety, and effortless melodic invention. The universal recognition of Mozart's genius during the two centuries since his death has never wavered among professional musicians, amateurs, and the general public, although those who preferred the larger-than-life qualities of Beethoven would fail to hear the proto-Romantic element amidst the Classic aesthetic in Mozart. In his music, smiling simplicity was combined with somber drama; lofty inspiration was contrasted with playful diversion; profound meditation alternated with capricious moodiness; religious concentration was permeated with human tenderness.

Mozart was the first great child prodigy. At a nursery age he knew public acclaim and the praise of kings and potentates. There was a sweetness and serenity in Mozart as a child unmatched by any other musical child in history. He was a miraculous player, and he was a composer of alluring charm even in his works written before he reached early adolescence.

Mozart's older sister, Maria Anna ("Nannerl"), took harpsichord lessons from their father, Leopold, and Mozart as a very young child eagerly absorbed the sounds of music. He soon began playing the harpsichord himself, and later studied the violin. Leopold was an excellent musician, but he also appreciated the theatrical validity of the performances that Wolfgang and Nannerl began giving in Salzburg. In 1762, he took them to Munich and Vienna to play for royalty and in 1763 to Frankfurt, where Wolfgang showed his skill in improvising on the keyboard. In November 1763 they arrived in Paris, where they played before Louis XV; it was in Paris that Wolfgang's first compositions were printed (four sonatas for harpsichord, with violin ad libitum). In April 1764 they proceeded to London; there Wolfgang played for King George III.

In London he was befriended by Bach's son Johann Christian Bach, who gave exhibitions improvising four-hands at the piano with the child Mozart. By that time, Mozart had tried his ability in composing serious works; he wrote two symphonies for a London performance, and the manuscript of another very early symphony, purportedly written by him in London, was discovered in 1980. Leopold wrote home with undisguised pride: "Our great and mighty Wolfgang seems to know everything at the age of seven that a man acquires at the age of forty." Knowing the power of publicity, he diminished Wolfgang's age, for at the time the child was fully nine years old. In July 1765, they journeyed to the Netherlands, then set out for Salzburg, visiting Dijon, Lyons, Geneva, Bern, Zurich, Donaueschingen, and Munich on the way.

Arriving back in Salzburg in November 1766, Wolfgang applied himself to the serious study of counterpoint under the tutelage of his father. In September 1767, the family proceeded to Vienna, where Wolfgang began work on an opera, *La finta semplice*. His second theater work was a singspiel, *Bastien und Bastienne*, which was produced in Vienna at the home of Dr. Franz Mesmer, the protagonist of the famous method of therapy by means of "animal magnetism," later known as mesmerism. In December 1768 Mozart led a performance of his Missa solemnis in C Minor before the royal family and court at the consecration of the Waisenhauskirche.

Legends of Mozart's extraordinary musical ability grew; it was reported, for instance, that he wrote out the entire score of the Miserere by Allegri, which he had heard in the Sistine Chapel at the Vatican only twice. Young Mozart was subjected to numerous tests by famous Italian musicians; he was given a diploma as an elected member of the Accademia Filarmonica in Bologna after he had passed examinations in harmony and counterpoint. In 1770, the pope made him a knight of the Golden Spur. He was commissioned to compose an opera and conducted three performances from the harpsichord.

Two of his finest symphonies—No. 35 in D Major, the "Haffner," written for the Haffner family of Salzburg, and No. 36 in C Major, the "Linz"—date from 1782 and 1783, respectively. From this point forward, Mozart's productivity reached extraordinary dimensions.

In 1785, Mozart completed a set of six string quartets, which he dedicated to Haydn. Unquestionably the structure of these quartets owed much to Haydn's contrapuntal art, and Haydn himself paid tribute to his genius. Leopold Mozart reports Haydn's words about Mozart: "I tell you as an honest man before God that your son is the greatest composer I have ever known personally or by name. He has taste and, what is more, supreme science of composition." Despite the fact that Haydn was almost twice Mozart's age at the time, their friendship was on an equal footing. Haydn was generally accepted as the creator of the Classical quartet, a form that Mozart faithfully followed. But there was no condescension on Haydn's part when he expressed his opinion of Mozart's greatness, and there was no feeling of subservience on the part of Mozart. In short, the Haydn-Mozart relationship is a rare example of unaffected friendship between two men of greatness. It is interesting to add that both were members of the order of Freemasons. Mozart joined the Vienna Lodge in December 1784, and Haydn followed early in 1785.

Wolfgang Amadeus Mozart's Werke.

Kritisch durchgesehene Gesammtausgabe.

Serie 14.

QUARTETTE
für Streichinstrumente.

Serie 14.		Köchel's Verz. Nº	Seite.	Serie 14.		Köchel's Verz. Nº	Seite.
1.	Quartett G dur ¾.	80.	I.	13.	Quartett D moll C.	173.	96.
2.	Quartett D dur C.	155.	8.	14.	Quartett G dur C.	387.	106.
3.	Quartett G dur ⅜.	156.	15.	15.	Quartett D moll C.	421.	124.
4.	Quartett C dur C.	Für 157.	21.	16.	Quartett Es dur C.	Für 428.	137.
5.	Quartett F dur ¾.	2 Violinen, 158.	29.	17.	Quartett B dur ⅜.	2 Violinen, 458.	152.
6.	Quartett B dur C.	Viola 159.	36.	18.	Quartett A dur ¾.	Viola 464.	168.
7.	Quartett Es dur C.	und 160.	45.	19.	Quartett C dur ¾.	und 465.	186.
8.	Quartett F dur C.	Violoncell. 168.	52.	20.	Quartett D dur C.	Violoncell. 499.	206.
9.	Quartett A dur ¾.	169.	60.	21.	Quartett D dur C.	575.	226.
10.	Quartett C dur ¾.	170.	69.	22.	Quartett B dur ¾.	580.	242.
11.	Quartett Es dur C.	171.	77.	23.	Quartett F dur C.	590.	258.
12.	Quartett B dur ¾.	172.	86.				

A great number of Mozart's instrumental works were the products of commissions by wealthy patrons. This circumstance influenced even the form of Mozart's instrumental works. Thus, instrumental divertissements, serenades, and similar compositions often provided several extra minuets or other dances to fill in the time if the particular festivity for which such works were written lasted longer than expected, much as contemporary incidental music for movies provides extra sections, or is so arranged that the separate sections can be easily spliced.

Mozart's life and Mozart's music form an interlocking commentary. It is a strange reflection on eighteenth-century society that Mozart could not maintain the security that his early successes seemed to augur, and that in his later life he should have been dependent entirely on his commissions as composer, and when these failed to materialize in sufficient numbers, on borrowing without repayment and on undisguised begging. Composers have not been self-supporting at any time in any society based on profit, and have always been dependent on the benefactions of those in political or economic power—the kings in monarchical Europe, the wealthy art patrons in other parts of the world. But performers finding favor with the public were in a far better position than creative musicians. Why Mozart could not provide for himself and his family as a performer or a teacher is a puzzle not explained by the historians of musical society.

Still, melodramatic stories of Mozart's abject poverty are gross exaggerations. He apparently felt no scruples in asking prosperous friends for financial assistance. Periodically he wrote to Michael Puchberg, a banker and a brother Freemason, with requests for loans (which he never repaid); invariably Puchberg obliged, but usually granted smaller amounts than Mozart requested.

In literature, Mozart has been the subject of several novels and plays. Pushkin presented a tragic Mozart in a play, *Mozart and Salieri*, in which the Italian composer Antonio Salieri (1750–1825), the court Kapellmeister in Vienna, poisons Mozart to stop the flow of celestial harmony: "What if Mozart is allowed to live on and to reach new heights?" asks Salieri. "Will the art be maintained at that height? It will fall again as soon as Mozart disappears—he will not leave an heir. Like a cherub, he has brought down a few songs from paradise, which will only excite a wingless desire in us, the children of the dust, and he will then fly away. Fly then! and the sooner the better." Rimsky-Korsakov set Pushkin's tale of Salieri the poisoner to Mozartean music; his opera ends with Mozart playing his own Requiem. Salieri himself thought so seriously about the rumors he had had a hand in Mozart's death that in 1825 he sent a deathbed message to the pianist Ignaz Moscheles: "I did not poison Mozart." At least, Moscheles so reports. A fanciful dramatization of the Mozart-Salieri rivalry was made by Peter Shaffer into a successful play, *Amadeus*, and gained wider currency through a film version in 1984.

The notion of Mozart's murder also appealed to the Nazis: in the ingenious version propagated by some German writers of the Hitlerian persuasion, Mozart was a victim of a double conspiracy of Masons and Jews who were determined to suppress the flowering of racial Germanic greatness. In this version, the Masons were outraged by his revealing of their secret rites in *Die Zauberflöte* (*The Magic Flute*), and allied themselves with plutocratic Jews to prevent the further spread of his dangerous revelations.

Another myth related to Mozart's death that found its way into the majority of Mozart biographies and even into respectable reference works was that a blizzard raged during his funeral and that none of his friends could follow his body to the cemetery. This story is easily refuted by the records of the Vienna weather bureau for the day. It is also untrue that Mozart was buried in a pauper's grave; his body was removed from its original individual location because the family neglected to pay the mandatory dues.

The parallel between Mozart and the Renaissance painter Raphael is often drawn. Both lived short lives. Raphael died on his thirty-seventh birthday; Mozart did not even reach his thirty-sixth. Raphael's art was marked by logical simplicity, and so was Mozart's. Raphael's subjects are serene and natural; Mozart, too, portrayed carefree moods in a carefree manner. This parallel was drawn for the first time by Franz Niemetschek in a biography of Mozart written a few years after his death and is sufficiently plausible to have engaged Mozarteans in successive centuries.

We are so familiar with the picture-book presentation of Mozart, a genius unconscious of his own powers, an eternal child with an angelic face in a frame of artificial curls, that it is naturally shocking to discover he could be mischievous in his art. He could be mischievous and sly also in his human relations. From the evidence of his letters, an entirely new Mozart emerges, cunning, shrewd, and not above borrowing money under false pretenses. Yet this Mozart is much more human than the tinseled creature of conventional biography.

Mozart used dissonances and forbidden progressions on purpose in a little parody that he called "A Musical Joke" ("Ein musikalischer Spass," subtitled "Die Dorfmusikanten," "The Village Musicians"), and which he wrote on the afternoon of June 14, 1787, for the amusement of friends. In this musical joke, Mozart deliberately used consecutive fifths and a whole-tone scale in the violin cadenza and, to top it off, finished the piece in five different keys. He could hardly foresee that the employment of several keys in simultaneous harmony would be taken seriously a hundred-odd years thence, and that it would even receive a scientific-sounding name—polytonality.

The variety of technical development in Mozart's works is all the more remarkable considering the limitations of instrumental means in his time; the topmost note on his keyboard was F above the third ledger line, so that in the recapitulation in the first movement of his famous C-Major Piano Sonata, K. 545, the subject had to be dropped an octave lower to accommodate the modulation. The vocal technique displayed in his operas is amazing in its perfection; to be sure, the human voice has not changed since Mozart's time, but he knew how to exploit vocal resources to the utmost. This adaptability of his genius to all available means of sound production is the secret of the eternal validity of his music.

ORCHESTRAL MUSIC
Symphony No. 25 in G Minor, K. 183 (1773)

Mozart's Symphony No. 25 is dated October 5, 1773, that is, when Mozart was only seventeen years old. This is not too surprising, considering that he wrote his first symphony at the age of eight. Haydn's influence is easily detected in this Twenty-fifth Symphony, but there are also points of contact with Johann Christian Bach, the "London Bach," who showered attention on the child Mozart during the journey of Mozart's family to England. The presence of fine dynamic nuances in the work indicates Mozart's awareness of the innovations introduced by the Mannheim masters.

The symphony is in four Classical movements. The first movement, Allegro con brio, in the principal key of G minor, in $\frac{4}{4}$ time, opens with a strong rhythmic subject with repeated notes in syncopated rhythm. Its development follows the outline of sonata form, and there is a clearly defined recapitulation. The second movement, Andante, is in E-flat major, in $\frac{2}{4}$ time. Here the interest lies in a balladlike sequential construction of the main theme for muted strings. The third movement, Minuetto, is in the traditional ternary form. The minuet proper is in G minor, the trio is in G major. The Finale: Allegro, in G minor, in $\frac{4}{4}$ time, is a vivacious rondo. Once more, the construction by simple tonal sequences arrests attention.

Symphony No. 32 in G Major, K. 318 (1779)

Mozart wrote this work in Salzburg in 1779, when he was twenty-three. It is sur-mised that he intended it to be used as an overture to one of his operas planned for production there, which may explain the unsymphonic character of the work. It is in three movements, Allegro spiritoso; Andante; Tempo primo. There is no minuet. The finale constitutes a shortened recapitulation of the first movement, and it is played without a pause after the slow middle movement. The sequence of tempi—fast, slow, fast—is the formula of an overture rather than a symphony. There are dramatic incidents in the music—mounting crescendos over protracted pedal points, horn calls and tremolos in the strings—that suggest stage action.

Symphony No. 36 in C Major ("Linz"), K. 425 (1783)

On the way back from Salzburg to Vienna in late October of 1783, Mozart and his wife stopped over at the house of Count Thun in Linz. Mozart wrote on October 31, 1783: "On November 4, I am giving a concert at the town theater here, and since I do not have a single symphony with me I must work neck-and-head at a new one, which must be ready before then." It was indeed ready—the composition, the copying of the parts, and the rehearsals, all accomplished in four days. The work was performed on schedule and became known, rightly so, as the "Linz" Symphony.

The work is one of Mozart's most classically perfect compositions. It is in C major, and contains four movements. The first movement consists of an introductory adagio in $\frac{3}{4}$ time, leading to Allegro spiritoso, in $\frac{4}{4}$, which evolves with poetic animation within the confines of Classical sonata form.

The slow movement, Poco adagio, in F major, in $\frac{6}{8}$ time, is an air in the rhythm of barcarole. There follows a minuet, which moves along with typical Mozartean grace. The finale is a Presto in $\frac{2}{4}$ time in rondo form, with the vivacious principal theme returning afresh after an intermittent series of melodious countersubjects.

Overture to Der Schauspieldirektor, K. 486 (1786)

While working on *The Marriage of Figaro*, Mozart took time off to write an engag-ing little theater sketch, *Der Schauspieldirektor* (*The Play Director*), dated February 3, 1786. It was a commissioned work for a performance at the orangery of the royal palace in Schönbrunn, in Vienna, at a reception given by Joseph II for the visiting general-governor of the Netherlands. The slender story, from a contemporary play, dealt with a rivalry between two *prime donne*, in which the Impresario becomes embroiled, much against his will. They were named in the cast of characters Mlle Herz ("heart") and Mlle Silberklang ("sound of silver"). One of the parts was sung by Mozart's sister-in-law.

The score consists of an overture in C major (presto, $\frac{4}{4}$ time), an arietta, a rondo, a vocal trio, and the finale. The text is in German. The most amusing num-ber is the trio, in which the two *prime donne* sing in canon: "I am the prima donna, I am universally acclaimed, no other singer can approach me... adagio, allegro, alle-grissimo, piano, pianissimo..."

The overture remains a popular item on concert programs. It is typically Italian in structure, and its vivacity is contagious. Several attempts have been made to titi-vate the simple story and the score for scenic purposes. A version of 1845 had Mozart himself put on the stage as a supernumerary character. The Italian title *L'Impresario* was adopted in the middle of the nineteenth century. In 1953 Eric

SYMPHONY No. 36
in C Major, K.425 ("Linz")

Composed November 1783 in Linz.

Blom published a witty English version under the title *An Operatic Squabble, or The Impresario Perplext*, naming the warring singers respectively Mrs. Heartfelt and Miss Silvertone.

Overture to The Marriage of Figaro, K. 492 (1786)

Le Nozze di Figaro: dramma giocoso in quadro atti; poesia di Lorenzo Da Ponte, aggiustata dalla commedia del Beaumarchais, "Le Mariage de Figaro" was written by Mozart in Vienna in 1786. It was performed at the Imperial Royal National Court Theater in Vienna on May 1, 1786. Amazingly enough, the performance ran into all kinds of obstacles on account of the immorality of the comedy itself. Lorenzo Da Ponte reports in his memoirs that Mozart wrote the music as fast as the libretto was being prepared, and that the entire opera was completed in six weeks.

The librettist, Lorenzo da Ponte, decided to approach the Emperor Joseph II himself for permission to have the opera performed. "But you know that I have already forbidden the German theatrical company to have this piece performed," the emperor told Da Ponte. The librettist acknowledged that it was so, but pleaded with the emperor, pointing out that he had cut out all objectionable scenes in making the Beaumarchais play into an opera libretto. He assured the emperor that nothing would be left that might shock the sensibility of the public. He courteously reminded the emperor of the high opinion in which Mozart's musical talent was held in the city.

The emperor relented and ordered the score to be sent to the copyists. Later, Mozart himself was summoned to the palace to play some numbers from the opera for the emperor in private. Joseph II was delighted by the music, and *The Marriage of Figaro* started on its glorious road through the opera houses of the world.

The overture itself, in D major, is a presto. The basic movement remains unaltered throughout the overture, but marvelous contrasts and subtle variety of moods are created by rhythmic and melodic changes of musical phrases. The form is a projection of luminous symmetry. After the main themes have been stated, there is a reprise, culminating in a brilliant coda.

Symphony No. 38 in D Major ("Prague"), K. 504 (1787)

Mozart always loved Prague, and Prague loved him. He knew greater triumphs and heart-warming welcome in Prague than in his native Salzburg or in his adopted hometown of Vienna. Within the German and Austrian sphere of influence, Prague was a great cultural center in the eighteenth century. Confident of success, Mozart, accompanied by his wife and several friends, gladly undertook the tedious three-day journey from Vienna to Prague (150 miles, about twenty minutes by plane today) to conduct his freshly composed symphony, which came to be known as the "Prague" Symphony.

The *Prager Oberpostamtszeitung* (*Prague Post Office Newspaper*) reported on January 12, 1787:

> Last night our great and beloved composer Herr Mozard [a common spelling in Mozart's time] arrived here from Vienna. We do not doubt that in honor of this man, the well-loved work of his musical genius, *The Marriage of Figaro*, will be performed again and that the discerning inhabitants of Prague will surely assemble in large numbers, notwithstanding that they have already heard the piece frequently. We would dearly like to be able to admire Herr Mozard's playing for ourselves.

Mozart did not disappoint the expectations of Prague's music lovers, and he conducted a special performance of his opera. So delighted was he by the reception that within the same year, he gave Prague the honor of the first performance anywhere of his greatest opera, *Don Giovanni*, and came again to Prague to conduct it.

Mozart filed a necessary application "to hold a musical concert," which was duly granted by the office of the governor of Bohemia. On January 19, 1787, he conducted the "Prague" Symphony and, in response to applause, obliged with three improvisations on the piano. Mozart left Prague on February 8, arriving in Vienna, by stagecoach as before, in four days.

Mozart entitled the work simply Eine Sinfonie. A sad postscript: in the latest edition of Köchel's catalogue, there is an annotation: "Manuscript lost since the end of the war." Some Mozart lover in the Army of Occupation must have taken the "Prague" Symphony as a war souvenir from one of the deposits in various German towns where the manuscripts of the old Prussian State Library were distributed by faithful German librarians during the last days of the Third Reich.

The first movement begins with an adagio in D major, in $\frac{4}{4}$ time, with dramatic upward runs in unison. The violin has a plaintive melody, echoed in the woodwinds. The mood darkens, with a shift to D minor. A syncopated figure, punctuated by the strokes of the kettledrum, alternates with light flourishes of the violins. The modulations are tense and follow a chromatic progression toward an extensive cadence. The principal Allegro opens with a syncopated figure on a repeated note in the first violins. The wind instruments enter, by way of contrast, and the strings return, while the oboe plays a short melody. The figure of the repeated note soon develops into a rhythmic pattern. The orchestra, now in full strength, plays a vigorous marching theme, leading to the dominant key. Again the figure of the repeated note appears, in different instruments and different keys, ending on a quiet cadence in the dominant.

The first violins carry a quiet melody. There is a sudden darkening into a minor key, with the bassoons echoing the violin theme. The major key returns, and the violins play a lively theme, leading toward the marching theme, this time in the dominant. This concludes the principal part of Allegro in sonata form. The development section that follows opens with a curious canon in the violins. The same canonic device is then taken up in the low register. The marching theme appears in different keys, in combination with the figure of the repeated note. There is a prolonged pedal point on the deep A, and the repeated note returns in the first violins: this is the recapitulation. However, in sonata form, recapitulation is literal repetition only in very orthodox writing. This is not early unsophisticated Mozart; and he is not content with unchanged forms. Accordingly, there are new modulations, and characteristic shifts from major to minor on the same keynote. This section ends on the quiet theme in the tonic, corresponding to the preceding quiet theme in the dominant.

From now on, the recapitulation follows its appointed course with little change. Again, there is a darkening into the minor key. The expressive violin theme reappears, and the animated marching section leads to a brilliant ending.

The second movement, Andante, follows after a brief pause. It is in $\frac{6}{8}$ time, in the key of G major, with a rhythmic lilt suggesting a barcarole. The tenseness of the mood is indicated by frequent chromatic progressions. There is canonic imitation between the violins on the one hand and cellos plus the basses on the other. The modulatory scheme is bold, and there is a feeling of unrest. Finally, there is an intense drive toward the key of D, with the violins and the woodwinds playing preparatory figurations.

A new phrase of pastoral character is heard in the violins. The mood is sustained by the echoing of woodwind instruments. The violins play a concluding theme, and the exposition is ended. The development elaborates on the ideas already presented. There are darker colors, frequent shifts from one key to another. The chromatic upward runs intensify the dramatic effect. The scoring is more full, and the contrasts are emphasized by dynamic changes.

A few remaining bars of the development lead to a recapitulation. But once more, recapitulation is here no literal repetition. The orchestration is supplemented, the coloring is sharper. However, the succession of keys follows the traditional formula. Both the principal and the second, pastoral theme are now played in the tonic key. The movement ends gently, in pianissimo.

The third and final movement, Presto, is appropriately optimistic. The tonality is clear D major, and there are no tortuous chromatics. The tempo, in $\frac{2}{4}$, is light, the scoring diaphanous. Particularly fine are the color effects of woodwind interludes. The division of musical periods is symmetric: four, eight, or sixteen bars each. The melodic flow is free, the phrasing natural and simple. It is the Mozart of *Figaro*, intent on amusement, not the philosophical Mozart of the first two movements of this symphony.

The strings open the movement with the four-note principal theme. After a symmetric sixteen-bar period, the orchestra enters in full. By way of contrast, there follows a section in the woodwinds, imitating the principal theme in a modulatory period, from D minor to F major. The full orchestra is sounded again, and there is some darker, dramatic coloring here. Now the strings play the second theme, and the flute, accompanied by a bouncing bassoon, finishes it off. The interplay of these elements is repeated. The woodwinds play the principal theme in the dominant key of A major, and the strings enter in imitation.

Again, the full orchestra enters dramatically, in a minor key. The violins play the principal theme, varied in rhythm and intervals, and descending arpeggios bring the first section to a close. Full orchestra chords announce the second section, and there is alternation with woodwind. The contrasts are sharp. A prolonged development, with keys shifting frequently in a wide modulation range, leads to the return of the second theme in the violins. Again, as in the first section, the woodwinds finish off the phrase. The tonality is now D major, the key of the entire symphony. The descending arpeggios bring the Presto (and the symphony) to a brilliant close.

Symphony No. 39 in E-flat Major, K. 543 (1788)

June 1788 was a very busy month in Mozart's life. On June 17, he moved with his wife and children to new lodgings in suburban Vienna, at Wäringergasse no. 135, at the sign of the Three Stars. He had left the previous quarters on the Landstrasse under unpleasant circumstances, for the landlord compelled him to pay the back rent before they moved out. Mozart liked the new rooms, which were comfortable and, what was particularly important, cheap. True, he had to pay the fiacre ten kreutzer to drive to town, but then he was more free to work, because visitors were less frequent at this distance from town. And he did accomplish in ten days in the new lodgings more than he had in two months in the old.

Mozart's Symphony in E-flat Major is the first of the stellar symphonic trilogy created in a state of quiet inspiration during the summer of 1788. The second and the third symphonies of the cycle are the intimate G Minor and the Olympian C Major.

SYMPHONY No. 39
in E-flat Major, K.543
Composed June 1788 in Vienna.

The E-flat Major Symphony can be seen as a musical equivalent to the golden section in architecture. In it, each phrase relates to its associative period as that period relates to the entire movement, and as each movement relates to the entire work. There is an abiding symmetry in the noble macrostructure as in the minimotives of each of the four movements of the work. An opening adagio serves as an earnest declaration of purpose, introducing the main division of the first movement, Allegro. Its principal theme is built on the three notes of the tonic triad of E-flat major, exquisitely arranged in convoluted undulations.

A contrasting figure follows with a doubled quantitative rhythmic content. Then an energetic new motive makes its entry. These thematic elements engage in a lively interchange until the exposition is completed. There is no formal development; each variation, each modulatory digression, appears as a newly born idea, melodically and rhythmically associated with the basic subjects of the movement. The provocative suggestion of a famous modern composer that Mozart's symphonies could have been vastly improved by the elimination of the development section does not apply. The music here is irreducible in content and in impact.

The second movement, Andante, in ⅞ time, in the key of A-flat, is a romanza with varied contrasting clauses. Its syncopated rhythmic pattern lends itself to canonic imitation. The modulatory scheme is remarkably bold; by dint of artful enharmonic equations, the entire cycle of scales is circumambulated and the remotest keys are reached, before returning to the home base.

The Minuet: Allegretto, is far from a conventional courtly dance. The initial theme is arrayed in wide intervallic steps encompassing two octaves in a single measure. It is in this minuet that Prokofiev must have found the model for the brusque skipping melodies of his *Classical Symphony*. In the middle section of the minuet—the trio—the clarinet and the flute conduct a melodious dialogue.

The Finale: Allegro, is a rondo. The main motive, with its vigorous upbeat, sets the tone of Classical directness. The alternation of numerous ancillary motives provides variety without impeding the strong pulse of rhythmic motion. Canonic imitation between strings and woodwind instruments proceeds vivaciously. There are frequent excursions into distant tonalities, and they are effected without resort to the diminished-seventh chord, that passe-partout of enharmonic modulation. The ending is remarkable; the initial motive of the finale serves as the concluding measure of the symphony. Here the principle of cyclic construction finds its perfect application.

Symphony No. 40 in G Minor, K. 550 (1788)

Sacha Guitry, the French actor and playwright, who wrote a play about Mozart, said that Mozart flew across the skies of music like an archangel with wings of gold. In Pushkin's drama *Mozart and Salieri*, Salieri pours poison into Mozart's wine murmuring "So fly away to Paradise from whence you came." (This Mozartocidal tale is an unmitigated fantasy not supported by an atom of realistic evidence.)

The real Mozart, as revealed in his correspondence, had little of an angel in him. He was an honest artisan trying hard to earn enough money to support himself and his growing family. He was even, horribile dictu, given to profanity. His scatological canons have been issued on records, now that there is no censorship of German four-letter words. Nor is Mozart's music uniformly serene. There is enough drama in its somber harmonies and its throbbing rhythms to conjure up a vision of Mozart the Tragedian.

Mozart's Symphony in G Minor, his fortieth, was written in the summer of 1788, after the one in E-flat major, and preceding the great C-Major Symphony, the "Jupiter." The creation of three symphonies, each one sublime in its art, within a single year was an unparalleled achievement even for Mozart. The four movements of each of these three symphonies are in the Classical mold: a fast first movement, Allegro molto, followed by an Andante, a Minuet, and a rapid Finale: Allegro assai.

The symphony opens with Allegro molto, in G minor. Its palpitating principal subject sets the tone for the entire movement. The form is that of a sonata allegro, which is worked out with superlative clarity and dramatic contrasts. The second movement, Andante, in the key of B-flat major, is characteristic of Mozart's "Italian" style, songful and decorative in its ingratiating melodic variations. The third movement, Minuett, in the principal key of G minor, is uncommonly brief. The middle part, trio, is based on the fanfare figures of hunting horns. The movement is set in a Classical three-part form, without elaborations or variations.

SYMPHONY No. 40
in G Minor, K.550

Completed July 25, 1788 in Vienna.

The Finale: Allegro assai, is full of kinetic energy. In the development section, there are bold enharmonic modulations to remote keys. The diminished-seventh chord (which the Italians called *accorde di stupefazione*, "chord of stupefaction") plays a crucial role in the modulatory scheme. In one intriguing episode, three mutually exclusive "chords of stupefaction" form a series of twelve different notes, used consecutively in various instruments of the orchestra. Some modern commentators cite this section as a prophetic anticipation of dodecaphonic usages. Mozart, it appears, was a composer for all seasons. And in his music there are to be found roots of future idioms and future techniques.

CONCERTOS
Concerto for Violin No. 5 in A Major, K. 219 (1775)

In 1775, at the age of nineteen, Mozart wrote five violin concertos, probably intended as exercises to satisfy the paternal urgings of Leopold Mozart, himself an eminent violinist and teacher, and possibly with a view toward a performance by a Salzburg virtuoso. The manuscript of the Fifth Violin Concerto is now in the Library of Congress in Washington; it was formerly owned by the famous violinist Joseph Joachim (1831–1907), and before that by the publisher Johann Anton André, who acquired it from Mozart's widow.

The Fifth Concerto is a fine distillation of Mozart's stylistic qualities, a paradigm of his instrumental art in composition. There is the characteristic vivacity of a musical optimist in the rapid portions of the music; elegiac inspiration in songful passages; and a graceful gait of a court dance in the finale.

The first movement, in A major, is set in the energetic meter of $\frac{4}{4}$. It comprises three sections: an "openhearted" allegro aperto, in which the subject based on the notes of the tonic triad is introduced jointly by the soloist and orchestra; a brief adagio, with an expressive theme in the solo part accompanied by the shimmering murmurations of innumerable semi-demi-quavers; and another "open" (aperto) allegro, not as a literal recapitulation, but as a greatly expanded presentation of germane thematic materials in a new melodic and rhythmic mold.

The second movement, Adagio, in E major, in slow $\frac{2}{4}$ time, is remarkable for its varied melodic figurations, in which Mozartean syncopation seems to reinforce the main beat by metrical anticipation. A series of tonal sequences leads to an unaffected ending.

The third and last movement, in A major, is a minuet, an unusual selection for a finale. The violin solo introduces the gentle dancing theme, with an upbeat and a note échappée, falling down on the unprepared suspension on the leading tone. The place of a traditional trio is taken by an allegro set in a totally different metric scheme, in $\frac{2}{4}$ time, in the minor tonic. Melodic patterns are most curious in this middle section; there is a fascinating ascending chromatic phrase within a tetrachord, reciprocated by a symmetric descending chromatic phrase, in a manner suggesting a peasant stomping dance of Central Europe.

In fact, some musicologists have published learned essays on Mozart's utilization in this and other violin concertos of such peasant dance tunes. However that might be, the effect produced by this display of elastic resilience in chromatic progression is extraordinary. The Tempo di minuetto re-returns, and the concerto concludes with reverberating gusto.

Concerto for Three Pianos in F Major, K. 242 (1776)

Mozart composed his Concerto for Three Pianos in Salzburg a few days after his twentieth birthday, as a commission for Countess Antonia Lodron and her two daughters. Mozart's father, always mindful of the prime necessity of pleasing aristocratic patrons, wrote out a flowery dedication in Italian: "Dedicated to the incomparable merit of Her Excellency the Signora Contessa Lodron and her two daughters, Countesses Aloisa and Giuseppa, by their most devoted servant Wolfgang Mozart." But apparently the three ladies never performed the concerto. The first hearing was given in Augsburg on October 22, 1777. Mozart played the second piano part, with a local organist at the first piano, and a piano manufacturer at the third.

Like so many of Mozart's concertos, this concerto consists of three movements, Allegro, Adagio, and Rondeau, the latter marked Tempi di minuetto. The first and last movements are in F major, and the slow movement is in B-flat major. The concerto has 565 bars, of which Allegro numbers 280 bars, Adagio 73 bars, and Rondeau 212 bars. Although the slow movement has the smallest number of bars, the reduced tempo equalizes it with the fast movements in duration.

Concerto for Flute and Harp in C Major, K. 299 (1778)

A major part of Mozart's meager revenue came from commissions to write music for amateur musicians of the nobility, dukedom, or royalty. The Concerto for Flute and Harp was composed in April 1778 for the duc de Guines and his daughter. The duke played the flute and the daughter, the harp. Mozart wrote in a letter that the duke was a very good flutist and that the little duchess played the harp "magnifique." Being a superior workman capable of satisfying any kind of customer, Mozart adopted in his concerto a French salon manner. He was also careful not to write passages that might overtax the technique of the duke and the duchess, and he wrote the concerto in the key of C major unencumbered by sharps or flats in the key signature. But despite all of Mozart's eagerness to please, the duke was uncivil enough to have delayed the payment for the commission for fully four months after the delivery of the manuscript, a fact of which Mozart, always pressed for money, complained to his father.

The concerto is in three movements, Allegro, Andantino, and Rondeau (the latter spelled in French in the manuscript). Mozart had written cadenzas for both the flute and the harp in the concerto, but they were lost. The concerto numbers 775 bars of music in all, Allegro taking 265 bars, Andantino 118 bars, and Rondeau 392 bars.

Sinfonia Concertante for Violin and Viola in E-flat Major, K. 364/320d (1779)

So brief was Mozart's life that Mozartologists are compelled to classify his successive styles and manners of composition in periods of a very few years each. Mozart's productivity was prodigious. Neither the heartaches of his amorous youth nor disheartening failures to obtain satisfactory employment interfered with the steady flow of music from his magical pen. It may be said that composition for Mozart was a bodily function, as natural as respiration and the oxygenation of venous blood.

Mozart's gifts were universal. He was superb in all genres of musical composition: opera, symphony, chamber music, solo works for various instruments, and concertos. He mastered the art of keyboard playing to perfection; but he was also an expert violinist; at one time he applied himself to the viola, and played in a string quartet with Haydn. His double concerto for violin, viola, and orchestra, known as Sinfonia Concertante, bears testimony to his ability to write for these instruments with a virtuosity based on personal practice.

The work, written in 1779, is the culmination of a series of double concertos that Mozart wrote between the ages of twenty-one and twenty three, and is regarded as one of his greatest achievements in this particularly difficult form. He wrote it upon his return to his native Salzburg from a visit to Paris. On his way he stopped over in Mannheim, a locality of great importance in music history, for it was there that the "Mannheim sound," characterized by a wealth of dynamic instrumental effects, originated; among these the total orchestral crescendo and diminuendo were of particular expressive power. Mozart was very much taken with the Mannheim innovations and adopted them in his subsequent works.

In Salzburg, Mozart held a position with the archbishop's court and drew a modest salary. His letters indicate that he had little love for his employment there; he wrote to his father that "the Archbishop cannot pay me enough for this Salzburg slavery."

The Sinfonia Concertante in E-flat Major is more in the nature of a concerto grosso than a symphony. The two solo instruments perform the function of the concertino, contrasted with the tutti of the orchestra. It is in three movements: Allegro maestoso, Andante, and Presto. The work opens with a declaration of tonality in assertive chords of the tonic E-flat major. A procession of triadic tones in the solo violin supports this declaration. The immediacy and the freshness of the thematic material have forced the critics to exhaust their supply of superlatives. The tonus of the music is muscular, determined by the prevalence of major keys. It is in this movement that the "Mannheim crescendo" makes its debut with great effect. Another remarkable feature is the proliferation of persistent pedal points on the dominant, with chromatic passing notes forming the connective tissue for modulatory digressions. After a double cadenza for the soloists, the movement comes to a close.

The second movement, Andante, is in C minor. It is in the nature of a ballad, with expressive melodic suspensions imparting a poignant sentiment to the melody. The tonality is gradually turned toward E-flat major through a series of daring cross-relations. There are truly Beethovenian anticipations in the somberness of sonorities reposing on deep pedal points.

The Finale: Presto is a festival of rhythm, a dance of many connected refrains. Both soloists and orchestra are active in melodious and harmonious cooperation. As in the preceding movements, the pedal point on the dominant occupies a strategic position in the progress of the music. The ending reasserts the declaration of tonality in the basic E-flat major.

Concerto for Piano No. 24 in C Minor, K. 491 (1786)

Mozart completed this concerto in Vienna on March 24, 1786. It represents his "dramatic" period, notable for the somber quality of his harmonies and a considerable increase of enharmonic modulations in comparison with his earlier works. There are fascinating points of similarity between the material of this concerto and some arias and orchestral ritornellos of *The Marriage of Figaro*, which occupied Mozart's creative imagination at about the same time as the concerto. In fact, the opera bears the next K. number, 492. The resemblance between the two formally unrelated works is revealed sometimes in the intervallic turn of the melodic phrase, sometimes in characteristic tonal sequences, sometimes in harmonic progressions, and quite often in rhythmic figures. One can almost hear an echo of an aria from *The Marriage of Figaro* in the concerto, and the Italian words almost fit some of the concerto's themes.

There are three movements in the concerto. The first, Allegro, in C minor, in ¾ time, opens with a long orchestral introduction. Owing to the basic minor key and the prevalence of chromatic modulations, the coloration of the music appears to be in the dark part of the tonal spectrum. The piano enters without accompaniment, and soon plunges into a series of energetic passages of a fine rococo character. In the recapitulation, the principal theme of the movement appears in the relative major key; the second theme is, as required by tradition, in the tonic key of C minor. The movement ends quietly.

The second movement, Larghetto, is set in E-flat major, in alla breve time. The piano solo again appears without accompaniment; the mutual responses between the soloist and the orchestra set the mood of the music, in antiphonal dialogue. The thematic materials are developed in fluent variations, and the movement concludes without ostentation.

The third and last movement, Allegretto, in C minor, alla breve, is a rondo with variations. The themes are stated with utmost clarity, with variations developing by rhythmic diminution so that the number of notes within a given beat increases steadily and produces a state of tension, which is further enhanced by the use of chromatic modulations. Then, with characteristic Mozartean ease, the intensity of the musical texture is suddenly relaxed. The concerto comes to a close without undue prolixity or Baroque garrulity.

Concerto for Piano No. 25 in C Major, K. 503 (1786)

Mozart was very punctilious in noting down the exact date of completion of most of his works, but he never numbered his symphonies and concertos, which makes the task of cataloguers difficult and leads to discrepancies and duplications. Considering also the influx of spurious scores ascribed to Mozart and later exposed as not authentic, the numeration of his works becomes even more complicated.

Mozart completed his Piano Concerto in C Major in Vienna on December 4, 1786, and played its first performance at the Vienna Academy on March 7, 1787. A Ph.D. thesis ought to be written on the significance of C major in Mozart's music, but the writer should be careful to take into consideration the important fact that the standard of pitch was much lower in the eighteenth century than it is now. Mozart's C-Major Concerto as played by himself in 1787 would sound somewhere between B and B-flat major to most American musicians accustomed to the high pitch of American orchestras. Conversely, it would register in Mozart's ear higher than D-flat major were he to hear it as performed in America. The symbolism of C major, the key that Robert Browning described as the essence of life, its immaculate whiteness, its chaste freedom of all chromatic impurities, is largely a matter of notation: no sharps, no flats in the key signature, only white keys on the piano keyboard.

The concerto is one of Mozart's most ingratiating scores, pre-Raphaelite in its natural simplicity. It is in three movements. The first movement, Allegro maestoso, in gentle ¼ time, introduces the principal theme, which is derived from the component tones of the C-major triad. A development follows, with thematic phrases embellished by graceful arabesques. Occasionally the tonality darkens; the mediant and the submediant are flatted, and the key assumes the somber coloring of C minor. There are numerous piano vignettes, replete with pearly scales and flowing arpeggios.

The second movement, Andante, in F major, in ⅜ time, is a songful eclogue. It evolves as a theme with variations. The flute, the oboe, and the clarinet are given prominence, contributing to the pastoral character of the music. The third movement, Allegretto, in C major, in ⅔ time, is a vivacious rondo. Once launched, it progresses with unabated celerity toward a brilliant ending.

At the time of the composition of the concerto, Mozart's financial situation was far from being in C major. It was rather in F double-sharp minor, what with sharp reminders from his Vienna landlord regarding the payment of past due rent. In his distress, Mozart turned for help to a friendly banker, one Michael Puchberg, who was a fellow member of Mozart's in the Vienna branch of the Free Masonic Order, which gave Mozart an opportunity to address him as a fraternal soul. Once, receiving no reply from Puchberg to one of his begging letters, Mozart enclosed a pair of pawnbroker's tickets as collateral. Mozart never asked for outright gifts, but always termed his requests as applications for a loan. As far as can be established, Puchberg never got back a kreutzer.

But in exchange for his florins Puchberg received a measure of immortality in the name index of Mozart's biographies. In fact, had he bequeathed Mozart's begging letters to his descendants, they would have made a fortune selling them to autograph dealers for several thousand times the sum originally asked by Mozart. The finances of Mozart's family did not improve much after his death. Mozart's widow could not even place many of his manuscripts with publishers. She printed the C-Major Concerto in 1798 at her own expense.

Concerto for Piano No. 27 in B-flat Major, K. 595 (1791)

The manuscript of this piano concerto, the last that Mozart wrote, is dated January 5, 1791. Mozart played it in Vienna at a concert of the clarinetist Josef Bähr on March 4, 1791. He died at the end of that year.

The concerto is in three movements, in the key of B-flat major. The first movement, Allegro, in ¼ time, is thematically evolved from a simple triadic formation in the gentlest Mozartean manner. Musical phrases are formed in symmetric tonal sequences, and the periods are usually binary.

The second movement, Larghetto, in ¼ time, is in E-flat major. Here, too, utmost serenity prevails. No diminished-seventh harmonies, so conspicuous in Mozart's dramatic works, darken the diatonic lucidity of the thematic design, and the melodic and harmonic progress is charmingly predictable.

The third and last movement, Allegro, in the key of B-flat major, in § time, is a vivacious rondo, which has an air of bucolic festivity. It forms a perfect counterpart to the more spacious first movement, rounding off the formal equilibrium of the cyclic structure.

The original manuscript of the concerto was preserved in Berlin for a century and a half after Mozart's death. The 1964 edition of the Köchel catalogue of Mozart's works carries the melancholy note, "Missing since the end of the war."

Concerto for Clarinet in A Major, K. 622 (1791)

Mozart's production was of a universal quality. He was equally resourceful in opera, symphony, chamber music, and solo works. He composed concertos for piano, for violin, for flute, for clarinet, for bassoon, for horn. His concerto for clarinet and orchestra is his last written for any instrument; he composed it in the year of his death, 1791.

In Mozart's time, the clarinet was a relative newcomer in orchestral usage, and Mozart himself did not include clarinets in the scene until his later symphonies. It is therefore all the more remarkable that he was able to use the entire range of the clarinet, particularly its deep register, with such beauty and perfection. The concerto became a model for subsequent works for solo clarinet and orchestra, and firmly established the clarinet as a fine solo instrument in operatic overtures, in symphonies, and in chamber music.

CHAMBER MUSIC
String Quartet No. 15 in D Minor, K. 421 (1783)

Before Mozart's time string quartets were a novelty. The more common forms of instrumental writing in four parts were the so-called *sinfonie a quattro*, in which each instrumental part could be played by any number of similar instruments. It was Haydn who established the now familiar composition for two violins, viola, and cello. Goethe poetically described his impressions of quartet playing in a remark to the composer Carl Friedrich Zelter on February 9, 1829: "We hear four intelligent people converse with one another; we seem to profit from their discourse, and, at the same time, become acquainted with the characteristics of each instrument." The composer Carl Maria von Weber (1786–1826) described the string quartet as a "musical consommé" in which the expression of every musical idea is reduced to its most essential property, a musical idea in four-part harmony.

As for the succession of movements, the string quartet in the form that it assumed in the hands of Haydn and Mozart is similar to the symphony. This similarity was brought about by the inclusion of the minuet (or scherzo, in Beethoven), and by the use of sonata form in the opening movement.

Mozart composed his first quartet at the age of fourteen. At that time he was entirely under the influence of Italian masters. The subsequent development of Mozart's style is closely connected with the guiding direction of Haydn's quartets. Hermann Abert, in his illuminating article on Mozart in *Cobbett's Cyclopedic Survey of Chamber Music*, suggests that Mozart was entirely independent of extraneous considerations only in his chamber music. He wrote his operas for the public; his concertos were expressions of his vital energy; his symphonies, a manifestation of masculine energy; but his chamber music, and particularly this most intimate and least spectacular form of chamber music—the string quartet—was the revelation of his inner soul. Harmonically speaking, Mozart's string quartets contain the boldest progressions he ever applied. Abert also finds in the quartets a premonition of the tragic Mozart—the brooding, contemplative, fatalistic Mozart.

Mozart acknowledged his great indebtedness to Haydn in the dedication to him of six quartets written between the years 1782 and 1786, when Mozart was in his late twenties. Haydn himself greatly praised these quartets, and Mozart's father credibly reports that Haydn spoke to him of these quartets as being without rivals.

The D-Minor Quartet is the second of the six quartets dedicated to Haydn, and the only one in a minor key. Its companions breathe energy in various forms: the first quartet, in G, is masculine; the third, in E-flat, romantic; the fourth, in B-flat, aggressively energetic, with the hunting-song theme; the fifth, in A, glowingly gay; and the sixth, in C, vigorous and buoyant.

Opening of Mozart's String Quartet No. 15 in D Minor, K.421

The Quartet in G Minor was written in Vienna in June 1783, when Mozart was twenty-seven years old. The first movement is an Allegro in ⁴⁄₄, and in recognizable sonata form. The first subject is stated at once by the first violin, and repeated an octave higher. The harmonic progressions follow the Classical alternation of the tonic and the dominant, but soon the Mozartean plaintive harmonies of the augmented sixth appear, with their inevitable resolutions into the octave.

Simultaneously with the chromaticization of the harmonic texture, the rhythmic pattern is quickened in the second section of the exposition. There are bold modulations in the development, transitions to remote keys, at one juncture connecting E-flat minor and A minor by a sudden chromatic move. It is of such enharmonic changes that Robert Browning wrote:

> And music: what? that burst of pillar'd cloud by day
> And pillar'd fire by night, was product, must we say
> Of modulating just by enharmonic change,
> The augmented sixth resolved.

The variety of keys in this section of Mozart's D-Minor Quartet, and the persistent enharmonicism, are revelations of a Mozart who was not all sweetness and light. The recapitulation of the Allegro is, however, entirely on the Classical model.

The second movement, Andante, is in § time. The harmonic succession of keys is here characterized by an alternation of major and minor. The third movement is a Minuet, following the example set by Haydn. The trio is written in the folksong style, and the last movement, Allegro ma non troppo, is a set of variations in the key of the quartet, D minor.

String Quartet No. 17 in B-flat Major ("Hunt"), K. 458 (1784)

Mozart's "Hunt" Quartet is the third of the six dedicated to Haydn. It was written in one day, on November 9, 1784, in Vienna. Mozart sold all six quartets to the publishers for 100 ducats, and they were published almost immediately.

Sending his six quartets to Haydn, Mozart wrote, in Italian, in an affected, half-humorous manner:

> A father who had once decided to send out his sons into the great world deemed it his duty to entrust them to the protection and guidance of a man of great fame who, moreover, was also his best friend. In like manner I send my six sons to you, most celebrated and very dear friend. They are indeed the fruit of a long and painstaking endeavor; but the hope, corroborated by many friends, that this toil will be in some degree rewarded, flatters me and encourages me in the belief that some day these children may prove a source of consolation to me.
>
> During your last stay in this capital you, my very dear friend, personally expressed to me your approval of these compositions. Your kind opinion encourages me to present them to you, and lets me hope that you will find them not entirely unworthy of your favor. I pray you, then, receive them kindly, and be a father, guide, and friend to them. From now on I surrender my rights over them to you. I beseech you not to be severe to faults that may have eluded a father's partial eye, and to preserve your generous friendship toward one who so highly treasures it.

The sobriquet "Hunt" is justified by the opening theme of the first movement, which is based on a well-known figure of the so-called horn fifths, based on the natural tones of a hunting horn; they are used whenever it is intended to picture a hunting episode, a journey, or leave-taking. Schubert uses it in his song "Die Post," from Schwanengesang (Swan Song), Beethoven in his "Les Adieux" Piano Sonata, Mendelssohn in his "Hunting Song" from the Songs Without Words. And it is inter-

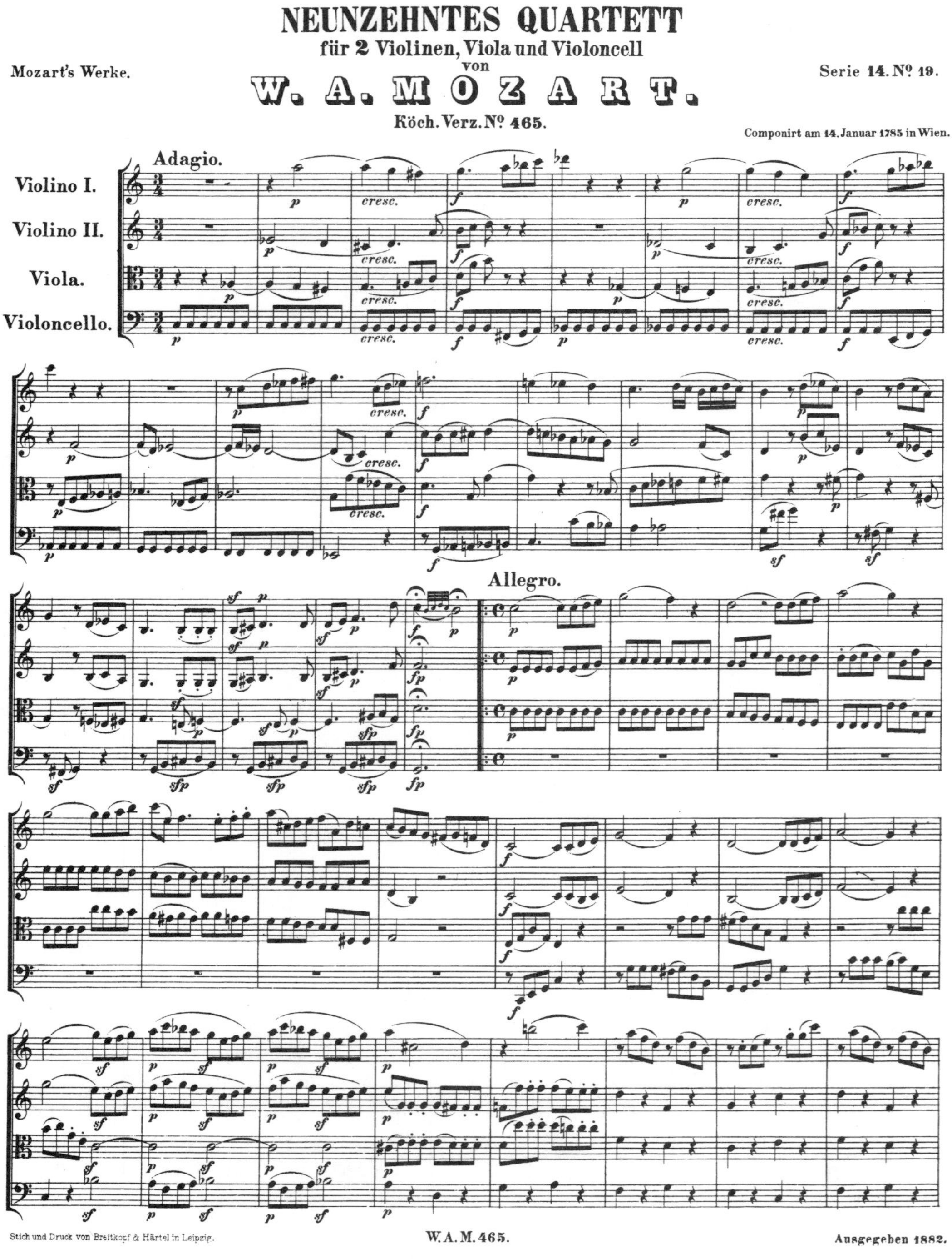

Opening of Mozart's String Quartet No. 19 in C Major, K. 465

esting to observe that these hunting-horn intervals are mostly used in the key of B-flat major, the key in which natural bugles, trumpets, and postilion horns were actually constructed. It is not unnatural, then, that Mozart's "Hunt" Quartet is written, too, in the key of the hunting horn.

The "Hunt" quartet follows the Haydn model. There are four movements. The first and the last movements are fast, and the two middle movements are, respectively, a Minuet and an Adagio. There are no unusual harmonic procedures, no dissonant tonal encounters that baffled early Mozarteans, and moved some of them to the thought of correcting these rough spots in order to achieve smoothness in harmony. It is a serene Mozart, free from the strife and preoccupations of his later life.

String Quartet No. 19 in C Major ("Dissonant"), K. 465 (1785)

Mozart's Quartet in C Major, the last of the six quartets he wrote for Haydn, was composed in Vienna in one day, January 14, 1785. Mozart's earliest biographer, one Franz Niemetschek, a teacher at the Prague Gymnasium, wrote: "Mozart could not honor Haydn more with any other work than with these quartets, which are a treasure of the finest thought, a model, and a lesson in composition."

The C-Major Quartet is a celebrated one in the annals of Mozartology. In the opening adagio, Mozart uses combinations of chromatics that create what is known in harmony textbooks as "cross relations." Natural and altered tones brush each other in closest proximity, and there is a strange feeling of the absence of key. C major is expressed only by the initial tonic in the cello, while the viola and the two violins hover perilously on the fringe. All kinds of subtle explanations have been advanced to account for these chromatic vagaries, but Haydn, to whom the quartet was dedicated, merely remarked: "If Mozart wrote it, he must have had a good reason to do so."

After the quartet's famous ambiguous introduction, the key of C major asserts itself in an Allegro in common time ($\frac{4}{4}$). The following slow movement, in triple time, Andante cantabile, is regarded as one of the finest examples of Mozart's lyricism. Then follows a minuet in C major. The last movement is a brilliant Allegro in duple time.

"Eine kleine Nachtmusik" (Serenade in G Major), K. 525 (1787)

The year 1787 was crucial in Mozart's life. His father Leopold, who was also his teacher and partly a provider, had died. Also, one of Mozart's infant sons died, following the natural average of infant mortality in those days. In 1787, Mozart wrote his greatest opera, *Don Giovanni*. He made a successful visit to Prague, where he conducted his new Symphony in D ("Prague," K. 504). It was one of the few lucrative engagements that Mozart ever had in his life. Upon his return to Vienna, he was appointed chamber musician by the emperor.

And yet he remarked to the Bohemian composer Adalbert Gyrowetz that he envied him his concert engagements in Italy and elsewhere, for Mozart himself could make his living only by teaching and by writing occasional pieces to be played at social functions. Even the appointment as chamber musician did not secure a necessary minimum for Mozart and his growing and ailing family. The emperor was strangely frugal despite the success that Mozart had in Prague. When some time later the king of Prussia offered Mozart a better salary and a more enviable position, Mozart refused out of loyalty to the emperor and to Vienna, but the gesture was little appreciated.

Great as was Mozart's fame even in his day, it seems from contemporary reports that he was not the most successful composer in Vienna as far as public reception and appreciation is concerned. A Vienna correspondent, writing in the *Magazine für Musik* in 1788, gives the palm of priority to Leopold Koželuh (1752–1818): "Koželuh's works hold their ground and are always acceptable, while Mozart's are not by any means as popular." Incidentally, Koželuh succeeded Mozart, after his death, as chamber musician, and at a higher salary. And where is Koželuh now? One finds him only in very complete music dictionaries.

Mozart composed the so-called "Eine kleine Nachtmusik" in Vienna on August 10, 1787, as a piece of the order we now would call *Gebrauchsmusik*, "utilitarian" music, to be played by students or amateurs. "Eine kleine Nachtmusik" is classified as a serenade, which in Mozart's usage was not much different from a little symphony. In fact, the piece is entirely symphonic. It is built in four movements. The initial Allegro in G major, and in common time ($\frac{4}{4}$), is couched in the orthodox sonata form. The development is exceedingly brief, and there is nothing experimental in the use of different keys. The second, slow, movement, Romanze, is in C major, in duple time. It is in ternary form. The phrases are sharply subdivided into four-bar phrases, or their multiples. The middle section of the Romanze is in C minor, with characteristic simple figures imitated by one instrument after another. Then the C-major theme returns, and the movement is concluded with the feeling of a perfect ending.

The following movement is a Minuet in G major, with a trio in the dominant. The minuet is repeated, according to usual ternary form. The last movement is an allegro, which is called Rondo by Mozart himself, although the structure is close to sonata form. The initial vivacious theme dominates the movement, appearing in the tonic, then in the dominant, and in the middle section also in other keys. The movement is further consolidated by an extended coda.

LUDWIG VAN BEETHOVEN
(1770–1827)
The Fervent Genius

The greatest musical names have a harmonious sound all their own, as though they were intentionally shaped to impress themselves on the minds of humanity. The family name of Beethoven possesses such a ringing sound; yet it is derived from nothing more lofty than the Dutch word for a beet field. Beethoven's grandfather was a Dutchman who settled in Bonn, where Beethoven was born. Beethoven's family was a democratic one; yet Beethoven was proud of his nobiliary particle "van," which had an air even more aristocratic than the German "von."

Many musical biographies begin with the words: "His father opposed music as a profession and desired his son to be a lawyer." Beethoven's early biography needs no such negative introduction. His father was himself a musician in the employ of the prince-elector of Cologne, and he thought highly of his social position. When he discovered that Beethoven had instinctive musical ability, he taught him to play the violin and piano and to read music. Often Beethoven would stray away from the notes before him and play some inventions of his own. His father would then discipline him and admonish him to attend to the printed music.

Soon father Beethoven decided that it was time to present his young son to the world. He arranged a joint concert for him with another of his pupils, a contralto singer, and announced in the local press that his "little son would give complete enjoyment to all ladies and gentlemen" with his playing on the piano. Beethoven progressed rapidly; when he was thirteen years old, he wrote three piano sonatas. His father, always mindful of practical matters, arranged for publication of these youthful works with a flowery dedication to the prince-elector, in which the young composer (aided no doubt by his father) expressed himself with becoming modesty and deference to princely powers:

> May I venture, most illustrious Prince, to place at the foot of your throne the first fruits of my youthful inspiration? And may I venture to hope that you will bestow on them the benevolent paternal mark of your encouraging approval? Accept them as a pure offering of childlike homage, and look graciously on them, and on their young author.

Beethoven was not quite fourteen when he was appointed assistant court organist, while his father held the position of first organist. Young Beethoven was given a salary, which was a token of recognition of his professional standing. Three years later he had enough funds to undertake a journey to Vienna. There he was introduced to Mozart, and played for him, not from written music as he was told to do when he was a child, but from his own unfettered imagination. To improvise freely was a mark of true musicianship in the age of Mozart and Beethoven. Mozart listened to the passionate and artful roulades from another room with some friends. "This young man will soon make much clamor in the world! Watch him in the future!"

His first works are Mozartean in melody and in gentleness of harmonies. Gradually the untamed passion of Beethoven's musical spirit would break through the eighteenth-century grace. And yet he was still a student; he felt that he needed more musical and general education. He settled in Vienna, where he took lessons from Haydn, at eight groschen each, a sum that corresponded to about twenty-five cents. He wrote exercises in counterpoint, which Haydn patiently corrected. Beethoven's artistic independence grew. "I wish to learn the rules well, the better to break them," he confessed to a friend.

Beethoven's refusal to bow before men of power found expression in another story: one summer, when Beethoven met Goethe in the spa town of Teplitz, Archduke Rudolph passed by in a carriage. Goethe stopped, took off his hat, and bowed deeply; Beethoven pulled his hat down, buttoned up his overcoat, and folded his arms. Then he explained to Goethe that they, as men of intellect and imagination, should not defer to men whose only greatness resides in their uniforms and titles. Perhaps this story, too, is an elaboration of what might well have happened. But even an imaginary episode has its place in a great man's biography if it is in character. It is undoubtedly true that to Beethoven, aristocracy of the mind was at least as important as nobility of title. When his brother came to visit him and, not finding him at home, left a note signed "Carl van Beethoven, landowner," Beethoven returned the visit and, his brother being absent, left a similar note, signed "Ludwig van Beethoven, brain owner."

Beethoven was a giant, and he was a child. He was constantly oppressed by the consciousness of his insufficient education. He had some Latin in school, and he learned to write ungrammatical French and passable Italian, but arithmetic was his nemesis, and he could never manage to compute his domestic expenses. Having already reached fame, he surreptitiously acquired a book entitled *The Easiest Method of Teaching Arithmetic to Children in a Pleasant Way.* His nephew, of whom he was very fond and whose guardian he eventually became, explained to him that multiplication was a simplified form of addition, but this Beethoven could never manage to master. And when he attempted complicated rhythmic divisions in one of his later sonatas, the note values did not add up correctly, a fact that a contemporary critic scornfully pointed out.

Then came the severest trial in any musician's life. Beethoven had known for a long time that his hearing was failing; at the peak of his creative activity, he became almost totally deaf and was forced to resort to a "conversation book" for communication with friends. A greater misfortune can hardly be imagined, and yet, by an extraordinary self-assertion of genius, Beethoven wrote sublime music, which he himself could not hear. The mighty Fifth Symphony, the joyful and poetic Pastoral Symphony, the transcendental "Choral" Symphony (the Ninth), were all written during the period of external deafness. But it was also the time of inner illumination, and it enabled Beethoven to form musical images of striking power and beauty.

Considering the fact that Beethoven had many friends and worshipful followers who realized the opportunity that fate had offered them in being with Beethoven, irritatingly little is known about Beethoven's intimate life, his method of work, or even the dates of his compositions. His conversation books are singularly lacking in important details. Beethoven wrote relatively few letters, and most of them were business communications, or letters relating to his incessant personal quarrels. There is, of course, one celebrated exception in Beethoven's correspondence: his letter addressed to an unknown woman, whom he called the "Immortal Beloved." Who the Immortal Beloved was still remains unsolved by the Beethoven scavengers (the expression was used by the American music historian Oscar Sonneck in his painstaking but futile 1927 essay "The Riddle of the Immortal Beloved").

The advent of Beethoven in music history marked the transition from pure classicism to a more concentrated, more expressive type of music, which we know as romanticism. Nothing illustrates Beethoven's romantic musical nature better than the progressive change of style and idiom from his early works to his last instrumental compositions, which presage the development of modern music. Mozart and Haydn wrote symphonies in quantity, and the style of these symphonies remained within a general concept without transcending the established tradition. Each Beethoven symphony, however, each successive piano sonata or string quartet, is a step forward in the direction of a new musical language. Excelsior! For Beethoven could not conform, not even to his own greatness, nor to his own reputation in the world of music. He was the passionate genius who broke the bounds of conventionally pleasurable art to reach the realm of musical expression yet to come.

SYMPHONIES
Symphony No. 3 in E-flat Major (Eroica), *Op. 55 (1804)*

On August 26, 1804, Beethoven wrote to his publishers, Breitkopf & Härtel, in a letter accompanying the shipping of several new works, among them the Third Symphony: "The symphony is really entitled Bonaparte, and, in addition to the usual instruments, there are three obbligato horns. I believe it will interest the musical public." Breitkopf & Härtel, however, declined the symphony, and it was subsequently published by the Verlag für Kunst und Industrie, with the new title "Sinfonia Eroica composta per festeggiare il sovvenire di un grand' Uomo," that is, "Heroic Symphony, composed to celebrate the memory of a great man." On the title page of the manuscript used for publication there were two words after the title, which were carefully erased. But the second word is legible: it is "Bonaparte." The first word, in all probability, is "Napoleon."

Between the completion of the symphony and its publication occurred the most celebrated episode in music history: the dramatic elimination of the title *Bonaparte* from the symphony. The story is related in substantially identical features by two intimates of Beethoven: Ferdinand Ries and Anton Felix Schindler. "The original idea of the symphony is said to have been suggested by General Bernadotte, who was then French Ambassador at Vienna," writes Schindler,

> ...and had a high esteem for Beethoven, so I was informed by several of his friends. Count Moritz Lichnowsky, who was frequently with Beethoven in Bernadotte's company, and who is my authority for many circumstances belonging to this period, gave me the same account. In his political sentiments Beethoven was a republican; the spirit of independence natural to a genuine artist gave him a decided bias.... He lived in the firm belief that Napoleon entertained no other design than to republicanize France.... Hence, his respect and enthusiasm for Napoleon. A fair copy of the musical work for the First Consul of the French Republic, with the dedication to him, was on the point of being dispatched through the French Embassy to Paris, when news arrived in Vienna that Napoleon Bonaparte has caused himself to be proclaimed Emperor of the French. The first thing Beethoven did on receiving this intelligence was to tear off the title-leaf of this symphony and to fling the work itself to the floor, from which he would not allow it to be lifted, with a torrent of execrations against the new French Emperor, against the new tyrant. It was a long time before Beethoven recovered from the shock and permitted this work to be given to the world with the title of Sinfonia Eroica.... I shall only add that it was not till the tragic end of the great Emperor at St. Helena, that Beethoven was reconciled with him, and sarcastically remarked that, seventeen years before, he had composed appropriate music to this catastrophe, in which it was exactly predicted musically, alluding to the Funeral March of the symphony.

It must be noted that Schindler himself was a mere boy at the time and in his story relies entirely on Ries and Lichnowsky. There is no evidence that Ries recorded the story before he published his short memoir of Beethoven, that is, before 1837. Napoleon was proclaimed emperor in May 1804, and the news must have reached Vienna within a fortnight after the event. It is quite possible that between 1804 and 1837, Ries might have unconsciously embellished the incident. The evidence of the manuscript score with the dedication to Napoleon laboriously erased, and Beethoven's calm mention, in his August 1804 letter to the publisher three months after Napoleon assumed the title of emperor that the symphony was entitled *Bonaparte*—all this points to a different interpretation. Ries asserts in his memoir that the copy he saw on Beethoven's table bore Napoleon's name in the Italian form, "Buonaparte," at the extreme top of the title page, and, at the extreme bottom the signature, also in the Italian form, "Luigi van Beethoven." Yet it is very unlikely that Beethoven would have used the Italian form, which at the time was not in favor with the adherents of Napoleon, and this alone lessens the reliability of Ries's testimony.

The Third Symphony was finally dedicated to Beethoven's patron, Prince Franz Joseph Lobkowitz, and was performed numerous times at his palace. Ries records an occasion when Beethoven conducted and became so confused in the second half of the first movement, where the half notes are tied over the bar line, going against the beat, that the orchestra had to stop and start over again. The first public performance took place in Vienna on April 7, 1805, under Beethoven's direction. The symphony was announced simply as "a new grand symphony," and the key was given, curiously enough, as D-sharp instead of E-flat. The audience and critics thought that the symphony was too long, and that Beethoven was not sufficiently courteous to the public in acknowledging the applause. This complaint caused Beethoven to write on the violin part of the symphony: "As this symphony somewhat exceeds the usual length, it should be played nearer the beginning rather than the end of a concert, after an overture, an aria, or a concerto lest it lose some of its effect on an audience fatigued by preceding pieces." In the same letter from Beethoven in Vienna to his publishers, Breitkopf & Härtel in Leipzig, in which Beethoven referred to the composition of the *Bonaparte* Symphony, he also wrote:

> I hear that the symphony which I sent you last year and which you returned to me has been roundly abused in the *Musikalische Zeitung*. I have not read the article, but if you think that you do me harm by this, you are mistaken. On the contrary you bring your newspaper into discredit by such things—all the more since I have not made any secret of the fact that you sent back this symphony.

The article referred to was a review published in the May 21, 1806, issue of the *Allgemeine Musikalische Zeitung*, which was the house organ of Breitkopf & Härtel. "It is to be hoped," the article stated, "that this symphony makes no claim to be included among Classical works. It begins with a March à la Russe, after which follows an Allegro which is the very essence of wantonness, where trumpets and drums reign supreme, and where all other instruments are thrown into dust by this domination."

The *Eroica* is in four movements. The first, Allegro con brio, is the heroic movement par excellence. Interestingly enough, it is in triple measure, not in the martial accents of ⁴⁄₄ time. The famous opening theme is derived with utmost simplicity from the triadic configurations of the E-flat chord. The form is that of sonata; the traditional sections include a full-fledged recapitulation and an extended coda.

The most significant movement of the *Eroica* is the Marcia funebre: Adagio assai. The story is told that when Napoleon died in exile on St. Helena, Beethoven exclaimed, "I predicted this catastrophic end when I wrote the funeral march in the Eroica!" Formally, the Funeral March is a set of variations; the miracle of its composition is that it never loses its mournful beat through all the harmonic modulations and rhythmic modifications of the music. The Marcia funèbre is followed by a lighthearted Scherzo. The Finale: Allegro molto is the most complex movement of the entire work. It contains elements of variations with numerous episodic interpolations suggesting the form of a rondo; in addition there are fugal developments of great intricacy. The coda, presto, provides a fittingly heroic ending.

Symphony No. 5 in C Minor, Op. 67 (1807–8)

"So knocks Fate on my door!" This famous exclamation, supposedly made by Beethoven to describe the opening theme of the Fifth Symphony, belongs to a rapidly expanding anthology of spurious winged phrases. Beethoven himself denied that he had ever used the simile. Upon investigation, it appears that the rhythmic pattern of the theme, consisting of three short notes followed by a long one, occurs in a number of Beethoven's works dating from the period of the composition of the Fifth Symphony: the "Appassionata" Sonata for Piano in F Minor, Op. 57; the Fourth Piano Concerto in G Major, Op. 58; and the String Quartet in E-flat, Op. 74. Most remarkably, the tonalities of these works are related to C minor, the key of the Fifth Symphony. It is obvious, therefore, that it was present in Beethoven's mind as a purely musical invention for a long time, free of any psychological or phraseological associations. Another theory of the origin of the motive is that Beethoven used the notes of a birdcall, specifically of a goldfinch. Beethoven did use birdcalls in the *Pastoral* Symphony, which was written at the same period as the Fifth, and so the hypothesis is not entirely improbable.

The most natural supposition is that the four notes are of a purely musical, nonprogrammatic origin. The catalogue of all Beethoven's themes, published by the Beethoven House in Bonn in 1932, lists nineteen examples of the rhythmical figure of the Fifth Symphony, under the heading of "triple repetition in the upbeat, followed by a skip." It must be assumed, therefore, that this rhythm was part of Beethoven's natural vocabulary. However, there is no instance of the use of this rhythm in Beethoven's works with the downward skip of a major third, in a minor key, from the dominant to the mediant, except in the Fifth Symphony.

Beethoven was thirty-eight years old when the Fifth Symphony was presented to the public, but sketches of the symphony refer to a considerably earlier period. The original four notes are present in the earliest jottings in Beethoven's notebooks, but other thematic material is amazingly different from the final shape.

The Fifth Symphony occupies the midway point in Beethoven's creative life. In it the link with the eighteenth century is not entirely severed. The traditional form of a Classical symphony is observed, yet there are constantly erupting flames of the Beethoven of the last, his greatest, period, the Beethoven who used the medium of music to express the drama of turbulent emotion, the essence of human struggle, rather than the formulas and usages of the Classical art, however exquisite. There are coloristic effects, such as the kettledrum episode in the protracted deceptive cadence of the Scherzo, before the clarifying explosion of the C-major fanfare of the finale, when, for the first time, the trombones enter the scene. There is the accumulation of power through the persistent repetition of notes and figures, pursued even where the laws of contrast might dictate a different course, as, for instance, in the use of the same four-note motive in the second subject, with a change of interval and key.

er Beethoven's death, young Mendelssohn visited the aged Goethe, and irst movement of Beethoven's Fifth Symphony for him. "This is very great, he remarked, "and quite mad. One fears that the house would come down on us if all instruments were to play it together." Schumann wrote after hearing a performance of the symphony: "So often heard, it still exercises its power over all ages, just as those great phenomena of nature, which, no matter how often they recur, fill us with awe and wonder. This symphony will go on centuries hence, as long as the world and world's music endure."

And Berlioz, the great Romantic and great individualist, saw in the Fifth Symphony the revelation of Beethoven's soul: "He develops in it his own intimate thought. His secret sorrows, his concentrated rage, his reveries charged with a dejection, oh, so sad, his visions at night, his bursts of enthusiasm—these furnished him the subject; and the forms of melody, harmony, rhythm, and orchestration are as essentially individual and new as they are powerful and noble." He saw in its first movement, Allegro con brio, a conglomeration of "disordered sentiments which oppress a great soul." He compared the syncopated alteration of chords in the wind instruments and strings to hiccups, and their dynamic contrasts to a sudden change from the breathing of a dying man to a desperate outburst of human violence. The coda of the first movement represented to him "two burning unisons forming twin torrents of lava."

The first performance of the Fifth Symphony took place in Vienna on December 22, 1808. The program must have been an exceptionally long one, for it included, in addition to the Fifth Symphony, Beethoven's Sixth Symphony, the *Pastoral* (but the numbers were exchanged, so that the Fifth, the C-Minor Symphony, was billed as No. 6, and the *Pastoral* as No. 5), and the Fourth Piano Concerto, with Beethoven as soloist.

The first movement is in Classical sonata form. The instrumentation of the "fate" motive is surprising: it is scored for two clarinets and strings in unison. The entire melodic material of the exposition is evolved from this basic phrase. The second subject is lyrical in nature, but the "fate" figure lurks in its contrapuntal background. The development follows the Classical model with the inevitability of a syllogism. The recapitulation arrives in a blaze of symphonic glory. The coda is succinct and energetic.

The theme of the second movement, Andante con moto, in A-flat major in $\frac{3}{8}$ time, is one of the most beautiful slow melodies created by Beethoven. When a scientific melometer is perfected, we may be able to define in concrete terms the secret of esthetic gratification derived from such melodies. The form of the movement is that of a set of variations, combined with the characteristics of a rondo.

The third movement, Allegro vivace, in C minor, is a brilliant essay in scherzo form. The extraordinary rapid figuration in the trio, when the cellos and double basses make a virile entry in the bland key of C major, reminded Berlioz of "the gambols of a frolicsome elephant." The rhythm of the "fate" motive is heard again. There follows a mysterious kettledrum solo in steady triple rhythm, holding the listener in mounting suspense, which is resolved by the climactic fanfare inaugurating the finale, Allegro, in C major, in festive duple time.

It is in the Finale: Allegro that the trombones make their tremendous appearance for the first time in a Beethoven symphony. A comparison with the ominous trombones that announce the terrifying presence of the statue of the Commendatore in Mozart's *Don Giovanni* suggests itself. The scherzo is recollected with its thematic four-note motive. Then the Allegro returns, leading to a precipitous coda, presto. The ending constitutes the most emphatic reiteration of tonic triads in symphonic literature. Here the music creates the sense of psychological subjection, a melosomatic catharsis.

Symphony No. 7 in A Major, Op. 92 (1811–12)

Wagner called Beethoven's Seventh Symphony the apotheosis of the dance, with reference to the last movement, in which, so Wagner thought, nature itself danced with Beethoven. Other romantic commentators solemnly examined the score and found in it the expression of exultation at the deliverance of Europe from French domination; the famous second movement, in which the melody grows out of the rhythmic pendulum on a single note, inspired visions of the catacombs to some. Beethoven left no hint as to pictorial or literary associations with the music, and so deprived his admirers of authorized speculation.

Beethoven began the composition of his Seventh Symphony in 1811, and dedicated it upon completion to the "High-born Count Morits von Fries." The first performance of the Seventh Symphony took place in Vienna on December 8, 1813. There was a previous private hearing at the Archduke Rudolph of Austria's palace in Vienna on April 20, 1813.

The public performance of the Seventh Symphony was given on the same program with a curious work that Beethoven wrote to celebrate the victory of the duke of Wellington over the French, written especially for a mechanical instrument, called the panharmonicon, an invention of Johannes Nepomuk Maelzel. Both Maelzel and Beethoven hoped for great financial rewards, which failed to materialize, despite the musical flattery to Great Britain, with quotations from "God Save the King" and "For He's a Jolly Good Fellow." The Seventh Symphony, without such artificial fanfares, survives as a great work, while *Wellington's Victory* is relegated to a museum of musical curiosities.

Maelzel was also the inventor of the metronome, and his name is immortalized in the markings "M. M." (Maelzel's Metronome) preceding the figure indicating the number of beats per minute. Beethoven was very much taken by Maelzel's invention, and in his letter to him expressed his determination never to use the old-fashioned Italian designations of tempo. He even set metronome marks for all of his symphonies. But his enthusiasm was short-lived. In one of his works he indicated a metronome figure, but added a word of caution, that "feeling also has its tempo and cannot be entirely expressed in figures."

The first movement of the Seventh Symphony opens with poco sostenuto, in $\frac{4}{4}$ time, serving as an introduction to the main part, Vivace, in $\frac{6}{8}$. The music is full of kinetic energy accentuated by dotted rhythms. The progress is interrupted on several occasions by extraordinary silences of two bars each, silences that give Beethoven an opportunity for instantaneous modulations into remote keys.

The second movement is marked Allegretto, but it registers in the listener's perception as being slow, as a result of an aural illusion produced by the measured progress of quarter notes and eighth notes and a sustained growth of the theme from a single note. The form is ternary, with a section in A major embanked between the principal divisions in A minor. An interesting fugato develops toward the recapitulation.

The third movement, Presto, is a scherzo, with the trio section containing characteristic horn calls of the type used by Beethoven in all his symphonies.

The Seventh Symphony ends with the impetuous dance movement, Allegro con brio. The two contrasting melodic and rhythmic themes, the dance theme and an explosive figure in dotted rhythms, constitute the elements of sonata form. The main rhythm of the dance returns with tremendous vigor. The symphony ends, indeed, as an apotheosis of nature dancing.

Symphony No. 8 in F Major, Op. 93 (1812)

Beethoven wrote his Eighth Symphony in 1812 in his brother Johann's house in Linz. He revised and completed it while traveling by stagecoach to various health resorts, because his doctor recommended hydrotherapy to relieve the ailments from which he suffered all his life. A feud between the two brothers started in that year, when Beethoven objected to his brother's marrying a woman whom he violently disliked. In his letters, Beethoven often referred to his hated sister-in-law as the Queen of the Night, with the allusion to the sinister character in Mozart's last opera, *The Magic Flute*.

The Eighth Symphony was first performed in Vienna on February 27, 1814. The Seventh Symphony was also played on the same program. It was already familiar and well liked, and was received with considerable enthusiasm. An account of the concert in the prestigious musical journal *Allgemeine Musikalische Zeitung* noted that the new symphony had aroused much interest and expectations, which were not quite gratified. The writer explained this adverse reaction on the part of the audience by the length of the program featuring two symphonic works.

The Eighth Symphony is in four movements, a traditional division of Beethoven's symphonies. The first movement, Allegro vivace e con brio, justifies its designation: it is gay, vivacious, and noisy. The noise is euphonious, of course, with shining brass and dancing violins. This is the music of Beethoven in his rustic mood. A typical postilion's horn, always a favorite with Beethoven and so easily imitated by natural French horns, is a leading motive here. Beethoven must have heard this call very often while changing his stagecoach.

The principal theme of the second movement, Allegretto scherzando, a sort of circular canon, is supposed to have been inspired by Maelzel's metronome. Beethoven was enthusiastic about Maelzel's invention, and liked him personally. An apocryphal story goes that Beethoven improvised a text for this canon: "Ta, ta, ta, Lieber Maelzel," containing the word "metronome" in another line. But there is an anachronism involved, because Maelzel's rhythm machine was originally called a musical chronometer, and only much later was patented under the name "metronome."

The third movement, Tempo di menuetto, does not present any innovations. But it departs from the traditional melodic and rhythmic figurations of the old court dance and suggests rather a scene of merrymaking in the country. The last movement, Allegro vivace, is set in a festive mood. Some commentators believe that there is a Gypsy mood in the finale, inspired by itinerant Gypsy bands that Beethoven might have heard at country fairs.

Beethoven himself described the Eighth Symphony as "a little symphony." Posterity disagreed. Berlioz had this to say about the work: "It is one of those inspirations for which there is no antecedent. Such music falls directly from heaven into the composer's brain."

Symphony No. 9 in D Minor ("Choral"), Op. 125 (1822–24)

First performed in Vienna on May 7, 1824, the program described the Ninth Symphony, Beethoven's last, as a "Grand Symphony with a finale in which solo voices and chorus enter, on the text of Schiller's Ode to Joy." The choral ending is notoriously difficult to sing, because its tessitura lies very high. Attempts were made to obviate the difficulty by transposing the chorus a tone lower, but there is no record of an actual performance using such a device. There are indications that the choral ending was an idea that came to Beethoven when the preliminary sketches of the symphony were already written. The sentiments expressed by Schiller must have been dear to Beethoven, for the "Ode to Joy" preaches the universalization of humanity in joy and happiness.

Wagner, in his book on Beethoven, interprets the Ninth Symphony as the culmination of all instrumental music and a natural transition to a Wagnerian music drama. But music critics in Europe and in America found much fault with it. An American publication had this to say in 1853:

> If the best critics have failed to find the meaning of Beethoven's Ninth Symphony, we may well be pardoned if we confess our inability to find any. The last movement appeared to be an incomprehensible union of strange harmonies. Beethoven was deaf when he wrote it. It was the genius of a great man upon the ocean of harmony, without the compass which had so often guided him to his haven of success; the blind painter touching the canvas at random.

The violinist Ludwig Spohr (1784–1859), a great musician and a close contemporary of Beethoven, wrote in his autobiography:

> The fourth movement of the Ninth Symphony seems to me so ugly, in such bad taste, and the conception of Schiller's Ode so cheap that I cannot understand how such a genius as Beethoven could write it down. I find in it another proof of something I had always suspected, that Beethoven was deficient in aesthetic imagery and lacked the sense of beauty.

Beethoven had intended to dedicate the Ninth Symphony to Czar Alexander I of Russia, the conqueror of Napoleon, but changed his mind and inscribed the score to the king of Prussia, Friedrich Wilhelm III. The king sent to Beethoven a diamond ring as a token of gratitude. But when the ring reached Vienna, it turned out to be a less precious stone, and Beethoven sold it to a local jeweler for three hundred florins. What happened to the original diamond ring? Possibly the Prussian functionaries to whom the affair was delegated substituted a cheaper stone. It is also possible that the Viennese customs officers made this profitable switch.

When the Ninth Symphony was first performed by the Philharmonic Society of London, it was advertised as a "New Grand Characteristic Sinfonia, in manuscript, with vocal finale, composed expressly for this society." Obviously, Beethoven must have promised the first performance to both Vienna and London; he was always confused in his practical arrangements. In 1827, when the news reached London of Beethoven's grave illness, the Philharmonic Society sent him one hundred pounds. The money was used to pay a portion of the funeral expenses.

The opening measures of the first movement, Allegro ma non troppo, in D minor, with a time signature $\frac{2}{4}$, are arresting. The theme consists of falling fourths and fifths, before committing itself to a complete triadic progression in D minor. A development follows by the process of accumulation, typical of Beethoven's music. Eight distinct motives can be found in the first movement, but they are so closely interwoven that an impression of continuous motion is firmly maintained.

The second movement, Molto vivace: Presto, is still in D minor, in $\frac{3}{4}$ time. It corresponds to a scherzo, and is marked by a forceful rhythmic pulse with energetic syncopation. The third movement, Adagio molto e cantabile, is in B-flat major, in $\frac{4}{4}$ time. There are two discernible themes, each giving rise to a series of variations. Beethoven reversed the order of the middle movements in the traditional symphony, in which the slow movement follows the opening section, and a minuet or a scherzo is the third movement.

The finale is like an oratorio in its magnitude. It contains numerous sections, instrumental and vocal, opening with a chord of tremendous majesty, containing as it does every note of the D-minor harmonic scale. Of course, it resolves immediately into a D-minor chord, but the combination dismayed many musical purists. After recitatives in the cellos and double basses, the baritone enters with an exhortation to humanity to raise their voices in song. The tenor has a solo in an episode marked vivace alla marcia. The chorus becomes active, first in allegro assai and then an andante maestoso. An adagio follows, yielding soon to an allegro energico. There are many adumbrations to the famous tune of the "Ode to Joy," materializing in its entirety in the final prestissimo. There are several false endings which may mislead the audience into premature applause. The coda is a veritable festival of D-major chords.

OVERTURES
Overture to The Creatures of Prometheus, *Op. 43 (1801)*

It is difficult to imagine Beethoven in the role of a ballet composer, but he did write danceable music. Of his ballet *Die Geschöpfe des Prometheus,* only the overture survives in frequent performances. The libretto is based on one of the several myths concerning the legendary bringer of fire. Prometheus molds two beautiful human figures out of clay and water. He steals the fire from the sun to animate them, and sends his creations to Apollo. The latter in turn sends them to the muse Melpomene, who teaches them the art of dramatic emotion. The muse of comedy, Thalia, shows them how to laugh, and the muse of choreography, Terpsichore, instructs them in dancing. To complete their education, Bacchus initiates them into wine drinking. But Prometheus realizes that all men are mortal and is saddened by the thought of the inevitable death that awaits his creations.

Beethoven wrote the ballet in 1801 on commission from the famous Italian dancer Salvatore Vigano (1769–1821). The score contains an overture, an introduction, and sixteen ballet numbers. The original opus number was 24; when Beethoven revised the score, it was assigned a later opus number, 43. Vigano produced the ballet in Vienna on March 28, 1801; it was described in the program as a "heroic-allegorical ballet in two acts." Interestingly enough, much of the material that eventually went into the finale of the Eroica Symphony was originally written for *The Creatures of Prometheus.*

The overture is in C major. It opens with an adagio. The main part of the overture is the Allegro molto con brio, a movement charged with kinetic energy. There is a contrasting lyrical subject. The development of the materials is businesslike and unfailingly effective. A series of tonic chords marks the ending.

Leonore *Overture No. 3, Op. 72a, no. 3 (1806)*

Beethoven wrote only one opera, but he supplied it with four overtures. The title of the opera is *Fidelio,* but only the fourth overture bears that name. The remaining three overtures are known respectively as Leonore Overtures Nos. 1, 2, and 3. The riddle of the double name is easily solved when we recall that in the opera, Fidelio is the male pseudonym of Leonore, the faithful wife (as the derivation of the word Fidelio implies, *fides* being Latin for "faith") of an unjustly imprisoned man; *Leonore* was also the original title of the opera. Leonore, dressed as a youth, secures the position of an assistant to the warden and succeeds in saving her imprisoned husband's life by interposing her own body between him and a murderous governor of the fortress. The rescue comes to both husband and wife when a trumpet is heard from afar (in the overture this trumpet call is usually sounded off-stage for better effect), and the Minister of State arrives to reestablish justice, and Leonore's happiness. There is a minor complication when the warden's daughter falls seriously in love with the transvestite Leonore.

Beethoven was not the first composer to write an opera to this highly romantic and highly incredible story. An opera, *Léonore, ou l'Amour conjugal,* was produced in Paris on February 19, 1798, music by Pierre Gaveaux, libretto by Jean Nicolas Bouilly. Then Ferdinand Paër wrote an Italian opera, *Leonora, ossia L'Amor conjugale,* which was produced in Dresden on October 3, 1804. Beethoven used a German text by Josef Sonnleithner, and the opera was produced in Vienna on November 20, 1805, under the name of Leonore's male avatar, Fidelio. That was a few days after the occupation of Vienna by Napoleon's armies, and the audience consisted mainly of French officers and diplomatic agents. The opera ran for three performances, and its incomplete success was attributed not only to the French occupation, but also to the fact that it was longish. Beethoven was persuaded, after a long night session with persons concerned about the production, to cut the opera from three to two acts. This curtailed version was produced in Vienna on March 26, 1806, and ran for five days. It was revived at the Vienna Opera on May 23, 1814, in a considerably revised version, and with a new overture, which Beethoven composed specially for the revival. This was the Overture No. 4, the only one that is known as the *Fidelio* Overture. It was in E major, in contradistinction to the three Leonore Overtures, which are in the key of C major. Beethoven conducted, as on previous occasions, but in 1814 he was considerably deafer, and the synchronization of his gestures and the orchestra's playing was much more difficult. As a safety measure, the regular conductor, Michael Umlauff (1781–1842), was stationed behind Beethoven's back, and it was to him that the orchestra looked for guidance in emergency.

The overture opens with a scale majestically descending in unison. A lyrical phrase is heard. The flute plays ascending arpeggio figures, imitated by the violins. They gradually gather force, and lead to a climax, with powerful chords alternating in the strings and wind instruments. The mood changes suddenly, in the typical Beethoven manner; a tender phrase is sounded in the woodwinds, and is repeated with more insistence. The adagio ends in the air of anticipation of the principal movement, Allegro.

The principal theme in C major is presented in the violins. It is full of action, incessantly striving forward. Its rhythmical aspect (dot-dash-dot, in $\frac{4}{4}$) enhances its melodic dynamism. From a cautious pianissimo it grows to brilliant fortissimo in the high register of the strings. Then the woodwinds take over the theme. The key shifts, and heavy accents underscore the syncopated rhythm. A horn call ushers in a lighter mood. The violins, and then the flute, sound a lyrical phrase, but soon a tension appears, and the dot-dash-dot rhythms are telescoped in canonic imitation. The dynamics are in black and white, sudden outbursts of power contrasted with brief periods of calm.

The Allegro is in a mood of transition. The basses mount chromatically, still preserving the familiar rhythms of the principal theme. There are running scale passages, presaging a significant entry, and the long trumpet call is heard, which in the opera signals the advent of the Minister of State, and the liberation of the prisoner. The trumpet call is repeated after a lyrical phrase in slow, even notes. After the second trumpet call there is an increase in tempo, the even notes appear in double, then quadruple, time, in preparation of a new entry. The flute introduces the principal theme in G major, instead of the customary C. The solo of the flute is of considerable length. Then the strings in pianissimo start a chromatic trek upward, which eventuates in the reentry of the principal theme in full orchestral splendor.

The allegro is the recapitulation, the repetition of the principal section, the exposition. As the regulations of the sonata form prescribe, the recapitulation is in the original key throughout. But there is also some additional material. The flute plays in short insistent phrases, which are echoed, with more emphasis, by the strings, oboe, and bassoon. The violins play a figure of three ascending notes which seem to spell "excelsior." Then the violins, violas, and cellos with basses, one group after another, break forth in rapid scale passages, leading to a triumphant coda.

The three *Leonore* Overtures and the *Fidelio* Overture were performed on one program by Mendelssohn in Leipzig on January 9, 1840. Schumann delved deeply into the relationship between the overtures: "Here the composer can be plainly watched in his own workshop. What he altered, what he discarded, what ideas he followed, what instrumentation he used, all is revealed to us. How unwilling he is to give up the trumpet call backstage! To observe and to compare is a most fascinating and instructive task for any student of the art."

Coriolanus *Overture, Op. 62 (1807)*

Beethoven wrote the overture to *Coriolanus* in 1807. It was not inspired by Shakespeare's play of that name, but by the tragedy of a minor poet, Heinrich Josef von Collin. Coriolanus, the valiant Roman soldier of the fifth century B.C., turned against Rome and remained deaf to the entreaties of his family to lift the siege. In Collin's play, Coriolanus commits suicide. Some writers speculate that Beethoven felt a spiritual kinship with the Roman hero in his intransigence, pride, self-assertion, and self-righteousness. Like Coriolanus, Beethoven believed that his genius was not appreciated. He wrote to Collin, urging him to collaborate on a grand opera: "Take my music for your poetry, and you can be sure that you will gain thereby." The opera project did not materialize, but the overture is acknowledged as one of Beethoven's finest works.

The overture, in the key of C minor, is in one continuous movement, Allegro con brio. It is set in martial time of $\frac{4}{4}$. The opening is announced by unisons on C in the strings, dramatically enhanced by powerful and resonant chords in the full orchestra. The first theme seems to portray the turmoil of the soldier's heart. The second theme is in the relative key of E-flat major. There is femininity in the lyrical passion of this melody, and it may well represent the implorations of Coriolanus' wife. The time-honored form of sonata, much modified, is in evidence here, for there is a development section and a full-fledged recapitulation, in which the first subject returns in the key of F minor and the feminine theme appears in C major. There is an elaborate coda, and the mighty chords of the opening are heard again. The closing bars are in C minor, suggesting a lament at the death of the hero.

Egmont *Overture, Op. 84 (1810)*

Beethoven's musical mind was that of a giant, and his creative imagination encompassed the loftiest and noblest visions in sound. He was a symphonic philosopher. The music of the theater was not his chosen domain; his opera *Fidelio* was a symphonic drama. But being Beethoven he injected some of his profoundest thoughts into incidental music for the theater. Such was the score he wrote for Goethe's

Overture to *Coriolanus*, Op. 62

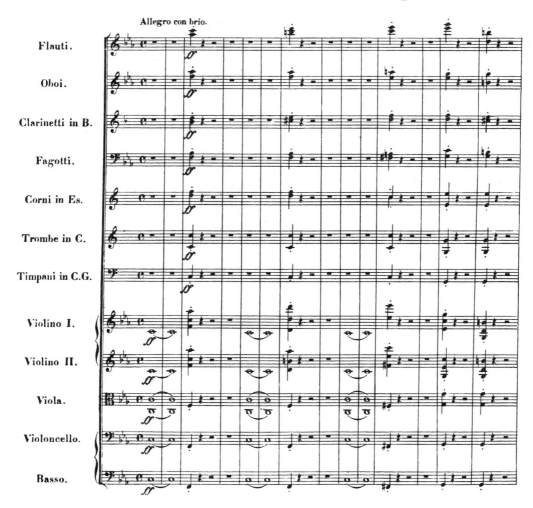

drama *Egmont*. Its subject was close to Beethoven's heart, for it concerned the struggle for freedom. Count Lamoral d'Egmont was a Dutch patriot who led the people of the Netherlands against the oppressive Spanish rule. He was tried for treason by the infamous Council of Blood and was executed in 1567. But his martyrdom spurred his countrymen to continued action against tyranny, resulting in the eventual liberation of the Netherlands.

Goethe's drama with Beethoven's music was first performed in Vienna on May 24, 1810. The score comprised an introduction, four interludes, two songs, and a concluding "Triumph Symphony." From these materials Beethoven fashioned an overture, which became a standard piece of symphonic concert repertory. The opening measures, in F minor, in ¾ time, set the tone for dramatic action. The ponderous chords, separated by pregnant silences, reflect Egmont's brooding spirit on the eve of his decision to lead his people against the oppressor. This serves as a preamble to the main section of the overture, Allegro, in ¾ time. The first subject is rhythmically agitated, portraying the mass action on the political scene. The second theme is

Overture to *Egmont*, Op. 84

a courtly sarabande, which may be interpreted as the symbol of the Spanish duke of Alva, for a sarabande is reputedly a dance of Spanish origin. Some literal-minded analysts attempt to follow the fortunes of Egmont through the thematic development of the music, so that the falling octaves in the violins at the interval of a perfect fourth at the end of the principal section of the overture are taken as illustrating the beheading of Egmont. The concluding part of the overture, allegro con brio, in F major, in ¼ time, depicts the triumph of the people, with jubilant fanfares carrying the oriflamme of victory in the brass, reinforced by the penetrating sound of the piccolo like a full-throated voice of the people in the streets.

Overture to King Stephen, *Op. 117 (1812)*

Beethoven wrote occasional pieces for the theater, among them a score of incidental music for the opening of a grand theater in Pest, the capital of Hungary. The opening took place on February 9, 1812, with a drama by the famous German playwright August von Kotzebue, dealing with St. Stephen, king of Hungary, who fought the pagan noblemen in the early eleventh century. Beethoven's overture to *King Stephen* was performed after the drama, as a postlude; his overture to *The Ruins of Athens* (also by Kotzebue) served as a prelude to the drama.

In a letter to his older brother, who was often an intermediary between him and his publishers, Beethoven specifically mentioned the honorarium for the overture and other incidental music for the occasion. There were twelve numbers in all; Beethoven wanted 20 ducats each for four of them; 10 ducats apiece for seven others, and only 5 ducats for the shortest number. Adding them up, Beethoven arrived at the *summa summarum* (Beethoven used the Latin words), 155 ducats.

The overture opens with a preamble in C minor, in a deliberate slow tempo. Martial fanfares are heard in the horns introducing the main section, Presto, in E-flat major. The brass instruments are very busy, maintaining a rapid march tempo. While the work is not of major importance in Beethoven's catalogue, there are some interesting features in the score. Particularly intriguing are the passages in the violins anticipating the main theme of the choral finale of Beethoven's Ninth Symphony, almost note for note. After a return to the initial section in C minor, there is a decisive recapitulation in E-flat major, continuing in rapid tempo to the end, with drums and brass playing fortissimo supported by the entire orchestra.

Overture to The Consecration of the House, Op. 124 (1822)

Beethoven wrote the overture to the play *Die Weihe des Hauses* for the opening of the Josefstadt Theater in Vienna, and it was performed on that occasion on October 3, 1822. Beethoven conducted the orchestra himself. He could still hear a little with his left ear, and he directed the performance from the piano bench, turning his good ear toward the stage. But he could not command the players unassisted. Fortunately, his disciple and biographer Anton Schindler was at his side, leading the violin section and helping to maintain the proper tempo. Socially, the opening of the Josephstadt Theater was a great success. Four hundred reserved seats and fourteen boxes were sold in advance, and the crème de la crème of Vienna society was in attendance.

The overture is set in a festive mood; its hymnal strains are positively Handelian in their lofty utterance. There are some melodic and rhythmic figures reminiscent of the *Pastoral* Symphony, and there are other earmarks of Beethoven's familiar style. The ending is a joyous celebration in the immaculately white key of C major.

CONCERTOS
Piano Concerto No. 2 in B-flat Major, Op. 19 (1785; revised 1794–95, 1798)

In 1852, a Latvian-born Russian writer of German descent named Wilhelm von Lenz published in St. Petersburg a book in the French language entitled *Beethoven et ses trois styles*. In it he arbitrarily divided the creative catalogue of Beethoven's works into three periods: from Opera 1 to 21, entirely Classical in style; from Opera 22 to 95, truly Beethovenian in spirit and noble in expression; and the last, from Opus 96 on, marked by an attempt to scale unattainable heights. This artificial but convenient division's obvious defect relates to the fact that Beethoven distributed his opus numbers not chronologically but according to the publishers' convenience. As a result, wide divergences exist between the opus numbers and the time of composition in Beethoven's list of works. For instance the two "easy" piano

Piano Concerto No. 2 in B-flat Major, Op. 19

sonatas, which are among Beethoven's earliest works, bear the incongruous opus number 49.

Beethoven's Second Piano Concerto in B-flat Major, is assigned the opus number 19, and thus belongs to the first "Classical" period. In fact, it was written before the First Concerto in C Major, which bears an earlier opus number, 15. Beethoven completed his Second Piano Concerto when he was twenty-three; it was one of the earliest works he wrote in Vienna after his arrival there from his native city of Bonn. The title of the first edition, published in Vienna in 1795, reads in the original French: "Concert pour le pianoforte avec deux violons, viole, violoncelle et basse, une flute, 2 hautbois, 2 cors et 2 bassons, oeuvre XIX." There are no clarinets in the score. This abstinence is indeed very Classical, pre-Mozartean, in fact. The original orchestration has reduced strings, according to eighteenth-century usage.

The B-flat Major Concerto has no number in the original edition. Its classification as the Second Piano Concerto was adopted in later editions. To reverse the numbering in order to reestablish proper chronology is now impractical. (Incidentally, the numbering of Chopin's two piano concertos is also reversed; his Second was written before the First.)

The concerto is set in three movements, in the cyclic succession of tempi: fast, slow, fast. The first movement, Allegro con brio, opens with a lengthy introduction for orchestra, bringing out the dotted rhythm characteristic of the principal theme of the first movement. The piano enters with a brief episode and then plunges into the energetic exposition of the subject. The contrasting lyrical theme appears in the dominant, according to the time-honored sonata form. In the development, the modulatory scheme carries the music to more remote keys. The recapitulation contains a number of episodes in which great rhythmic variety is achieved by the use of two, three, four, and six notes to a beat. Beethoven wrote a special cadenza for this movement, in which the dotted rhythm is greatly emphasized.

The second movement, Adagio, is an air with variations. The tonality, E-flat major, remains firm throughout; the thematic material is distributed antiphonally between the solo piano and the orchestra. The ending is in pianissimo.

The third and last movement, Allegro molto, is a rondo. It starts brilliantly in piano solo, and is set in jig time with strong off-accents. The orchestra picks it up, while the piano provides a background in bravura passages. The alternative themes of the rondo, lacking the sharp accents of the opening, are more serene. The conclusion is terse and vigorous.

Piano Concerto No. 3 in C Minor, Op. 37 (1800)

Beethoven wrote his Third Piano Concerto during the last year of the eighteenth century. He completed the score on December 15, 1800, on the eve of his thirtieth birthday. The piano writing of the concerto represents a transition between the facile virtuosity of the era of Mozart and Haydn and the dramatic, massive style of the mature Beethoven. The nature of melody and harmony is also indicative of this transition. Time and again, in the midst of a hedonistic development, there is a glimpse of the somber image of Beethoven of his future tragic years. The first performance of the concerto took place in Vienna on April 5, 1803. Beethoven himself played the piano part.

The concerto is in three movements, with a slow movement placed between two fast sections. There is a lengthy orchestral introduction, which summarizes, like an overture to an opera, the entire content of the first movement, Allegro con brio. Both principal subjects, the dramatic first theme in C minor and the romantic contrasting subject in E-flat major, are explicitly stated. After the introduction is completed, the piano enters without accompaniment. As the exposition progresses, the piano and orchestra share the thematic substance. The movement ends brilliantly in unison.

The second movement, Largo, in E major, in $\frac{3}{8}$ time, is unmistakably marked with Beethoven's stylistic expression. The piano solo introduces a songful theme supported by resonant deep harmonies. The melody is decorated with harmonious arpeggios and melodious trills. As the piano falls silent, the orchestra, with strings muted, echoes the subject. This dialogue forms the substance of the music. Gradually, the piano intensifies the rhythmic variety of its filigree ornamentation.

So fine does the fabric become that Beethoven is impelled to use passages of quin-tuple-stemmed 128th-notes, so that the full complement of these microrhythmic notes numbers 48 units in a single minuscule bar of $\frac{3}{8}$.

The finale is a rondo; the tempo is Allegro; the time signature is $\frac{2}{4}$. Here Beethoven is completely unbuttoned, speeding in a rustic mood with hardly a pause to prepare for the next step. After an extraordinary cadenza, traversing the entire range of the piano from bass to treble, the concerto ends in a display of sonorous fireworks.

Romance in G for Violin and Orchestra, Op. 40 (1802)

In 1802 Beethoven's brother, who took care of his affairs, wrote to his publisher: "We have also two Adagios for violin with accompaniment for several instruments, which will cost 135 florins." One of these adagios was a piece published subse-quently under the title "Romance, Op. 40." There was no dedication, an unusual omission among Beethoven's works. This Romance preceded by three years the composition of Beethoven's Violin Concerto. There is, however, very little in the music of the Romance that presages the concerto. Rather, the composition of the Romance should be set down as an addition to the supply of short solo pieces for the then growing class of virtuoso performers on the violin.

The score of the Romance opens with a passage for violin unaccompanied, with double stops that suggest a kinship with the opening of the "Kreutzer" Sonata (Op. 47), composed at about the same time. The violin passage is repeated by the orchestra. In this, too, there is analogy with a similar procedure in the "Kreutzer" Sonata, where the piano and the violin are antiphonally treated. Further develop-ment includes ornamentations and variations of the theme. The melodic interest is sustained throughout; the treatment is concise and clear, and the ending is simple, without superfluous climaxes.

In Beethoven's biography, the year 1802, when the Romance was composed, was one of the darkest. It was the year of the Heiligenstadt Testament, in which he expressed his despair that he was growing deaf, a document that revealed Beethoven as being close to suicide. It would be futile to try to find a counterpart to this gloomy testament in music composed at the same time. Certainly, there is nothing of the Heiligenstadt philosophy in the innocent Romance for Violin and Orchestra. But it is psychologically interesting that this Romance was written immediately before or immediately after these lines penned by Beethoven on October 6, 1802: "You men who think or say that I am malevolent, stubborn, or misanthropic, how greatly do you wrong me. O how harshly was I defeated by the doubly tragic experience of my bad hearing, and yet I could not say to people, speak louder, shout, for I am deaf. Ah, how could I possibly admit an infirmity in the one sense which should have been more acute in me than in others, a sense which I once possessed in highest perfection, a perfection such as surely few in my profession enjoy or have enjoyed!"

Concerto in C Major for Violin, Cello, and Piano, Op. 56 (1804)

Beethoven wrote his triple concerto for violin, cello, piano, and orchestra in 1804, the year of the *Eroica*, but its melodic and harmonic style bears the hallmark of an earlier period. There is a Baroque dalliance in symmetric rhythmic sequences and in the luscious display of expansive arpeggios in the piano part. The antiphony of the violin and the cello is clearly outlined. But the orchestra participates in the proceedings to a much greater degree than in the traditional Baroque ensembles, and has a distinctly symphonic character.

The concerto is in three movements. The opening Allegro, in C major, is in sonata form. The violin and the cello assume a virtuoso character as soon as the main themes are introduced, while the piano occupies a subsidiary position. The development section and the recapitulation are elaborated according to tradition, but Beethoven's hand is revealed in bold modulations led by chromatic expansions in enharmonic progressions. A roulade of decorative melodic figurations leads to the coda on the pedal point. The ending is assertive.

The second movement, Largo, in A-flat major, is a typical Beethoven romance, with a long protracted melody serving as the point of departure for instrumental variations in filigree texture. The dynamic design is a model of Classical perfection, providing a natural alternation of moods. After a stationary and foreboding passage there is a transition without pause to the last movement, Rondo alla polacca. The propulsive rhythm of the polonaise is struck immediately, imparting a festive air to the music. The sonorities are enhanced by a cascade of scales in the solo instruments, gradually subsiding into a series of echoes, followed by coquettish trills and ponderous unisons. Once more there is a discursive interlude; meaningful diminished-seventh chords create a temporary suspense, and a brilliant coda is launched in vigorous $\frac{2}{4}$ time. The last hurrah is sounded, bringing the triple concerto to a most satisfying close.

Piano Concerto No. 4 in G Major, Op. 58 (1805–6)

Beethoven began his Piano Concerto No. 4 in the year 1805, but apparently the composition proceeded slowly. He was in the habit of writing several works concurrently and intermittently, without a definite chronology, in which respect he was very unlike Mozart, Haydn, or Schubert, who turned out symphonies in a matter of days, rarely weeks. Thus, while at work on the concerto, Beethoven was engaged in the composition of the Fourth and Fifth Symphonies; and it is probable that the similarity between the rhythmical figure of the first phrase of the concerto and the famous "knocks" of the Fifth is not just a coincidence. In 1805 Beethoven was thirty-five years old. His deafness was already a serious affliction, he was dramatically conscious of it, and he had already confided his fears to friends. In his everyday affairs he was highly irritable, and suspicious of everyone. Yet these years marked the peak of his powers.

Beethoven disliked playing his own compositions in public. When the Fourth Concerto was completed, he asked his pupil and friend Ferdinand Ries to play it. There were only five days left for Ries to learn it before the performance, and Ries begged Beethoven to let him play the C-Minor Concerto instead. But the great man could tolerate no opposition to his desires. He left Ries in a rage, and turned to another young pianist, who agreed forthwith. At the last moment, however, the audacious pianist demurred, and substituted in the program the selfsame C-Minor Concerto that Ries wanted to play. Beethoven, though raging, had to submit. The first performance of the Fourth Concerto took place much later—at one of Prince Lobkowitz's palace concerts, in March 1807—and Beethoven played the piano part. The orchestral parts were published in 1808. The concerto was dedicated to the Archduke Rudolph.

Piano Concerto No. 4 in G Major, Op. 58

The concerto opens in an unusual manner, with the piano solo. The theme has a rhythmic pattern similar to the opening of the Fifth Symphony, without its dramatic significance. The strings imitate the rhythm, with immediate modulation. Gradually the entire orchestra is brought into play, while the principal theme undergoes various modifications, until only two notes of it remain, alternating in vigorous rhythmic figures. After the climax there is a moment of calm, and a curious modal transition brings in a new theme in a minor key, given first to the violins. Then the oboe is heard, and the flute, seconded by the bassoon. The sonority grows, the rhythm is more incisive, the accents are sharper, and the rumbling basses prepare another climax, punctuated by the full chords in the orchestra. As an aftermath, the woodwinds play the concluding figure, based on the pattern of the principal theme. Four energetic chords round off the orchestral interlude, and the piano finally enters with a rhythmic figure, again formed of four notes. There is brilliant passage work, the orchestra sounds four powerful chords in the key of the concerto, G major, and the piano resumes its solo. Now it is give-and-take between the soloist and the orchestra, with the principal subject embellished and varied. The piano part covers the entire range of the instrument and in one place the distance between the right and left hands exceeds five octaves. This is a typical device of Beethoven, met with also in the "Appassionata," composed at about the same time as the concerto.

Then the strings announce a lively theme. The bassoon and later the clarinet take it up, while the piano plays rhythmical figurations, trills, arpeggios, and freely rhythmed ornaments. The theme in a minor key, heard at the beginning of the movement, reappears, and merges with the four-note motto of the principal theme. The oboe and the bassoon hold the foreground, while the piano continues its passage work, spiced with vigorous cross-accents. After a four-octave chromatic run, the piano has a short interlude in the treble. There is a crescendo. The orchestra enters in full strength, and there is the concluding figure in the woodwinds. This section corresponds to the similar section in the middle of the first part. It is here in the key of D major, while at its first appearance the key was G major, the tonic. As before, the piano solo enters with the four-note motto, and there is a great deal of elaboration on this figure. A climax is reached with a chromatic run, followed by trills in the piano part. A quiet theme is sounded, punctuated by the four-note figure in the lower strings.

The woodwinds and the horns now have the four-note figure, with the piano still contributing the accompanying flourishes. The mood is quiet, but there are cross-accents. A quick and vehement crescendo brings about a climax. The orchestra is cut off, after a series of powerful chords, and the piano solo announces the principal theme, as in the beginning of the concerto. This is the recapitulation, but the theme is played an octave higher, and with considerable enhancement, rhythmic and melodic. Such highly modified recapitulations are characteristic of the middle and late period of Beethoven's art of form. The secondary theme appears in G minor and, through a series of modulations, is headed for a climax in G major. There are powerful chords in the full orchestra and a piano cadenza.

Beethoven composed two cadenzas for the first movement. As every cadenza should, each includes flourishes, arpeggios, and trills. All these ornaments bear a definite thematic relationship to the principal theme, and the four-note motto is clearly recognizable. After the cadenza, the piano continues playing, with the orchestra accentuating the thematic material. After some extended scale passages, the four-note motto is reiterated in the full orchestra, and the movement comes to an end.

In the second movement, Beethoven marked expressly in the score that the piano part should be played throughout with the soft pedal down. This fact alone imparts a characteristic color to the movement. To be sure, the orchestra is given a wide range of dynamics, from triple piano to forte. Even the piano part, in its final short cadenza, bears an indication, *"à 3 corde,"* which means, in effect, soft pedal off. Beethoven was notoriously inconsistent in such small matters, and would rarely observe his own specifications. The interesting feature of this movement is also the fact that the piano and orchestra do not play together, but alternate antiphonally. The orchestra is given a sharply rhythmed phrase, while the piano responds with a lyrical period. The key of the movement is E minor, the time, slow $\frac{2}{4}$.

The Rondo at the beginning of the third movement is in quick $\frac{2}{4}$ time. Thus, all three movements are in duple metrical division, which may be not without a special significance, as implying energy and vigor. The key is G major, but the incisive three-note motto opens in C major. There is an interchange of phrases between the strings and the piano, at an increasingly rapid pace. The full orchestra now plays the principal theme, and there is a new four-bar phrase, with the rumbling basses giving it vigor. The piano echoes the new phrase, and the interplay is repeated in another key. The contest between the orchestra and the piano is now narrowed to a one-bar figure. In this connection it is well to recall that the word "concerto" comes from the Latin word signifying a competition. This meaning of the word was very clear in the minds of the early composers of instrumental concertos; much later, Stravinsky deliberately revived the original meaning in his Concerto for Two Pianos.

The piano solo has a brilliant cross-accented passage in sixteenth notes, which subsequently slows down to triplets in eighths. Follows a quiet theme in the piano part, which is taken up by the clarinet and strings in pianissimo. Beethoven's rondo form was extremely flexible, and such interludes as this were quite in the manner. The piano solo now runs wide-ranged arpeggios, with incisive cross-accents in the woodwind. The motto of the Rondo is heard, the movement slackens, and the piano has a short cadenza: a C-major scale downward, and a chromatic scale upward. The Rondo is now resumed pianissimo in the strings, and follows the scheme of the beginning. There is an extensive modulation, and short rhythmic phrases are bandied from the orchestra to the piano. But the three-note Rondo theme persists.

The piano plays rapid figurations, corresponding to similar figurations in the first section of the Rondo. The movement slows down to triplets in eighth notes. The key is D, while the previous appearance of the triplet figure was in A. The quiet theme is heard, and once more the strings and the clarinet echo it in the orchestra. There are arpeggios, with syncopated chords in the woodwinds. The motto of the Rondo is heard again, and soon is proclaimed by the entire orchestra. The cadenza covers less range this time and, after a brief lull, with a clarinet solo against the background of plucked strings and percussive piano passages in broken octaves, the orchestra resumes with great vigor. The piano imitates the second phrase of the orchestra, and there is an alternation of lyrical phrases between the piano and the woodwind instruments. The strings repeat the quiet theme. Then the full orchestra sounds the phrase, modified and invigorated by cross-accents. Four short chords in fortissimo prepare the cadenza.

The cadenza was written by Beethoven himself. It is relatively short, containing references to the quiet theme, and there are some arpeggios. The piano continues with long trills. The Rondo theme returns, without the three-note motto, in the woodwinds, while the piano plays arpeggios in the treble. The movement becomes more animated, and once more there is a long trill in the piano. The concluding section is marked presto. Starting in pianissimo, the dynamic range is quickly covered up to fortissimo, and the Rondo theme is given in full by the orchestra. The piano then plays arpeggios in the treble, and once more there is a crescendo, reaching the final climax, the three-note motto being sounded with crashing effect.

Violin Concerto in D Major, Op. 61 (1806)

Beethoven wrote five piano concertos, but only one violin concerto. The latter was written for a popular Vienna violinist named Franz Clement. Beethoven inscribed the manuscript, in a mixture of Italian and French, "Concerto per clemenza pour Clement." Why did Beethoven have to beg Clement for clemency? There must have been a reason behind the pun. Perhaps he felt conscience-stricken, for he did not deliver the manuscript until the last moment for its first performance in Vienna, on December 22, 1806, and poor Clement had to play it practically at sight. The program was arranged in a most peculiar manner. Clement played the first movement of the concerto and, before going on with the work, presented a violin fantasy of his own, holding the violin upside-down. He completed the concerto in the second part of the program. Such interpolations of solo pieces of the "virtuoso" type between the movements of a concerto or a symphony were not uncommon at the time. Anyway, there is no evidence that Clement's fantastic stunt shocked anyone in the audience, or for that matter Beethoven himself.

The first movement, Allegro ma non troppo, in D major, in $\frac{4}{4}$ time, begins in a startling way, with four strokes on the kettledrum on the tonic D. A story is told that these drumbeats were inspired by a neighbor knocking at Beethoven's door late at night, but there is as little verisimilitude in it as in the legend that the initial four notes of Beethoven's Fifth Symphony represent Fate knocking at the door. (It may have been the same door, for Beethoven was working on the Violin Concerto and the Fifth Symphony at about the same time and in the same lodgings.) The orchestral introduction is unusually long; it forms a summary of the thematic content of the entire movement. The first theme is introduced by the woodwinds. The beautifully proportioned second theme is sung out by the violins.

A remarkable phenomenon occurs in the transition: four D-sharps, set at the same measured pace as the opening four drumbeats, and left in suspended animation without a resolution into their natural outlet on E. With malice aforethought, or so it seems, Beethoven leads them to a dominant-seventh chord of D major, in which the crucial E is misplaced; the four D-sharps are then repeated and intentionally misdirected to the dominant-ninth chord, again minus the hoped-for E.

The mystery deepens, and the plot thickens, when we discover that in the preliminary sketches of the Violin Concerto the impertinent D-sharps are enharmonically notated as E-flats—many arcs removed, on the quintal cycle of scales, from the basic tonality of this concerto. Then there is this neat circumstance that E-flat, as well as its enharmonic equivalent D-sharp, stands in the tritone relationship to the dominant of the principal key of the concerto, the tritone being the "diabolical" interval which the musical theologians of the Middle Ages called "diabolus in musica." There is enough material in this note grubbing for a musicophilosophical essay full of cavernous profundities. Fortunately, relief from analytical tension is provided on heuristic grounds: enharmonic substitution was common in Beethoven's notational modus operandi. To cite an amazing example, the *Eroica* was described in the announcement of its first performance as a symphony in D-sharp rather than E-flat major. Were it in fact set in that improbable key, the signature would have required nine sharps, two of them double! The Case of the Four D-sharps is solved at a later occurrence of the suspension in question, when they are pointedly led to their legitimate exit on E.

When the solo violin is at last introduced after the lengthy orchestral prolegomenon, its entrance is oblique, masked by allusive arpeggios and decorative scale passages. It is only after a great deal of virtuosic perambulation that the soloist gains prominence in melodious presentations. The orchestra accommodates itself to the harmonious soloist, and the movement concludes without prolixity or supererogation.

The second movement, Larghetto, is set in G major, in $\frac{4}{4}$ time. As in the first movement, the thematic initiative is given to the orchestra, which states the principal subject in muted strings. Once again the soloist assumes the role of the exterior decorator, furnishing some exquisite purfling. But when in due time the solo part rises to its rightful dominance, it resounds with magnificent eloquence. A cadenza perlustrates the pertinent thematic materials, leading to a decisive plunge into the third and last movement, Rondo, in D major. Here Beethoven finds himself in his natural environment, under the open harmonious skies, happily pursuing a pastoral echolalia in the folkish rhythm of $\frac{6}{8}$.

The music is full of fanfares, suggesting the sound of a postilion horn announcing the departure of a stagecoach, or of a distant hunting scene. A poignant balladlike tune in a minor key brings about a change of mood. But soon the rollicking rhythms of the country dance reassert themselves. An upward run of two and a half octaves along the chord notes of the D-major triad in the solo part gives the signal for an applause-provoking ending.

Piano Concerto No. 5 in E-flat Major ("Emperor"), Op. 73 (1809)

Beethoven wrote his fifth, and last, piano concerto in Vienna in 1809. The city was under the siege of Napoleon's armies in August of that year, but surrendered quickly after the French howitzers opened fire. Beethoven spent most of the time during the bombardment in the cellar of his brother's house with pillows pressed against his ears to protect him from the noise of the artillery.

The E-flat Major Concerto has somehow acquired the nickname "Emperor" Concerto, perhaps in connection with the fact that it was composed during Napoleon's drive on Vienna. An imperial link may also have been suggested by the "military" tonality of E-flat major, the key of the *Eroica* Symphony, which was inspired by Napoleon. Incidentally, the concerto's nickname, "Emperor," is unknown in Germany and Austria.

The first performance of the concerto took place in Leipzig on November 28, 1811; it had its first Vienna hearing on February 12, 1812, when Carl Czerny, famous for his piano exercises, who was a pupil of Beethoven's and the teacher of Liszt, was the soloist. The Vienna concert was a social affair, and its ostensible purpose was a benefit for the Charitable Society of Noble Ladies. Popular entertainment was provided on the same program by three living tableaux representing paintings by Raphael, Poussin, and Troyes. For this type of audience the music of the concerto was too difficult, and it was indifferently received.

The concerto is in three movements. The orchestra strikes a powerful tonic chord in the first movement, Allegro, and it triggers a sonorous display of arpeggios in the piano part. Another orchestral chord, in the subdominant, is struck, and the piano responds with a series of harmonic figurations. The dominant follows, and once more the piano fills in the harmonic outline. The introduction is completed with the resolution into the tonic. The orchestra then presents the principal "imperial" subject in its most authoritative utterance, set in martial $\frac{4}{4}$ time, in the main key of E-flat major. A lyric melody in G major in the piano part serves as the second subject. Bravura passages follow, with a piano and orchestra fully engaged. Chromatic sequences provide colorful elaboration of the principal subjects, but the key of E-flat major dominates the harmonic scheme in its porphyrogene majesty.

The second movement, Adagio un poco mosso, in $\frac{4}{4}$ time, is in the key of B major; it is set in the form of instrumental variations on a chorale-like melody. A remarkable modulation is effected at the end of the movement through the enharmonic identification of the tonic of B major with the flatted submediant of E-flat major. The spirit of improvisation reigns in the transitional chords, softly played by the pianist, in anticipation of the main subject of the finale, Rondo. There is a sudden dash forward, unleashing an explosive series of tonic chords and harmonic embellishments, allegro ma non tanto. The tonal scheme of the finale is crystal clear. Cascades of chords and arpeggios, cataracts of scales, rivulets of pearly figurations fill the air with music. The piano reaches the high E flat in the treble, a key that had not been available to Beethoven on the instruments he used to compose his early works. The "Emperor" Concerto ends with a coruscating scattering of brilliant sonorities.

Piano Concerto No. 5 in E-flat Major, Op. 73 ("Emperor")

CHAMBER MUSIC
String Quartet No. 1 in F Major, Op. 18, No. 1 (1799–1800)

Beethoven was a late beginner in composition. He wrote his first string quartets at the age of twenty-nine. At the same age, Mozart had already gone through more than half his voluminous catalogue of works. Also, Beethoven worked laboriously. While Mozart could turn out a string quartet in one afternoon, it took Beethoven months to bring his early quartets into shape, after many revisions.

The Quartet in F Major, Op. 18, No. 1, is the first of Beethoven's published quartets, although not the first in the order of composition. Opus 18 includes six quartets in all, dedicated to Beethoven's friend and financial benefactor, Prince Franz Joseph Lobkowitz, who was an amateur musician and patron of the arts. Many of Beethoven's instrumental compositions were performed for the first time at Lobkowitz's home. Such private performances arranged by a rich music lover were very frequent in the Vienna of Beethoven's time, whereas public performances in public halls were rather exceptional.

Beethoven's notebook reveals five attempts at the composition of the very first theme of this quartet. Curiously enough, they were all in $\frac{4}{4}$ time, while the final product crystallized itself in $\frac{3}{4}$. Beethoven completed the composition of the quartet on June 25, 1799, but a year later, in June 1800, he wrote to Karl Friedrich Amenda, his friend to whom he had given the manuscript: "Don't play my quartet—I have modified it very much. I am only now learning how to write quartets, as you will observe when you receive the music." And Beethoven was already in his thirtieth year at the time!

In his student days Beethoven practiced strict counterpoint diligently, using for a textbook the famous Latin treatise on counterpoint, *Gradus ad Parnassum (Steps to Parnassus),* by the celebrated composer and theorist Johann Joseph Fux (1660–1741). Beethoven's own music book with 245 exercises, some of them corrected by Haydn, who was Beethoven's teacher for a time, is extant, and testifies to the fact that he applied himself thoroughly to the science. But strict counterpoint never appealed to Beethoven, although he felt great admiration for master contrapuntists of his day. In actual composition Beethoven made use of counterpoint as he saw fit, without being much concerned about the strictness of the interval and the pedantry of the science. He humanized counterpoint. In quartet writing, he individualized separate instruments by lending melodic interest to their parts and, in common with all contrapuntal practice, he made ample use of the device of imitation. But it was mostly imitation of pattern rather than strict transposition of intervals.

The Quartet Op. 18, No. 1, is in the orthodox four movements. The first movement, Allegro con brio, in F major, in $\frac{3}{4}$ time, is based on one single motive, which is used 102 times in 313 bars, an amazing proportion for a movement that is not a set of variations. This rhythmic theme appears in every instrument, in various melodic forms. There is a contrasting second theme and a development—a fact which makes it possible to approximate this movement to sonata form.

The second movement, Adagio affettuoso ed appassionato in D minor, in $\frac{9}{8}$, is also in sonata form, but with considerable modifications. Thus the return to the first time in the original key is embellished with figuration, which serves to enliven the closing part of the movement. We catch a glimpse of the future nineteenth-century Beethoven in characteristic explosions of dynamic force and lightning flashes of rapid notes. We find here also an instance of the use of extremely rare 128th notes. Amenda tells us that this movement was inspired by the scene in the tomb in Romeo and Juliet; this statement is plausible in view of the fact that a sketch of this movement, dated 1799, bears the programmatic designation *"Les derniers soupirs,"* "the last sighs," as the end.

The third movement, a Scherzo, is used by Beethoven in place of the Classical minuet. As in the minuet there is a trio, so named because in the original Classical form three instruments used to play the middle section. The Scherzo is in the key of the quartet, F major, and the trio is in the dominant, C major, in conformity with common usage. The principal part of the Scherzo is repeated, completing the ternary form. Donald Francis Tovey is the authority for the statement that Beethoven always used the word "scherzo" in its etymological sense, the German *Scherz,* or "jest," thus suggesting a humorous composition.

The last movement is a lively Rondo, in duple time, in F major. The principal theme returns three times, and there are episodes with new material between the appearances of the principal theme. The coda is extensive, and leads to a brilliant close.

String Quartet No. 8 in E Minor, Op. 59 ("Razumovsky" Quartets), No. 2 (1805–6)

The tenuous thread existing between the Immortal Beloved and the three Op. 59 Quartets (called the "Razumovsky" Quartets) hangs on the question of chronology. Beethoven was extremely careless in his dates. The letter to the Immortal Beloved was dated Monday, July 6, but without the year. Among the years in which July 6 fell on a Monday, the most probable is 1807, that is, if Beethoven was not mistaken in setting down the day of the week. Now on April 20, 1807, Beethoven signed an advantageous contract with the London-based Italian composer and publisher Muzio Clementi, by the terms of which he sold Clementi the British rights on his Quartets Op. 59, the Fourth Symphony, the Overture to *Coriolanus,* the Fourth Piano Concerto, and the Violin Concerto for the sum of two hundred pounds sterling. But the quartets were in the hands of Count Franz von Brunsvik, and Beethoven, eager to deliver all the items to Clementi in due time, wrote in May 1807 an urgent note to Brunsvik requesting him to return the quartets to him at once. This letter contains the phrase "Kiss your sister Therese." This kiss, taken in conjunction with the letter to the Immortal Beloved written two months later, makes Therese an important candidate.

Psychologically it is unlikely that Beethoven should have included this kiss in a letter of prosaic contents, if it had any emotional significance, but confronted with the riddle of the Immortal Beloved, Beethoven scavengers are willing to grasp at a straw. No Beethoven scholar has considered the most likely solution of the riddle: that Beethoven played with his own fantasy, as he very often did; that he invented a nonexistent voyage which he described in that letter, and that he did not destroy the letter precisely because it had no object in the real world.

The three Quartets, Op. 59, are usually known under the name "Razumovsky" Quartets. Count Andreas Razumovksy was the Russian ambassador to the Austrian court in Vienna. He was also an amateur violinist, who played the second violin in a quartet he organized for his pleasure. That the quartets were written at Razumovsky's request, or were without such a request destined for Razumovsky, is shown by the fact that Beethoven introduced Russian themes in the music. The dedication to Razumovksy appears in the third printing of the quartets, in these characteristic words in French:

Trois Quatuors très humblement dédiés a son Excellence Monsieur le Comte de Razumovksy, Conseiller, privé actuel de Sa Majesté l'Empéreur de toutes les Russies, Senateur, Chevalier des ordres de St. André, de St. Alexandre-Newsky, et Grand-Croix de celui de St. Vladimir de la 1re Classe, etc., etc., par Louis van Beethoven.

There is no trace of any money transaction between Beethoven and Razumovksy, but it may be assumed that this dedication, and the joint dedication of the *Pastoral* Symphony to Count Razumovksy and Prince Lobkowitz, were made in consideration of a sum of money. This was a perfectly legitimate and sanctioned procedure, no more objectionable in Beethoven's time than in our own.

The Russian melodies that Beethoven used in the Quartets Op. 59 were taken from a collection of Russian songs compiled by one Ivan Pratch and first published in Russia in 1790. Beethoven must have had a copy of this compilation, for he adhered to the type of the melody faithfully. In the Quartet Op. 59, No. 2, he makes use of the same Russian tune that was later used by Modest Mussorgsky (1839–1881) in the coronation scene of *Boris Godunov*. Pratch has this tune in $\frac{3}{8}$ time and in A major. Beethoven uses it in the trio section of the third movement, alternately in E major and A major, setting the time signature as $\frac{3}{4}$. The theme is treated fugally, with a stretto toward the end. The accompanying figure of the tune is in triplets, and the entire presentation is extremely logical and symmetric. Thus, the subject appears in each of the instruments, and is kept in its original melodic form. The Russian words of the theme—which Beethoven could not have understood, for there were no translations given in Pratch's collection—are in conflict with Beethoven's light conception. The song is in fact a hymn to the glory of the czar, and was used on solemn occasions in Russia: "Glory be to you, our Lord in Heaven! Glory be to our Czar on this earth. His beautiful robes will not be worn out! His faithful servants will not grow old! His valiant steeds will not tire out! We sing this song to our Lord! We render him his glory."

A brief notice in the *Allgemeine Musikalische Zeitung*, published after the performance of the quartets in Vienna, referred to them as "of great length and difficulty." The view was expressed that they "will be found perhaps too obscure for general acceptance, though finely constructed and deeply conceived." The quartets were performed in St. Petersburg at a private house early in 1812, a few months before Napoleon unleashed his armies on Russia. In 1857, the Russian writer Alexander von Oulibichef, in his book on Beethoven directed against Wilhelm von Lenz, the initiator of the theory of three styles of Beethoven, assailed the quartets of Beethoven's later period in vehement language:

Few people liked the quartets at the time of their first appearance in St. Petersburg. Today the Op. 59 are called the "great" Beethoven quartets; soon the Opp. 127, 130, 131, 132, and 135 will be called the very great. These titles will undoubtedly be exact since the score of the longest in Op. 18 is thirty pages in length, the longest in Op. 59 is thirty-eight, and the longest of the last, sixty-two. Certainly no one can quarrel with this arithmetic.

String Quartet No. 13 in B-flat Major, Op. 130 (1825–26)

Beethoven's string quartets marked by opus numbers 127, 130, 131, 132, and 135 are usually bracketed under the group of "last" quartets or "late" quartets. They belong to Beethoven's last three years, and in them the greatness of inspiration is reflected in the greater length of the music itself, as though Beethoven needed a larger canvas and more manuscript paper to develop the dramatic expression of his last period.

The tragedy of Beethoven's last years of life, his "quartet years," was not only the Grecian tragedy in which the most precious line of communication, from the ear to the brain, was destroyed. His was also the lesser tragedy, the annoying lack of funds, which was magnified by Beethoven's inability to manage his daily life, and his susceptibility to minor distress. His hopes were set on England, the proverbial land of shopkeepers, which proved unsuspectingly and amazingly the land of generous and far-sighted customers for culture and genius.

In a letter dated September 20, 1824, Charles Neate wrote to Beethoven on behalf of the Philharmonic Society of London, offering him three hundred guineas to come to London to conduct the performance of the Ninth Symphony, which had been written for the Society. Beethoven asked for one hundred guineas more, to buy a coach in which to travel in greater comfort. For this extra money, he offered Neate a string quartet. Neate was receptive to this suggestion: "If you bring the quartet, it is as good as one hundred pounds more," he wrote, "and you can be quite sure, I see no obstacle to it that you should earn a sufficient sum of money to take back with you, enabling you to pass your whole life pleasantly and free from care."

This quartet was the B-flat Major Quartet, Op. 130. Beethoven was agitated by the thought of possible prosperity: "If God would only give me health, I shall be able to accept all commissions I receive from every country in Europe and even from North America." Beethoven's sketchbooks show that he went on from one quartet to another almost without an interval. It was a state of feverish activity; the extraordinary rhapsodic quality, the un-Classical fluidity of modulation, the innovating spirit of instrumental writing of the last quartets are explained by the fact that Beethoven ran a musical temperature when he was writing them. He was eager to market them, of course; but the pressure of work freed Beethoven from restrictions that he might have imposed on himself were he writing for familiar patrons who, as he knew, preferred a Mozartean Beethoven to the truly Beethovenian one. But his old patrons were gone. New patrons were from England, from Russia. They were not parading as benefactors, but approached Beethoven in full appreciation of his greatness.

The Quartet Op. 130 is the thirteenth in the order of Beethoven quartets. It was sketched in the spring and summer of 1825, and the scoring was completed by November of the same year. As so often in Beethoven's creative habits, he was working on all movements at once. The fourth movement of the B-flat Major Quartet, the Danza tedesca, was originally sketched in A major and apparently was to be made part of the A-minor Quartet, but later was transposed into G major, and entitled "Allemande," the French word for the Italian *tedesca,* a German dance; but the Allemande has also a special function and character as the opening dance in the Classical suite. The *Grand Fugue,* Op. 133, was originally intended as the finale of the B-flat Major Quartet, but its length (745 bars) and its polyphonic grandeur were regarded as deterrents to success by the publisher, who persuaded Beethoven to compose another finale. Beethoven followed the publisher's advice. The new finale was probably the last thing Beethoven wrote. He sent it to the publishers on November 26, 1826, four months before he died. The B-flat Major Quartet was performed with the original *Grand Fugue* for the first time on March 21, 1826.

The B-flat Major Quartet is in six movements, and the order of these movements is unusual. The first and the last movements are Allegros, the second movement is a Presto; the third movement is an Andante scherzoso; the fourth movement, an Allegro assai. The only truly slow movement is the fifth, Adagio molto espressivo. The characteristic markings of Beethoven's last period are observable in this quartet even to the eye: the shifting key signatures, the expressive silences, the dramatic instrumental solos. The first movement is in sonata form, with its two themes anticipated in the slow introduction in a truly Beethovenian manner. The Presto is a scherzo in the tonic minor, with a trio in the tonic major. The third movement, in the remote key of D-flat major, has been called by Schumann an "intermezzo." Harmonically, melodically, rhythmically, it is extraordinary, anticipating as it does the future development of Romantic music. There is drama in the uncertainty of key, in the shimmering use of tremolo, in the abrupt ending.

The fourth movement is the Danza tedesca of the sketchbook. There is no organic connection between this German dance and the rest of the quartet. It is an insertion, an interpolation.

The fifth movement is a Cavatina (short aria or song). Beethoven's friends reported that it was written in tears and agony. An indirect confirmation of this may be seen in Beethoven's expression mark *Beklemmt* ("agonized"), with which he marked an episodic passage.

The finale is in the original key of B-flat major. Like the Danza tedesca, this finale might well bear a lower opus number. It is a rustic dance in $\frac{2}{4}$ time, with a contrasting lyrical theme in A-flat major. The climactic coda is in Beethoven's first style, imaginative and brilliant, with episodic ideas constantly brought into play. This finale, written in Beethoven's last months of life, demonstrates that the division of Beethoven's music into three styles, originated by Lenz and accepted by all Beethoven scholars, is at best a convenient chronology. In his third period, Beethoven had not relinquished the youthfulness, vigor, and simplicity of the first.

String Quartet No. 14 in C-sharp Minor, Op. 131 (1825–26)

Immortality was available at the price of fifty ducats in Vienna before 1827. Beethoven, who lived and died there, in a state of constant financial insecurity, was willing to dedicate an overture or a string quartet to anyone rich and beneficent enough to pay. And a Beethoven dedication was a ticket to immortality. Who would now retain the name of a Russian ambassador to Vienna during Napoleonic times, were it not for the fact that Beethoven wrote the "Razumovsky" Quartets? An even more obscure Russian, one of the innumerable tribe of princes, Nikolas Galitzin, also bought a ticket for immortality. His case is particularly interesting because he did not even pay in full for the privilege. Beethoven dedicated three quartets to him, at fifty ducats each, but never collected the entire money, for Galitzin went to war in Persia, and failed to keep his promise to send Beethoven the rest of the money through his bank in St. Petersburg. The inability to get this money preyed on Beethoven's mind during the months of his illness. After Beethoven's death, Galitzin tried to prove that the money had been paid, but finally closed the controversy by sending the required sum to Beethoven's heir, his unworthy nephew, Carl.

Beethoven was not as poor as he made himself out to be. After his death, several Austrian securities were found in the drawer of his desk. He could have lived better than he did, and that he did live in poverty during his last years cannot be doubted. Carl Maria von Weber's son, who visited him, described "a bare and poorly furnished room in terrible disorder: money, clothes, all scattered on the floor; a pile of linen on the bed, dust thick on the piano, cups and cracked plates strewn over the table."

Beethoven was constantly writing letters to friends bemoaning his condition. He wrote to the Italian composer Cherubini in 1823: "My situation is so critical that I can no longer keep my eyes fixed on the stars; I have to concentrate upon the barest necessities of life." He received no reply to this letter. While appealing for help, Beethoven would not yield in any of the disputes that he was getting into, and spent money on litigations with his brother's wife for the custody of his nephew, Carl; with the heirs of Prince Lichnowsky; even with the inventor of the metronome, Johannes Maelzel.

During the last ten years of his life, Beethoven wrote his greatest works, the Ninth Symphony and the "last quartets." Yet his life, his health, and his mental state were in the worst condition imaginable. His deafness was almost complete. His domestic life was made intolerable by his nephew, custody of whom he won after a court fight. We catch glimpses of the nephew's character from Beethoven's letters and notes. "Last Sunday, you again borrowed money from the housekeeper, that cheap old harlot," he writes to his nephew in desperation. But when his nephew shot himself in an unsuccessful suicide attempt, Beethoven forgot everything and begged him to come back to his "loving father Beethoven." He always signed his notes to his nephew as a loving father, not a mere uncle.

The String Quartet in C-sharp Minor, Op. 131, one of the "last quartets" embodying Beethoven's "third style" of creative development, had an indirect bearing on his nephew. Beethoven asked his publishers, in a letter written two weeks before his death, to inscribe the score to Baron von Stutterheim, the colonel of the regiment in which Beethoven's nephew was enlisted. The quartet had been completed and sent to the publishers in October 1826, a few months earlier. In several of his letters, Beethoven refers to having finished this quartet, but his statement often was the expression of a determination, not the actual fact.

Musically speaking, the Quartet in C-sharp Minor represents the highest development of Beethoven's new style. It contains elements of innovation, extraordinary for his time. The selection of the key itself was unusual, if not unprecedented. The quartet has seven movements, linked so that there is no distinct separation between the component parts, but a liquid transition from one mood to another. There is an element of experimentation in the use of such effects as the violoncello playing on the bridge in the high treble register, or pizzicato in isolated notes, creating the impression of an intrusive drumbeat. The form is extremely free, and yet in the Presto Beethoven reverts to his manner, and employs a simple harmony and rhythm of a country dance.

That the quartet was conceived, on the whole, as an expression of Beethoven's brighter side is borne out by Beethoven's own inscription on the manuscript: "zusammengestohlen aus verschiedenem diesem und jenem": "fashioned [literally, "stolen together"] from various this and that." Beethoven was in the habit of writing several movements, or several different pieces, at once, and the seeming eclecticism (or synthesis, if a more dignified word is desired) may be explained exactly by Beethoven's "zusammengestohlen."

The opening movement is Adagio ma non troppo e molto expressivo, in common time ($\frac{4}{4}$), in C-sharp minor. It is a fugue with episodic development, ending on the tonic major. Wagner described this movement as "revealing the most melancholy sentiment ever expressed in music." The following movement is Allegro molto vivace, in D major, in $\frac{6}{8}$ time. The third movement is Allegro moderato, in B minor, in common time ($\frac{4}{4}$). A short adagio serves as an introduction to andante ma non troppo e molto cantabile, which is a theme with variations, which Wagner characterized as "the incarnation of perfect innocence, revealed in countless aspects." The fifth movement is Presto, starting in E major, in common time, "a vision embodied in material form," to quote Wagner once more. This movement is similar in character to the Scherzo from the Ninth Symphony, composed during the same period. There is surprising boisterousness in this movement that belies the picture of Beethoven as an unchangeably gloomy hypochondriac.

The concluding part is an adagio in the key of the quartet, C-sharp minor, in triple time, leading to the final Allegro in cut time ($\frac{2}{2}$), which suggested to Wagner the picture of "the indomitable fiddler, whirling us on to the abyss."

String Quartet No. 16 in F Major, Op. 135 (1826)

The String Quartet Op. 135 is the last complete work written by Beethoven. It bears the date in Beethoven's hand: October 30, 1826. Beethoven died on March 26, 1827. The quartet was performed posthumously in Vienna, on March 23, 1828. This quartet has caused more flow of commentators' ink than all the rest put together, mainly because of Beethoven's curious inscription at the head of the last movement, over the musical quotation of the two principal themes: "Muss es sein? Es muss sein!" ("Must it be? It must be!"). The musical quotation bears a special title, also written in Beethoven's own hand: "Der schwer gefasste Entschluss" ("the very difficult resolution").

Schindler offers a prosaic explanation of this mysterious quotation. Beethoven's housekeeper had asked him for money. "Must it be?" Beethoven inquired. "It must be," the housekeeper answered with emphasis. An alternate explanation, also offered by Schindler, is that Beethoven had asked his publishers for money and, anticipating a query, answered it in a musical theme. A more probable version is offered by Maurice Schlesinger, the son of Beethoven's publisher, namely that Beethoven did not care to write this quartet, which is, in its extension and inner significance, on an inferior scale to the quartets opp. 127, 130, 131, and 132, but, needing money, and having promised the work to the publisher, was conscience-bound to write it. The difficulty in accepting Schlesinger's version lies in the fact that he stated it thirty-two years after the event, and quoted from memory a letter that Beethoven was supposed to have written to the publishers in explanation of the "must it be" quotation, a letter that was lost during a fire at the publisher's premises, and of which no copy was kept. A simpler explanation suggests itself in the absence of plausible report, namely that Beethoven, thinking about the possibilities of the themes already selected by him, fitted the question and answer to them, and set them down in the spirit of a ponderous joke of the kind to which he was addicted.

The first movement is an Allegretto. This is the only quartet that opens with an Allegretto; the rest begin with an Allegro in sonata form, sometimes prefaced with a slow introduction. This departure from rule indicates the lighter nature of the quartet as a whole. The mood is established at once by a whimsical melodic squib in the viola. This melodic fragment has a questioning character underlined by its harmonization. Half a dozen more motives appear in free succession. There is hardly any development, and the form as well as the mood here point toward late Romantic music; this Allegretto might well be regarded as a direct predecessor of Richard Strauss' *Till Eulenspiegel*, which is also in the key of F major.

The following movement is a Vivace, and corresponds to a scherzo. It is in fast

⅜ time. The movement opens in canon so that the two violins and the viola enter on different beats, while the cello plays an independent melody staccato. The middle part contains a succession of forty-seven bars with an unchanging figure in the second violin, viola, and cello, while the first violin disports itself over this insistent background. Beethoven's early critics saw in this display of Beethovenian humor a sign of mental decline, and the consequences of deafness. Yet, this repetition of figures is obviously part of a design, and is quite in keeping with the spirit of the whole scherzo.

The slow movement is a different Beethoven. Joseph de Marliave, in his book *Les Quatuors de Beethoven,* which is a model of conscientious presentation of facts and careful analysis, here gives way to the besetting temptation of all writers on music, and explains the movement as a premonition of approaching death. Even if unconscious knowledge of the end has come to be accepted, there is no more evidence in this particular movement than in any other slow movement in Beethoven's music that he felt that it would be his last Lento. If anything, a case can be made against all powers of premonition in Beethoven's life. When he wrote his last will and testament, he did not die. And his last quartet has three movements full of life and gaiety, as against one contemplative movement. The very last music he wrote, a new finale to the Quartet Op. 130, overflows with youthful energy. The slow movement of the present quartet had better be analyzed without excursions into the mysteries of foreknowledge.

Lento assai, cantante e tranquillo is in the remote key of D-flat major, with the middle part in a minor key on the same tonic, enharmonically changed to C-sharp. This short middle part is dramatic, even mysterious; there are gaps or silences typical of Beethoven's third style of writing. When the movement is resumed in the major key, the pastoral mood reigns, with flashes of distant lightning in the first violin. Beethoven's sketchbook bears these words in relation to this Lento: "gentle song of peace."

The finale is based on the motives "Must it be?" and "It must be," the first with an upward and questioning inflection, the second, in the affirmative interval of a fourth, in downward movement, resting on F, the tonic of the quartet. There are rapid changes of mood, alternating between doubt and affirmation. The casual and light nature of the movement is emphasized by Beethoven's note at the end of the development: "The second part to be repeated if desired." Elsewhere, in his sonatas and quartets, Beethoven is much more categorical about his repeats.

Beethoven's last quartet opens the era of Romantic music. Beethoven's near contemporaries condemned the quartet for its looseness in construction, and judged it a work of the decline. Others acclaimed it as a prophetic vision of the Romantic future. Perhaps it is neither. The quartet is typical Beethoven, and there are elements of his great style, as exemplified in the Lento, and also the lesser art of brilliant humor. Although Beethoven noted "the last quartet" at the end of the manuscript, he could not foresee it was to be his last work. This quartet was Beethoven's intermezzo, which death converted into a finale.

PIANO WORKS
Piano Sonata No. 14 in C-sharp Minor ("Moonlight"), Op. 27, No. 2 (1801)

The writer of the Beethoven entry in the ninth edition of the *Encyclopedia Britannica,* published when there were still people alive who had known Beethoven, describes Beethoven's relationship with women in the following manner:

> Although by no means insensible to female beauty, and indeed frequently
> enraptured, in his grand chaste way with the charms of some lady,
> Beethoven never married, and was, in consequence, deprived of that feel-
> ing of home and comfort which only the unceasing care of refined wom-
> anhood can bestow.... He was a favorite with the ladies of the court, and
> many of the reigning beauties of Vienna adored him and would bear any
> rudeness from him. These young ladies went to his lodgings or received
> him at their palaces as it suited him. He would storm at their least inat-
> tention during their lessons, and would tear up the music and throw it
> about. He may have used the snuffers as a toothpick in Madame Ertmann's
> drawing-room, but when she lost her child, he was admitted to console her.
> He was constantly in love, and though his taste was very promiscuous,
> Beethoven made no secret of his attachments.... One thing is certain, that
> his attachments were all honorable, and that he had no taste for
> immorality.

Afterwards, Beethoven's famous letter addressed to the Immortal Beloved was
published. The greatest confusion was precipitated by it among Beethoven biographers. The letter was never sent, and possibly was never intended to be sent, but
who was the presumptive addressee? One of the strongest candidates was
Beethoven's pupil, Giulietta Guicciardi, later the Countess Gallenberg. To her
Beethoven dedicated his most poetic and most personal work, the "Moonlight"
Sonata. The nickname originated with the Berlin music critic and publisher Johann
Rellstab (1759–1813) who, in his criticism of the work, said it reminded him of the
moonlight on Lake Lucerne.

Beethoven wrote the Sonata quasi una fantasia in C-sharp Minor, Op. 27, No.
2, as the "Moonlight" Sonata is properly titled, in 1801, in the full vigor of his
manhood, at the age of thirty-one. Was this sonata a musical declaration of love?
The theory was destroyed by the Countess Gallenberg herself, who told Alexander
Thayer (1817–1897), Beethoven's greatest biographer: "Beethoven gave me the
Rondo in G, but wishing to dedicate something to the Princess Lichnowsky, he took
the Rondo away and gave me this Sonata in C-sharp minor instead." The dedication was thus a makeshift gift, and nothing more.

The first movement, Adagio sostenuto, was principally responsible for
Rellstab's impression of the moonlight. The tranquil mood of this Adagio sostenuto is established by the slow, wavy motion of harmonic progressions in the right
hand against the deep organlike octaves in the left. The melody, sounded above
these harmonies, is built on only two essential notes, followed by a cadence.
Depending on where the cadence leads, the key shifts with the conclusion of every
phrase. Soon the melody ceases, and the underlying harmonies spread over several
octaves in an ever-heightening emotional sweep. Then the calm mood returns. But
while in the beginning the melodic direction was downward, toward lower keys,
here the melody strives higher and higher, before coming to rest on the tonic. The
characteristic pulse of the melody is then heard in the bass, under the wavy harmonies of the right hand. The close is in a perfect mood of tranquillity.

The second movement, Allegretto, in D-flat major, is written in a light manner.
It is a scherzo, regularly constructed, with a trio for a middle part. What makes it
typically Beethovenian is the use of cross-accents, which inject new vigor into the

rhythmic scheme. Dynamic contrasts in this movement are essential to the music.

The third and last movement, Presto agitato, is in true sonata form. There are two contrasting sections, the stormy first and the lyrical second. The scheme for modulation also follows the broad lines of the Classical sonata form, with such modifications as Beethoven applies in all but his very early sonatas and symphonies. Thus, there is not one first theme, but several subjects that can be bracketed together to form a first section.

The second subject is more easily isolated and recognized. But it appears over the bass of rapid passages which characterize the whole mood of the movement. It is heard variously, in the left hand and in the form of syncopated octaves in the right hand. In Beethoven's later sonatas, the development section is the scene of much contrapuntal activity, canonic imitation, and fugal interlocking. In this sonata there is no formal complexity—new themes are added freely as the inspiration prompts. The sonata's title, Sonata quasi una fantasia—"Sonata in the style of a fantasia"—suggests the procedure. The mood of a fantasia is magnificently displayed in the final section of the last movement. Technically, it takes the place of a coda, but as Beethoven conceives this final section, it is a long meditation on the themes of the sonata. It abounds in cadenzas, trills, arpeggios, meaningful pauses, dramatic transitions.

It is often said that Beethoven is the most personal composer among the great, and that one can read his soul in his music. The stormy pages of the conclusion of the "Moonlight" Sonata seem to justify this common notion. It is easy to connect this music with the picture of Beethoven as presented by Romantic painters, deep in meditation, with flashes of explosive power anticipated in the knitted brow. Even if Beethoven's features had never been seen, painted, or described, his physical appearance could have been plausibly reconstructed from his music.

Piano Sonata No. 28 in A Major, Op. 101 (1816)

In 1816 and 1817, in the wake of the Napoleonic Wars, there was in Europe a general resurgence of the national spirit. One trait of this resurgence was the emphasis laid on the purity of national languages. Beethoven, who always followed, in his impetuous way, the changes of political sentiments, decided that in music, too, the vernacular should be used in preference to the internationally accepted Italian terms. He had experimented in this direction, and even coined some substitute words, such as *Luftsang* for aria, *Kreisfluchtstück* for canon, and *Grundsang* for bass. In January 1817, Beethoven, in a formal letter, announced his decision to change the Italian term *pianoforte* to *Hammerklavier*. It was not a translation, but a mere designation of the type of sound production, by hammers, actuated from a keyboard. The first composition designated for the Hammerklavier was the Piano Sonata No. 28, Op. 101. Apparently, Beethoven felt there were compelling reasons for the change, for he expressed willingness to pay for a new title page of the sonata, which had been engraved with the use of the word "pianoforte." The indications of tempo and mood were given in both languages, and the German was usually more explicit and more expressive. Beethoven used the term "Hammerklavier" for three sonatas, and after that apparently lost interest in verbal quibbles, letting his publisher use the commonly established phraseology.

Dorothea von Ertmann, to whom the sonata is dedicated, was a Beethoven pupil, and one of the best interpreters of his music. There is a tendency among biographers to seek romantic implications in every dedication Beethoven made to a woman. In the case of Dorothea von Ertmann, there were definitely no such developments. She was married to an Austrian Army officer. When Mendelssohn visited the Ertmann family in 1831, this officer, now a general, gave some interesting sidelights on Beethoven's habits, such as, for instance, the use of candle snuffers for a toothpick during a music lesson with Dorothea. Less authenticated is the story that when the Ertmanns lost a child, Beethoven invited Dorothea to his house and played for an hour, talking to her in tones instead of words.

To place the Sonata Op. 101 in Beethoven's creative catalogue, it should be sufficient to note that it was written during the long interval of years between the Eighth and Ninth Symphonies. The exact dates of composition are unknown, but may be tentatively given as 1815, 1816, and/or 1817. Beethoven was not in the habit of dating his manuscripts, and was careless in dating his letters, particularly in the early months of every year, when he would inadvertently set down the year just passed, a habit which worked havoc with the Beethoven chronology, and confused his biographers.

The indications in German for the first movement read, "somewhat lightly, and with innermost feeling." The time signature is $\frac{6}{8}$. Although the key of the sonata is A major, the tonic triad does not make its appearance until the last section of the first movement. The opening phrase begins in E major, considered as the dominant of A, but the cadences are deceptive, leading into minor keys, and away from the designated key of the sonata. From the musical, and even psychological, point of view, such studied ambiguity is interesting, particularly since it is not found in any of Beethoven's other sonatas. The rhythmical scheme of the movement is a slow barcarole-like motion, which is reduced in transitional passages to a series of syncopated chords, without the main beat. The initial phrase furnishes most of the thematic elements used in the first movement. The coda is unusually extensive.

The indication in German for the second movement is "lightly, marchlike." The movement is energetic, suggesting a drumbeat rhythm. The key is F major. The middle section, in the subdominant, is written in the form of a two-part canon, which imparts a quality of sparseness. In canonic imitation, the right hand leads, the left following a half bar behind; then the left hand leads, and the right follows a whole bar behind; and after a brief noncanonic interpolation, the left hand leads the right by half a bar, using the subject of the first period of the canon, where the right hand led the left by the same length. These formal devices are characteristic of the Beethoven of the last sonatas. After the middle section, the march is repeated without modification.

The indications, in German, for the third movement are "slow, and full of yearning." The adagio serves as an introduction to Allegro. The initial phrase is repeated in various forms, accumulating strength with every repetition. There is a slow cadenza. Then, the opening phrase of the first movement is quoted, as if to point out the unity of the whole sonata. Three long, chromatically rising trills lead to the Allegro, in A major, in $\frac{2}{4}$ time, which is launched vigorously. The indications, in German, read: "fast, but not excessively so, and with determination." A figure of a falling third, from the upbeat to the downbeat, is the motto of Allegro, which is used later in the fugue. The structure is canonic, the right and left hand moving in free imitation. There is an emotional melodic section, warningly marked "non lirico," "not lyrically." After another canonic episode, the second theme of a spirited character is played in the dominant, which is in agreement with Classical usage. A cadence confirms the dominant key.

In the fourth movement, a short interlude is played; instead of a development, as in Classical forms, there is a fugue, based on the figure of the falling third, the motto of the principal subject of Allegro. But Beethoven's fugues were no mere exercises in polyphony. Beethoven himself is quoted (and the remarks sound authentic) in these words: "To make a fugue requires no particular skill. But the imagination ought to assert itself, and a new poetic element should be injected into the traditional form." In the fugue of this sonata, the subject and the answers do not follow the absolute rule of the tonic and dominant. Instead, they appear on various degrees of the scale, as used in the middle section of the Bachian fugue. The freedom of the form contributes to the cumulative dynamic force; the voices telescope; there is a stretto, a narrow progression of thematic fragments. The dominant is reached in the bass, preparatory to the return of the initial section of the Allegro. As usual in Beethoven's later sonatas, the recapitulation has many additional details. The succession of keys is, however, according to the Classical formula. The "nonlyric" theme of the first section, then heard in the tonic, now recedes into subdominant, and the spirited second theme is played in the tonic, bringing the sonata to an easy conclusion. The coda is built on a swelling trill in the deep bass, and the ending is in fortissimo.

Piano Sonata No. 29 in B-flat Major ("Hammerklavier"), Op. 106 (1817–18)

The full title of Beethoven's Sonata op. 106 is Grosse Sonate für das Hammerklavier. Its principal key is B-flat major. The name Hammerklavier is nothing more than the German word for "hammer keyboard," which Beethoven adopted as a concession to the rising tide of German nationalism of the post-Napoleonic times. The "Hammerklavier" Sonata is the longest of all Beethoven's sonatas. Its tonal range exceeds six octaves, and extends from D in the low bass register to F in the highest treble, over an octave more than the range available to Beethoven on the pianos of earlier manufacture.

The extension in length and tonal range are the outward attributes of the inner grandeur of conception, a fullness of development, a complexity of detail, which characterize the last period of Beethoven's creative life, to which the "Hammerklavier" Sonata belongs.

Contemporary critics mistook this vastness of design and multiplicity of ideas for a confusion in Beethoven's mind in his last years. The picture of the master, almost totally deaf, untidy in his dress, unable to organize his daily life, anxious over his financial insecurity, was projected by such critics onto the music of Beethoven's last period, and the conclusion was drawn that it was the music of the decline. More astute commentators saw the beginning of the new era in this music as yet so strange. They argued that deafness itself might have led to greater concentration on fundamental problems of style, and that Beethoven's indifference to the social necessities of life was easily explained by his preoccupation with loftier tasks. On the other hand, Brahms denied that there is any departure from the established forms in the music of Beethoven's last period, and that, to the contrary, Beethoven was never more rigorous in his adherence to the fundamentals of the science of music as in these titanic creations.

It is quite understandable why some of Beethoven's critics demurred his novel usages. They seemed whimsical, avoidable, unnecessary. Why, for instance, leave the unresolved leading tone before going into C minor in the bridge passage in the recapitulation of the first movement? Why shift the octave progression in the left hand at the return of the Scherzo, instead of reproducing the passage as it was played the first time, and so as to avoid the grating semitones? Hans von Bülow

(1830–94), an enlightened musician and a great respecter of Beethoven even when there is a suspicion of a slip of the pen, accepts these caprices of the master, but rebels at the superposition, in the thirty-eighth bar from the end of the "Hammerklavier" Sonata, of the passing F and G over the minor third, E-flat and G-flat in the left hand, claiming that the resulting effect is barbarous. His proposed emendation of F and G in the right hand to F-sharp and G-sharp would indeed eliminate the acoustical unpleasantness, were it not thematically a monstrosity.

The "Hammerklavier" Sonata offers as many stumbling blocks to the pianist. Difficult inner trills, uncomfortable crossings of hands at a very close range, so that the fingers collide on a single key, chords demanding unnatural extension, all these usages are doubtful inducements to frequent performances. Besides, the contrapuntal technique of writing, reaching its culmination in the *Grand Fugue* of the finale, presents additional difficulties, necessitating the subtlest possible use of dynamics in order to "orchestrate" the several voices.

This fugue of the finale embodies formal devices that are exceedingly difficult to bring out in an effective manner. In it the subject is presented in a variety of transformations, following the Bach tradition, namely in augmentation (played twice as slowly), inversion (playing ascending notes in descending, and vice versa), crab motion (playing the theme backward), and inverted crab motion (which is tantamount to reading the music upside down). The application of the term "crab" to retrograde progression is derived from the mistaken notion that crabs walk backward.

At the climactic point of the fugue, all these forms are combined in triple counterpoint, the fugue being in three voices, and are further telescoped in a stretto. But Beethoven's tempestuous temperament animates all this artifice, turning it into a medium of personal expression. The abstract architecture of fugal style gives way to a new conception, a Romantic fugue.

In the first three movements, the "Hammerklavier" Sonata follows the Classical model, with such modifications and extensions as are foreordained in Beethoven's earlier works. The first movement is in sonata form, with two contrasting subjects, a vigorous principal theme, and a lyrical subsidiary. But between the two themes, there is a wealth of material that is far from episodic. The development section of the movement contains a fugato on the rhythm of the principal vigorous subject. A meaningful interlude in quickly changing moods, dramatized by explosive rhythmic power, serves as a bridge to the final fugue. When the fugue has run its impetuous course, the conclusion is brief and assertive.

THE FELICITOUS FELIX MENDELSSOHN
(1809–1847)

The spirit of German musical romanticism is embodied in Felix Mendelssohn (1809–47) to the point of textbook clarity. His life harmonized beautifully with the Zeitgeist of the Romantic century, but he was spared personal anguish. He was born into a prosperous family: his father was a banker, his grandfather a philosopher. The ugly specter of anti-Semitism did not touch him with its black wings, for his parents became converted to Christianity long before he was born. Apart from his great gifts as a musician, he was endowed with a fine intellect, a scholarly disposition, linguistic ability, and a distinctive talent for landscape painting. Unlike most composers, he possessed great social charm and perfect manners in company. He was the darling of the Continent. He was beloved in England, where he traveled often, and he was the favorite composer of Queen Victoria. He was happy in his marriage. He was free from the besetting demon of the majority of creative men and women, that of overweening ambition. He never nurtured personal animosities. He was a friend of everyone he knew in his profession. His given name, Felix, spelled felicity. Fate that governs the lives of musicians could not, it seems, tolerate the existence of such an untroubled career. Mendelssohn died at the age of thirty-eight.

Mendelssohn was a true Romantic. His music is evocative; it flows as a facile narrative; it appeals directly to the heart. Its mastery is impeccable; nothing imperils the smooth progress of his melodies, harmonies, and rhythms. He excelled in instrumental music. His symphonies and chamber music are masterpieces of Romantic art. One should not seek profound manifestations of musical philosophy in these works, but one will never fail to find in them a true artistic sentiment, beautifully expressed.

Mendelssohn received his first piano lessons from his mother and also studied violin, foreign languages, and painting. His most important teacher in his early youth was Carl Friedrich Zelter (1758–1832), an influential figure in the Berlin musical world, who understood the magnitude of Mendelssohn's talent and in 1821 took him to Weimar and introduced him to Goethe, who took considerable interest in the boy after hearing him play.

Mendelssohn had another world besides his native country, and that other world was England. He loved England, and he loved London, even the London fog. "That smoky nest is fated to be now and ever my favorite residence," he wrote to his sister Fanny from sunny Naples. He wrote from London amusingly:

> London is the most formidable and the most complicated monster on the face of the earth. In the whole of the last six months in Berlin I have not seen so many contrasts and so many varieties as in these three days. Just walk with me from my home down Regent Street; see the splendid broad avenue filled on both sides with pillared halls, unfortunately enveloped in fog. See the shops with signs as high as a man's head, and the omnibuses on which human beings tower up into the air…. See how a long row of coaches is left behind, stalled by some elegant equipage ahead; see how a horse rears, because the rider has some acquaintance in the house… and the thick John Bulls, each with two pretty and slender daughters on his arm. Oh, those daughters! But there is no danger from that quarter. The only danger is at the street corners and crossings, and I often say to myself to be careful and not to get run over in the general confusion.

England paid him back with adulation almost surpassing that accorded to Handel and Haydn, for whom London was also a second world. Every concert Mendelssohn played in London from his young days was a great social ceremony. One of the lengthiest articles in the 1879–89 Grove's *Dictionary of Music and Musicians* is devoted to Mendelssohn, in which a worshipfully meticulous account is given of his daily activities, visits, and sayings. Mendelssohn profoundly influenced the development of English music in nineteenth-century England, and the great vogue of English oratorios was developed from the success of Mendelssohn's choral works.

Mendelssohn was not only a precocious musician, both in performing and in composition, but what is perhaps without a parallel in music history is the extraordinary perfection of his works written during adolescence. He played in public for the first time at the age of nine, and wrote a remarkable octet at the age of sixteen. At seventeen, he composed the Overture to Shakespeare's *A Midsummer Night's Dream*, an extraordinary manifestation of his artistic maturity, showing a mastery of form equal to that of the remaining numbers of the work, which were composed fifteen years later. He proved his great musicianship when he conducted Bach's *St. Matthew Passion* in the Berlin Singakademie on March 11, 1829, an event that gave an impulse to the revival of Bach's vocal music.

Professional music historians are apt to place Mendelssohn below the ranks of his great contemporaries Schumann, Chopin, and Liszt. George Bernard Shaw, writing in 1889, gave an impartial but keen appraisal:

> Mendelssohn, though he expressed himself in music with touching tender-ness and refinement, and sometimes with a nobility and pure fire that makes us forget all his kid glove gentility, his conventional sentimentality, and his despicable oratorio mongering, was not in the foremost rank of great composers. He was more intelligent than Schumann, as Tennyson is more intelligent than Browning; he is, indeed, the great composer of the century for all those to whom Tennyson is the great poet of the century.

The innate gift of music is an instinct, akin to the natural gift of language. Mythology may be closer to truth than musicology in that some men, women, and children are endowed with a divine spark of tonal imagination. Of all musicians known to history, Mendelssohn possessed the instinct of music in its purest form. Not even Mozart as a child had his genius developed to a perfection found in Mendelssohn's earliest works. A number of his string symphonies, written during his adolescent years, later came to light, revealing an extraordinary mastery of musical technique. This is not to say that the quality of Mendelssohn's music is comparable to Mozart's; rather, his art was an example of perfection that appears to be attained without gradual learning.

There were no tempestuous outbursts of drama or tragedy in Mendelssohn's symphonies, chamber music, piano compositions, or songs. His works could serve as a manual of proper composition of his time; his modulations were wonderfully predictable in their tonal fusion. His melodies were born on the wings of song; his counterpoint was never obtrusive; his orchestration was euphonious in its colorful harmony. Yet the very perfection of Mendelssohn's musical canon was the cause of the gradual decline of his popularity among musicians of the succeeding sesquicen-tenary. His music became associated with the spirit of Biedermeier: too facile, too fulsome in its *Gemütlichkeit* (good-naturedness).

Mendelssohn did not create disciples of his imitators; he could only attract epigones. But in performance by orchestras and instrumentalists, his music is ever alive; his symphonies, notably the "Scotch" and "Italian," maintain their smiling flow; his *Songs Without Words* are favorites of amateur and professional pianists alike. The popularity of his Violin Concerto remains undiminished among students and virtuosos. His trios and other chamber music are radiant in their communal cohesion. In sum, Mendelssohn was the musical personification of German roman-ticism.

Symphony No. 3 in A Minor (Scottish), Op. 56 (1830–42)

The Third Symphony in A Minor is known as the *Scottish* Symphony, inspired by Mendelssohn's journey to Scotland in 1829. Some elements of Scottish songs are discernible in the finale of the symphony. Mendelssohn himself conducted its first performance on March 3, 1842, with the Gewandhaus Orchestra in Leipzig.

The *Scottish* Symphony is in four traditional movements. The first movement, Andante con moto, followed by allegro un poco agitato, is typical of Mendelssohn's style: Romantic, smoothly flowing, melodious, and harmonious. The second move-ment, Vivace non troppo, is written in the manner of a scherzo: agile, propulsive, and energetic. There follows the slow third movement, Adagio, in which a languorous theme undergoes numerous transformations while the rhythm is increasingly complex. The last movement is Allegro vivacissimo. It is syncopated and songful by turns. The coda, allegro maestoso assai, is in A major, homonymous of the *Scottish* Symphony's main tonality, A minor.

Symphony No. 4 in A Major (Italian), Op. 90 (1833)

Mendelssohn's Fourth Symphony is known as the *Italian*, perhaps because its composition followed his Italian journey in 1831. Mendelssohn completed it in 1833 in Berlin, and conducted its first performance in London with the Philharmonic Society, to which the score is dedicated, on May 13, 1833. At the same concert he appeared as soloist in a Mozart piano concerto, scoring a double triumph with London music lovers as composer and pianist.

For some reason Mendelssohn was not satisfied with the work and revised the score in 1837. Its Italian quality has been questioned by critics. In fact, Schumann mistook Mendelssohn's *Scottish* Symphony for the *Italian* and wrote exuberantly about the wrong work that the music might well provide an aesthetic substitute for actual travel in Italy. Thus musical geography can be confounded even in a most sensitive listener's mind, and misty Scotland can play the role of sunny Italy.

The *Italian* Symphony is in the traditional four movements. The first movement, Allegro vivace, in § time, starts energetically with an impulsive rhythmic subject in A major in the violins. The contrasting theme, more leisurely than the first, appears in the woodwinds, in E major. A vigorous development follows, leading to a comprehensive recapitulation in which the second theme is taken over by the strings.

The second movement, Andante con moto, in ¼ time, is an elegiac interlude in D minor. Some commentators have suggested that the stately procession of the melody represents a march of pilgrims in Rome, providing a clue to the Italian associations of the work.

The third movement, in A major, ¾ time, is marked Con moto moderato, and has the character of a symphony minuet. There is a brief middle section corresponding to a trio; the principal part then returns in a different instrumentation.

The last movement is entitled Saltarello: Presto, emphatically confirming the Italian derivation of the symphony. The *saltarello* ("leaping dance") is similar in spirit to the tarantella. It may have been inspired by Mendelssohn's sojourn in Rome during Carnival. "I was driving along the avenue," Mendelssohn wrote, "when I was suddenly pelted by a shower of sugar confectionery. I looked up and saw that they were thrown at me by a group of young ladies. I took off my hat and bowed, and they proceeded to pelt me even more determinedly." This scene may well be regarded as the stimulus for the colorful finale of the *Italian* Symphony.

Overture to A Midsummer Night's Dream (1826)

Mendelssohn was an assiduous reader of Shakespeare in the excellent German translations by the playwright Johann Schlegel and the playwright and author Ludwig Tieck, which are regarded by Shakespearean scholars as the nearest approach to the essence of Shakespeare in any foreign language. Mendelssohn was only seventeen when he wrote the Overture to *A Midsummer Night's Dream*. The overture, Allegro di molto, in E major, in ⅜ time, opens with a progression of four long chords in the woodwind instruments, which somehow imparts an authentic

Shakespearean flavor, redolent of fable, mystery, and wonderment. The action is then taken over by the strings, followed by "fairy music" in E minor. There are several allusions to the characters of the play; it is also said that the quick descending passages in the cellos were suggested to the boy composer by the buzzing of a large fly in the Mendelssohn family garden in Berlin.

Seventeen years later, at the command of King Friedrich Wilhelm IV of Prussia, Mendelssohn wrote additional music for the play, scored for solo voices, small orchestra, and chorus. He conducted the music at the king's palace in Potsdam on October 14, 1843. Several themes were taken from materials already found in the overture.

By far the most celebrated number in the score is the "Wedding March" in Act IV, which has since bestowed musical blessings on millions of married couples all over the world. It was in England that the Wedding March began to be used to accompany the bridal procession; the first such use of the work was for the marriage of Tom Daniel and Dorothy Carew at St. Peter's Church, Tiverton, on June 2, 1847. It became particularly fashionable, however, when it was played at the wedding of the princess royal to the crown prince of Prussia, the future Emperor Friedrich III, held at Windsor Castle in 1858.

Overture in B Minor, The Hebrides (Fingal's Cave), *Op. 26 (1832)*

Mendelssohn's overture *The Hebrides (Fingal's Cave)* was written under the impression of his visit, in 1829, to the island of Staffa, in Scotland. Fingal's Cave, the island's chief attraction, is 227 feet long and 42 feet wide. Mendelssohn wrote to his sister: "You will understand how the sight of the Hebrides affected me from the following," and he jotted down a few measures of his future overture. For some reason, after this spontaneous inspiration, Mendelssohn waited a long time before completing the score. He presented the manuscript to the Philharmonic Society of London at Covent Garden, which gave its first performance there on May 14, 1832.

The key of B minor seems to be peculiarly fitting to the tone painting of a dark cave in a northern climate. The contrasting theme is set in the relative key of D major, bringing light and the air of the open sea into the music. Formally, *Fingal's Cave* is a paragon of structural solidity. The instrumentation is remarkable; the rolling passages in the low strings give a vivid illustration of stormy turbulence of wind and water. Yet Mendelssohn himself commented that the elaborate development section smelled more of counterpoint than of seagulls and saltwater fish.

Capriccio brillant *for Piano and Orchestra, Op. 22 (1832)*

Mendelssohn composed the *Capriccio brillant* during his second visit to London, in 1832, when he was twenty-three years old. The score was completed on May 18, 1832, and Mendelssohn played it with an orchestra for the first time in London a week later. The work starts with a slow introduction in B major for piano solo. The principal theme is played with the light accompaniment of strings and, later, woodwinds. The main movement, Allegro con fuoco, introduces a lively subject in the solo piano part, which, in the process of development, appears in many keys, major and minor. The movement is sustained with unabated vivacity, and the ending is in minor, a procedure that is the reverse of the common practice of concluding a minor-key composition in a major key.

Overture *to* Ruy Blas *in C Minor, Op. 95 (1839)*

The music of Mendelssohn is lacking in all artifice and pretension. He composed, to use a German expression, "as a bird sings." There is no evidence in his manuscripts of any hesitancy in the transference of musical ideas to their final realization. Such technical facility often bespeaks mediocrity. But Mendelssohn was never mediocre. He imparted congenial expression to the human quality in music. He gave to music lovers a sentiment, an emotion, an aesthetic object which fitted perfectly into the artistic trends of the time. He contributed to the general musical repertory a number of perennial favorites, among them *Songs Without Words*, cherished by five generations of piano teachers, and the euphonious Wedding March.

No more romantic subject could be imagined than that of Victor Hugo's play *Ruy Blas*, purportedly a historical drama from the reign of Charles III of Spain (1716–88). In it, a Spanish nobleman removed from the royal court through the intrigues of the Queen is determined to avenge himself. He introduces his personable valet, named Ruy Blas, to the Queen as his cousin and contrives an assignation between them. But just as the ploy is about to come to fruition, Ruy Blas, a faithful subject of the Queen, refuses to go through with the iniquitous scheme, kills his master, and poisons himself.

Mendelssohn was asked to contribute incidental music for a performance of *Ruy Blas* at the Leipzig Municipal Theater, as a benefit for widows of deceased members of the theater orchestra. He was reluctant to comply, because he found the subject of Hugo's play distasteful, but an earnest appeal by interested parties to his eleemosynary feelings overcame his scruples. Working at great speed, he wrote an overture in three days, and conducted it on March 8, 1839. He intended to call the score *Overture to the Dramatic Fund,* with reference to the purpose of the commission of the work. It was only after his death that it was published under the title *Ruy Blas*, and an opus number was assigned to it.

The music of the overture is unrelated to the action of *Ruy Blas*, but it is dramatic in quality and can be fitted to any operatic subject. It has its usual share of melodramatic suspense portrayed in the ominous murmurations of the massed violins and in the solemn fanfares in the wind section of the orchestra. The cellos sing with ingratiating lyricism. The contrasts are expertly drawn, and the overture concludes in brilliant sonorities.

Concerto in E Minor for Violin and Orchestra, Op. 64 (1844)

Mendelssohn composed his Violin Concerto in 1844 for the famous violinist Ferdinand David, who gave its first performance in Leipzig on March 13, 1845. The concerto is in Mendelssohn's favorite key of E minor, a tonality that lends itself naturally to the disposition of the violin strings. It is in three movements. The first, Allegro molto appassionato in E minor, in $\frac{2}{2}$ time, opens with a decisive beat, and the solo violin enters immediately. The theme is ingratiatingly euphonious, and is developed in decorative passage work. The orchestra enhances it in full sonority. The second theme is presented softly in the woodwinds. The violin is given a brilliant cadenza; there are cascades and roulades outlining the harmonic scheme. The ending summarizes the various thematic ingredients.

The second movement, Andante, evolves without pause from the first. It is in the bright key of C major. Considerable animation is encountered in the middle part of the movement, and then the original melody is returned.

The third and last movement opens with a brief introduction, allegretto non troppo, in the basic key of E minor, in $\frac{4}{4}$ time. The key is then changed to E major in the principal section of the movement, Allegro molto vivace. There is a great deal of activity in the wind instruments, imparting the sense of a pastoral landscape. The form is that of a rondo with variations, with elements of sonata. The finale reaches the level of fortissimo, and the dash toward a logical and dynamically rich ending has the feeling of inevitability.

Octet in E-flat Major, Op. 20

Octet in E-flat Major, Op. 20 (1825)

Child prodigies of the piano and violin are fairly common, but youthful composers are rare. Mozart and Schubert were marvels of precocious creative genius. Though Mendelssohn cannot be compared to them in sheer greatness, his technical facility in composition at a very early age was even more phenomenal. He seems to have achieved a mastery of counterpoint, harmony, and orchestration intuitively, for there are no signs of hesitancy in the manuscripts of his boyhood. Among his discarded juvenilia there are several full-fledged symphonies and operas. He was only seventeen when he wrote the remarkable Overture to *A Midsummer Night's Dream*. Still earlier, at sixteen, he composed his first explicitly polyphonic work, the Octet for Strings. In a marginal note, Mendelssohn specifies that the piece "must be played in true symphonic style." Indeed, the octet is a symphony in miniature, which can be performed by a full string orchestra without impairing its chamber music quality.

The octet adheres to the classical form of four movements. The first, Allegro moderato, ma con fuoco, in $\frac{4}{4}$ time, opens in media res, with a strong statement based on the three notes of the tonic of E-flat major, the principal key of the work. There is a considerable amount of thematic deployment before the appearance of a contrasting subject in the dominant. Numerous ancillary motives become the substance of momentary variations and fleeting canonic configurations. A rhythmic episode in palpitating syncopated patterns introduces a dramatic element. In the recapitulation, the first theme is treated in full, while the second, in the tonic, as required by the conventions of sonata form, is compressed without congestion.

The second movement, Andante, in $\frac{6}{8}$, is set in C minor. It begins mysteriously with naked open fifths in the lower strings; the mediant in the violas subsequently completes the tonic triad. A sudden transition to D-flat major follows. The emotional tonus is intensified. There are characteristic modulating sequences, Neapolitan cadences, and chromatic ascensions that are to become the hallmarks of Mendelssohn's mature style. New melodic materials are added. A rhythmic precipitation of syncopated passages in rapid sixteenth-notes leads to a coda in C minor.

The third movement, Allegro leggierissimo, in G minor, $\frac{2}{4}$ time, is a scherzo. This scherzo must be played "pianissimo and staccato," Mendelssohn specifies in the score. The injunction is imperative in order to achieve the requisite lightness indicated in the tempo mark of the movement. In writing this scherzo, Mendelssohn was inspired by the final stanza in the "Walpurgis Night" in Goethe's *Faust*. It is interesting to note that Goethe introduces this stanza with the words, "Orchestra, pianissimo":

> Clouds above and mist below
> Form an airy ocean,
> Through the leaves soft zephyrs blow,
> Starting a commotion.

Luminous plumes of melodic vapors rise from the music. Gentle undulations with light trills and swift tremolos limn the tonal picture of fairyland. Goethe was still living when Mendelssohn wrote the scherzo, which provides a perfect illustration for his romantic verse.

The last movement, Presto, in E-flat major, in alla breve ($\frac{2}{2}$) time, is a brilliant polyphonic study. A fugal theme arises from the deep register of the cellos, spreading to the violas and the violins in orderly procession. Gradually the entire ensemble becomes engaged. A series of modulatory sequences leads to a climax, which is followed by a détente. The fugal section is recalled, and the octet concludes with a concise coda.

THE PARADOXICAL RICHARD WAGNER
(1813–1883)

Lord Beaverbrook, no opera buff, was induced to attend a performance of *Tristan und Isolde*. "This Wagner," he inquired after sitting through the opera, "was he a clean-living man?" The answer should have been in the negative. By all accepted moral standards, Richard Wagner (1813–83) was not a clean-living man, in his relationships with women, in his financial transactions, or in his friendships. He stole Liszt's daughter from his friend, the champion of his music Hans von Bülow, while the latter was busy rehearsing *Tristan und Isolde*. When she bore Wagner's daughter, he named her Isolde. (In 1911 Isolde sued her own mother for a share in Wagner's royalties as Wagner's natural daughter, but the German tribunal ruled that inasmuch as her mother was still sharing von Bülow's bed and board at the time of conception, Wagner's paternity could not be legally proved.)

But Wagner was also a genius, the greatest creative artist of the nineteenth century, according to Thomas Mann, not merely as a composer but as a thinker who by the sheer power of his novel ideas revolutionized the concept of opera as music drama. Great revolutionaries in art have usually advanced by depicting contemporary life rather than sanctified subjects of mythology and ancient history. Wagner made his revolution by delving further into the symbolic world of the past. He called his art the "music of the future," and in this he propounded his greatest paradox. His critics accepted him at his word. It was the music of the future that they opposed.

The very vagueness of Wagner's stories as told in his music dramas allowed for varied interpretations of their meaning. George Bernard Shaw, who like Wagner loved paradox, proffered the most astonishing of these interpretations. Because Wagner was briefly engaged in the revolutionary movement of 1848, Shaw suggested that the struggle of the gods in *The Ring of the Nibelung* was a symbolic characterization of the revolutionists who had once been Wagner's comrades in arms. Some ardent Wagnerites believe that the texts, or librettos, that he wrote for his music dramas are as great from the literary standpoint as the music itself, but this opinion was discredited when professional literary critics dissected Wagner's bombastic jargon, arranged in curious syntax and overladen with strange neologisms.

From the beginning of his career, Wagner became the center of tremendous controversy. He acquired fanatical followers who regarded him as the liberator of art from the shackles of tradition. From the other side of the barricade, he was the target of ridicule and denunciation. Cartoonists exercised their wit, showing Wagner in the process of conducting the siege of Paris during the Franco-Prussian war with a battery of musical guns. An American cartoon, entitled "Music of the Future," showed an orchestra supplemented by braying donkeys and a row of cats whose tails are pulled by a special operator. At the conductor's feet, a discarded score bears the inscription "Wagner—Not To Be Played Much Until 1995."

A tide of Wagnerophobia rose among musicians in the second quarter of the twentieth century as a reaction against turgid romanticism in general, but Wagner came back with a vengeance with another shift of popular taste, and was enthroned once more as an irresistible magician of musical color and theatrical drama. It remains true, however, that no contemporary composer chose to imitate Wagner. Stravinsky dismissed Wagner's era as "a lamentable chapter in music history."

Wagner's first significant opera was *Rienzi* (1840), inspired by Edward Bulwer-Lytton's historical novel of the same name dealing with the last Roman tribune Cola Rienzi, who flourished, and perished, in fourteenth-century Rome. In *Tannhäuser*, written in 1845, Wagner entered the domain of mythology, which was to remain the foundation of his music dramas. Tannhäuser was a real personage, a minstrel who flourished in the thirteenth century. Among medieval legends surrounding his name was a religious fantasy of his intimate association with Venus, his penitence, and his redemption. The Paris première of *Tannhäuser* was one of the great debacles in music history. The newspapers were full of bitter invective. Rossini remarked, "Wagner has some good moments but also bad quarter hours." One musician emerging from the theater was heard to remark, "Well, anyway, I have survived!" Wagner voluntarily withdrew the opera, and no further performances of *Tannhäuser* were given in Paris for some time.

Tannhäuser was followed by *Lohengrin*. The action takes place in and around the royal castle in Antwerp in the tenth century; Lohengrin, a knight of the Holy Grail, arrives in a boat drawn by a swan, to claim the hand of Elsa, the king's ward. She violates his injunction not to ask who he is, and Lohengrin is compelled to depart. The prelude to the third act of *Lohengrin* is a brilliant symphonic piece. It is followed in the opera by the famous wedding march, actually the Bridal Chorus. Millions of happy couples (and some unhappy ones) have been led to the altar to the strains of the *Lohengrin* wedding march, in stiff competition with the even more celebrated matrimonial piece by Mendelssohn. (A reputable statistical survey indicates that marriages performed to Mendelssohn's music are usually durable, while those sped to marital bliss by Wagner are likely to end in divorce.)

Lohengrin was scheduled for performance in Dresden, but in the meantime Wagner had become embroiled in a revolutionary movement in Saxony during the turbulent year 1848. The production of *Lohengrin* was canceled, and printed announcements were posted bearing Wagner's likeness, ordering his arrest as a fugitive from justice. Wagner went into temporary exile in Switzerland, and it was Franz Liszt, his comrade-in-arms in "the music of the future," who brought out the opera for the first time in 1850.

The *Mastersingers of Nuremberg* (*Die Meistersinger von Nürnberg*, 1868) is an exception among Wagner's operas, for it has a distinct element of comedy. Yet, as in Wagner's previous operas, it has a historical foundation. Set in sixteenth-century Nuremberg, the story deals with a singing contest instituted by a guild of mastersingers. The principal contenders are Walther von Stolzing and the clerk Beckmesser. The latter was given by Wagner some pedantic traits of the celebrated anti-Wagnerian critic Eduard Hanslick; in fact, the part was assigned to a character named Hans Lick in Wagner's early sketches of the libretto.

In *The Ring of the Nibelung*, by Wagner's description a "festival play for three days and a preliminary evening," the center of contention is the magical ring of gold, coveted by gods, dwarfs, giants, and heroes. "The Ride of the Valkyries" from the second opera, *The Valkyries*, is the most celebrated symphonic episode in the entire tetralogy, representing the horsewomen of the mountains carrying slain heroes to their shrine, Valhalla. In the third music drama, *Siegfried*, Wagner projects his hero as a victor who obtains the coveted ring of the Nibelung and penetrates the magic fire surrounding his destined bride, Brünnhilde, one of the Valkyries. Siegfried himself is fated to be slain in the last opera of the tetralogy, *Twilight of the Gods*, in which Valhalla itself is consumed by flames.

Wagner's role in music history is immense. Not only did he create works of great beauty and tremendous brilliance, but he generated an entirely new concept of the art of music, exercising an influence on generations of composers all over the globe. Wagner had two great epigones: Anton Bruckner, who was called "the Wagner of the symphony," because his music embodied Wagner's harmony in lengthy symphonic works; and Richard Strauss, whom the German conductor and composer Hans von Bülow (1830–94) called Richard the Second (Wagner being Richard the First). Strauss accepted the Wagnerian idea of continuous melody, and expanded Wagnerian harmonies to the utmost limit of complexity in his symphonic poems, using leading motifs and vivid programmatic descriptions of the scenes portrayed in his music. (For this, Strauss was the recipient of invectives almost as violent as those hurled against Wagner himself.) Even Rimsky-Korsakov, far as he stood from Wagner's ideas of musical composition, reflected the spirit of *Parsifal* in his own religious opera, *The Legend of the City of Kitezh*. Arnold Schoenberg's first significant work, *Verklärte Nacht*, is Wagnerian in its color. When Wagner rejected traditional opera, he did so in the conviction that such an artificial form could not serve as a basis for true dramatic expression. In its place he gave the world a new form and new techniques.

In the domain of melody, harmony, and orchestration, Wagner's art was as revolutionary as was his total artwork on the stage. He introduced the idea of an endless melody, a continuous flow of diatonic and chromatic tones; the tonality became fluid and uncertain, producing an impression of unattainability, so that the listener accustomed to classical modulatory schemes could not easily feel the direction toward the tonic. The prelude to *Tristan and Isolde* is a classic example of such fluidity of harmonic elements. The use of long unresolved dominant-ninth chords and the dramatic tremolos of diminished-seventh chords contributed to this state of musical uncertainty, which disturbed critics and audiences alike. But Wagnerian harmony also became the foundation of the new method of composition that adopted a free flow of modulatory progressions. Without Wagner, the chromatic idioms of the twentieth century could not exist.

Rienzi: *Overture (1840)*

Wagner took the subject of *Rienzi* from Edward Bulwer- Lytton's well-known historical romance, which Wagner read in the German translation. There was some social significance in the story. Rienzi was the last of Rome's popular tribunes, defender of the poor against the overbearing nobles. The happy ending is made possible when the nobles submit to the will of the people. The music of the opera contains some early Wagnerisms, which the *Gazette musicale de Paris* of April 11, 1869, described as Wagner's "trademarks." But in the main it is still conventional opera, not unlike Meyerbeer's, with arias, ensembles, and choruses, designed to give the singers an opportunity to exhibit their talents to best advantage.

He completed the overture on October 23, 1840. The opera itself was practically ready by the time the overture was composed. The fact that the overture (literally, "opening") should be composed after the main body of the opera is completed is no more strange than that the table of contents should be compiled after the book is finished. An overture is commonly a musical table of contents, including the most important musical paragraphs from the opera, with the vocal arias and choruses arranged for orchestral instruments.

The overture, in $\frac{4}{4}$, in D major, begins with a trumpet call, which in the opera serves as a summons to arms against the nobles. After some recitative in the low strings and a brief chorale in the wind instruments, the violins, supported by the cellos, enter with the principal theme taken from Rienzi's prayer in the fifth act. Incidentally, there has been a controversy as to whether the gruppetto (turn or trill) of the theme should be played from above (D, E, D, C sharp, D), or from below (D, C sharp, D, E, D). No less a person than von Bülow instructed his players to take the turn from below, which is wrong, as he himself admitted a few years later. The theme grows in sonority and is soon taken up by the powerful ensemble of wood and brass. The violent brush-strokes in the strings are easily recognized as early Wagnerisms. Another trumpet call is sounded, and the orchestra begins the rapid movement, Allegro energico, on the theme of the chorus, "Gegrüsst sei hoher Tag" ("Greet the great day"), ending with the brass proclaiming the motto of the battle.

The orchestra continues in fortissimo. The brasses proclaim a martial theme. There is a transition to a calmer mood, and the cellos round off a falling cadence, of the type that the *Gazette musicale de Paris* called Wagner's trademark. The first violins now take up the principal theme of Rienzi's prayer, played nearly three times as fast as in the beginning of the overture. This, and the leaping accompaniment in a quick-step tempo, changes the character of the theme entirely. The brass has a sonorous interlude, and the full orchestra plays a new marching theme in A major. After a series of vigorous climaxes, the section concludes with the battle cry in the brass.

Overture to
Rienzi
der Letzte der Tribunen

Molto sostenuto e maestoso. (♩ =66)

Flauto I.
Flauto II.
Flauto III.
Oboe I.
Oboe II.
Clarinetto I in A.
Clarinetto II in A.
Fagotto I.
Fagotto II.
Serpent e Fagotto III.
Corno I in F.
Corno II in F.
Corno III in F.
Corno IV in F.
Tromba I in A.
Tromba II in A.
Trombi III & IV in A.
Tromboni I & II.
Trombone III.
Tuba.
Timpani in D & A.
Tamburo militare.
Tamburo rollo.
Triangle.
Gran-cassa e Piatti.
Violino I.
Violino II.
Viola.
Violoncello.
Contrabasso.

Molto sostenuto e maestoso. (♩ = 66)

NB. Zugleich für vereinfachte Besetzung, eingerichtet von Fritz Hoffmann. Bei kleiner Besetzung werden stets die in den Stimmen mit • bezeichneten Noten der nicht vorhandenen Instrumente gespielt.

NB. *Adapted for smaller Orchestras by Fritz Hoffmann. With small orchestras, the notes representing the absent instruments (indicated by • in the parts) must be always played.*

The now familiar trumpet call prepares for the recapitulation of the Allegro theme, this time to be played "a little more vivaciously." Again there is the battle cry in the brass, and the joyful marching theme returns in the key of the overture, D major. This return of a theme which previously was heard in the dominant key of A major indicates the sonata form, common to most classical overtures. The section marked molto più stretto is a coda (literally, "tail"). Here successive climaxes are reached by chromatic ascension toward the keynote, D. The overture ends with ten full D major chords, and one final D in unison.

Tannhäuser: *Overture and Bacchanal*

Tannhäuser was no mythical personage. There lived in the thirteenth century a minnesinger named Tanhuser, who wrote poems. He also went to the Holy Land as a Crusader. In folktales he has been made into a legendary knight who comes to Venusberg or, in terms of actual geography, Hörselberg in Thuringia, and meets the German counterpart of Venus in a mountain cavern. He remains with Venus but, after some time, recalls his higher ideals, and goes to Rome to beg forgiveness from the pope. He is told that forgiveness for the sin of consorting with a pagan goddess is as impossible as the flowering of a bare rod. But Tannhäuser's rod does blossom forth, and he now knows that he can die in peace. The aria "Dich, teure Halle," known also as "Elisabeth's Greeting," opens the second act of *Tannhäuser*, in which Elisabeth apostrophizes the Hall of Song in the Wartburg Castle, happy at Tannhäuser's return from his pagan adventures.

Such is the folk legend, which was used by several German poets before Wagner. In his brochure *Drei Operndichtungen (Three Librettos)*, published in Leipzig in 1852, Wagner relates the story of his writing of *Tannhäuser*. The deciding moment came when Wagner thought of connecting the Tannhäuser story with another story, that of a "singers' competition" at Wartburg. Hence the full title of the opera, *Tannhäuser und der Sängerkrieg auf Wartburg (Tannhäuser and the Contest of Song at the Wartburg)*.

Although Wagner called *Tannhäuser* a "romantic opera" rather than "music drama," it was a harbinger of the Wagnerian era. He wrote the text himself, establishing a unity of music and drama that became the foundation of his aesthetics. The characteristic Wagnerian idiom is here clearly recognizable, with its triadic expansion, melodic chromaticism, and opulent orchestration. *Tannhäuser* opened Wagner's opera cycle based on Germanic folklore, and in it he clearly outlined the importance of stage setting. He describes the events that led him to the composition of *Tannhäuser* in the following words:

> My third trip to Dresden took me through the valleys of Thuringia, from where one can see Wartburg towering above. How near was that sight to my heart! Yet, strangely enough, it was not until seven years later that I visited Wartburg for the first time, and it was from Wartburg that I cast the last glance at the German soil, which I had trod with heartfelt joy, and which I had to abandon as an outlaw, a refugee.

The reference to his status as an outlaw is explained by the fact that Wagner went into exile as a participant in the Dresden Revolution of 1848. As late as 1852, he was talked about in Germany as "that red revolutionary." When the question of a production of *Tannhäuser* at the Munich Opera House came up, an article in the press suggested that "the proper place for the Orpheus who, during the May revolt in Dresden, raised barricades with his lyre, is not the Munich Opera House, but prison."

Wagner's idea of *Tannhäuser* was far from pietistic. He describes his state of mind during the composition of the opera in vivid prose:

> How silly are the critics who, amidst their wanton living, have suddenly become spiritual, and who impute to my Tannhäuser a specifically Christian, impotently celestialized tendency.... I was in a state of highly

sensuous agitation which brought my blood and my nervous system to the point of feverish excitement when I conceived and carried out the composition of the music…. From this high state my eager vision became aware of a Woman; the Woman for whom the Flying Dutchman hankered from the sea-depths of his misery; the Woman who showed Tannhäuser the way to Heaven, and the one who brought Lohengrin from the sunlit heights down to the warm breast of the earth.

Wagner himself conducted the first performance of *Tannhäuser* at the Dresden Opera on October 19, 1845. The first performance of the overture as a concert piece was given at the Gewandhaus in Leipzig on February 12, 1846, with Mendelssohn conducting it from manuscript. Wagner provided a description of the overture. Briefly summarized, it appears as follows:

The chant of the pilgrims is heard; it draws near, swelling into a mighty torrent of sound, and passes finally away. Magic sights and sounds emerge at night; a rosy mist fills the air. Shouts of exultation assail the ears, followed by a voluptuous dance. The seductive powers of Venus attract the senses, and she herself appears before Tannhäuser. After a night of revelry, the chant of the pilgrims is heard again, winning salvation for Tannhäuser. The songs of pagan worship are joined with the hymns of God. Spiritual devotion and sensuous passion, God and nature, unite in a kiss of hallowed love.

It is difficult to imagine that the music of *Tannhäuser*, which impresses the modern listener as a charmingly innocuous score, full of mellifluous harmonies and melodious sequences, should ever have impressed anyone as unusual and strange. Yet the critic of *The Times* of London wrote the following incredible lines in 1855:

So much incessant noise, so uninterrupted and singular an exhibition of pure cacophony, was never heard before. And, all this is intended to describe the delight and fascinations which lured the unwary to the secret abode of the goddess of beauty. We sincerely hope that no execution, however superb, will ever make such senseless discords pass, in England, for manifestation of art and genius.

The enlarged version of the orchestral Bacchanale was added to the score for the Paris performance of March 13, 1861, a performance that made history because of the hostile manifestations in the audience, which forced the withdrawal of the opera after the third performance. The Paris humor periodical, *Charivari*, printed a cartoon representing a young woman playing the piano, and her mother sitting in a chair in the same room. "You are playing wrong notes," says the mother. "But, Maman, I am playing *Tannhäuser*," the young lady replies. "Oh, that's different," remarks Maman.

The fiasco of *Tannhäuser* in Paris in 1861 made history. "*Tannhäuser* has passed by, and the 'music of the future' was no more," wrote a French music critic. "Imagine a Hindu god with seven arms and three heads enthroned in a Greek temple: this is the emblem of the incongruous opera of Herr Wagner. His score is nothing but musical chaos. The unintelligible is its ideal. It is a mystic art proudly dying of inanition in a vacuum." The famous French writer Prosper Mérimée, the author of the original story of Bizet's *Carmen*, contributed to the chorus of condemnation for Wagner's opera. "*Tannhäuser* was a colossal bore," he wrote. "I believe that I could write something similar tomorrow, inspired by my cat walking on the piano keyboard."

Overture to
Tannhäuser
und der Sängerkrieg auf Wartburg

Tristan and Isolde: *Prelude and Liebestod*

Wagner was fascinated by Nordic legends of gods and godlike men and women. He wrote his own texts, often using peculiar neologisms and forming compound nouns to express an idea containing two related concepts. From the words *Liebe* ("love") and *Tod* ("death") he coined *Liebestod* (love-death). For *Tristan and Isolde*, Wagner took the subject from an old Cornish legend, in which Tristan is sent by the

Tristan und Isolde
Prelude and Liebestod

(Prelude and Love-Death / Vorspiel und Isoldens Liebestod)

king to bring his, the king's, bride, Isolde, to his side. But a love potion inflames both Tristan and Isolde with mutual love. Tristan dies of the wounds inflicted on him by the king's henchmen and Isolde follows him in death, which becomes the supreme fulfillment of their love, Liebestod. The first performance of *Tristan and Isolde* was given in Munich on June 10, 1865, with Hans von Bülow as the conductor. It was then that Wagner became infatuated with von Bülow's wife, Cosima, a daughter of Liszt, whom he married after her divorce. He named their daughter, who was born premaritally of this union, Isolde.

The opening phrase of the prelude, marked "slow and languorously," is famous. It is intoned by the cellos, and consists of an ascending sixth followed by chromatically falling notes. The resulting theme is the leading motive for the love potion. It is echoed by the oboes in ascending chromatics, symbolic of yearning. The entire prelude is evolved from these initial figures, depicting voluptuous love as only Wagner could incarnate it in music. Through the prelude and Liebestod, tidal waves rise and fall, swelling to fortissimo and receding to pianissimo.

This new chromatic music was unacceptable to the musical establishment. *Tristan and Isolde* was particularly irritating to listeners who were accustomed to an Italian type of opera, in which the arias and the recitatives were clearly delineated. Eduard Hanslick, the venomous anti-Wagnerite, wrote that the prelude to *Tristan and Isolde* reminded him of an old Italian painting of a martyr whose intestines were slowly unwound from his body on a reel. A German professor of music denounced the opera as "modern cat music, which can be produced by hitting black keys and white keys of the piano keyboard at random."

In America, too, the anti-Wagnerian tide threw up a lot of angry words. John Sullivan Dwight, the editor of *Dwight's Journal of Music*, declared *Tristan and Isolde* to be "the very extreme of the modern extravagance and willfulness in the spasmodic strife to be original in music. In its expression, its reiterated, restless, fruitless yearning and monotonous chromatic wail, we find it simply dreary and unprofitable."

For modernists, on the other hand, the prelude was a prophetic vision of atonality. Alban Berg inserted the opening measures of the prelude in his atonal *Lyric Suite*. But Debussy, whose attitude toward Wagner was ambivalent, made fun of the famous opening in his whimsical "Golliwog's Cakewalk" from Children's Corner. After quoting the ascending minor sixth and the descending chromatic notes in the same key and in the same rhythmic pattern as in the Prelude, he followed it with a group of derisively sounding chords. He added insult to injury by marking the passage *avec une grande émotion* ("with great emotion").

The Mastersingers of Nuremberg: *Prelude*

The Mastersingers of Nuremberg was performed for the first time in its entirety in Munich on June 21, 1868. Wagner wrote the score to his own libretto, as he did in most of his operas. The central character of the opera, the mastersinger Hans Sachs, a cobbler by trade, was an actual historical figure. In the opera he arranges a competition for the best song composed and sung by one of the town citizens, and the prize is the hand of Eva, the daughter of a local goldsmith. The winner is Walther, who sings a song about love in springtime. His chief rival is Beckmesser, an envious town clerk without talent, who loses out in the end.

Wagner wrote the prelude (or overture) in 1862. The opera was performed for the first time in its entirety in Munich on June 21, 1868. The prelude opens with a magnificent marching tune in C major, the theme of the guild of the mastersingers.

The second theme is Walther's prize-winning song; it is introduced by the flute, and imitated by the oboe and the clarinet. The fanfares of the march return. A development follows, in which the principal themes are ingeniously elaborated. Particularly remarkable is the interlude for woodwinds, in the manner of a scherzo. As the music progresses, the polyphonic network achieves a triumph of technical mastery. The overture ends in a glorious display of C major sonorities.

Overture to
Die Meistersinger von Nürnberg

The Ring of the Nibelung—The Valkyries: *Act I; Act III, Ride of the Valkyries*

Few musicians of Wagner's time could remain neutral when confronted with his music. Many were fanatically worshipful; others were repelled. Tchaikovsky wrote to his friend the Russian composer Sergei Taneyev in 1877,

> I heard *The Valkyries*. If indeed Wagner is destined to be regarded as the greatest figure in music of our time, one may well despair of the future. Can it be that his operas represent the last word in composition? Can it be that this pretentious, pompous, and uninspired trash will be the delight of the coming generations? If so, it will be terrible.

Anti-Wagnerian literature is rich in invective:

> Being a Communist, Herr Wagner is desirous of forcing the arts into fellowship with his political and social principles. In his music the true bases of harmony are cast away for a reckless, wild, extravagant, and demagogic cacophony, the symbol of profligate libertinage! This man, this Wagner, this author of *Tannhäuser*, *Lohengrin*, and so many other hideous things, this preacher of the Music of the Future, was born to feed spiders with flies, not to make happy the heart of man with beautiful melody and harmony. Who are the men that go about as his apostles? Men like Liszt—madmen, enemies of music to the knife, who, conscious of their impotence, revenge themselves by endeavoring to annihilate it. These musicians of young Germany are maggots that quicken from corruption.

The foregoing tirade appeared in *The Musical World of London*, on June 30, 1855. As a matter of fact, calling Wagner a Communist was not entirely without foundation. Wagner was involved in the revolutionary agitation in Dresden in 1848, the year of the *Communist Manifesto* of Karl Marx, and he was forced to flee; the police posted announcements, with Wagner's likeness, ordering his arrest.

Some of the most brilliant articles inveighing against Wagner belong to the famous Vienna critic Eduard Hanslick, a master of degrading metaphor. Here is his description of Wagner's method of composition: "A little motive begins, but before it is allowed to develop into a real melody it is twisted, broken, raised and lowered through incessant modulations and enharmonic shifts, with scrupulous avoidance of all closing cadences, like a boneless tonal mollusk, self-restoring and swimming into the horizonless sea."

Wagner could well afford to look down on his detractors with a smile of worldly success. He had had his share of trials and tribulations. He had spent a month in a debtors' prison in Paris; he had untold troubles with women. But sometimes his greatest disasters turned into triumphs by default. The fiasco of *Tannhäuser* in Paris became a *scandale du siècle*.

The compensation for these misfortunes was ample. Wagner found a fairy-tale prince in the person of the youthful King Ludwig II of Bavaria, who became his ardent admirer. It was Ludwig who, before he went completely insane, laid the foundation for a festival theater in Bayreuth, which became the home of the famed Wagner Festival.

Wagner's supreme achievement was *The Ring of the Nibelung*, "a stage festival play for three days and a preliminary evening," according to Wagner's own description. It may be regarded therefore either as a tetralogy or a trilogy with a prelude. The "preliminary evening" is *Das Rheingold* (*The Rhine Gold*), which serves as a prologue to the trilogy that followed: *Die Walküre* (*The Valkyrie*), *Siegfried*, and *Götterdämmerung* (*The Twilight of the Gods*). The prologue outlines the struggle among the gods, the heroes, and the mortals. Wotan, the lord of the gods, plans the building of Valhalla. For its defense Wotan begets nine Valkyries, powerful horsewomen who ride in the clouds. Wotan also procreates earthlings, among them Siegmund and Sieglinde, whose fate unfolds in *The Valkyries*.

The introduction to *The Valkyries* depicts a storm in the forest, with a main motive ominously sounded in the low strings. As the curtain rises, Siegmund, exhausted from wandering, stumbles into the hut of Hunding, the husband of Sieglinde. Siegmund and Sieglinde do not know that they are brother and sister. The leading motive of their love is one of the most impassioned melodies Wagner ever wrote. At Sieglinde's instigation Siegmund draws the magic sword which Wotan had left deeply sunk in a tree trunk. Hunding appears, and they engage in a fight. But Wotan intervenes and breaks Siegmund's sword in two with his spear, which allows Hunding to kill Siegmund.

The third act opens with the celebrated symphonic episode, Ride of the Valkyries. Brünnhilde, Wotan's favorite Valkyrie, gives the news that Sieglinde is to bear a son by Siegmund, the hero Siegfried. His theme is one of the most important leading motives in the entire *Ring*. Wotan punishes Brünnhilde for her intercession in Sieglinde's behalf by putting her on a rock encircled by flames. The opera ends as Brünnhilde slumbers amid the rising flames of the Magic Fire.

The Ring of the Nibelung—Twilight of the Gods: *Siegfried's Rhine Journey*

Twilight of the Gods is the last music drama of Wagner's great tetralogy, *The Ring of the Nibelung*. All four dramas are unified by a fantastically intricate network of leading motives, each of which identifies a character on the stage, an object, an event, or an abstract concept. A computerized analysis of these identification tags reveals that they are mutual permutations and inversions of a certain limited number of basic melodic configurations and rhythmic values. Moreover, it appears that by readjusting the motivic parameters of *The Ring of the Nibelung* it is possible to obtain the motives of practically all Wagner's operas. It may come as a shock to discover that the theme of erotic love in *Tristan and Isolde* is topologically congruent with the motive of faith in *Parsifal*, but the result is not surprising, considering that Wagner's thematic vocabulary was functionally derived from major and minor triads ornamented by chromatic passages. A deeper analysis of the structure of Wagner's music, with the aid of Boolean algebra, would prove that ultimately each of these seemingly independent motives is an idempotent.

No computer programming, however, can help much in disentangling the darksome deeds and misdeeds in Wagner's libretto of *The Ring*. Human and supernatural beings are here coiled in a musical Möbius strip. In *Twilight of the Gods* the curse of the ring of the Nibelung brings about the destruction of Valhalla and the downfall of the gods. The leading motives of the hero Siegfried, of the ring, of the flying horsewomen, the Valkyries, of the Rhine Maidens who kept the gold from which the ring was to be forged, of love, hate, death, fate, all pass in review in kaleidophonic variety.

The music of Siegfried's Rhine Journey forms the interlude between the prologue and the first act of *Twilight of the Gods*. Siegfried's horn call is heard as he leads his horse down from the rock of the Valkyries. His journey down the Rhine ends with his fateful encounter with Hagen, the sinister offspring of the Nibelung dwarf Alberich, the original forger of the ring. As Siegfried, under the influence of magical potions, relates the story of his love for the Valkyrie Brünnhilde, Hagen stabs him in the back. Siegfried cries out for Brünnhilde and dies.

Parsifal: *Prelude to Act I*

Wagner was drawn to the Christian romance of medieval poetry as strongly as to the darksome sagas of the Teutonic North. In his early opera *Lohengrin*, he evoked the mystery of the Holy Grail, the legendary chalice used by Christ at the Last Supper. Lohengrin, a knight of the Holy Grail, was the son of Parsifal, the figure Wagner selected as the central character of his last opera, which he described as "sacred festival drama." *Parsifal* was produced in Bayreuth on July 26, 1882, at the music dome decreed for Wagner by the "mad king of Bavaria," Ludwig II. It was a perfect consummation of Wagner's great career, which began with the operatic glorification of Nordic heroes and concluded with the apotheosis of mystical Christianity. A few months after the production of *Parsifal*, Wagner died.

The story of Parsifal and the knights of the Holy Grail is intimately interwoven with Arthurian romance. A link with King Arthur's court at Camelot is provided in the medieval epics, according to which Joseph of Arimathea, who received the body of Christ at the Crucifixion, preserved drops of sacred blood in the Holy Grail and carried the chalice to England, where it came into the possession of the knights of the Round Table at King Arthur's court.

Stories of the origin of the Holy Grail were not confined to the Last Supper or the Crucifixion. According to one version, the Holy Grail was a fragment of a crown that sixty thousand angels made for Lucifer. The archangel Michael struck it from Lucifer's head, and when it fell to the ground a part of it became the Grail. The symbolism of a sacred vessel characterizes many folktales. Often a vase is a token of victory. Cups given to winners at sports events are the mundane descendants of the Grail. The etymology of the word itself is not clear. It has been explained as an altered form of *sang real* ("royal blood"), or *sangraal*. Another derivation is from the Provençal word *grial*, "vessel," with the vowels transposed (not an uncommon philological phenomenon), resulting in the spelling *grail*.

In writing *Parsifal*, Wagner followed the epic romance *Parzival* by the German minnesinger Wolfram von Eschenbach, changing the spelling to Parsifal on the assumption that the name came from the Arabic words fal parsi ("pure fool"). In the romantic hagiography of the Middle Ages, only "a pure fool made wise through pity" can be qualified to become the keeper of the Grail. Wagner was long fascinated with the figure of Wolfram, who appears in *Tannhäuser* and sings the famous invocation to the Evening Star, Venus.

There are three acts in *Parsifal*. The knights of the Holy Grail congregate in Monsalvat, in Spanish Galicia. Amfortas, the keeper of the Grail, suffers from a mysterious wound that can be healed only by the touch of the sacred spear with which Christ's side was pierced on the Cross. Parsifal is apprehended for killing a wild swan, and is expelled. In the second act Parsifal wanders into the domain of the sinister magus, Klingsor, in Moorish Spain. Seductive "flower girls" surround Parsifal, and the floweriest girl of them all, the lascivious Kundry, implants a penetrating kiss on Parsifal's inexperienced lips.

Prelude to
Parsifal

Being a "pure fool," Parsifal recoils in horror. It is suddenly revealed to him that the wound of Amfortas must have been the punishment for his surrender to Kundry's blandishments, and that the sacred spear must be in Klingsor's possession. In the most pregnantly succinct line ever uttered in any opera, he exclaims, "Amfortas! The wound!" Klingsor appears and, furious that his stratagem in corrupting and thus neutralizing "the pure fool" has failed, hurls the spear at him, but it remains suspended in a spiritual magnetic field generated by Parsifal's mystical halo of goodness. Parsifal seizes the spear and makes the sign of the Cross with the scabbard. Thereupon Klingsor's unholy realm dissolves in ruins.

In the third act Parsifal returns to the kingdom of the Grail carrying the spear and heals Amfortas with its touch. The Holy Grail is then revealed to him and he holds it aloft. He is anointed as the king of the Holy Grail. Kundry, who was condemned to perdition for having mocked at Christ, is baptized by Parsifal, but she can no longer receive the charisma of redemption and falls lifeless on the ground, as the Holy Grail shines above in mystical light.

The dramatic action in *Parsifal*, as in other Wagner music dramas, is guided by a system of leading motives, serving as identification tags for the characters of the stage, symbolic inanimate objects, and abstract ideas. Incidentally, the term "leitmotiv" was never used by Wagner himself, who preferred the designation *Grundthema* ("basic theme"). For a private performance of the prelude to the opera, given for Ludwig II, Wagner provided a commentary on the symbolic meaning of the music. The opening motive is that of Love, which is identified also with the Last Supper. Wagner quotes the words of Christ: "Take, eat; this is my body.... Drink ye all; this is my blood, which is shed for many for the remission of sins." The theme is a throbbing musical phrase, in a gently syncopated rhythm, outlined melodically by an ascending major triad followed by a conjunct upper tetrachord.

The second cardinal motive is that of the Holy Grail, melodically encompassing the interval of an octave from the dominant to the dominant. The ending of the phrase is an ancient formula of Saxon liturgy, known as the "Dresden Amen," and it appears also in Mendelssohn's *Reformation* Symphony. There can be no question of Wagner's borrowing either from Mendelssohn or from liturgy. An ending of this nature is a natural cadence in a chorale.

A change of tempo leads to the announcement of the important theme of faith, a strong unambiguous utterance in the modal configurations of medieval chants. The motive appears four times in succession, in unprepared modulations by minor thirds, Wagner's favorite formula, much in evidence also in *Tristan and Isolde*. Analytically, it is significant that the successive tonics in such modulations by minor thirds form a chord of the diminished seventh, the *accorde di stupefazione* of Italian opera composers, used at melodramatic climaxes to depict sinister supernatural agencies and so instill *stupefazione* in the listeners.

Wagner never quite shook off such old-fashioned theatrical effects in his harmonic scheme. Thus Kundry's motive in *Parsifal* consists of a rapid descending passage along the tonal lines of a diminished-seventh chords sensitized by expressive appoggiaturas. Klingsor's motive is also derived from the "chord of stupefaction." The music of the Good Friday Spell is taken from the symphonic portion of the third act of *Parsifal*, in which Parsifal, arriving in Monsalvat on Good Friday to be anointed, surveys the pastoral scene of the land. The themes of Parsifal, the Holy Grail, and faith are blended in an enfilade of euphony in this music. The Wagnerian principle of endless melody receives here its finest realization. It is an apotheosis of redemptive Christianity.

Siegfried Idyll

Wagner planned his own life as if it were a heroic music drama. He placed himself above the common standards of nineteenth-century morality. Never in his writings or in his conversation did he show any evidence of regret about his ways with loyal friends and trusting women. He had no compunctions in luring away Liszt's daughter Cosima from her husband, Hans von Bülow, while the latter was ardently rehearsing *Tristan und Isolde*. When a daughter was born to Wagner and Cosima, still Bülow's wife, Wagner named her Isolde.

In June 1869 Cosima bore Wagner a son. "Ein Sohn ist da! Der musste Siegfried heissen!" ("A son is here! He must be called Siegfried!") Wagner proudly wrote in a dedicatory poem to Cosima. She obtained her divorce from von Bülow shortly after Siegfried's birth. Wagner and Cosima were finally married in August 1870. For Cosima's thirty-third birthday, on Christmas Eve, 1870 (Wagner was twenty-four years her senior), Wagner arranged a performance of his "symphonic birthday greeting" entitled "A Tribschen Idyll"—Tribschen was the name of Wagner's villa near Lucerne, Switzerland, where he stayed with Cosima—"with birdsong and orange sunrise, offered to his Cosima by her Richard." The work subsequently became known as *Siegfried Idyll*, in sentimental allusion to Wagner's baby son, and also to the hero of the third opera in the *Ring* tetralogy, which he was composing at the time, and which provided most of the thematic materials for the *Idyll*.

Wagner organized the rehearsals for a surprise performance of *Siegfried Idyll* in great secrecy in a Lucerne hotel. Early in the morning of Christmas Day, 1870, the musicians were assembled at Tribschen, on the stairs leading to Cosima's room. Wagner conducted standing at the top, with the orchestra men occupying the steps, and the first performance was played at seven-thirty in the morning. Several more performances were given during the day.

The themes of *Siegfried Idyll* derive mainly from the love duet between Siegfried and Brünnhilde in the closing scene of the opera, except for a lullaby, "Schlaf, mein Kind," which is a folk song. The tonality, E major, is the Siegfried key in *The Ring*. The orchestration is economical, comprising, besides the strings, one flute, one oboe, two clarinets, one bassoon, and two horns. The musical texture is lucid and transparent. *Siegfried Idyll* is perhaps the most truly Romantic piece written by Wagner, and one of his few purely orchestral compositions. *Siegfried Idyll* is one of the most tender musical expressions in all instrumental literature. Even the most violent critics of Wagner could scarcely call it loud or inharmonious.

JOHANNES BRAHMS
(1833–1897)
The Third B of Music

I knew that someday soon someone would suddenly appear as the greatest expression of our time in an ideal manner, one who would develop his mastery not by gradual unfolding, but suddenly, like Minerva springing from Jupiter's head in full armor. And he has come, a young blood, at whose cradle Graces and Heroes kept their vigil. His name is Johannes Brahms.

In these words, in an article entitled "New Paths," Robert Schumann introduced to the world the twenty-year-old Brahms. He gave a vivid description of Brahms the pianist:

Sitting at the piano, he began to discover wondrous regions. We were carried deeper and deeper into enchanted circles. There was genius in his playing that made an orchestra out of the piano, with plaintive and jubilant voices. There were sonatas, or rather veiled symphonies, songs whose poetry is understood without knowing the words. And then, it seemed, he united all these in a roaring torrent rushing toward a waterfall, with a rainbow in the waters streaming downward accompanied by butterflies and nightingales.

Johannes Brahms (1833–1897) appeared on the musical horizon at the height of the German Romantic movement. At that time, romanticism was something more than the word connotes today. It was imagination run free in luxuriant fantasy, in which the borderline between fancy and reality was adjustable according to the intensity of emotion. Schumann was a great Romantic musician, and he believed that Brahms belonged to the same exciting company.

But there was a great difference between Schumann and Brahms. Schumann wrote programmatic music, in which the written notes reflected passing moods, with fanciful titles to express these moods. Brahms, on the other hand, wrote absolute music. The titles of his works merely designate the form—symphony, sonata, rhapsody, intermezzo—without any hints as to their emotional content. Only in his expression marks did Brahms lift the veil from his inner feelings, as for instance in the indication "Con intimissimo sentimento"—with the most intimate sentiment.

And so Brahms became the bearer of the classical tradition, the third B in the august company of Bach and Beethoven. The man who gave him this proud title was Hans von Bülow, the great conductor, pianist, and wit extraordinary. There was symbolism in his famous pronouncement. His favorite key, von Bülow explained, was that of Beethoven's *Eroica* Symphony, with three flats in the key signature for E-flat major. In German, flats in general are sometimes called B's. The three B's of the *Eroica* were to the conductor Hans von Bülow the three great musical names: Bach, Beethoven, and Brahms. He elaborated the point when he called the first symphony of Brahms the "Tenth Symphony," an artistic successor to Beethoven's nine symphonies.

Brahms spent his youth in Hamburg, a bustling port that stimulated practical energy rather than flights of imagination. His father was a professional player on flute, violin, and horn, but played the most unromantic instrument in the Hamburg Philharmonic, the double bass. Brahms studied piano, and appeared in public at the age of fourteen. He began to compose with circumspection, and published his early works under assumed names. His first professional position was as a choral director and piano teacher. He also directed a ladies' choir, consisting of his students and their friends, for which he drew up a humorous set of rules, with a recurrent admonition: "The members of the ladies' choir must be present, that is to say, they shall arrive punctually at the appointed time."

The name of Brahms gradually became known outside his native city. He received invitations to appear as pianist-composer and conductor elsewhere in Germany and then in Vienna, which eventually became his hometown. Devoted to his parents and to his youthful memories, he paid several visits to Hamburg. He learned that his father was not doing very well in his profession, and he left a note for him: "Father, music is the best consolation. When in need, read carefully your score of Handel's *Saul,* and you will be comforted." In that score, Brahms had left several banknotes of high denomination.

With his friends, Brahms was charming and sentimental, but with unwanted admirers and ambitious composers he was often gruff. There are many stories illustrating these contradictory qualities in his character. Once Brahms was walking in the countryside near Vienna, when a gentleman approached him and, with many flattering words, asked for his autograph. "Oh, you probably want my brother, the composer," said Brahms. "Just wait here, and he will be back soon from the village." Then Brahms continued his walk in peace. When a social snob accosted Brahms at a summer concert in a Vienna park, Brahms whispered to him: "Please be silent! They are playing my piece!" The snob stopped conversation at once, and after the number was over, he became effusive in his compliments. But the piece was a march by a popular composer, Gungl. Brahms was quick at double-edged repartee. Once a musical friend sharply criticized an instrumental work written by a local German duke. Brahms cautioned him: "Be careful in your judgment—one never knows who is the real composer of the duke's piece."

Impatient with ambitious and arrogant colleagues, Brahms admired works by his contemporaries even from an entirely different camp, stylistically speaking. He went to many performances of *Carmen* in Vienna and inscribed a few notes of the "Blue Danube Waltz" on a fan belonging to Strauss's wife Adele with the following inscription: "Unfortunately, not by me." But he said of the Swiss-German composer Joachim Raff, who enjoyed great fame at the time, that only Raff's pupils should be subjected to the hearing of his symphonies as a punishment for their foolhardy decision to study with him.

Earnestness of purpose and stateliness of form distinguish the music of Brahms, but there is also a mildness, a musical loving-kindness, and pervading sentiment that imparts a feeling of intimacy. And there is also variety. Brahms is the composer of the ingratiating Lullaby, but he also wrote the fiery Hungarian Dances. Those infatuated with the sensuous charm of French music are apt to reject Brahms. When fire exits were placed in the new Symphony Hall in Boston in 1900, the quip made the rounds that these should have been marked "Exit in Case of Brahms." But Brahms survived that particular fire, and when a famous orchestra opens its season, as likely as not, it is a symphony of Brahms that resounds over the musical portals. This "Entrance in Case of Brahms" demonstrates that audiences as well as performers have long accepted Brahms as a legitimate successor to Bach and Beethoven in the triad of "the three B's of music."

ORCHESTRAL MUSIC
Symphony No. 1 in C Minor, Op. 68 (1855–76)

Brahms undertook the composition of a symphony at the age of twenty, but abandoned it when he felt unequal to the task. Portions of the work found their way into his First Piano Concerto. It was not until he reached the age of forty that he completed a symphony started in his late twenties. This time he carried it out, and the completed work was the great Symphony in C minor. It was first performed in Karlsruhe on November 4, 1876, with Otto Dessoff conducting the orchestra from manuscript. A few days later, Brahms himself conducted the work in Mannheim.

Once more, the conductor Hans von Bülow launched a winged phrase when he described the First Symphony of Brahms as the Tenth Symphony, the rightful successor to Beethoven's nine symphonies. There are some parallels in the lives of Beethoven and Brahms. Both were born in North Germany: Beethoven in Bonn, Brahms in Hamburg. Both went to Vienna to live, to write music, and to die. Both were symphonists of universal expression; yet their inspiration was nurtured on the melodic and rhythmic patterns of Central European folk songs.

Much musicological rhetoric has been expended on the origin of the noble horn melody that appears out of nowhere with such splendid illumination in the last

Symphony No. 1

in C Minor, Op. 68

Un poco sostenuto

movement of the First Symphony of Brahms. Some attempted to trace it to the chimes of Westminster Abbey in London. The solution of the riddle is found in the published correspondence between Brahms and Clara Schumann. Vacationing in the Austrian Alps, Brahms sent a postcard to Clara, dated September 12, 1868, in which he jotted down the C-major horn theme note for note, just as it appears in the symphony. "The Alpine horn blew this today," he inscribed. And he set this salutation to the tune: "Hoch auf'm Berg, tief im Tal, grüss' ich dich viel tausend-mal" ("High on the hill, deep in the vale, I greet you many thousand times"). The presence of F-sharp in this bland C-major tune is easily explained, for it corresponds to the eleventh overtone of C in the natural harmonic series as sounded on an Alpine horn, bugle, or shepherd's pipe.

The First Symphony enjoyed excellent success in Europe, but for some strange reason it ran into a storm of critical abuse in America. A Boston critic delivered himself of this curious dictum: "Johannes Brahms is a modern of the moderns, and his C-Minor Symphony is a remarkable expression of the inner life of this anxious, introverted age." Another American critic declared that the work was "mathematical music evolved with difficulty from an unimaginative brain." Philip Hale, the cultured annotator of the Boston Symphony concerts, described the symphony as "the apotheosis of arrogance."

The symphony is in four movements arranged in the classical order: fast, slow, neither fast nor slow, fast. The first movement, un poco sostenuto, in C minor, is set in § time. Romantic German analysts are wont to describe the opening as the "music of destiny," and the slowly rising melody of the violins as an arduous effort to escape the gravity pull of the tonic pedal point in the double basses and the double bassoon. However that might be, the ensuing Allegro tears itself free of the shackles of destiny. Musical motion becomes more fluid and is constantly refreshed by rhythmic cross-currents. The relentless syncopated rhythms create a sense of tension, until the protracted stand on the dominant signals the advent of the recapitulation. A magisterial coda follows, and the movement concludes in resonant C major.

The second movement, Andante sostenuto, is in E major, in ¾ time. Its opening theme is one of Brahms's finest melodic inspirations. Here rhythmic prosody has a natural ring, and the harmonies, with their constant lowering of the mediant, suggest a crepuscular mood. The movement is an eclogue of poetic modalities.

The third movement, Un poco allegretto e grazioso, in A-flat major, in ¾ time, is a bucolic scherzo. The clarinet sets the pastoral tone, which the oboe echoes. In the graceful trio, the wind instruments and the strings engage in a genial dialogue.

The finale is in C minor, in ¼ time. An introductory adagio creates a somber mood in a chromatically embroidered chorale. The tempo is gradually accelerated to Più andante. It is here that the horn solo makes its clarion call, the melody Brahms heard in the Alps. It is echoed by the flute in the high register; a canonic development ensues, leading to a grandiloquent peroration, allegro non troppo ma con brio. The Alpine horn tune is recalled momentarily; an insistent drumroll presages the return to the major tonic of the symphony. After a chorale-like episode there is a coda saturated with sonorous energy. Although the final cadence is plagal, the concluding series of C-major chords provides full satisfaction to classically attuned ears.

Symphony No. 2 in D Major, Op. 73 (1877)

George Bernard Shaw, writing when Brahms was not yet canonized as the third great B of music, said bluntly: "Brahms is enjoyable when he merely tries to be pleasant or naively sentimental, and insufferably tedious when he tries to be profound." Brahms's followers were derisively labeled "Brahmins," so as to give full measure of dignity, and perhaps stuffiness, to their ideals.

Strangest of all, Brahms himself was convinced that his music brought little cheer to the world. Even with regard to his Second Symphony, conceived in the pleasant surroundings of rural Germany in the summer of 1877, and permeated with pastoral lightness, he wrote to his publisher: "I have never written anything quite so sad. The score should be printed with black edges." He repeated the same estimate in almost identical words in another letter. If it was a joke, then indeed Brahms must have been a sorry humorist. It is more plausible to suggest that Brahms was not the impulsive genius type, that the source of his inspiration was more like an evenly flowing river than a geyser, and that he himself failed to realize the lighter side of his genius. Also, it is quite possible that in making this estimate of his symphony, he thought chiefly of the adagio, which is indeed profoundly meditative, if not hopelessly sad.

Clara Schumann, who was a critical friend, wrote this in her diary after Brahms played some of the work for her: "Johannes came this evening, and played the first movement of his second symphony in D major, and it delighted me.... Also, he played some of the last movement, which gave me great joy. This symphony will bring him more success than the first, and its genius, and marvelous workmanship will impress the musicians, too."

The Second Symphony was completed in only a few months, which was remarkable, considering that it took Brahms fully fifteen years to compose the First Symphony. He was anxious to hear it performed, but there were obstacles. Finally, a performance was announced in Vienna, but the copyist could not finish the orchestral parts in time, which resulted in a three-week postponement. The symphony was eventually played by the Vienna Philharmonic on December 30, 1877, under Hans Richter. Brahms himself conducted it later in Leipzig, but was dissatisfied with the reception. Three days after that performance, he wrote to his publisher and asked him whether the first movement should be rewritten. Characteristically, he inquired whether, in the publisher's opinion, the new movement should not rather be in a minor key. However, the doubts soon abated, and there was no more thought of rewriting.

The symphony opens in ¾ time, in the key of D major. After an opening bar in the cellos and basses, with a figure of three notes, the tonic, the leading tone, and again the tonic, the horns play the theme. The woodwinds answer it. The horns restate the theme in the supertonic, and once more, the woodwinds give an answer. The entire statement is symmetrical, each of the four periods having four bars. This grouping of bars in twos and fours remains characteristic for the entire movement. The violins and violas play a transitional episode. There is a kettledrum beat, and the opening three-note figure is heard, which appears to be of no incidental significance. Then the violins introduce a new theme of a light character, which is immediately imitated by the flute, and then more insistently, in overlapping rhythms. Cross-accents signal a further increase in tension, but it is suddenly discharged by light passages in the woodwinds. Then the cellos and violas proclaim an emotional subject in minor, which is repeated by the woodwinds. An energetic development follows, with syncopated figures. Syncopation is now stabilized in a dash-dot figure, against which the rest of the orchestra leads in groups of ascending three notes, on the main beats. There is a climax, and a cascade of violins brings the music to a calmer level.

The violas and second violins play the emotional theme in a major key, while the flute weaves a counterpoint in triplet figurations. Then the woodwinds take over the theme, while the violins furnish the triplet counterpoint. This is the end of the exposition, and the beginning of the development. The function of the development is to make a review of all the themes presented in the exposition, using different keys, changed intervals, and new tone color. We hear the horn theme, and the three-note figure of the opening bar of the symphony, which latter is here extended into a sequence. The flutes repeat the horn theme, and the three-note progressions overlap in canonic imitation. The long-silent trombones join the orchestra. The rhythmic tension grows, with numerous cross-accents underlying the feeling of unrest. Fragments of the horn theme assume apocalyptic proportions, as proclaimed by the woodwinds and the brass, with the support of percussion. The light theme of the beginning now appears in minor, fortissimo. There are Beethoven-like transitions from darkness to light and, characteristically, fortissimo is associated with the minor keys, pianissimo with major. The climax is reached, and the flute and clarinet drop in a descending scale, to prepare for the recapitulation.

In the recapitulation, the horn theme is given to the oboes. The emotional cello-viola theme is now in B minor, the relative key of the tonic. It is repeated in the woodwinds. As in the exposition, the rhythms thicken, the syncopated figures appear, and, once more, a cascade of notes falls to bring the music to a quieter range. The woodwinds now play the original cello-viola theme in a major key, and this time it is the viola that furnishes the triplet counterpoint. The roles are exchanged once more, so that the cellos and violas are assigned their original theme, with the flute playing the counterpoint. The music grows more tenuous, and there is a feeling of approaching conclusion. The horn theme reappears in a dynamic outburst and the light theme of the beginning is inconspicuously recalled. The violins play a cadential form of the horn theme, while the lower strings move importantly in three-note figures. The woodwinds flash the dancing motive, against plucked strings. The mood is now serene, the horns begin their theme, but leave it unfinished. A full chord completes the movement.

Beginning the second movement, the cellos present a long, meaningful subject, in a slow falling cadential figure, with the counterpoint of the bassoons, surging against the cellos. The violins take up the theme, but play only the first four bars. The wind instruments follow with an interlude, in which a characteristic seesawing fragment of the theme is developed in the horn, oboes, and flutes. The cellos and basses imitate the swaying figure. There is a lull, and the woodwinds play a graceful interlude, in ⅛, gently moving forward, in slow syncopated figures. The strings develop this rhythm, but soon the main beat asserts itself over the syncopated progressions. The pace of the movement doubles. Parallel to this rhythmic acceleration, there is a dynamic expansion, until a climax is reached

The thematic elements now include the initial motive, the three-note figure, and the rhythmic figurations in double time. The principal theme is played by the strings, and then taken up by the wind instruments, solo and in groups. Its faithful counterpoint accompanies the theme. There are variations, and the second portion of the theme, not heard since its initial appearance, is now given in full by the violins. After a short episode, this section of the theme is sounded in a modified form, against the rapid figurations of the violins. The theme is quoted here and there, and the quiet ending is now near. The surging scale of the contrapuntal figure is heard to the last, seconded by the muffled kettledrums. The final chord is in B major, the key of the movement.

The third movement is full of rural grace. It is in G major, ¾ time, and the accent on the last beat gives it a quasi-Slavic tang. The slow dance tune, in woodwinds, is accompanied by plucked cellos. Suddenly, the tempo changes to presto, in ¾. This is simply a variation of the dance theme, using the same intervals, and the characteristic accent on the upbeat. A new modification of the theme appears in a vigorous section in C major, but here the tune is not only altered rhythmically, but also inverted, so that the thematic interdependence is hardly noticeable. The movement slackens, with the fatuous lights still flickering on the pointed cross-accents in the woodwinds. Then the original tempo returns, with slight variations of the theme. Soon, only the tail end remains of the theme, and there is a half-cadence. The tempo is now a rapid ⅜, another remote variation of the inverted theme. It passes quickly in alternations of strings and woodwinds. Finally, the original theme returns in a new key of F-sharp major. But a modulation to the original G major is easily effected. There is a moment of silence, and the movement ends quietly.

The fourth movement is a typical fast finale. It is in the key of the symphony, D major, in cut (⅔) time. The restless theme is sounded in unison by the strings. The woodwinds join for the second section of the subject. After a brief lull, the entire orchestra plays the opening bars, but the rest of the theme is modified melodically as well as rhythmically. Again there is a slackening, brightened up by rapid arpeggios in the clarinet, and a new theme appears in the dominant key. It passes from the strings to the woodwinds, and soon develops into an energetic rhythmic episode, marked by strong syncopation. There are running scales, in thirds, in the woodwinds. The syncopation spreads to the entire orchestra. Then the original theme comes back, appearing in various keys. The tempo subsides; there is an episode, marked tranquillo, in triplet figures, ultimately traceable to the intervals of the opening subject.

The tranquil episode is developed, with the indication, sempre più tranquillo. The movement is still in triplets. Then the falling fourths, characteristic of the second section of the theme, appear in doubly slow tempo, that is, in the augmentation. The recapitulation is announced by the strings in unison, identical with the beginning. But immediately after this identification, the recapitulation deviates from the course of the exposition, and the orchestration is new. Then the second theme appears in the tonic. Again we hear the running thirds, the syncopated chords. The trombones enter significantly, and then the kettledrums, presaging the climax. The coda is long and brilliant.

Symphony No. 3 in F Major, Op. 90 (1883)

Brahms completed the Third Symphony in the summer of 1883, shortly after the death of Wagner, his great rival in musical aesthetics. To Brahms and to the "Brahmins," this symphony was a reassertion of the Classical faith. The symphony was performed for the first time at a Vienna Philharmonic Society concert on December 2, 1883, under the direction of Hans Richter. Eduard Hanslick, the powerful Vienna critic, declared that the Third Symphony was superior to the first two, "the most compact in form, the clearest in the details, and the most plastic in the leading themes."

There were several attempts by Brahms's friends to affix a durable subtitle to this symphony. Both Hanslick and Richter suggested "Eroica," but admitted that the parallel with Beethoven's Third was not complete: the heroic element lacked defiance and tragedy. Clara Schumann thought the best name would be "Forest Idyll," and even wrote a tentative program to fit the description. Finally, Max Kalbeck, the author of the most worshipfully detailed biography of Brahms, declared that the symphony was inspired by the sight of the statue of Germania at Rüdesheim. Though it is true that Brahms believed in the great destiny of the German race, particularly its North German branch, it can be questioned whether he needed a statue of stone for musical inspiration.

After Brahms conducted the Third Symphony in Berlin on January 16, 1884, Carl Lachmund, one of the last American pupils of Liszt, wrote enthusiastically from Berlin to *Freund's Weekly*:

Symphony No. 3

in F Major, Op. 90

Brahms has been visiting Berlin. He came to conduct his new symphony. I can hardly find words to express the high praise it deserves. Everything is expressed in a clear and concise form. Though the themes are fine, the beauty of the work lies more in the development. Brahms has a wonderful gift for developing manifold beauties out of his motives or short themes, and in this respect he strongly resembles Beethoven. The symphony, on the whole, may be termed pastoral, though the last movement is decidedly heroic. The third movement is especially charming, and had to be repeated at the rehearsal as well as at the concert.

It is an interesting fact that Brahms did not think it prejudicial to repeat a movement of the symphony. When Hans Richter did exactly that at the first performance in London, on May 12, 1884, an English critic complained bitterly:

> Is it really necessary to inform Herr Richter that the four movements of a symphony constitute an organism, and that to make one part of that organism twice as long as it was designed by the author is to destroy the harmony of the whole? If we should be informed that similar abuses have been practiced at Vienna in the presence and with the tacit consent of Brahms himself, such a fact would only prove that where personal vanity comes into play, a grave German composer is as open to temptation as a French soubrette.

J. S. Shedlock, an English critic of some eminence, coupled Brahms with Antonin Dvořák (1841–1904) as preservers of the classical tradition against Wagner's newfangled theories of art. He termed the Third Symphony "a noble and earnest work" and its production in England "an event of no small importance."

The first American performance of Brahms's Third Symphony took place at one of Van der Stucken's Novelty Concerts in New York, on October 24, 1884. Shortly afterward, on November 8, 1884, it was given by the Boston Symphony Orchestra. The American critics were as receptive to Brahms as their English and German colleagues. The *Boston Evening Transcript* wrote:

> Now that Wagner is dead, there is no composer in the world from whom a new work in one of the larger musical forms is looked for with such deep interest. Brahms stands almost alone today as a composer who, although wholly modern in spirit and style, seems to feel that nothing impels him to relinquish the traditional musical forms, and to strike out into a wholly new path. The time has fully come for the people who are fond of talking about Brahms's brains, to think well what they are saying. Thank heaven, the man has brains, an article of which no one can have too much.

But there was some dissension. The *Boston Traveller* wrote:

> Brahms occupies a position in music similar to that held by mathematics in the common curriculum of study. To the majority of students who sincerely desire to cultivate music from an art standpoint, Brahms represents a school of composition abstract and cold. He often forgets beauty of sound in an absorbing earnestness of form; the characteristics of his intelligence prevent his music taking hold upon our sympathies.

The *New York Evening Post*, which had always hewn to the Wagnerian line, condemned the new symphony unequivocally: "If this Symphony is to be accepted as evidence, Brahms has said his last word in music. There is nothing of striking originality in the whole work. Repeated hearing is not likely to reveal hidden beauties as everything in it seems clear and superficial." The *Musical Gazette* of Boston made the common reproach of too much science:

> The Symphony is of course dignified in character, but, like the great mass of the composer's music, it is painfully dry, deliberate and ungenial. Its

themes are brief according to the method of Brahms, and he no sooner evolves four bars of melody than he sets to work to develop it, and keeps it aggravatingly meandering through labored counterpoint and twisted rhythm.... We yearn for more tune in Brahms, even at the loss of something of his persistent masterly development. There is something else in music besides mere science.

Ten years later, Edgar Stillman Kelley, then a young composer and a critic for the *San Francisco Examiner*, roundly condemned the Third Symphony, and all of Brahms, in his column of May 9, 1894:

> After the weary, dreary hours spent in listening to the works of Brahms I am lost in wonder at the amount of devotion accorded him and the floods of enthusiasm with which he is overwhelmed. I try to console myself that this last light of the classic school exerts a valuable conservative influence at a time when music, if it were allowed to follow in the lines marked out by Wagner, would soon fall into utter disintegration. But no! Mistaking Brahms's un-beauty for a new line of thought, his followers amuse themselves with seeking in what a variety of means they, too, can twist and torture a series of commonplace tones and chords.

All these stirrings, pro and con, throw an interesting light on the status of music at the time when Wagner's school of composition was naturally opposed to the classical tradition. In our day, the acceptance or nonacceptance of Brahms is submerged in the larger question of postclassical heritage in music. By a curious twist of music history, Brahms is now classified not with the classicists, but with the Romantic composers of the nineteenth century. The tendency of present-day classicists is to go further back in search of true classical art. In new music Brahms is not an influence, but to every musician he nonetheless remains a constant companion.

Symphony No. 4 in E Minor, Op. 98 (1884–85)

Brahms wrote his Fourth Symphony in 1884–85, under the fresh impression of his fourth trip to Italy, where he was an observant student of Roman antiquities. It is also known that at the time he was reading the Greek classics in a translation. The Fourth Symphony may not have been directly conditioned by Brahms's interest in classical art, but a certain congeniality of inspiration, a certain austerity of expression may have been the result of these classical leanings.

At the time of composition of the Fourth Symphony, Brahms was in his early fifties. After an ardent youth and formative middle age, Brahms had now reached the philosophical period of his life. He was serene, secure in the knowledge of his own powers, working systematically and evenly. He had recently grown a flowing beard. When his friend Joseph Widmann saw him bearded for the first time, he found in Brahms's appearance "a symbol of perfect maturity of his powers." During Brahms's travels in Italy, he invariably attracted attention in the streets, in the railway carriage, in the museums. To the Italians he was a picture of genius, but he was more often taken for a sculptor or a university professor than a musician. Brahms himself derived a great deal of amusement from the fact that a school book of geography used his photograph as an illustration of a perfect type of the Caucasian race.

The Fourth Symphony is indeed a symbol of perfect maturity of Brahms's genius. Hans von Bülow, the friend and interpreter of Brahms's orchestral music,

Symphony No. 4

in E Minor, Op. 98

referred to it reverently as the Thirteenth Symphony, taking Beethoven's nine symphonies into the count, and continuing with Brahms's four. "No. 4 is colossal," wrote von Bülow, "It breathes inexhaustible energy from A to Z."

Brahms himself had no such reverence for his music. He jocularly called the Fourth Symphony the "Waltz and Polka affair," the waltz being the last movement, and the polka the third. But he liked it better than any other of his works. He also liked to conduct the Fourth, although he was no match for von Bülow in the art of orchestral conducting. For the first performance, which took place at Meiningen on October 25, 1885, Bülow prepared the symphony at painstaking rehearsals, but let

Brahms conduct the concert. Richard Strauss, who was assistant conductor at Meiningen at the time, tells that Brahms, as conductor, made no great impression, but "one did hear the music." Brahms subsequently went on tour with the orchestra as guest conductor of his symphony, and precipitated a minor quarrel with von Bülow when he agreed to conduct a second performance at Frankfurt.

Unlike Wagner, Brahms was never the target of criticism as an innovator. But he was often accused of being overscientific. It was said that Brahms's themes, at least in symphonic and chamber music, were derived from the development, which was formed in his mind first. The triumph of Brahms as a scientist of music comes in the last movement of the Fourth. It is a Passacaglia, variations over a continuously repeating motive, never departing from the key of the symphony, E minor, and representing a numerically perfect concatenation of thirty-two periods of eight bars each, up to the coda. The theme, an eight-note motto, one note to a bar, is derived from the bass of the chaconne from Bach's Cantata No. 150.

Elisabeth von Herzogenberg, a friend of Brahms and herself a fine musician, was dismayed by the technical complexity of the last movement when she played it in a piano arrangement. "It is more for the lens of a microscope," she wrote to Brahms, "for the erudite and the scientific than for an average music lover." But when she heard it in the orchestra she forgot her misgivings: "The movement might as well be three times as long, and the audience would have enjoyed it, even without knowledge and understanding of passacaglia and such things as that."

Not every listener was as understanding as Elisabeth von Herzogenberg. Hugo Wolf, at that time a young Wagnerian, wrote with bitter irony about Brahms's *Krebsgang* ("crab walk," a technical term for retrograde imitation where the melody is read from right to left): "Art to compose without inspiration has surely found in Brahms its chief protagonist. Like the Lord himself, Brahms knows the trick of making something out of nothing." Yet Brahms was not an anti-Wagnerian. In the Third Symphony, written shortly after Wagner died, there is a distinct musical reference to Wagner's Venusberg music from *Tannhäuser*. In the Fourth Symphony, the second subject of the first movement comes, without purpose or quotation, amazingly close to Hunding's leading motive in *The Valkyries*, particularly in its rhythmical formula.

Brahms had the heart of a genial peasant and loved the countryside of Austria. His lighter symphonic movements reflected the peasant side of his creative talent. Elisabeth von Herzogenberg gave a description of the scherzo of the fourth movement, to which Brahms jocularly referred as a polka: "What a sweep in your scherzo! It seems as if you wrote it down holding your breath, or in one sustained breath. One has a feeling of growing bigger and stronger listening to it." However, there is "science" in this movement, too, or at least great adroitness in handling the simple theme in different keys, and also in the inverted form.

Shortly before his death, Brahms attended a performance of his Fourth Symphony by the Vienna Philharmonic Society. Racked by cancer, emaciated and weak, he responded to the applause of the audience after each movement. Florence May, the English pianist who lived many years in Germany and Austria, described the scene:

> Tears ran down his cheeks as Brahms stood, shrunken in form, with lined countenance, strained expression, white hair hanging lank; and through the audience there was a feeling as of a stifled sob, for each knew that they were saying farewell. Another outburst of applause, and yet another; one

more acknowledgment from the Master, and Brahms and Vienna had parted forever.

Concerto for Piano and Orchestra No. 1 in D Minor, Op. 15 (1854–58)

Schumann wrote in his diary after young Brahms showed him his first compositions: "Brahms came in today: a genius." He followed this private endorsement with an enthusiastic article in which he welcomed Brahms as a new great force in music. To Brahms, this accolade was the guiding event in his career. Brahms inherited the spirit of Schumann's romanticism, which found its expression in the gentility of mood, the euphony of harmony, the fluidity of rhythm, and the dynamic quality of his music, still preserving a strict classical attitude toward the formal aspects of composition. To him, music was human thought expressed in tones. Each of his instrumental works seems to represent a musical syllogism, in which themes are premises, and deductions are made according to unchallengeable laws of musical esthetics.

Brahms was a classicist in a Romantic century. To Eduard Hanslick, he was the paragon of the "beautiful in music." But to critics seeking sensuous enjoyment from the sounds of music, his Romantic classicism lacked emotion and artistic humanity. It is amazing to read the reviews of Brahms at the height of his inventive powers and fame, that described his music as strained, unnatural, unimaginative, pedantic, fragmentary, disjointed, cold, tiresome, dry, morbid, even unintelligible! George Bernard Shaw, whose first profession was that of a music critic, wrote disdainfully: "Brahms takes an essentially commonplace theme; gives it a strange air by dressing it in the most elaborate and far-fetched harmonies; keeps his countenance severely; and finds that a good many wiseacres are ready to guarantee him as deep as Wagner, and the true heir of Beethoven."

The battle of rival aesthetic codes that raged in the nineteenth century between the followers of Brahmsian classicism and Wagnerian romanticism has long subsided. Brahms has been firmly established as a master craftsman. Despite the many misguided prophecies of his inevitable decline, his music remains a mainstay in concert programs today.

Brahms wrote two piano concertos, separated by an interval of twenty years. The first, in D minor, was the by-product of a two-piano sonata turned symphony that Brahms planned to write in 1854, when he was twenty-one years old. Some materials from this sonata-symphony went into the initial two movements of the concerto. This early work also incorporated a scherzo originally destined for the decomposed symphony, but for some reason Brahms did not transplant the scherzo into the concerto, which would have been a fourth movement.

Despite the synthetic origin of the concerto, it holds together remarkably well as a self-consistent composition. The only sign of its heterogeneous origin is the relatively unvirtuosic appearance of the solo piano part. The tragic character of the opening of the concerto and of the second movement, Adagio, is explained by the circumstance that Brahms wrote them under the impression of Schumann's attempting suicide by jumping into the Rhine River from a bridge.

The first movement of the concerto, Maestoso, retains its original symphonic grandeur. The principal theme introduced by the orchestra is built on large vaulting intervals. The dramatic character of this subject is enhanced by abrupt trochaic endings of each member of the musical phrase, over a sustained pedal point. It brings a Romantic response from the piano part. There is a great deal of thematic deployment. The songful second subject, in F major, presented by the piano solo, has a distinct Schumannesque quality in its narrative, balladlike exposition. There follows a protracted development. The recapitulation is classically outlined, and the ending is in rousing fortissimo.

The second movement, Adagio, in D major, in ⅜ time, was originally subtitled by Brahms with the Latin words carved over the doorway of the Benedictine monastery at Kanzheim in the novel *Kater Murr* by E. T. A. Hoffmann: "Benedictus, qui venit in nomine Domini." The slow movement is meant to be a portrait of Clara Schumann, as Brahms told her in a letter. The main theme appears in the muted violins, with the piano providing artful counterpoint. After an elegiac interlude, there is a quiet ending.

The third and last movement is a brilliant rondo, Allegro non troppo, in D minor, in ⅔ time. This is the only movement in the concerto that was written independently from the material of the incomplete symphony. The rondo assumes the form of variations with some interesting rhythmic translocations. A piano cadenza leads to a brilliant ending in D major.

The first performance of the concerto was given, from manuscript, in Hannover on January 22, 1859. Brahms himself was the soloist, and his friend the famous violinist Joseph Joachim conducted the orchestra. The Hannover correspondent of the important German music periodical *Signale für die musikalische Welt* reported that each movement was applauded and that the "young artist was tumultuously recalled at the end of the concert." But when five days later Brahms played the concerto with the prestigious Gewandhaus Orchestra in Leipzig, the same periodical described the concerto as "unhealthy" and proceeded to take it to pieces:

> One can hardly speak of organic development and logical elaboration. Like infusoria, seen in a drop of water through a microscope, the musical ideas, barely born, devour each other, and vanish. One must absorb this unfermented mass, and as a dessert, swallow a dose of shrieking dissonances and cacophonous sounds.

Serenade No. 2 in A Major, Op. 16 (1858–59)

The contrapuntal complexity, the depth of musical expression, the somewhat haughty academicism of Brahms's last period are not in evidence in the music written during his youthful years. His Serenade in A major belongs to this early period. It was sketched when Brahms was in his middle twenties, and was slightly revised in his early forties. The result is a relatively simple work with a superinduced technical elaboration.

The Serenade is interesting first of all because it is scored for an orchestra without violins. This imparts a certain somber quality to the tone color; it also enhances its Romantic character. In the absence of the violins, the horns and the woodwinds assume a greater importance. Romantic devices inaugurated by Weber, fanfarelike progressions of instruments in pairs, lend special color to the music. In the first movement, the clarity of the principal theme is contrasted with the chromatic meanderings of the second subject. A new group of melodic motifs introduces dancelike rhythms. These thematic ingredients enter a skillful contrapuntal game in the development section. The original subjects return in an almost orthodox recapitulation.

The ensuing scherzo is cast in the key of C major. Its rhythmic pattern is determined by the presence of off-beat accents that overlap the metrical divisions in a characteristically Brahmsian cross-rhythm. The slow movement, Adagio ma non troppo, in A minor, opens as a gentle barcarole. The smooth flow of the music is, however, interrupted by dramatic episodes in diminished-seventh harmonies, recalling similar passages of the First Symphony. The musical motion is doubled in frequency, creating a contrapuntal network of considerable complexity. Modulations carry the music far afield along the cycle of keys, before coming to rest on the major tonic.

The next movement is marked Quasi minuetto, implying a departure from the parent form of the classical minuet. Its tonal pattern is simple, and the expressive chromaticisms of subsidiary melodies do not transgress the basic tonality. The final Rondo signals the resumption of simple harmonic procedures of Brahms's youngest days. Again there are fanfare-like figures; the propulsive rhythm carries the movement along with but a few reflective moments of lyrical recollection. The movement concludes on an optimistic proclamation of musical romanticism.

Variations on a Theme by Joseph Haydn, Op. 56A (1873)

The title may well be misapplied. The theme itself, originally called "St. Anthony Chorale," was used by Haydn in one of his so-called Zittau Divertimentos, but in all probability it was a traditional hymn of unknown provenance. Indeed, these divertimentos, or *Feldpartiten* (suites for wind band) are now considered spurious. Whatever the source of the theme itself, Variations represents a development of great significance in the career of Brahms as a symphonic composer. It was written in 1873, prior to the composition of his First Symphony, but it embodies the distinctive traits of his symphonic style. The orchestral treatment in the Variations preserves the main features of the "Zittauer divertimenti," with an emphasis on wind instruments, as in band arrangements.

There are eight variations and a finale. Analytically, the variations are of the "characteristic" type, stemming from Beethoven's example, rather than from the formal "ornamental" variations of the Baroque and Rococo. Each variation possesses a distinctive character in its modality, dynamic distribution of instrumental timbres, and individual rhythmic patterns. The theme, Andante, is in B-flat major, as in Haydn's original score. It is brought out by the woodwind instruments, with the lower strings providing a discreet accompaniment in pizzicato. All odd-numbered variations are in B-flat major; all even-numbered variations are in B-flat minor, with the exception of variation 6, which is in B-flat major, as is the finale.

Variation 1, Poco più animato, is distinguished by a typically Brahmsian combination of four notes against six notes in a bar of $\frac{2}{4}$, which imparts to the music a sense of stimulating fluidity. Variation 2, Più vivace, is marked by a punctuating syncopation of the principal rhythmic pattern of the subject. Variation 3, Con moto, is a pastoral eclogue, with delicate crewel-work in the contrapuntal background, dolce e legato. Variation 4, Andante con moto, in $\frac{3}{8}$, is a locus classicus of invertible counterpoint in the twelfth, with the countersubject appearing in the low register and then transposed an octave and a fifth higher, without a change in the theme itself. The perturbations resulting from this polyphonic salto mortale are stupendous, for consonances become dissonances and vice-versa—but Brahms was a supreme master of this sort of thing.

Variation 5, Vivace, in $\frac{6}{8}$ time, is a scherzo in a fine filigree texture, in which passages in pianissimo are vitalized by recurrent puffs of off-beat sforzando. Variation 6, Vivace, in $\frac{2}{4}$ time, is an incisive instrumental movement, opening in throbbing pianissimo and reaching fortissimo at the climax. Variation 7, Grazioso, in ⅜ time, is a gentle barcarole. The cross-accents result in a rhythmic interference in the implied dual meter of ¾ and ⅜, imparting to the movement a Spanish character. Variation 8, Presto non troppo, in B-flat minor, has the sonority of Romantic precipitation that Brahms favored in the rapid movements of his symphonies. A pause separates this variation from the Finale, which is the longest part of the entire set. Its form is that of a passacaglia, with a short theme of five bars in the ground bass recurring eighteen times in succession, while a cornucopia of florid counterpoint descends upon it from the upper voices. The principal theme returns in the coda, and the Variations conclude in a blaze of B-flat major chords.

Concerto for Violin and Orchestra in D Major, Op. 77 (1878)

The Violin Concerto belongs in the symphonic period of Brahms. It was composed in 1878, a year after the Second Symphony, and it is written in the same key of D major. But apart from this there are no thematic points of contact between the two works. The Violin Concerto was written for the violinist Joseph Joachim, a great friend of Brahms's and a famous virtuoso. Brahms had some trouble with the organization of the concerto. He planned originally to write four movements, including a scherzo, but was dissatisfied with the result, and eliminated the extra movement. Joachim made all kinds of suggestions for the improvement of the violin part, but Brahms proved to be uncommonly reluctant to make changes, and followed Joachim's advice only in technical matters of bowings, accents, rests, etc.

Joachim played the first performance, with Brahms himself conducting, at a Gewandhaus concert in Leipzig on January 1, 1879. Reports of the quality of performance differ. Florence May, in her Brahms biography, wrote: "Joachim played with a love and devotion which brought home to us in every bar the direct or indirect share he has had in the work." But Max Kalbeck, the author of the voluminous life of Brahms, was critical of Joachim and found his performance even technically inadequate. Brahms himself was enthusiastic. "Joachim played my concerto more and more magnificently with each rehearsal," he wrote to a friend. "The cadenza produced such an effect that the audience applauded right through the coda." An amusing episode brought snickers to the listeners. Brahms, never a careful dresser, forgot to fasten his unbuttoned suspenders and, semaphoring the orchestra in large gestures of his short meaty arms, he had to fight the downward movement of his trousers, and his shirt showed under the waistcoat.

The concerto eventually became a standard work of the violin repertory, but there were skeptical voices in Germany and elsewhere about the enormous difficulties of the work. A famous quip had it that the Brahms Concerto was not for violin and orchestra, but against the violin.

The first movement, Allegro non troppo, in D major, in ¾ time, opens with a broad subject in the low register of the orchestra, establishing at once a Brahmsian mood of declarative elegance. A contrasting subject, dynamically tense and sharply syncopated, in D minor, is introduced and developed. After a very long orchestral introduction the violin solo comes in with a cadenzalike passage. It assumes the role of an exterior decorator (not unlike the style of Beethoven's Violin Concerto), beautifying the thematic developments in the orchestra with florid ornamentation. When it finally takes over the main theme, it does so in a grand manner, in the high treble, with double stops. A cozy waltzlike theme introduces the warm environment of Viennese gemütlichkeit. The recapitulation is maintained in vigorous tones. There is a formidable cadenza, composed by Joachim for the first performance, and the movement comes to a satisfying close.

The second movement, Adagio, in F major, in $\frac{2}{4}$ time, is bucolic. The oboe announces an elegiac subject. The violin solo elaborates the theme in countless variations. There is a contrasting middle section, and the pastoral mood returns for a soft ending. The Finale: Allegro giocoso ma non troppo vivace, is a rondo with melodic material suggesting a festive Gypsy tune. There is a constant interplay between the soloist and orchestra; the solo part here reaches the height of virtuosity. It provides a fitting ending to a nobly conceived but mundanely effective work.

Academic Festival Overture, *Op. 80 (1880)*

There is no other composer to whom the title of doctor would apply as perfectly as to Brahms. But he had to wait for his doctor's degree until his fame made it imperative for a German university to award him an honorary title. It was the University of Breslau that gave Brahms the honorary doctoral degree on March 11, 1879, and it is quite certain that far from adding to Brahms's stature by this honor, the Breslau University added to its own academic standing by its act.

The Latin wording of the degree described Brahms as "Artis musicae severioris in Germania nunc princeps." The translation is best made from the last word to the first to render the Latin word order more intelligible: "The first now in Germany in serious musical art." The word "severioris" literally means "more severe, stronger," the inference being that Brahms was the greatest German composer in the severe polyphonic style. Some critics belonging to Wagner's circle discerned in this work an implied condemnation of opera. Brahms never wrote any works for the stage, and the phrasing of the degree seemed to recommend his abstention from the less "severe" art of the theater.

The Breslau University faculty made it plain to Brahms that, in lieu of a doctoral thesis, they expected from him a "doctoral symphony" or, at the very least, a festive song. Brahms replied with professorial humor that he would be glad to come to Breslau and to take part in a doctoral banquet and some ninepin games. Breslau University finally got a musical doctoral thesis from Brahms: the *Academic Festival Overture*, Op. 80. Some of Breslau's professors thought the title was too dry and academic, and suggested *Viadrina*, which was the Latinized name of Breslau University, with reference to the river Oder (in Latin, *Viadua*), on which Breslau is situated. But Brahms decided to stick to the original name.

He spoke of the overture as a "potpourri on students' songs à la Suppé," but then he was notoriously irreverent to his own music. Max Kalbeck, Brahms's Boswell, whose four- volume biography of the master sets all records for minuteness and detail, finds in the *Academic Festival Overture* more than a token of appreciation for an honor. He believes it is an ode to the spirit of freedom, comradeship, and joy of living of the old German universities. He finds in the opening theme of the overture a double reminiscence of the Rákóczy March (the Hungarian "Marseillaise" of 1848) and the Paris Entrance March of 1813, symbolizing the emergence of the spirit of liberation from the armies of military conquest and from the oppressive reaction in post-Napoleonic Europe. The concluding song, "Gaudeamus Igitur," was indeed a symbol of students' rebellion against the police surveillance in German universities.

Four student songs are used in the *Academic Festival Overture*, apart from original thematic material. The first song, "Wir hatten gebauet ein stattliches Haus" ("We had built a stately house"), makes its appearance, after a long drumroll, in the brass, softly, as if from afar. This theme is in the key of C major, suggesting the famous horn theme of the First Symphony, which is also in C major. The second song is "Der Landesvater," in the key of E major. If the C-minor opening of the overture is regarded as the first theme, and the C-major song as the second theme, then "Der Landesvater" may be construed as a second movement, an Andante. The third movement in all of Brahms's four symphonies is a Viennese scherzo. In the *Academic Festival Overture*, the scherzo effect is provided by the "Fuchslied" ("Fox Song"), introduced, appropriately enough, by the laughing bassoons. This song is a hazing song for a freshman, who is asked impertinent questions about his family, and then is given a pipe too strong for a freshman's lungs. It is in quick polka time; it is bandied about from the bassoons to the oboes, from the basses to the flutes, from the violins to the brass, and further appears in various combinations of these instruments, until it is finally sounded by the whole orchestra. If the symphonic interpretation of the overture is valid, then the concluding song, "Gaudeamus Igitur," is the finale. This finale parallels the coda of Beethoven's Fifth Symphony, with which it has the key, C major, in common.

The orchestration of the *Academic Festival Overture* is interesting. Brahms accords in it more place to percussion instruments than in any of his other symphonic works, and adds metal sonorities of the cymbals and the triangle which are somehow alien to the accepted picture of Brahms as the greatest composer in the "severe type of musical art." But then, Brahms's intention was not to justify his doctorate, but rather to assert his consanguinity with the German student body, with a perceptible undertone of self-mockery.

Brahms went to Breslau to conduct the overture himself, and the first performance took place at the university on January 4, 1881. Other performances followed immediately, and very soon, the *Academic Festival Overture* became an orchestral favorite the world over. The *Overture* may not be the revelation of Brahms at his greatest, but it is an expression of his less solemn and, paradoxically, less professorial self.

OTHER WORKS
Intermezzos for Piano (1871–78)

Brahms used to write piano pieces in batches, several at a time. In writing these pieces, he often was influenced by the anticipated opinion of his two women friends, both eminent pianists, Clara Schumann and Elisabeth von Herzogenberg. Clara Schumann was seventy-four years old at the time Brahms sent her his last batch of Four Piano Pieces, Op. 119.

The Intermezzo Op. 76, no. 3, is one of the shortest pieces Brahms ever wrote. It is in A-flat major, and comprises only thirty bars. There are two musical subjects, alternating in simple succession, without a trace of development: a, b, a, b. The first subject is characteristically syncopated; the second is in gently moving triplets. Huneker describes this intermezzo in his impressionistic language as a "tender wreath of moonbeams and love." Edwin Evans all but gives up the task of analysis: "Too ethereal for description in the terms of every-day employment." But he does comment upon the form: "Notwithstanding its shortness, it is divided into two portions, which are practically a repeat of one another. But the repetition only seems to respond to the listener's longing to hear the lovely strain again, and in doing so to make it even more charming than before."

The Intermezzo Op. 76, no. 4, is remarkable for the use Brahms makes of tonality. The key signature is in two flats, and the opening bar is the dominant seventh of B-flat major. But having implied the principal key by aural harmony and visual time signature, Brahms shuns the tonic in a most deliberate manner. He veers momentarily toward G minor, in a deceptive cadence, as it were, and then proceeds enharmonically to remote keys, farther and farther away from the tonic. It is only in the second section that the tonic makes its appearance in the pedal, and even then as the bass of the minor subdominant. Clear and unadulterated B-flat major appears for the first time only in the last two bars. This deceptive procedure is characteristic of Brahms; other instances of similar avoidance of the tonic are found in the second movement of the First Clarinet Sonata, where the tonic triad does not appear until the twenty-second bar, and in the Second Rhapsody for Piano, Op. 79, in which the principal key of G minor does not appear until the eleventh bar. The Intermezzo Op. 76, no. 4, is thus the extreme instance of Brahms's tonofugal idiosyncrasy, for here the tonic triad is not reached until the very last bars.

The Intermezzo Op. 116, no. 4, is an adagio in the clearly expressed key of E major. The first section is marked by a wavy motion in triplets on the first beat. This rhythmic accentuation is intensified in the second section, where the movement is in sixteenth notes. But the upbeat is always free from the accentuating waves. The piece is thus a study in acceleration and retardation, secured not by the actual increase and decrease of tempo, but by the quicker rate of motion in a given metrical unit. Harmonically and melodically, the important effect is that of the upward resolution of the augmented triad in the opening phrase.

The Intermezzo Op. 118, no. 6, is in E-flat minor. In this intermezzo Brahms delights in long appoggiaturas, projected upon the harmony notes at close range, so that a sensation of acute discord is created. Brahms applied this method consciously. Writing to Clara Schumann about another piece similarly constructed (Intermezzo in B Minor, Op. 119, no. 1), he confesses: "It teems with discord. These may be all right and quite explicable, but you may not perhaps like them," and adds with a touch of Brahmsian humor, "and if so, I might wish that they were less right and more pleasing to you." Apart from the conscious use of discord, the Intermezzo in E-flat Minor is extremely pure in its form, which is ternary. The middle section is in the relative key of G-flat minor, and is distinguished by quick pulsating rhythms, in thirty-second notes. Edwin Evans, in his extraordinary handbooks to Brahms's complete works, comprising altogether 1,581 pages in four volumes, has this to say about this intermezzo: "This is a movement portraying the utmost grief and passion.... There is no bending of the form to his will; nothing (except maybe a highly refined pianism) to point particularly to Brahms." The pianism is indeed quite extraordinary, almost acrobatic, in that Brahms makes the left hand cross the right in light arpeggios, at times in the identical register, to the point of collision and coincidence.

The Intermezzo Op. 119, no. 2, is another instance of Brahms's tonofugal harmony. Ostensibly the piece is in E minor, with a middle section in E major. But the E-minor triad never appears at all, and when the final cadence seems to lead to the tonic, it is the major tonic of the middle section that provides the resolution. The movement is toccata-like with both hands alternating in quick groups of two notes. The second section is, rather unexpectedly, a Viennese waltz, as charming as any by Brahms. The concluding section is almost an exact repetition of the first, and the ending is in E major.

Three Rhapsodies for Piano—Nos. 1 and 2, Op. 79 (1880); No. 3, Op. 119 (1892)

On a concert tour, Brahms stopped at Leipzig one day in 1879, and called on his dear friends, the von Herzogenbergs, to play for them his two newly composed piano pieces. Heinrich von Herzogenberg was a plodding composer of sorts, but his wife, Elisabeth, was an excellent and intelligent pianist, the type of German woman of taste that inspires the great among German men of genius. Brahms maintained with her an epistolary *amitié amoureuse* typical of his relations with women.

The original titles of the two Op. 79 pieces were Capriccio: Presto agitato and Capriccio: Molto passionato. Brahms decided to rename them, and asked Frau von Herzogenberg what she thought of "rhapsody" for a title. He also added playfully that he could not possibly improve on the dedication, which was made to her. She replied, after an outburst of gratitude and admiration, that she felt the simpler title Klavierstücke (Piano Pieces), would suit the pieces better, and that the music did not conform to the general idea of a rhapsody, but she quickly admitted that "rhapsody" was the best of the descriptive titles.

"This B-minor Rhapsody," James Huneker wrote in the preface to the selected edition of Brahms's piano works, "sounds as if its composer were trying to make a harsh pragmatic statement; in it there is more intellectual acrimoniousness than rhapsody. . . . Acrid as the patina on antique metal, this first rhapsody is for the head rather than for the heart." This judgment, coinciding in part with that of Frau von Herzogenberg, is puzzling: the musical analysis would tend to show that the First Rhapsody is much more "human" than the second. It is in perfect three-part form; the main section, which is repeated in full in the third part of the piece, is tonally clear, and the modulations take place only after the fundamental key is established. There is a touch of humor in the lyric D-minor phrase, which is a quotation from Grieg's theme in "The Death of Ase" from the *Peer Gynt* Suite, No. 1. Brahms no doubt intended it as an amortization of the melody loan Grieg had made for his Piano Concerto from Brahms's E-flat Minor Scherzo, Op. 4.

Huneker liked the Second Rhapsody as much as he disliked the first: "A wonderful, glorious, bracing tone-picture, in which Brahms, the philosopher, burns the boats of his old age and becomes for the time a youthful Faust in search of a sensation. A hurricane of emotion that is barely stilled at the end, this Rhapsody reminds me of the bardic recital of some old border ballad. . . . It is an epic in miniature." In the same letter in which Elisabeth von Herzogenberg suggested the title Klavierstücke, she gave a vivid account of a "G-minor night," which she spent trying to recall the music of Brahms's Second Rhapsody before she received the manuscript: "a night like that is terrible to live through, and the Almighty, if he is at all musical, should show us mercy. Scraps of the glorious music pursue you, and you vainly try to put them together. Then suddenly, a phrase breaks through the fog, then another.... In despair, you count one hundred to fall asleep, but sleep eludes you." Indeed, the Second Rhapsody is hard to remember from a single hearing: in fact, the key of the "G-minor night" does not appear until the eleventh bar and, even then, only as the minor subdominant of the key of D major.

The last rhapsody is the fourth piece of the Four Piano Pieces, Op. 119, and is the last original piano piece that Brahms composed. He wrote arrangements and piano exercises, but the inspiration for the piano as a medium of Romantic self-expression was gone. He composed this last rhapsody in 1892, the year of the death of Frau Elisabeth von Herzogenberg.

Sonata for Piano and Clarinet (or Viola) No. 1 in F Minor, Op. 120, No. 1 (1894)

The register of the clarinet practically coincides with that of the viola. The lowest note of the viola is C, an octave below the middle C, and the lowest note of the clarinet in B flat for which Brahms's sonatas are written is D. It is, therefore, possible to play on the viola a part written for the clarinet. But in discussing Brahms's sonatas for viola and piano it should not be forgotten that they were originally intended for the clarinet, and that the viola was a second thought, and is indicated on the title page in parentheses.

Brahms composed the two Clarinet Sonatas, Op. 120, in the summer of 1894 at Ischl. He gave the first performance of the sonatas in Vienna on January 7, 1895, playing the piano part. He was sixty-one years old and at the height of his fame. With his famous beard, he looked like a venerable professor, or a celebrated artist, but these sonatas were to be his last important instrumental works: he died in Vienna on April 3, 1897. Despite Brahms's absolute recognition in the musical world, the two clarinet sonatas were not accepted by the critics with uniform kindness. Otto Floersheim wrote after the Berlin performance in October 1895:

> The compositions themselves were grievously disappointing, at least for those who anticipated much of anything from the Johannes Brahms of today. Brahms is completely *ausgeschrieben*; these two sonatas prove it beyond the shadow of a doubt. The first one in F minor is the less unimportant of the two, and is in four movements, of which the slow one in A flat is the most, and the first movement the least disappointing.

The English critics were much more deferential to the great Brahms. When the clarinet sonatas were performed in London in June, 1895, the reviewer of the *London Atheneum* wrote:

> With regard to the merits of the work, definite judgment must be reserved, for Brahms does not write carelessly and should not be hastily criticized. But there need be no hesitation in saying that the sonatas are well worthy of his reputation as the most gifted representative of classical music. They are noteworthy for freshness and geniality, and do not in the least smell of the lamp.

The clarinet sonatas were given the first American performance in Boston by Arthur Foote, the American composer, and Pourtau, the clarinetist of the Boston Symphony Orchestra, on November 25, 1895. Wrote Philip Hale in the *Boston Journal*, referring retrospectively to the Leipzig performance of January 27, 1895:

> Dr. Johannes Brahms, pianist—and what a pianist! one of ten thumbs— appeared with the clarinetist, Richard Mühlfeld of Meiningen, at a chamber concert in the Gewandhaus, Leipzig, and they then played two new sonatas for clarinet and piano. Neither of the sonatas made much of an impression, and in the conventional notices of the concert, yawns were heard between the lines.

Then turning to the occasion, Hale went on:

> The first movement is priggish; it is entitled passionate, but here Brahms's imagination dropped. The second movement has more color, and is at least suggestive of the mood. The third movement promises something at first,

but after a few measures, it is nothing but notes, notes, notes. The finale is drearily academic. What an absurd theme is that given first to the clarinet! Not even Mr. Pourtau could make anything out of the gurgle, gurgle. It is idle now to inquire into the cause of Brahms's late passion for the clarinet, or to ask whether the upper tones of this instrument blend readily with the tones of a piano, even when the pianist has an agreeable touch. It is only necessary to regret that in this sonata Brahms gives an example of premature senility.

Speaking analytically, the two Sonatas for Clarinet (or viola), Op. 120, are representative of Brahms's last period, which includes the Fourth Symphony and the intermezzos and rhapsodies for piano. Brahms's harmonic style is here characterized by a spirit of free modulation. The First Clarinet Sonata gives many instances of this modulatory technique. The first movement, Allegro appassionato, in ⅜ time, is in the key of the sonata, F minor, but almost immediately a G flat is introduced, which confutes the impression of the principal key. However, F minor is explicitly shown in the first subject. In the development section there are instantaneous shifts toward the sharp keys, and the return to the principal key is effected by enharmonic change. This procedure of clockwise modulation over the entire cycle of scales when the principal key is in flats, as in this movement, and the converse procedure by modulating counterclockwise when the principal key is in sharps as in the Fourth Symphony, is characteristic of Brahms's harmonic technique.

PETER ILYICH TCHAIKOVSKY
(1840–1893)
Poet of Cheerful Melancholy

The world of Peter Ilyich Tchaikovsky was confined and compressed within himself, and the music that he wrote was an explosive complaint that somehow gave him the sense of full life and even exaltation. He composed an enormous amount of music in a great variety of forms, and yet every work seemed to come to him as a trial.

An indefatigable correspondent, he poured out his feelings in his letters with extraordinary frankness. He also gave an insight into his philosophy of work. "The worst is to yield to the reluctance to work," he wrote. "I have set myself a rule to force myself to accomplish something every morning until I achieve a favorable frame of mind for work."

And again:

A true artist cannot sit idly on the pretext that he is not inclined to work. If one waits for an inclination, it is easy to lapse into laziness and atrophy. One must be patient and have faith that inspiration will surely come. This phenomenon happened to me this very morning. Had I succumbed to my lack of desire for work, I would not have accomplished anything. But faith and patience never abandoned me, and I became possessed with this incomprehensible fire of inspiration, which comes no one knows whence, and thanks to which I know in advance that everything I write today will have the faculty of penetrating the heart and leaving a lasting impression. I have learned how to conquer myself.

He adds an interesting observation on Russian composers at large: "I am happy to say that I do not follow in the footsteps of my Russian colleagues who, lacking self-confidence and tenacity, prefer to take a rest and to put off their work at the slightest provocation."

The struggle with himself was the principal motive of Tchaikovsky's music. He was obsessed with the idea of inexorable fate. One of his earliest symphonic works is entitled *Fatum* (fate). The theme of fate permeates his Fourth Symphony, his Fifth, and his Sixth, the *Pathétique*. To Tchaikovsky, happy times were always in the past, misery in the present, with Fatum in the future. But if despair is the rule of the world and of art, then what is the source of the gay dances and sparkling scherzos in Tchaikovsky's symphonies? Even in the *Pathétique*, which ends on a tone of depression, in the lowest reaches of the instrumental range, in pianissississimo (pppp), there is a scherzo full of infectious exhilaration and rhythmic fire.

If we were to compile a table of musical statistics, then Tchaikovsky's music would show a mournful mood, as exemplified by a decisive preponderance of minor modes and drooping cadences, with the main melodic line constantly falling in symmetric sequences. The overture to Tchaikovsky's opera *Eugene Onegin* contains perhaps the longest falling sequence of this nature in any musical composition, and of course the key is minor. But somehow Tchaikovsky's melancholy muse has brought artistic satisfaction, and hence happiness, to millions of people everywhere.

Tchaikovsky had many devoted friends, and he loved company, but he was afraid of strangers, and was particularly wary of admirers who thrust themselves at him with compliments that he detested. Once in Hamburg, when he was enjoying a happy anonymity, a Russian tourist sought him out, dispensing fulsome expressions of admiration. Tchaikovsky decided to leave town earlier than he expected, just because of this unwelcome encounter.

Among Tchaikovsky's intimates were his brothers, his sister and her family, some of his colleagues, his former pupils, and that extraordinary woman who played such a role in Tchaikovsky's life, Nadezhda von Meck. Tchaikovsky's correspondence with her began as a result of a commission that she asked him to accept, at a plainly exorbitant fee. In subsequent years she sent Tchaikovsky a regular and very generous subsidy, which enabled him to work and travel without financial worries. The relationship was strange. It was mutually agreed that they should never see each other face to face, but it appears from Madame von Meck's letters that she was not at all averse to a personal meeting. When they both happened to live in Florence at the same time, she even suggested that Tchaikovsky should visit her villa while she was absent. But Tchaikovsky's morbid fear of social involvements made him refuse all these advances, as gently as he could. "One should not see one's guardian angel in the flesh," he explained, and their correspondence continued by messenger across the city.

There are composers who address their creations to the world with deliberate intent, in quest of universal acceptance. They eliminate subjective elements as a price of coveted success. But as often as not they do not succeed, because communicative power cannot be adjusted. Tchaikovsky wrote music out of his full heart, even when he wrote pieces commissioned for a special purpose, such as his ballets. And his very personal art became cosmopolitan in its appeal. His first ballet, *Swan Lake*, demanded a combination of dance music in the Italian style prevalent in Russia at the time, with some elegiac qualities. The story, taken from a German folktale, was tragic, which gave Tchaikovsky an opportunity to write music in his favorite symphonic style. The theme of the swan, with its poignant minor cadence, is one of Tchaikovsky's simplest and yet most profound inspirations. But *Swan Lake* also abounds in wonderful waltzes and other dance episodes; the ballet of little swans, in the lightest instrumentation, is one of the most popular numbers in the score. Tchaikovsky wrote another ballet from the world of fairy tales, *The Sleeping Beauty*. And one of his most cheerful works, the children's ballet *The Nutcracker*, was written at the same time as his most tragic score, the *Pathétique*.

Symphony No. 4 in F Minor, Op. 36 (1877–78)

Tchaikovsky began the composition of his Fourth Symphony in Moscow in May 1877, and finished it in Italy during the season 1877–78. The composition of the symphony was interrupted by a tragic event in Tchaikovsky's life, his unnatural marriage. Some commentators explain the disparity of treatment between the dramatic opening and ostentatiously gay finale as paralleling Tchaikovsky's moods of dark gloom, when he determined to marry, and his relief when he was liberated from his marital bonds. However, it must be remembered that sketches of the symphony were made before the wedding ceremony, and that the rest of the work was devoted to details and orchestration without changes in the original conception.

The symphony is dedicated to Madame von Meck, although her name does not appear on the title page. The dedication merely reads, "To my beloved friend." In his letter to Madame von Meck of February 17, 1878, Tchaikovsky explained the introductory motive as the nucleus of the entire symphony, a Fatum, something less than inexorable fate, and more than an accident of misfortune. The only salvation from Fatum is the life of dreams, which is characterized by a livelier rhythmic motive of the first movement.

The second movement of the symphony is merely another phase of nostalgia and melancholy. It is full of reminiscences of the young days and the realization that life has passed. The third movement, a Scherzo, in which an extraordinary effect is achieved by strings playing pizzicato, is a reflection of capricious moods. "All of a sudden a group of tipsy moujiks appears in the picture, and there is a street song." (This description corresponds to the trio of the Scherzo.) "Then, somewhere far off, passes a military parade." (This refers to tempo primo, after the Trio, before the second appearance of the principal motive of the Scherzo.)

The finale of the symphony opens with a joyful theme, which is alternated with a theme of the Russian folk song "A Birch Tree Stood in the Meadow." The song is very old, and was first published in 1790 in the collection compiled by the Czech musician J. G. Pratsch. Tchaikovsky did not change either the melodic outline or the essential harmonization of the Pratsch version. He gave the description of the finale in these words: "If you find no reason for joy in yourself, look at others. Go to the people. See how they can make merry." But the theme of the Fatum intrudes again. The conclusion is a compromise: "Be gay with other people's joy. Life is tolerable after all." However, Tchaikovsky's program should not be accepted too literally. He wrote to Madame von Meck on the spur of the moment, but a month later, in a letter to Taneyev, he corrected himself: "My symphony is of course programmatic. But this program is such that it is utterly impossible to formulate it. It would arouse ridicule, and appear comical."

A mon meilleur ami

Fourth Symphony in F Minor, Op. 36

I

It is interesting to note the progress of Tchaikovsky's work on the symphony, which he reported in his letters to his brothers. He wrote to Anatol from Venice on December 15, 1877, "I slept very well, and from early morning set to work on the symphony." A few days later he wrote, "I am very much satisfied with the symphony. It is beyond doubt the best work I have written, but the progress is not without difficulty, particularly in the first movement." On December 23 he wrote to

Anatol, "I have finished today the most difficult part of my symphony, the first movement," and on the following day,

> My nerves have amazingly calmed down. I sleep very well, but every night, before going to bed, I drink beer or a couple of glasses of cognac. My appetite is as usual, that is, excellent. All this is thanks to the symphony, and also to the monotonous life in Venice and the absence of all distraction, which has enabled me to work so determinedly and assiduously. When I wrote my opera, I did not experience the sensation the symphony gives me. In the opera I write at random, reckoning that it may come off well, and then again it may not. But the symphony I write in full consciousness that this is a work quite out of the ordinary, and the most perfect in form of all my compositions.

On December 26 he informed Anatol: "I worked from morning to lunch, and from lunch to dinner time without respite, and only took a walk in between. I have almost finished the third movement of the symphony." On the next day he reported again: "Finished the Scherzo. Feel very tired." Finally, writing to Anatol from San Remo on January 7, 1878, he stated: "Yesterday and today I worked without getting up, and finished my beloved symphony. My health is perfect. I feel fine."

The first performance of the symphony took place in Moscow on February 22, 1878. Nikolai Rubinstein, the brother of Anton, conducted. Tchaikovsky was in Florence at the time, but Madame von Meck was present at the performance, and wrote Tchaikovsky enthusiastically about it. On November 25, 1878, the Czech conductor and composer Eduard Nápravník conducted the symphony in St. Petersburg. Modest Tchaikovsky described this performance in a letter to his brother:

> If it is at all possible that a symphonic work should produce a furor, then your symphony did it. After the first movement the applause was moderate, about to the extent of applause after the first movement of a Beethoven or Schumann symphony. After the second movement there was much more acclaim. Nápravník was compelled to acknowledge it by bowing. After the Scherzo there were outcries in fortissimo, stamping of feet, and demands for an encore. Nápravník bowed several times, but the noise would not subside, until he finally lifted his conducting scepter; then there was a silence, which yielded to your pizzicatos. After that there was more shouting, recalls, bows, etc. The concluding chords of the Finale were accompanied by handclapping, shouting, and stamping of the feet. Here I flew out of the hall like a bomb, and in fifteen minutes I was here in my study, with a pen in my hands.

When the Fourth Symphony was produced in Berlin in 1897, already after Tchaikovsky's death, the Berlin critics were uncommonly caustic. The *Kleines Journal* wrote: "Tchaikovsky's symphony is a tittle-tattle in motley orchestration, the contents of which look astonishing enough in the classical form.... I found the whole very boring. The external orchestral splendor could not conceal the inner bareness of the work. The tomfooleries of the Russian composer irritated me.... The chaotic brass and the abuse of the kettledrums drove me away." The *Berliner Tageblatt* was equally condemnatory:

Even if we ignore the traditions of our masters, there should be a limit if the word "symphony" is to have any meaning at all.... Tchaikovsky substitutes for a musical idea phrases, sometimes of the most formidable kind. Still worse are his melodies when they appear at all clearly. There were themes which might be pleasant enough in the operetta theater, but which under the circumstances affected me repulsively, so much more so because their contrapuntal treatment sought to lend them the false glamour of nobleness. Most disagreeable was also the obstinate adherence to repeated rhythmic figures, which seem to persecute the composer like fixed ideas. The same semi-Asiatic taste is shown in the instrumentation, which changed from distressing dullness to cheap gaudiness.

In America the Fourth Symphony was produced by Walter Damrosch, the pioneer conductor who introduced many great works to the American public. The first performance took place in New York City on the Friday "public rehearsal," January 31, 1890. The *New York Evening Post* wrote interestingly on the occasion:

The Fourth Tchaikovsky Symphony proved to be one of the most thoroughly Russian, i.e., semi-barbaric, compositions ever heard in this city. The keynote of the whole work is struck by the Rienzian blare of brass, which opens it, and which recurs at intervals. There is an extraordinary variety in the orchestral colors, some of which are decidedly too loud for a symphony. If Tchaikovsky had called his symphony "A Sleigh Ride Through Siberia," no one would have found this title inappropriate.

The reviewer of the *Musical Courier* commented:

Tchaikovsky's symphony was in parts a disappointment. One vainly sought for coherency or homogeneousness; indeed the work might better be labeled a suite, for all the organic variety appreciable in the four movements.... In the last movement the composer's Calmuck blood got the better of him, and slaughter, dire and bloody, swept across the storm-driven score. Then, as if to do penance for his musical sins, he winds up the work with a weak and vapid choral, in which musical platitudes abound.

At the first Boston performance, on November 27, 1896, the *Boston Globe* remarked: "At times the musical tumult is deafening and sound inharmonious. The kettledrums are liberally woven into the score, and there are musical combinations of an eccentric nature in abundance."

As late as 1904, Tchaikovsky's Fourth Symphony was still debatable. Louis C. Elson, reviewing a performance by the Boston Symphony Orchestra in the *Boston Evening Transcript* of March 28, 1904, called the symphony "labored and grandiloquent."

As is often the case with great composers and great works, they start out in the estimation of the official musical judges as barbaric and eccentric, and only later are universally accepted. When the point of saturation is reached, there is a feeling of surfeit, and the music is relegated to summer concerts for the large public. Then, after a pause of a decade or two, there is a rediscovery. In Russia Tchaikovsky was in decline after the Revolution, as a representative of gloomy defeatist moods, only to come back with a vengeance as the protagonist of the Internationale of universal human emotion. In the Anglo-Saxon countries, Tchaikovsky is a perennial companion whose glory has never been dimmed with the public. But it is only recently that serious composers of England and America have discovered that Tchaikovsky was not only a neurotic sentimentalist, but also a classic of Romantic emotionalism.

Manfred *Symphony, Op. 58 (1885)*

The *Manfred* Symphony was first performed in Moscow on March 23, 1886. Tchaikovsky wrote to his benefactress and epistolary friend Madame von Meck: "I believe that Manfred is my best composition." But Tchaikovsky expressed the same opinion about several of his other works, notably about the *Pathétique* Symphony. As it happened, *Manfred* never matched his other symphonic scores in musical significance or in public acclaim.

The subject of *Manfred* was inspired by the famous mystical poem by Lord Byron, who exercised tremendous influence on Russian poets and musicians. Tchaikovsky provided the following résumé of Byron's poem:

> Manfred wanders in the Alps. Beset by the fateful problems of human existence, tormented by the burning feeling of hopelessness and by memories of his hideous past, he suffers cruel distress. He seeks solace in the mysteries of magic and communication with the powerful force of Hell. But nothing can give him [the] oblivion he seeks in vain. The memory of dead Astarte, whom he passionately loved, gnaws at his heart. There are no limits, there is no end to Manfred's infinite despair.

Manfred is described as a symphony in four tableaux, but it is not ordinarily included in the catalogue of Tchaikovsky's symphonies. Like most of Tchaikovsky's programmatic works, *Manfred* is set in a minor key. The first movement consists of several episodes, clearly demarcated by protracted pauses. The first episode, lento lugubre, portrays Manfred with a strong leading motive in fortissimo; the second, moderato con moto, provides a moment of tranquillity; the third, andante, evokes memories of Astarte, bringing new tortures to Manfred's soul. The initial theme is invoked again. The movement concludes with spasmodic chords of ultimate despondency.

The second movement, Vivace con spirito, is a scherzo. While wandering in the mountains Manfred summons the fairy of the Alps, who appears in the rainbow of a waterfall; the music sparkles in Tchaikovsky's colorful instrumentation. The third movement, Andante con moto, set in the pastoral time signature of §, pictures the bucolic scene of rural life. The shepherd's pipe is heard in the woodwinds. Gradually a dancing spirit enters the music, and a climax is reached through continuous rhythmic escalation. A somber note is struck when Manfred makes his appearance. But the sound of the church bell brings about a mood of peace. The movement ends in diminutive pianississississimo.

The fourth and last movement, Allegro con fuoco, illustrates the orgiastic ritual of the subterranean world. Manfred enters during a bacchanal; this moment is signaled by the appearance of his leading motive. The infernal spirits try to expel him. An energetic fugato reflects the agitation provoked by Manfred's intrusion. Undeterred, he implores the rulers of hell to summon Astarte. She appears and promises to end Manfred's torments. A protracted harp cadenza suggests a celestial intervention. A solemn chorale, based on Manfred's motive, is heard, symbolizing the attempt of reconciling Manfred to the Church. There is a contrapuntal insertion of the medieval Doomsday chant, Dies irae. Manfred receives absolution and dies in peace.

Symphony No. 5 in E Minor, Op. 64 (1888)

In one of his notebooks, Tchaikovsky jotted down his ideas for the Fifth Symphony: "Introduction: Complete submission to Fate or, what is the same, to the inexorable judgment of Providence. Allegro: Doubts, laments, reproaches to X.X.X." Who was "X.X.X." to whom Tchaikovsky addressed his complaints? No biographer would venture a guess. "Should I perhaps throw myself into the arms of Faith?" Tchaikovsky asks. "A ray of light?" he notes in the sketches for the second movement of the Fifth Symphony, and he answers his query on the same page, in the bass part: "No, there is no hope."

All Tchaikovsky's symphonies, except the little-known Third Symphony, are set in minor keys, a characteristic trait for the melancholy composer. The Fifth Symphony is in E minor, in four movements. The first, Andante, in 𝄴 time, states the "fate motive" in the low register. The introduction is followed, after a pause, by allegro con anima, the theme of complaints and reproaches, in 𝄿 time. Chordal explosions—implosions would be a more fitting word—interrupt the progress of thematic development. The harmonic sequences are plagal, conveying the sense of obliquity and indecision. A "ray of light" shines through in a candid major tonality, but it is immediately polarized by rhythmic interference in its melodic phase, resulting in a disquieting syncopation, even though the tempo is marked molto più tranquillo.

The second movement, Andante cantabile con alcuna licenza, in D major, in 𝄵 time, sings out lyrically. It is contrasted by a bright theme in F-sharp major, which the eminent British musicologist Sir Donald Francis Tovey calls "the chief topic of the most impassioned climaxes in this movement." It comes therefore as a shock to find, on Tchaikovsky's own authority, that he used in this melody the street cry of a Moscow vendor of salami and sausages. Old Russians may still recall the familiar singsong: "Kol-ba-a-saaaa... Soo-see-ski..." Tchaikovsky marks the tune dolce espressivo. The idyll is disrupted by the new intrusion of Fatum. The salami-sausage theme is engulfed in the stream of ominous brass, and with it are swept away all tentative smiles and all gladness of heart.

The third movement, Allegro moderato, in A major, is a waltz, an unusual symphonic ingredient. But Tchaikovsky felt that a waltz was no less entitled to social recognition in a symphony than the minuet, which is a dance of the same measure. Tchaikovsky's waltz, of course, is not of the salon variety, but a melodic invention which is soon wrapped up in ingenious melodic and rhythmic variations.

The finale opens solemnly in an andante maestoso. The key is E major, a proper cyclic counterpart to the initial E minor of the first movement. It is followed by an Allegro vivace, containing four distinct themes, built in sonata form. The oppressive pessimism of the concept of Fatum is here seemingly dispelled by the marchlike tones of the music. But the melodic and rhythmic configuration of the march is the ubiquitous Fatum motive. A titanic struggle is waged in the concluding pages of the symphony. Whether humanity wins against the blind force of destiny remains a question for philosophical analysts to settle.

Symphony No. 6 in B Minor, Op. 74 (Pathétique) *(1893)*

Tchaikovsky, the "melancholy genius" of Russian music, was haunted in his life and in his work by the inexorable specter of fate. It is of psychological significance that five of Tchaikovsky's six symphonies are set in minor keys, traditionally associated with the feeling of sadness. For students of musical morphology, it may be of interest that the nuclei of the opening themes of the last three symphonies are all confined within the somber interval of the minor third. In his original outline of the work that was to become the *Pathétique*, Tchaikovsky planned to limn in tones the entire course of human life. "The first movement," he wrote, "is all in upswing,

Sixth Symphony in B Minor
("Pathétique"), Op. 74

I

self-assurance, action; the second portrays love; the third is disappointment; the finale is Death, ultimate dissolution." Other jottings in Tchaikovsky's notebook relating to the planned symphony are typical: "This motive asks the questions Why, What for, For what reason?"

He confided to his favorite nephew Bob Davidov, to whom the *Pathétique* was eventually dedicated:

> The program of my symphony shall remain an enigma to all. It is very subjective, and while composing it in my mind during my trip to Odessa I often wept bitterly. On my return home I set to work with such determination that in barely four days I had the first movement completely done. Half of the third movement was also finished. There will be much that is novel in the form. For instance, the finale will be not a loud Allegro, but a long Adagio.

Bob Davidov did not respond to his uncle's impassioned communications, and Tchaikovsky voiced his displeasure: "I intended to dedicate my new symphony to you, but now I must reconsider, to punish you for not writing for such a long time. But still I believe it is my best work, and I love it more than any of my musical children." Tchaikovsky did not carry out his threat; the score bears Davidov's name in the dedication.

The veil over the "enigma" of the *Pathétique* is lifted in a passage in the first movement, when suddenly, like a memento mori, the trombones intone the mournful chant from the Russian Mass for the Dead, "Let him rest in peace with the Saints." Was it a premonition of his own death? But Tchaikovsky was only fifty-three in 1893 when the Pathétique was completed, although he looked much older. (He was very much disturbed when an American reporter described his age as about sixty during his concert tour in the United States in 1891.) Professionally, socially, and musically, he was very active; in the summer of the fateful year 1893 he traveled to England to receive a doctor's degree in music at Cambridge University; a photograph taken of him in cape and gown shows a cheerful countenance.

Tchaikovsky asked his friend, the conductor Vasili Safonov, to play over the symphony with his orchestral class at the Moscow Conservatory in order to check on details and on the accuracy of copy. Apparently, the report was satisfactory, and Tchaikovsky went to St. Petersburg to conduct the first performance of the work. The premiere took place on October 28, 1893. The title, *Pathétique*, was suggested to him after the performance by his brother and biographer Modest, and Tchaikovsky accepted it at once.

What happened immediately after the performance was the essence of tragedy. A cholera epidemic was raging in St. Petersburg at the time. Tchaikovsky's mother had died of the disease. Apparently, Tchaikovsky incautiously drank a glass of unboiled water; the dread symptoms of the infection set in. Within a few days, Tchaikovsky was dead. Rumors spread almost at once that Tchaikovsky deliberately exposed himself to contamination. The "enigma" of the *Pathétique* became clear to morbidly romantic Russians; the "memento mori" of the trombones, the victory of death in the finale, all this must have presaged Tchaikovsky's determination to kill himself. Once before, he had defied Fatum when he walked into the chilly Moskva River with the intention of catching a deathly cold.

The opening adagio of the *Pathétique* sets a funereal mood. After a moment of eloquent silence, the principal theme becomes the nucleus of a moving musical particle in Allegro non troppo. The music plumbs the depths and scales the heights of Romantic lamentation. It is in the process of development that the chant from the Russian Mass for the Dead is heard. Then a contrasting lyric theme appears, letting a ray of sunlight enter the dark landscape. Despite the profound emotional turmoil of the music, Tchaikovsky observes the conventions of sonata form; the two contrasting themes are properly developed; there is an abundance of secondary motives. The recapitulation is opulent in its sonorities.

The second movement, Allegro con grazia, is in ⅝ time, unprecedented in symphonic annals, which moved the ineffable Vienna critic Eduard Hanslick to say that "it upsets both the listener and the player," and to suggest that Tchaikovsky could, were be not so perverse, have arranged it "without the slightest inconvenience" in ⅜ time by merely adding a beat to each bar and changing quarter notes to eighth notes. To Russians, on the other hand, there is nothing unnatural in ⅝ time, for it often occurs in Russian folk songs. If the second movement is a scherzoid waltz in quintuple time, the third, Allegro molto vivace, is a scherzo-march in tarantella time. The march is built on a progression of perfect fourths, a procedure not fully developed until the twentieth century. Here Tchaikovsky appears as a precursor of modern devices.

The finale, Adagio lamentoso, opens with a remarkable trompe l'oreille, in which the pathos-laden melody is divided in cross-counterpoint between the violins, with the lower strings similarly arranged. The entire movement is a continuous cry of despair, a musical portrait of Tchaikovsky sobbing on the train while thinking of the music to come. The melodies are in a state of perpetual fall along the notes of the principal scale of B minor, a key which in Romantic music is associated with sorrow and death. An ominous sound of the tam-tam enhances the mood of depression. In the coda the descending violins stop as if asphyxiated, one note short of the dominant, and the low wind instruments have to supply the missing F sharp below the violin range.

Piano Concerto No. 1 in B-flat Minor, Op. 23 (1875)

Tchaikovsky's First Piano Concerto had its world premiere not in Russia, not in any European country, but in Boston, Massachusetts! An extraordinary displacement, which occurred as a result of an equally extraordinary rebuke Tchaikovsky received from the director of the Moscow Conservatory, Nikolai Rubinstein, brother of the director of the St. Petersburg Conservatory, Anton Rubinstein.

Tchaikovsky describes the circumstances in a highly emotional letter to his financial benefactress, Nadezhda von Meck. "In December 1874 I composed a piano concerto," he wrote.

> Since I am not a pianist, I intended to consult a professional virtuoso for advice about technical details, pianistic writing, awkward passages, etc. An inner voice warned me against approaching Nikolai Rubinstein, as a judge of the purely mechanical aspect of my concerto, for I suspected that he would take an opportunity to show off his egotistical side. But he is the best pianist in Moscow, and I knew that he would have been deeply offended had I gone to someone else for advice. So I asked him to go over the concerto with me and give me advice regarding the piano part. It was on Christmas Eve of 1874. We both were invited to a Christmas party, and Rubinstein suggested to use the time before the evening to play over the concerto in a classroom of the Moscow Conservatory. I came with my

manuscript, sat at the piano and played the first movement. There was no response whatsoever on Rubinstein's part, not a single word. You cannot imagine the sense of intolerable foolishness when a person serves to a friend a dish of his own concoction, and the other eats it without saying a word!

Rubinstein's eloquent silence was significant. He seemed to be saying: "My good friend, how can I discuss details when the very essence of your music is repugnant to me?" I armed myself with patience and played the work to the end. Again silence. I rose and asked: "Well, what do you think?" Then Rubinstein let loose a torrent of words, at first in a soft tone of voice, but gradually assuming the thundering tones of Jove. My concerto, he said, was absolutely worthless, impossible to play; technical passages were trite, clumsy, and so awkward that they could not be fixed. Musically, too, my concerto was poor, banal, and furthermore borrowed from this or that work by someone else. There were perhaps two or three pages that could be salvaged, he went on, but the rest must be either discarded entirely or completely revised. A stranger happening to step in by chance would think that I am some sort of maniac, an incompetent and uneducated scribbler who annoys a famous musician with his trashy productions.

I felt stunned and insulted. I left the room in silence and went upstairs, unable to utter a word from excitement and anger. Rubinstein followed me and, noticing my distress, called me to another room. Then he reiterated his opinion that my concerto was impossible to play, and indicated numerous places which required radical alterations. He added that if I revised my concerto according to his requirements by a certain date, he would give me the honor of performing it at one of his concerts. To this I replied: "I will not change a single note and will have the work published as it stands now." And this is exactly what I did.

The original dedication of the concerto was to Rubinstein, but after the rebuke Tchaikovsky received from him, he rededicated it to the German pianist and conductor Hans von Bülow, who had previously shown interest in having Tchaikovsky's music performed. Von Bülow acknowledged the receipt of Tchaikovsky's manuscript and wrote him warmly about the high quality of the music. But apparently he hesitated to present it before the classically minded audiences in Germany. He was making an American tour, and took this opportunity to try out the new work on Americans, who might not be as sensitive as the Germans. And so it came to pass that on October 25, 1875, von Bülow played the world premiere of Tchaikovsky's famous concerto with a pickup orchestra in Boston.

But the Bostonians, nurtured on German music, did not take too kindly to Tchaikovsky's "Asiatic" melodies and wild rhythms. The cultured *Boston Evening Transcript*, read by all proper Bostonians, opined: "This elaborate work is, in general, as difficult for popular apprehension as the name of the composer. There are long stretches of what seems, on the first hearing at least, formless void, sprinkled only with tinklings of the piano." The *Boston Journal* voiced similar sentiments: "Tchaikovsky is unmistakably a disciple of the new school, and his work is strongly tinged with the wildness and quaintness of the music of the North. Taken as a whole, his Piano Concerto appeared interesting chiefly as a novelty. It would not soon supplant the massive productions of Beethoven, or even the fiery compositions of Liszt, Raff and Rubinstein."

Dwight's Journal of Music, published in Boston by John Sullivan Dwight, the eminently respectable arbiter elegantiarum of the Boston scene (and Boston was, of course, the "hub of the universe"), added a note of puzzlement: "This extremely difficult, strange, wild, ultra-modern Russian concerto is the composition of Peter Tchaikovsky, a young professor at the Conservatory of Moscow.... We had the wild Cossack fire and impetus without stint, extremely brilliant and exciting, but could we ever learn to love such music?" Bostonians, and Americans at large, ended up liking this music very much indeed. Its broad introductory theme was transmogrified by Tin Pan Alley into the popular song "Tonight We Love!" Bemoaning the fact that Tchaikovsky never profited by this posthumous fame, a Hollywood tunesmith put out a song entitled "Everybody's Making Money but Tchaikovsky!"

The key of Tchaikovsky's First Piano Concerto is listed as B-flat minor, but that tonality is outlined only at the very beginning of the concerto and is treated as the submediant of D-flat major, inaugurated by the piano solo with wide-ranging plangent tonic triads. Then the famous principal theme is sounded in the orchestra, while the piano continues to play its sonorous rhythmic chords. Then the soloist picks up the main tune, adorning it with melodic encrustations. There follows a brilliant cadenza. The initial section of the first movement, allegro non troppo e molto maestoso, concludes on a pause, and an Allegro con spirito is ushered in, in the nominal key of the concerto, B-flat minor. A tender-sweet flute introduces an expressive theme, which is further developed in one of the numerous piano cadenzas in the movement. The concluding part is in the homonymous key of B-flat major.

The second movement, Andantino semplice, in D-flat major, is a typically Tchaikovskian barcarole, swaying gently on the surface of the water. It is antiphonally constructed, with the flute and the oboe playing dolcissimo, accompanied by piano solo in syncopated rhythm. Even in this short movement Tchaikovsky finds room for several piano cadenzas.

The third and last movement of the concerto, Allegro con fuoco, in the principal key of B-flat minor, begins like a fiery scherzo. Gradually, it accumulates a tremendous amount of kinetic energy. There are several climactic points. Finally, a majestic coda is reached in the key of B-flat major, with pyrotechnical displays of bravura octaves in the piano solo. Von Bülow reported to Tchaikovsky that on his American tour he had to repeat the finale. Tchaikovsky was greatly pleased. "The Americans must have a healthy appetite," he wrote. "Imagine, von Bülow had to play the entire finale of my concerto as an encore! Nothing like that could ever happen in Russia!"

Francesca da Rimini, *Symphonic Fantasia*, Op. 32 (1876)

On October 26, 1876, Tchaikovsky wrote to his brother and biographer, Modest:

> I have just finished my new work, a fantasy on Francesca da Rimini. I wrote it with love, and the love came off rather well. As to the storm, one could write something that would come closer to Doré's drawing. [The French artist Gustave Doré made drawings to Dante's *Divine Comedy*, in which Francesca is a figure.] However, correct estimate of the piece cannot be made until it is orchestrated and performed.... Did I tell you that I began taking cold baths every morning? You have no idea how beneficial it is to my health. I never felt as well as now (knock wood). This circumstance (that is, the cold water) has and will continue to have influence on

my writings. If there is anything fresh and new in Francesca, it is due to a large extent to cold water.

In Tchaikovsky's original manuscript, now preserved at the Tchaikovsky Museum in Klin, there is the following program note, paraphrasing the episode from Dante's "Inferno":

Dante, accompanied by Virgil's shadow, descends into the second realm of hell's abyss. The air is here filled with lamentations, shouts, and cries of despair. The storm rages in gravelike darkness. An infernal whirlwind rushes through, carrying in its rounds the souls of those whose reason was darkened by a love passion in their lives. Among innumerable human souls, Dante's attention is attracted by two beautiful images, locked in embrace, Francesca and Paolo.

Deeply affected by the heart-rending spectacle of the two young souls, Dante addresses them, and wants to know what crime led to this horrible punishment. Francesca, in tears, recounts her sad tale. She loved Paolo, but was against her will given in marriage to the hateful brother of her lover, the one-eyed hunchback, jealous tyrant of Rimini. The yoke of a forced marriage could not eradicate Francesca's tender passion for Paolo. Once they read together the romance of Lancelot. "We were alone," Francesca said, "and we were reading in peace. Often we paled, and our anxious eyes met. A single moment was our ruin. When the happy Lancelot finally gained his first kiss of love, Paolo, from whom nothing will part me now, touched my trembling lips with his, and the book that opened to us the mystery of love fell from our hands." At that moment, Francesca's husband made a sudden appearance, and killed her and Paolo with his dagger. Having told her story, Francesca, still in Paolo's arms, is carried away by the savagely raging storm. Shaken by inexpressible pity, Dante faints, and falls down as one dead.

The program given in the printed edition of the score contains the Italian text from Dante's "Inferno," beginning with the lines: "Nessun maggior dolore che ricordarsi del tempo felice nella miseria" ("There is no greater sorrow than to remember the happy times in misery"). Tchaikovsky often quoted these lines in his letters to his brothers, particularly during the tragic interlude of his unsuccessful marriage.

The structural plan of *Francesca da Rimini* is simple. There are three divisions played without pause. The first and the third portray the fury of the storm, in chromatic harmonies and powerful dynamics. The middle section represents Francesca's sad story. It opens with an unaccompanied solo of the clarinet. The theme is later taken by the flutes with the oboes, the violins, and the cellos, and, finally, by the combined string instruments against the background of the rest of the orchestra. There is another motive, similarly developed, and there are rhapsodic episodes with harp passages. The fanfare is sounded, there is a crashing chord, and the storm breaks out with renewed fury.

Francesca da Rimini was performed for the first time in Moscow on March 10, 1877, with Nikolai Rubinstein conducting. The success was great. Even more successful was the performance in St. Petersburg on March 23, 1878. In the volume of Tchaikovsky's family letters published in 1940, we find the report of the St.

Petersburg performance written by Tchaikovsky's brother Anatol: "Francesca had enormous success, there was no end to the applause.... After the concert we had tea at the Davidovs [Carl Davidov (1838–89), the famous cellist and director of the St. Petersburg Conservatory]. Carl has asked me to write you that in his opinion Francesca is the greatest work of our time."

The composer and pianist Sergei Taneyev, to whom the score of *Francesca da Rimini* is dedicated, reported more opinions: Eduard Nápravník, who conducted the performance, liked the work very much, but found it a bit too long. The composer César Cui liked the introduction. Rimsky-Korsakov did not like the themes, but liked the work as a whole. Tchaikovsky's friend the critic Hermann Laroche was restrained in his estimate; he thought the music was too much like Liszt's, and that symphonic poems were not Tchaikovsky's genre.

Variations on a Rococo Theme for Violoncello and Orchestra, Op. 33 (1877)

The characterization "rococo" gives a clear indication of Tchaikovsky's intentions in this set of attractive variations for violoncello and orchestra. "Rococo" comes from the word *rocaille*, suggesting shell-like rock ornaments, elegant, charming, decorative, in soft blue or rose colors, like a girl's figure painted by Greuze or a pastoral landscape by Fragonard. The Variations had its first performance in Moscow on November 30, 1877.

After a brief introduction, the theme Moderato semplice, is sounded by the cello solo. Its rhythm suggests a gavotte, a dance favored during the innocent age when the Rococo flourished in prerevolutionary France. There are seven variations in all; they are all distinguished by simplicity and virtuosity. The first two variations are in the same tempo as the original theme. But the third variation, Andante sostenuto, assumes an air of Russian melancholy. The fourth variation, Andante grazioso, resumes its Rococo character. The fifth variation, Allegro moderato, affords the solo cello a display of easy virtuosity, with opulent cadenzas adding brilliance to Rococo elegance. The sixth variation, Andante, is by contrast a Russian meditation. The final, seventh, variation, Allegro vivace, serves as a coda, rushing forward with joyous precipitation.

Violin Concerto in D Major, Op. 35 (1878)

Tchaikovsky wrote his Violin Concerto during March and April 1878, at Clarens, a peaceful little town on Lake Geneva. The composition of the concerto followed immediately after the Fourth Symphony, and the opera *Eugene Onegin*. It was a very dramatic period of Tchaikovsky's life. He had just thrown off the burden of an unnatural marriage, and was obsessed with the fear that the true cause of its failure would become generally known.

Financially, Tchaikovsky felt secure through the rich annuity that the beneficent Madame von Meck was giving him, first under the pretext of commissioned works, and later as an outright gift. Madame von Meck's admiration for Tchaikovsky's genius was warmed by the sympathy she felt for his unsuccessful marriage, and in her letters she pictured Tchaikovsky's wife as a person unworthy of bearing his name, a person who failed to understand his greatness. In accepting this version of the story, Tchaikovsky nevertheless could not help feeling that he was something worse than a hypocrite. Only with his brothers he could be frank, for they knew. Thus, Tchaikovsky's life was split; the facade gave no hint of the interior.

By nature, Tchaikovsky was morbidly introspective. He found pleasure in condemning himself. In the Tchaikovsky Museum at Klin there is an old volume in Latin, in which Tchaikovsky wrote on the title pages "Stolen from the Palace of the Doges in Venice by Peter Ilyich Tchaikovsky, State Counselor and Conservatory Professor." This flaunting, in the privacy of his own self, of a minor criminal offense is very characteristic of Tchaikovsky's mentality. In his work, however, Tchaikovsky was amazingly efficient. No matter what his state of mind, he could write fast, without deviating from the original idea. Diffident and self-condemning though he was in life, in his art he was always sure of himself. The evidence of his manuscripts shows an orderly procedure, with no loose ends, no incomplete designs.

The Violin Concerto was dedicated to the famous violinist Leopold Auer. It is ironic that Auer should have shown so little interest in the work, and let it gather dust, until Adolf Brodsky picked it up, and played it in Vienna on December 4, 1881. For Leopold Auer was the teacher of a flock of Russian violinists, who made Tchaikovsky's concerto their favorite pièce de résistance. Brodsky's performance in Vienna was not an unqualified success. The Viennese critic Eduard Hanslick, famous for his invective, wrote harshly of it. Tchaikovsky said he could never forget this review, and no wonder; for Hanslick wrote that the violin was not played, but beaten black and blue. He also remarked that there is music that one can hear stink, and that the last movement of the concerto, so odorously Russian, belongs in that category.

The concerto opens with a theme of the first violins, in D major, ₄. After a short introductory period, the kettledrum, basses, cellos, and the bassoon play a tremolo on the dominant, a time-honored device to create suspense, in anticipation of the principal subject. Here the violins of the orchestra give away the rhythmic pattern of the coming violin solo. The solo begins with a few preliminary flourishes, and then announces the theme. There is a rapid development, with the soloist playing in virtuoso style. The orchestra sounds vigorously rhythmed chords. After a brilliant display of technique, the solo violin announces the second theme, of a lyrical character.

The movement grows, there are three, four, and six notes to a beat. The solo violin is now at the height of its virtuosity. The orchestra supports it by rhythmical chords, first on the beat, then syncopated. The flutes and violins sing out the lyrical theme, while the soloist carries on in virtuoso manner. There is more "business," to use stage parlance, and the entire orchestra strikes the first theme in the dominant, to the accompaniment of the fanfares of the wind instruments. The solo violin has a long period of rest, and then comes in with brilliant variations on the first theme, in a new key, C major. Once more the orchestra takes over the theme, this time in F. The soloist and the orchestra exchange vigorous chords. The orchestra now keeps the dominant A in the bass, a clear indication of the impending return of the original key.

The violin plays a brilliant cadenza, employing all its technical resources—double, triple, and quadruple stops, trills, and runs. The cadenza ends on a trill, and the flute announces the first theme of the movement. This is the recapitulation, but Tchaikovsky would not use this formality of a sonata form without coloring and embellishing it, to make the recapitulation a new edition of the exposition. But the outline is clearly recognizable. Once more, we hear the rhythmically spaced orchestral chords. And then comes the second theme, now in the tonic key.

The solo violin plays the lyrical second theme on the G string. A chromatic run brings the theme an octave higher, and higher still, to the limits of the effective range of the violin. We recognize the syncopated chords in the orchestra. Then the orchestral violins play the lyrical theme, chromaticized, and otherwise modified, while the soloist plays rapid passages. The tempo is stepped up, paralleling the corresponding section of the exposition, and the final portion of the movement is reached. It is marked allegro giusto. The square-by-square rhythm of the solo violin, four sixteenth notes to a quarter, is punctuated by the chords of the orchestra. The rhythm narrows to six notes to a beat. The concluding più mosso has some material similar to *Eugene Onegin*, the opera that Tchaikovsky wrote shortly before the concerto.

The lyrical second movement is more Italian than Slavic, and the Italian designation, Canzonetta, is not an accident. It opens with an introduction for wind instruments. Then the solo violin plays the unassuming theme, in G minor, ⅜ time. The flute repeats the theme with added trills. Then the solo violin resumes, playing a contrasting melody, to the accompaniment of the strings, and later of the woodwinds. After some transitional passages, the solo violin returns to the original theme of the Canzonetta, with parenthetical interpolations from the clarinet and the flute. The violin leaves off with a trill, and the woodwinds repeat the introduction. There is some interplay of instrumental colors in slow tempo, and the movement ends in pianissimo.

The finale enters at once, in the original key of D, in ⅞ time. The orchestra starts in vigorous dancing rhythm, and the solo violin plays a cadenza, preliminary to the main subject. The solo violin holds the foreground, with the woodwind instruments quick repartees, now and then. A running scale leads to a new, "Russian" theme, played by the solo violin against the thumping fifths of the violoncellos. It must have been this theme that moved Hanslick to remark that he detected the strong smell of Russian boots. However that may be, here is a dance for dance's sake. The theme is played over and over in the violins, the horn, and the bassoons. Then there is an interlude in a slow tempo, with the oboe and clarinet playing a lyrical theme, bearing only rhythmical affinity to the thumping Russian motive. The solo violin and the violoncellos echo this new lyrical figure. Then the solo violin whips up the tempo, and brings back the first theme of the finale.

The form is clearly a rondo, with two principal themes, and episodes, patterned after the themes. The orchestra presents the first theme in various keys, and modified to the intervals, while the solo violin interjects brilliant arpeggio passages. The "Russian" theme returns in G major. The flutes take it over, while the solo violin plays variations. But all resources of the violin technique are not yet exhausted, and the theme is played in octaves, and in harmonics. Once more, the oboe and the clarinet have their interlude, participated in by the solo violin. In the final section, both themes appear in various guises. The concerto ends in a rousing fortissimo.

Overture "1812," Op. 49 (1880)

Battle pieces are the most ancient, the most obvious, and the most profitable art forms. They always glorify, and they are always composed by nationals of the winning party. One of the best-known battle pieces, *The Battle of Prague*, continued inexplicably in popularity for a century after the composer, one Francis Kotzwara, a Czech-born violinist at the King's Theatre in London, had hanged himself in a London brothel, on September 2, 1791. Another popular battle piece was *Battle Gemmappe*, a sonata by François Devienne, who ended his days in an insane asylum near Paris. In America, Francesco Masi, "author of several fugitive compositions," wrote *The Battles of Lake Champlain and Plattsburg*, a Grand Sonata for the Piano Forte, respectfully dedicated to the "American Heroes Who Achieved the Glorious Victories." Finally there is the *Battle of Marengo*, a military piece by Bernard Viguerie, whose claim to pioneer achievement is the special effect for the sound of the cannons "to be expressed by stretching the two hands flat on the three lower octaves, the hand to be kept on the keys until the vibrations are nearly extinct." In all these pieces, galloping horses are portrayed by the device known in music history as the Alberti bass. Another feature is an "attack with swords" or, in later pieces, with bayonets. There is an obligatory section in a minor key entitled Cry of the Wounded. The end is usually a grand fanfare. The most famous orchestral battle piece is Beethoven's Wellington's Victory; in it the cannon is represented by two bass drums.

Tchaikovsky wrote the Overture "1812" in 1880 for the dedication of the Temple of Christ the Savior on Red Square in Moscow (be it noted parenthetically that Red Square was the ancient name of the Kremlin Square, in old Russian the word for "red" also meaning "beautiful"). The composition was written at the instigation of Nikolai Rubinstein. Tchaikovsky had no enthusiasm for writing the commissioned work. "There is nothing more distasteful to me than to compose music for special occasions," he wrote to Madame von Meck from Kamenka on September 28, 1880. "What can one write for an inauguration of an exposition except banalities and noisy commonplaces? But I have no heart to refuse Rubinstein's request and so, willy-nilly, I will have to embark on a disagreeable task." On October 10, he reports to Madame von Meck: "My muse is so benevolent to me of late that I have completed two pieces with great speed, namely, an overture and a serenade for string orchestra. I am orchestrating both pieces. The overture will be very loud and noisy, but I was writing it without a warm feeling of affection, and there will probably be no artistic value in it." The proposed performance on Red Square did not materialize. Yet with this public performance in mind, Tchaikovsky had included in the score a real cannon, such as is used in the theater for sound effects, and a battery of church bells.

The Overture "1812" depicts the epic event of the victory over the "invasion of twelve nations," as the Napoleonic armies were described in Russian popular phraseology. The faith in victory is symbolized by the opening prayer, "Save, O Lord, your people, and bless their treasure." Further, there appears the Russian song "At Father's Gates" and the Russian national hymn. On the French side is the "Marseillaise." The "Marseillaise" grows in volume until it reaches a climax, the occupation of Moscow in September 2, 1812. But the Russian song is heard undiminished. It is now a people's campaign. The invader is ejected. The "Marseillaise" now appears in minor, while the prayer and the national hymn return in triumph. Tchaikovsky was accused of anachronism for the inclusion of the "Marseillaise" and the Russian National Hymn. The "Marseillaise" was not the popular hymn of Napoleon's imperialist armies, and the Russian National Hymn was not composed until 1833. Tchaikovsky might have replied with the words of Tolstoy in the epilogue to *War and Peace*.

The discrepancy of my description of historic events with the account of historians is not an accident. It is inevitable. The historian and the artist depicting a historical era have two entirely different objectives. The historian is concerned only with the result of an event, while the artist is interested in the event by itself.

Coda: Tchaikovsky Rediscovered in His Dwelling Place—Notes of a Visit to the Tchaikovsky Museum in Klin

Klin is a small town near Moscow. Many changes have swept through Russia in the last century, but Klin has changed little. There were a few buildings of modern architecture when I visited the town in 1935, but it was an old-fashioned droshky that brought me from the railroad station. The rain fell on the horse with the same even rhythm that Russian rain has always possessed—nothing violent, nothing capricious, but a steady, determined precipitation.

There was a feeling of gratitude in my heart when I observed how little modern times had affected the quiet and, in itself, unimportant town. But it was important to me, as indeed it is to all musicians, since Klin was for many years the home of the great Russian composer Peter Ilyich Tchaikovsky. There he lived and worked. In Klin he composed his Sixth Symphony, the *Pathétique*. The cottage he occupied was lovingly preserved by the Russian people.

Entering that cottage, we are introduced into the private world of Tchaikovsky. On the wall over his bed there was a picture that had hung there for some sixty years. It was a landscape, painted by an artist who was not great but whose sincerity of sentiment made up for lack of mastery—a Russian woman who was deeply moved when she heard the nostalgic second movement of Tchaikovsky's Violin Concerto. Tchaikovsky was devoted to the picture, for he appreciated the sentiment that had inspired it.

There were objects connected with Tchaikovsky's daily activities, the incidental minutiae which help to reconstruct the temporal aspect of a great musician's life. There was his silk dressing gown, hanging from a peg near the bed; a pitcher and basin—there was no running water in Tchaikovsky's Klin; a kerosene lamp and some utensils of everyday use. Of more direct interest were the numerous photographs of Tchaikovsky's friends, inscribed to him. They left little space on the walls they decorated. The bookshelves were filled with books and the printed editions of Tchaikovsky's music. And, finally, in the center of the large drawing-room, stood an instrument of Tchaikovsky's muse, a grand piano.

I asked the custodian of Tchaikovsky's house—or perhaps I should call him curator, for the cottage was officially named "house-museum"—whether I might play on the piano. The curator himself seemed to be a personage of Tchaikovsky's world. His features strangely resembled those of the great musician to whose memory he dedicated himself. Perhaps instinctively, he trimmed his beard after the Tchaikovsky manner, because he thought it was the most dignified mode. Well, he cordially permitted me to run my fingers over the keyboard that had once felt the imprint of Tchaikovsky's hands. I played the C-sharp Minor Nocturne, which I had learned as a boy in Russia, and which to this day personifies Tchaikovsky for me more even than his symphonies. There is a perfection in this nocturne that is rarely matched, a cyclical form with two sections in minor, separated by a page in major. When the melody returns in the last part, it is sung by the left hand, while the right runs a measured scale upward and then downward in a swift cascade. As I played, the curator's Tchaikovskylike face smiled—in approval, so I hoped. Playing Tchaikovsky, in Tchaikovsky's house, on Tchaikovsky's piano, was a responsibility, even though there was no audience or music critic present.

But later on that day, there was an audience. It was a group of eager young boys and girls who were being conducted by the curator through the Tchaikovsky House-Museum, and introduced to the world of great music composed long before these young people were born. The curator played some of Tchaikovsky's music on a gramophone. It was an old machine that he used, with an old-fashioned loud-speaker of corrugated metal, and with that unearthly squeak that former genera-tions of phonograph enthusiasts must have ignored. And so did the present audi-ence, listening in reverence, without disparagement. Somehow that old gramo-phone, and even that squeak, seemed to strengthen the illusion of being near Tchaikovsky's world, an illusion that would have been destroyed by the incongru-ous perfection of a modern machine.

Toward the end of the day, the curator unlocked the metal containers in which Tchaikovsky's manuscripts were preserved, and I was allowed a glimpse into the inner sanctum of Tchaikovsky's musical thinking. Here was his opera *Pique Dame*. I knew every note of it. How strange: Could it be that this aria—which had always seemed to me something hewn unalterably from rock—could it be that Tchaikovsky had at first hesitated over the melodic line? There were other erasures and alter-ations that fascinated me. So that was the way such music was written!

I left Tchaikovsky's house with a feeling of having traveled into the past, of having been a member of Tchaikovsky's circle of friends. The house was a symbol of Russian culture, its strength, its poetry, its continuity. No storm, it seemed to me, would ever strike that unimpressive cottage, so far removed from the highways of modern life. But a storm did engulf Tchaikovsky's world. It was a man-made storm, led by men in uniforms riding on motorcycles. They reached Klin, in their sweep toward Moscow, as part of an ambitious plan to subjugate and repress the nation-al development of Tchaikovsky's homeland. In apprehension and anticipation of this invasion, the museum's curator had removed to a safe distance the manuscripts in metal containers, had tried also to send off Tchaikovsky's library. But there was no time for that. The invaders arrived, emptied the half-packed cases, and threw the books in the snow. They were not interested in either destroying or stealing Tchaikovsky's books and music. To them the house-museum was but a shelter for their bodies, a shelter for their motorcycles. They would have burned the house in their retreat from Klin, but they were driven off too rapidly to destroy.

Some weeks later, the invasion's tide receded and work was resumed in the museum. The rooms were cleaned; the broken-down motorcycle left behind by the invaders was removed from Tchaikovsky's drawing room. Again, during visitors' hours, came eager boys and girls to listen to Tchaikovsky's music. The pictures were once more restored to their accustomed places on the walls. Tchaikovsky's world, after a tempest, was once more returned to its calm and timeless existence.

Presenting the Great
NIKOLAI RIMSKY-KORSAKOV
(1844–1908)

"This is a composition by Rimsky, arranged by Korsakov," announced a disc jockey on the air. His naïve blunder was rather an understatement, for there is enough variety and color in Rimsky-Korsakov's music for several composers. No other composer can equal Nikolai Rimsky-Korsakov in the sheer brilliance of his orchestra, and the moderns, beginning with Debussy, followed his lead in treating instrumental colors. Yet to him music was music and nothing else, and he disliked extraneous explanations of his melodic phrases. When he conducted a concert of his works in Paris, early in the century, an enthusiastic lady asked him after the concert, "Please tell me, Maître, what was your clarinet saying?" Rimsky-Korsakov replied, with the greatest show of politeness, "It said, 'I am not an oboe.'"

In his autobiography, which is a model of modest yet informative writing, Rimsky-Korsakov tells us that he became conscious of music before he was two years old; at four, he could beat the toy drum strictly in measure while his father played the piano. In the spirit of a game, the elder Rimsky-Korsakov would suddenly change the tempo, but the boy would immediately catch on, and follow the new rhythm. He also had the sense of absolute pitch from his earliest childhood, so that he could name any note played for him on the piano without looking. Despite his unusual absorption with music, he was a lively boy who liked to climb on the roof and on trees. Indoors, he entertained himself by harnessing chairs for horses. He imitated a watchmaker by putting on eyeglasses, made of cardboard, and taking apart an old watch. He read books of adventure, and loved to spend time with geographic maps and astronomic charts.

At eighteen, Rimsky-Korsakov entered the naval academy and sailed abroad on the clipper *Almaz* ("amber"). He traveled to Gravesend, England, and later to America, visiting New York, Washington, and other coastal cities. He gratefully notes in his autobiography that "the Americans took us to Niagara Falls at their own expense as an act of hospitality accorded to Russians by their transatlantic friends." That was the time of the Civil War, and Rimsky-Korsakov followed the events with the greatest interest, all his sympathy being in favor of the Northern states and President Lincoln. The only musical instrument the mariner-musician took with him on board ship was a mouth harmonica. He found an American sailor, one Thompson, who could play on the violin, and together they amused themselves by playing American songs. The *Almaz* continued to Rio de Janeiro and then proceeded southward, intending to return to Russia via Cape Horn and the Pacific. But mechanical trouble developed and the clipper was summoned back by the Mediterranean route.

Upon his return in 1865, Rimsky-Korsakov began to compose music seriously and with great concentration. He became friendly with a group of young composers whose names are now familiar to every music lover—Mily Balakirev (1837–1910), César Cui (1835–1913), Alexander Borodin (1833–87), and Modest Mussorgsky (1839–81). Balakirev was the acknowledged leader of the group. Cui, of French descent, was an expert in military fortification, and music was to him a pleasant hobby; Borodin was a young professor of chemistry—he had a laboratory in the neighboring building, and would often interrupt composition and run over to see that his chemical utensils were in working order. Mussorgsky was employed in the Department of Forestry, and had little time to compose. The technique of composition was not coming easily to Rimsky-Korsakov, Borodin, and Mussorgsky; only Balakirev and Cui possessed the mastery of the art, and they were deferred to by the rest for their superior knowledge.

One fine day the group decided to present their symphonic works at a public concert. After that event, the Russian writer and lover of the arts, Vladimir Stasov, referred to the five composers as "the mighty little company [handful]." Rimsky-Korsakov thought this nomination was "tactless," but the variant form, "the Mighty Five," has been accepted by music historians. Among the composers who were grouped almost accidentally as the Mighty Five, Rimsky-Korsakov was the most professional, and indeed professorial. Curiously enough, Balakirev and Cui, who were regarded as superiors by their comrades-in-arms, have made little impact on subsequent musical developments; the mentor of the group, Balakirev, stopped composing midway in his long life. The stature of Mussorgsky, who was too erratic for a professional musician and always aware of his technical inadequacy, rose to extraordinary heights. Rimsky-Korsakov became one of the greatest masters of Russian music and a superb technician in the art of composition.

And so Rimsky-Korsakov became a master of music. Still in his twenties, he was appointed a professor at the St. Petersburg Conservatory, and later became its director. He was extremely conscientious in going over his students' exercises, which he read note by note, and offered detailed advice for improvement. Many of his students became important composers in their own right, and the traditions of Rimsky-Korsakov's teaching endured in Russia. Never a professorial pedant, he possessed a keen sense of humor. One of the most delightful compositions of Russian light music is a collection of variations written by Rimsky-Korsakov, Borodin, Cui, and others on the theme of the old-fashioned Chopsticks. In his contribution to this humorous collection, Rimsky-Korsakov managed to combine Chopsticks with a fugue on the name of Bach, which in German notation spells out the notes B-flat, A, C, and B-natural.

Tall, bespectacled, bearded, quiet in manner, friendly but not too convivial in company, a model husband, an affectionate father, Rimsky-Korsakov was the veritable personification of an old-fashioned Russian intellectual. Rimsky-Korsakov led a sedentary life in St. Petersburg. He was a modest man. He declined the proffered doctorate of Cambridge University, because he did not regard himself as a scholar. But he was unyielding in matters of principle. His personal integrity was absolute. When the czarist regime ordered the expulsion of a number of students at the St. Petersburg Conservatory who had been accused of holding an unauthorized political meeting, Rimsky-Korsakov registered a vehement protest, and as a result was himself relieved of his position as director and professor. But he refused to abandon his pupils and continued to give them private lessons at home.

Rimsky-Korsakov was adamantly against unauthorized cuts in his operas. When Diaghilev proposed drastic cuts in his Paris production of *Sadko*, because French audiences would not sit through a long opera, Rimsky-Korsakov wrote him in anger: "If to the dressed-up but feeble-minded Paris operagoers who drop in at the theater for a while and who are guided in their opinions by their venal press and their hired claque, my *Sadko* in its present state is too heavy, then I would rather not have it done at all."

Rimsky-Korsakov's musical conscience made him his own severest critic. Being human, he had his moments of creative fatigue, when he seemed unable to work productively, but he regarded such dereliction of duty as unwarranted self-indulgence. He was at his happiest in the final stages of orchestration. "What can be more satisfying than final scoring!" he wrote to a friend. "When I begin to orchestrate, everything becomes crystal clear and precise in harmony, rhythm, melodic line, even in secondary parts. The soul is calm for the thread of the composition has been woven in, and in a way the work already exists. And what a pleasure to correct unsatisfactory passages and polish up rough spots! As for the hopelessly bad sections, one simply gets used to them, and they cease causing irritation." This is, indeed, "an ode to professionalism and technique," as Rimsky-Korsakov's son Andrey described it.

The great innovation of Rimsky-Korsakov and his friends of the Mighty Five was the use of Russian national subjects in their operas and symphonic poems. Before them, Russian music followed the models of the Italian and German masters—even the great Glinka could not get away from Italianate inflections. But Rimsky-Korsakov did not slavishly borrow from Russian folk songs. Rather, he wrote new melodies that sounded like genuine folk songs. This fooled one of his critics, who asserted that the best melody in Rimsky-Korsakov's opera *The Snow Maiden* was the shepherd's song, which, so he said, was really a Russian folk tune. Rimsky-Korsakov wrote a letter to the editor of the paper, asking the critic to tell what Russian song that was. Of course, there was no reply to that.

Rimsky-Korsakov's music is extremely graphic. The growth of a magic forest is musically depicted in *The Snow Maiden* by a sequence of notes, one to a beat, then two, three, and four to a beat. In his symphonic suite, *Scheherazade*, the story-telling of the Sultan's wife is represented by a recurring motif of the solo violin which seems to articulate words in singing notes. In his *Capriccio espagnol* he catches the rhythm of Spain more effectively than any native Spanish composer ever did. The rhythmic waves of the ocean and the frolics of the fish in *Sadko* unroll a

musical seascape that one can almost perceive visually. Sometimes Rimsky-Korsakov imitated animal sounds as close to nature as the tempered musical scale could afford. His rooster's elaborate cock-a-doodle-doo could arouse a barnyard to sudden activity before daybreak. And there is also a family canary whose song he copied for another instrumental solo.

Rimsky-Korsakov's musical personality conceals a paradox. How could this typical Russian music teacher, who led such an uneventful life, have produced such resplendent pageants of sensuous color as *Scheherazade* and *Le Coq d'or*? The answer is that orientalism is part of the Russian musical heritage. Rimsky-Korsakov's Orient was the Near East, comprising countries with which Russia had a common frontier and a flourishing trade. This music was to Russia what Cuban dance rhythms are to the United States, an exotic stimulant. By a curious process of reversion, Rimsky-Korsakov's quasi-Oriental music spread in Asian countries by means of recordings and over the radio, and actually began to influence the lands that provided the original inspiration. The music of Rimsky-Korsakov is now, literally and figuratively, in the public domain. It is used and abused in pseudo-Oriental shows and in popular songs, its carefully balanced harmonies filled with extraneous notes, its flowing melodies deformed and cut to meet the exigencies of the medium, its masterly instrumentation blatantly inspissated. What a cry of anguish would Rimsky-Korsakov have emitted at such ignominious treatment at the hands of musical barbarians!

It is an accepted maxim that a deeply felt national art inevitably becomes universal art. Rimsky-Korsakov's music, so profoundly Russian, has spread to the four corners of the world. And now, his melodies speak as clearly to Americans as they do to Russians; to the English as to Italians; to Australians as to the Hindus. It is difficult for a foreigner to learn the Russian language; it is easy to learn and to enjoy Russian music as presented, in marvelous colors, by Nikolai Andreievich Rimsky-Korsakov.

Quintet for Piano, Flute, Clarinet, French Horn, and Bassoon in B-flat Major (1876)

Before Rimsky-Korsakov became a classic, he was regarded in some circles as almost a revolutionary. Eduard Hanslick, the famous Vienna critic, once described him as belonging to "the extreme left wing of the Russian school." The asymmetrical rhythms in Rimsky-Korsakov's operas caused great trouble to performers. Singers used to study the rhythms of eleven quarter-notes in some of his operatic choruses by reciting "Rimsky-Korsakov sovsen sumasoshol" (Russian for "Rimsky-Korsakov is completely mad"), which contains eleven syllables.

In order of popularity, the works of Rimsky-Korsakov range from his symphonic suite *Scheherazade* through excerpts from his operas to his songs. His chamber music is virtually unknown. One such forgotten work is his Quintet for Piano, Flute, Clarinet, French Horn, and Bassoon. It was written in 1876, for a contest of the Russian Musical Society. Rimsky-Korsakov describes, in *Chronicle of My Musical Life*, the nature of this work:

> I composed the quintet in three movements. The first was in the classical style of Beethoven; the second, Andante, contained a fairly good fugue for the wind instruments, with a free contrapuntal accompaniment in the piano part. The third movement, Allegretto vivace, in rondo form, contained an interesting passage: the approach to the first subject after the

middle section. The flute, the French horn and the clarinet by turns play virtuoso cadenzas, according to the character of each instrument, and each is interrupted by the bassoon entering by octave leaps. After the piano cadenza, the first subject finally enters in similar leaps.

Writing many years later, he admitted that the quintet did not express his real individuality. It was neatly copied and sent to the jury of the Russian Musical Society, along with another work, a sextet (Rimsky-Korsakov submitted two manuscripts to have a better chance to win). But the prize went to Eduard Nápravník, a Czech conductor and composer who settled in Russia. Rimsky-Korsakov's sextet got an honorable mention; the quintet received no reward at all. Rimsky-Korsakov explained that Nápravník's work, a trio, received an admirable performance by Leschetizky, though playing at sight from manuscript, whereas Rimsky-Korsakov's quintet was mangled by a poor pianist. "The fiasco at the contest was undeserved," Rimsky-Korsakov wrote, "for it pleased the audience greatly when it was subsequently performed at a concert of the St. Petersburg Chamber Music Society."

The May Night (1878–79)

The May Night is Rimsky-Korsakov's second opera. He wrote it in 1878–79, at a time when he was fascinated by stories of the fantastic and the supernatural. For his libretto he selected a tale by his favorite writer, Nikolai Gogol. The story deals with the youthful love of the Ukrainian boy Levko for the beautiful Hannah; Levko's father, the village elder, is himself infatuated with the girl and refuses to allow his son to marry her. There are several comic characters: the wine distiller, the scribe, the village drunkard. The fantastic element is represented by a drowned Polish maiden who comes out at night from the water and helps Levko in his romance by producing a magically contrived letter from the chief commissioner ordering Levko's father to have the marriage of Levko and Hannah celebrated without delay under heavy penalty for disobedience.

Rimsky-Korsakov used many passages of Gogol's prose without alterations in the recitatives and even in the arias. The result was that the opera acquired a colloquial flavor. There was no attempt at operatic realism in the manner of Mussorgsky, but rather an adaptation of the common speech to a melodic line written according to purely musical considerations.

The first performance of *The May Night* took place at the Mariinsky Theater in St. Petersburg on January 21, 1880, under the direction of the invariably strict and meticulous Czech conductor Eduard Nápravník. Rimsky-Korsakov, who once described Nápravník as "an inimitable wrong-note detective," was not particularly happy about the way the conductor interpreted his operas, and he resented the cuts made by Nápravník at subsequent productions of *The May Night*. The opera was not too successful at the Mariinsky Theater. It was revived by a Moscow opera company in 1892 and for a time attracted good audiences, but it was eventually replaced in the repertory by Leoncavallo's *I Pagliacci*, "a swindling score created by a modern musical careerist," as Rimsky-Korsakov ruefully described it.

Capriccio espagnol, Op. 34 (1887)

The most effective Spanish pieces for orchestra have been written by Frenchmen and Russians. Rimsky-Korsakov's Spanish suite of five pieces, played without pause and entitled, for want of a better description, *Capriccio espagnol*, is a particularly brilliant example of Russian Spanish orchestration. In a letter to V. Yastrebtzev, Rimsky-Korsakov's Boswell and "phonographic and photographic" biographer, as he was known in Rimsky-Korsakov's family, Rimsky-Korsakov writes: "How strange! It seems that I like to orchestrate better than to compose." In his *Chronicle of My Musical Life*, Rimsky-Korsakov points out the difference between a "well-orchestrated piece" and a "brilliant composition for orchestra." He puts his *Capriccio espagnol* in the latter category, a piece conceived for orchestra and inseparable from orchestral timbres. Instrumental cadenzas, the role of percussion, figurations and embellishments, all these, he maintains, are not mere elaborations and exercises in tone color, but integral parts of the whole.

The composition of *Capriccio espagnol* was completed on August 4, 1887. A year later, *Scheherazade* was written. These orchestral works mark the conclusion of a period in Rimsky-Korsakov's evolutionary style, which he defines by two characteristics, the attainment of a virtuoso style in orchestration, without Wagner's influence toward the enlargement of sonorous means, and the lessening of purely contrapuntal writing. In place of elaborate polyphony, Rimsky-Korsakov makes increasing use of melodic ornamentation, and its logical outgrowth, the art of variation. The first performance of *Capriccio espagnol* was given in St. Petersburg at one of the series of Russian Symphony Concerts, on November 12, 1887, conducted by Rimsky-Korsakov himself. (The date of October 31, 1887, given in the dictionaries and orchestral program notes, is the old-style date of the Russian calendar, which in the nineteenth century was twelve days behind the West's.)

Capriccio espagnol obtained a great success at its initial performance, and quickly became a repertoire piece. Its hispanicism is, of course, external, but the stylization of Spanish melodies and rhythms is remarkably effective. The name of the opening dance, Alborada (from the Latin and Spanish word *albor*, "whiteness, dawn") is often defined as "morning serenade." But since a serenade is itself an evening song, Alborada is a "morning evening song," which is as complicated a description as Erik Satie's *Crépuscule matinal (de midi)* ("morning twilight at noon"). Rimsky-Korsakov's Alborada is an explosive orchestral dance in A major, duple time, with several instrumental solos for contrast. It leads to a movement entitled Variations, in F major, in slow $\frac{3}{8}$ time. The horns announce the theme, and the first variation, given by the strings, is followed by an instrumental colloquy between the English horn and the French horn. Then the orchestra enters in full. A flute solo marks the transition to the next movement, which latter is a return of the Alborada, a semitone higher. The orchestration is, of course, different—a fact that justifies the repetition.

The next movement is a series of instrumental cadenzas under the general title Scene and Gypsy Song. The Gypsy-ness of the song is indicated by a sort of illegitimate Mixolydian or Hypoaeolian mode, derived from a minor scale, with the dominant serving as a tonic. This mode has done excellent service in nineteenth-century music as an "ersatz" for nontempered Oriental or Near-Eastern scales. There is a parenthetic flourish in the opening fanfare for horns and trumpets, and there is a flight of ornament in the ensuing violin cadenza. The flute and the clarinet play flourishes and ornaments in their turn, and finally the harp spreads a luxuriant foliage of scale passages with the triangle's metallic assistance. The Gypsy Song proper enters in the violins.

The movement gains in definiteness of rhythm, leading to the last number of the suite, an Asturian fandango, in A major, triple time, the theme announced by the trombones. The derivation of the name *fandango* has been traced by amateur etymologists to the playing on the lute (*fidicinare*), but it seems that the dance and the name were brought to Spain from the West Indies. The rhythm is similar to that of the bolero, but it has been said that while the bolero intoxicates, the fandango inflames. Rimsky-Korsakov felt the necessity of a well-rounded form very strongly, and could not resist the urge to return to the scene of the first act, to the initial theme and key. Accordingly, the Alborada returns suddenly, and the piece ends in the spirit of its beginning.

The treatment of Spanish melodies in Rimsky-Korsakov's *Capriccio espagnol* has become a model for some Spanish composers. Yet Rimsky-Korsakov himself borrowed his materials for this work from a collection of songs by the Spanish composer José Inzenga, retaining not only the melodies and the rhythms of the originals, but the harmonization as well, much as Bizet used the "Chanson Havanaise" by Yradier for his "Habanera" in *Carmen*.

Symphonic Suite: Scheherazade ("After 'A Thousand and One Nights'"), *Op. 35 (1888)*

A composer's physical appearance seldom provides a clue to his musical style. Rimsky-Korsakov's case confirms this adage. He wore a professorial beard, led a dignified life, was a good family man, and proved himself a fine administrator during his tenure as director of the St. Petersburg Conservatory. This is a drab life story, out of character with the luscious sound of his exotic music, filled to the brim as it is with quasi-Oriental melodies fashioned in serpentine spirals and colubrine convolutions.

In the total absence of filmable amours and licentious behavior in Rimsky-Korsakov's disconcertingly placid life, the caliphs of Baghdad-on-the-Hollywood-Hills, eager to make use of his technicolorful music, performed a pogonotomy on his chin and, dipping a greasy hand into a barrel of schmaltz, came up with a spectacular movie version of the Russian master's life. In it, a clean-shaven Rimsky-Korsakov lounges in an Algerian bistro and, enraptured by a sultry, dark-eyed ecdysiast, jots down on the back of a menu the score of a belly dance, which is performed the next night by a large Algerian orchestra. But what is this music? It is *Scheherazade*, electrically amplified, stuffed with saxophones and topped with bongos! This is the Rimsky-Korsakov Hollywood likes to chew gum by. Rimsky-Korsakov's family tried to protest against this outrage, but in vain. There is no copyright protection for Russian music, and it is wide open to such depredations.

Scheherazade is by far the most popular symphonic score by Rimsky-Korsakov. Its four movements represent tales told by Scheherazade to her uxoricidal Sultan Schahriar, who, with the nonchalance of a Henry VIII, puts his wives to death after their first night together. The sultana stays the hand of doom by a serial recital of 1001 Arabian tales, keeping the sultan in suspense at the most dramatic point of her story, so that his curiosity is aroused and he cannot afford to have her done away with.

The connecting link of all four movements is a violin solo representing Scheherazade's introduction to each tale. The action opens with a series of mighty unisons in the orchestra, portraying the stern sultan. It is followed by a series of modally disposed triadic progressions in the woodwinds. Scheherazade's violin solo introduces the first tale, that of "The Sea and Sinbad's Ship." The seas roll gently in barcarole time, ⁶₄, in the aquamarine key of E major. Tropical fish pass in colorful array in the woodwinds, as Sinbad's ship sails smoothly upon Rimsky-Korsakov's waters.

SCHEHERAZADE.
Suite symphonique.

I.

N.Rimsky-Korsakow,Op.35.

The second movement tells the story of "The Kalandar Prince." It is set in the maritime tonality of B minor, the key of yet another sea piece, Mendelssohn's overture *The Hebrides (Fingal's Cave)*. Scheherazade's violin solo is heard again. The main movement is a Scherzo, with the saturnine bassoon assigned the role of the narrator of the adventures of the exotic prince.

The third movement is a romance recounting the simple story of a sentimental love of a young prince for a young princess, projected by the violins in the bland key of G major, in gentle § time. In the background are heard the tintinnabulations of a tinkling triangle and a jingling tambourine.

The finale is a festive drama. Scheherazade and her violin open the curtains on the great festival of the fabled city of Baghdad, Allegro molto e frenetico, in the principal key of E minor, in barcarole time of §. But a tempest is brewing on the troubled ocean. A Leviathanlike trombone roars defiance of reckless sailors, and is echoed by an anxious trumpet. Sinbad's ship founders on the rocks with a fearful bitonal crash. As the storm subsides, the soft chords of the opening are heard again, and Scheherazade concludes her last Arabian tale on the highest harmonics of the violin.

It is hard to believe that *Scheherazade* was damned in the American press as an abomination of musical desolation. "The Russians have captured Boston!" cried the American music historian Louis Elson in 1905. "The Scheherazade engagement began with a bombardment of full orchestra, under cover of which the woodwinds advanced on the right. A furious volley of kettledrums followed, bringing up the trombone reserves and the remaining brasses. At this, the entire audience, including some very big guns, surrendered."

Le Coq d'or (The Golden Cockerel): *Introduction to the Wedding Procession (1906–7)*

Rimsky-Korsakov's opera *Le Coq d'or* was the last and musically most remarkable of his operas. The score introduces modernistic procedures far beyond the habitual language of Rimsky-Korsakov's music: whole-tone scales, polyharmonies, combining augmented triads and diminished-seventh chords, and arabesques teetering on the edge of atonality.

Rimsky-Korsakov did not live to see the production of *Le Coq d'or* on account of a squabble with the Imperial censorship office regarding some verses in the libretto, taken verbatim from a fairy tale of Pushkin's. Russia had just suffered a humiliating defeat in its war with Japan; a powerful revolutionary movement against the regime of the lassitudinous Czar Nicholas II was in full swing. The picture of a mythical czar, constantly dropping off to sleep (Nicholas II was somewhat narcoleptic), dallying with an Oriental princess (the affair of Nicholas II with the ballerina Kszesinska was freely reported in underground pamphlets), indulging in absurd diplomacy that led to disaster, was too close to Pushkin's tale and Rimsky-Korsakov's opera for comfort. The concluding verse, "The fable is false, but there is a lesson in it for certain people," was an invitation to draw embarrassing parallels, and the czar's censors wanted it deleted. Rimsky-Korsakov refused to submit to alterations, but they were finally made in the posthumous production of *Le Coq d'or* in Moscow on October 7, 1909. The original version was not restored until after the Revolution of 1917.

The coq d'or of the title refers to a weather vane in the shape of a rooster, presented to the czar by an astrologer (whose part is given to a countertenor singing falsetto, imitating the voice of a human gelding) to ward off aggression. The coq d'or is magically sensitive to movements of armies across the border. When all is well the cockerel crows the all-clear signal to the czar: "Reign lying on your bed!" But when hostilities threaten, it sounds a vociferous cock-a-doodle-doo, waking up the lackadaisical czar and alarming his somnolent kingdom. Elated, the czar promises the astrologer any reward he wishes, but is dismayed when the canny magician demands the czar's slinky bride in payment for his radar rooster. "What use is a girl to him?" asks the puzzled monarch. But the astrologer insists, and the czar, losing his patience, strikes him dead with his scepter. Thereupon the rooster takes off from his perch, alights on the czar's head and pecks him to death in the medulla oblongata.

GUSTAV MAHLER
(1860–1911)
Musical Prometheus

The life and music of Gustav Mahler can be fully understood only in the setting of his time and place, prewar Vienna, Januslike in its dual aspect of the gay capital of the waltz, and the seat of heavy intellectualism and searching philosophy. This was the city of Franz Lehár, and also of Freud; of the pleasure-loving royalty and of the tragic Mahler. It must be understood that at that time the Wagnerian wave was still rolling strong; composers did not merely write music: they created philosophies, founded religions. Although Mahler invariably denied that his symphonies had a program or a story behind them, each work was a chapter in his struggle with himself or, as he believed, a struggle with some mystical evil force.

Nietzsche once said that music of genius throws sparks of images. Mahler's music belongs to his category. Bruno Walter, the famous conductor, who was a protégé of Mahler, gives this evaluation of Mahler as a musician: "He was a great man whose visions, aspirations, and emotions reached to the utmost boundaries of human understanding. His musical inspiration came from his deep humanity and love of nature. But as a composer, he produced works that can be understood from a purely musical standpoint." As a composer, Mahler aroused controversy. Hostile critics assailed the alleged diffuseness of form and unconscionable length of his symphonies. Then the tide turned inexplicably and he came to be regarded as one of the greatest symphonists of his time.

Mahler's symphonicism is philosophical, proceeding from a guiding idea and developing as freely as human thought itself. He was not fearful of repetition when the musical ideas required emphasis, or of free association as a source of inspiration. His music was not all introspection and profundity; the emotional turbulence of his symphonic writing alternated with moments of hedonistic insouciance, signaled by the sudden intrusion of Viennese waltz tunes. In his philosophical moods, he probed eternal verities; in his topical digressions, he was an interested observer of the real world around him. For all his mystical strivings, Mahler retained in his music a vivid sense of local habitation, his beloved Viennese countryside. In each of his symphonies there is a welcome breath of fresh air from the fields, suggesting the simple melodic turns of rustic songs. In this, Mahler was a true heir of Beethoven, who also knew how to relax the philosophical profundity of his music with a gay rhythm or a folklike tune.

In selecting texts for his song cycles, Mahler, in common with his fellow Romanticists, was irresistibly drawn to poets obsessed by morbid hopelessness, grim anticipation, forlorn fatefulness. Yet these poets, and Mahler, who set their words to music, let a gleam of ultimate hope shine through the darkest of moods. Typical in this respect is Mahler's song "At Midnight." As the poet lies awake, no star smiles at him from the black firmament; he feels he is entrusted with the battle of all humanity, but his powers are too weak, and he surrenders the task into the hands of a greater power that keeps eternally the vigil of midnight. And the music, torn with long suspended dissonances, reflects this mood with trumpet sounds, concluding in a triumphant major key.

Mahler was the last Romantic composer in the last refuge of romanticism, Vienna. The First World War killed the spirit of old Europe, the nonchalant gaiety, the poetic sentimentality, and the Romantic conviction that subjective art has objective significance. His life and his music were two facets of the same spirit. Not as unsuccessful as his spiritual brother, Anton Bruckner, he made his life much more tragic than it was. Mahler was a great conductor and as such could gather financial rewards that would have been denied him had he been only the composer of complex and rarely performed symphonic works. But the afflatus of tragedy made Mahler's physical life precarious.

Universality of gifts is a Romantic ideal. Mahler approached this ideal, for he was a great interpreter of music at the conducting podium as well as a composer of extraordinary power. During his lifetime, he was known principally as director of the Vienna Opera, where he enjoyed great respect and wielded great power. Human frailty received little sympathy from Mahler. Once, when an opera soprano missed a rehearsal on account of trouble with her vocal cords, Mahler remarked: "What vocal cords? I never knew she had any." In Rome, he lectured the orchestra men on discipline and, with the aid of an Italian dictionary, accused them of *indolenza* and even *stupidità*, whereupon the orchestra went on strike. It took considerable diplomacy to patch up the quarrel and avoid the cancellation of the concert. As the musical director of the New York Philharmonic, Mahler had his difficulties with management and the all-powerful women's committee that held the purse strings and therefore ruled over the affairs of the orchestra. "In Vienna even the Emperor did not dictate to him," his wife Alma declared. "But in New York he had ten women ordering him about like a puppet." But Mahler never yielded to these pressures, and imperturbably maintained his Olympian air.

In the Romantic era, striving for greatness was quantitative. Berlioz and Liszt started the fashion by augmenting the orchestral and choral sources in their descriptive symphonic works. Wagner expanded the operatic form to tremendous proportions. Mahler's art owed much to Liszt and Wagner; to his symphonies he attached grandiose subtitles such as *Titan*, *Resurrection*, *The Giant*, and *Tragic*. His huge symphonies were often attacked as elucubrations of a self-deluded mind hermetically sealed from musical reality.

But in his own self Mahler was in a state of constant turbulence. In the margin of his unfinished Tenth Symphony he wrote: "Madness takes possession of me…. It destroys me, and I forget that I exist." Mahler's madness was not certifiable—it was the madness of a creative personality that tried to seize more fire from the heavens than Prometheus himself.

SYMPHONIES
Symphony No. 1 in D Major (Titan) (1883–88)

Mahler assigned programmatic titles to most of his symphonies, but later took them off and declared his works to be in the category of absolute music, independent of imagery or psychological content. He was twenty-eight years old when he completed his First Symphony, which he called *Titan*, with reference to the novel of that name by the Romantic writer Jean Paul Richter.

In its final form, following the classical model, Mahler's First Symphony is in four movements. (The original version of the work had five movements.) The tempo marks, in German: "Slowly, dragging"; "Powerfully turbulent"; "Solemnly and measured, without dragging"; and "Tempestuously stirring." Within these four movements, Mahler assembles a variety of sentiments and expressions, from the subjective and philosophical to folklike grotesquerie.

He gave the title "Spring Without End" to the first movement. Bucolic moments animate the score. There is even a cuckoo call. The second movement, a scherzo, includes rhythms of Moravian dances and a waltz, a reminiscence of his youth, for Mahler was born in Moravia, then a part of the Austro-Hungarian Empire. The third movement was originally entitled "March in the Manner of Callot," inspired by an engraving of the seventeenth-century French artist Jacques Callot, in which the body of a dead hunter is taken to the grave, accompanied by dancing animals celebrating their freedom from his hunt. The last movement represents the apotheosis of the human soul emerging from darkness.

Symphony No. 4 in G Major (Humoresque) (1899–1901)

For a long time after Mahler's death, his symphonies virtually disappeared from the concert repertory and were cultivated only by partisan admirers among conductors, principally Willem Mengelberg and Bruno Walter. Then the tide turned spectacularly. Mahler's music, so unashamedly Romantic in its essence and in its musical language, somehow found a resonance in the new generation. His symphonies were resurrected and he was proclaimed one of the greatest symphonists of all time.

Mahler gave grandiose programmatic subtitles to many of his symphonies; an exception was his Fourth Symphony, which he originally planned to name *Humoresque*. It was to be in six movements, each with a definite program: "The World as an Eternal Present"; "The Earthly Life"; "Caritas"; "Morning Bells";

"The World Without Trouble"; "The Heavenly Life." Some elements of this first scheme remained in the final product, which comprised four movements.

Mahler conducted the first performance of the Fourth Symphony in Munich, on November 25, 1901. The first movement is marked *Bedächtig, nicht eilen* ("Deliberately, unhurried"). It opens with an extraordinary exaltation of four flutes accompanied by sleighbells, conjuring up a pastoral scene so often represented in Mahler's symphonies. The main theme of the movement is in vigorous G major; the second theme, even more assertive, is in the dominant, thus suggesting the key relationship of orthodox sonata form. But within this traditional framework, Mahler indulges in a constant change of mood and manner, indicated by such romantic expression marks as "Fresh," "Broadly sung," "Flowingly." In the fortissimo ending, Mahler instructs the oboes and clarinets to hold bells up, a device common in horns and trumpets employed to achieve greater sonority, but rarely, if ever, applied to woodwind instruments.

The second movement, *In gemächlicher Bewegung, ohne Hast* ("In an easy motion, without haste"), is a leisurely scherzo, in ⅜, in the key of C minor. Here Mahler introduces an unusual innovation, a scordatura (i.e., discordatura, mistuning) in the first violin solo, with all four strings tuned a whole tone up in order to achieve greater brilliance. The violin thus becomes a transposing instrument. Scordatura is common in Baroque music (Vivaldi uses it in his violin concertos), but in symphonic works it is exceptional. Novelty always tempted Mahler. The mood of the scherzo is that of a wistful Viennese Ländler dance. A mournful horn signal is echoed by an angst-laden figure in the oboe. The lachrymal flatted submediant is in evidence when the movement modulates into a major key. Formally, there are five sections, three scherzolike expositions, and two triolike interludes separating them.

The third movement, *Ruhevoll* ("Peacefully"), in the key of G major, in ¼ time, is the one that Mahler described as "spherical," in the sense of a continuous surface of sounds, without a beginning or an end, an idea that is advanced by ultramodern composers of the last third of the twentieth century. Mahler's vision was prophetic. The movement is in the form of free variation, in five distinct divisions, each based on a theme bearing a morphological likeness to the other four. Regarding this movement, Mahler said to Natalie Bauer-Lechner that it represents the first set of true variations he had ever written, variations that really vary, as real variations ought to do. He described his own idea of the movement: "The music is pervaded by a divinely merry and profoundly mournful melody so that you can only laugh and weep listening to it."

The fourth movement, *Sehr behaglich* ("Very leisurely"), in ¼ time, is set in the principal key of the Symphony, G major. This is the movement that has a soprano solo, another unusual element. The words are from the collection of German folk songs *Des Knaben Wunderhorn*, arranged and rephrased by Mahler. A stern warning is inserted in the score: "It is of the greatest importance that the singer should be accompanied with utmost discretion." Among instrumental novelties there are glissandos in the cello part. The text justifies Mahler's visual impression of "perpetual cerulean blue" in the music, which was intended to portray "the heavenly life":

Wir geniessen die himmlischen Freuden, d'rum tun wir das Irdische meiden. Kein weltlich' Getümmel hört man nicht im Himmel! Lebt Alles in sanftester Ruh! Wir führen ein englisches Leben! Sind dennoch ganz lustig, ganz lustig daneben!

We enjoy the heavenly pleasures, thus we avoid the earthly things. No worldly strife is heard in Heaven! All lives in most gentle restfulness! We live an angelic life! Yet we are quite cheerful, quite cheerful as well!

Symphony No. 6 in A Minor (Tragic) *(1903–5)*

The Sixth Symphony is frequently referred to as Mahler's *Tragic* Symphony. He conducted its first performance in Essen on May 27, 1906. Romantic commentators found in it the expression of an unequal struggle of a human soul against a hostile destiny.

The work is in four movements. The first movement, Allegro energico, in $\frac{4}{4}$ time, is in the key of A minor. The principal theme is built on a vigorous descending melodic leap of an octave, which may be interpreted as the "motive of destiny." The development introduces seraphic melodies that form a contrasting group of thematic materials. Throughout, there is an alternation of minor and major triads, symbolizing the duality of pessimism and optimism.

The second movement is a scherzo. The rhythm undergoes a series of singular variations, suggesting a mischievous poltergeist at play. An ironic mood pervades this movement, with a sad smile behind the dancing notes. The third movement, Andante moderato, is a bucolic vignette, with an optimistic outlook depicted in the resonant major keys of E and E-flat. Hunting horns and tinkling cowbells paint a pastoral landscape in the background.

The finale is counterposed to the first three movements, equaling their combined length. There is an abundance of new thematic materials, interspersed among recollections of the motive of destiny originally sounded in the first movement. The strokes of a heavy hammer illustrate the finality of the unequal struggle. The thematic alternation of major and minor tonic triads emphasizes the conflict. The symphony ends in resigned submission.

Mahler was given an ovation at the first performance and was recalled eight times to the podium. The critics were not as enthusiastic. An American correspondent contributed a disdainful report in the *Musical Courier* of New York. "Mahler's Sixth Symphony," he wrote, "contains not one original thought. One hears a few notes of Tchaikovsky's B-flat-minor concerto, of *Carmen*, of the *Faust* Overture by Wagner. Mahler patches together these stray scraps from ancient and modern music with a conventional thread or two of his own, making a heterogeneous crazy quilt of music." This stood in open contradiction to an intelligent review in a Vienna newspaper written by Julius Korngold, who found in the symphony "a colossal structure built up in a thoroughly thematic style, and at the same time in a strict unity of sentiment, which Mahler designated as a tragic one." But even Korngold had misgivings. He thought that the music had a "nerve-wracking intensity that operates like an alarm.

Symphony No. 8 in E-flat Major (Symphony of a Thousand) *(1906–7)*

Mahler's Eighth Symphony, the last that he conducted himself, was advertised before its world premiere in 1910 in Munich as "The Symphony of a Thousand," for indeed the number of performers was in the vicinity of a thousand—an orchestra of 150, two mixed choruses aggregating to 500 voices, a children's choir of 350, and 8 soloists. The German papers grumbled against the high-pitched promotion, which they found in "echt amerikanischer" bad taste. But Mahler was above such mundane preoccupations, intent only on the adequate preparation of the immensely difficult and long work, rehearsing each instrumental and choral group separately for weeks before putting the whole ensemble together. The "Symphony of a Thousand" was not even a real symphony. It consisted of two parts, the first sung in Latin to the text of a medieval hymn, and the second in German to selected passages from the last act of Goethe's *Faust*, with its enigmatic conclusion: "All that passes is but a parable. All that is unattainable is the true event. The eternally feminine draws us near."

Its first performance was a triumph for Mahler; the large Exposition Concert Hall in Munich was filled with admirers, detractors, and the curious. Richard Strauss sat in the front of a box and read the piano score through a lorgnette. The musicians in the audience were impressed. The newspaper dispatches were purple with metaphors: "Flames seemed to dart from Mahler as he conducted. A thousand wills obeyed his will." But some professional music critics were openly derisive in their reviews. "Eight trumpeters and four trombone players stood up in a row at the top of the platform and blew for all they were worth into the faces of the audience," wrote an American observer. "There was also a gentleman who played on a large concert grand piano. He was very industrious. I know it because I saw him. Unfortunately, in the general clamor, none of his notes even got as far as my ear."

VOCAL MUSIC

Songs of a Wayfarer (Lieder eines fahrenden Gesellen) (1883–85)

The cycle of four songs, *Songs of a Wayfarer* was Mahler's first significant work, written when he was in his early twenties, to his own texts. They are songs of frustrated love, a frequent theme of German poetry. The music is remarkable, for it contains virtually all of Mahler's melodic, rhythmic, and harmonic elements later developed in his symphonies—the characteristic transitions from momentary exhilaration to depressive sadness, the use of folklike dance rhythms, the ambivalence of major and minor modes, revealed particularly in his predilection for the lowered subdominant in major keys.

The first song, "Wenn mein Schatz Hochzeit macht" ("When my Beloved Marries") portrays the distress of a lover whose beloved is married to another. Mahler described the various effects and actions on that sad day: "I go into my little room, darkened room, and I weep over my treasured one," but still he calls her "little blue flower" and "sweet little bird." But "all songs are now gone!"

The second song, "Ging heut' morgen übers Feld" ("This Morning I Walked over the Field"), is an ode to nature, a union with life in the fields. There are musical links in it with the finale of Mahler's Fourth Symphony and the "youth" movement in *The Song of the Earth*.

The third song, "Ich hab' ein glühend Messer" ("I Have a Glowing Knife"), pictures the poet with a glowing dagger of pain in his heart, that "cuts so deeply into every joy and every desire." When he looks at the sky he sees the two blue eyes of his beloved there; when he ventures into a yellow field he sees her again; and when he awakens from his dream, he hears her silvery laughter.

The fourth song, "Die zwei blauen Augen" ("The Two Blue Eyes"), is another variation on the theme of love: "The blue eyes of my dear treasure sent me out into the faraway world, into the silent night." He falls asleep under a tree, which bestrews him with blossoms. This brings him back to life, and everything is good again. But the final third in the music is the minor third.

Songs of a Wayfarer
Lieder eines fahrenden Gesellen

1 Wenn mein Schatz Hochzeit macht

Songs of the Death of Children (Kindertotenlieder) *(1901–1904)*

To Gustav Mahler, music was a language so profoundly human and at the same time so impenetrably arcane that he could fully accept Schopenhauer's aphorism that a person who can understand the message of music will achieve the knowledge of ultimate mysteries of the universe. Mahler's whole life seemed to exemplify this theomachy through music. He wrestled with the gods. The music he wrote was to him a phenomenon that might affect the destiny not only of himself, but also of others. He blamed himself for the death of his infant child, which occurred shortly after he wrote his *Songs of the Death of Children* to extremely morbid texts dealing with the death of small children. On the margins of the manuscript of his unfinished Tenth Symphony he scrawled: "Devil! Come and take me away with you, for I am accursed!" Even his sense of humor had a morbid turn. Asked whether he was satisfied with a performance of one of his works, he replied, "Do not speak of it! The very thought makes me turn in my grave!"

For the texts of his song cycle he selected five poems by Friedrich Rückert. Rückert, a nineteenth-century German poet, some of whose verses were set to music by Schubert and Schumann, wrote the poems after the death of his own two children from scarlet fever. Mahler set them to music in 1902, and arranged them for orchestra three years later. When Mahler's own daughter, Maria Anna, died, also of scarlet fever, at the age of four in 1907, he said that it was perhaps a defiance of fate to have written the songs. Indeed, the German originals touch the ultimate in irremediable grief. Here are the mottoes of the five songs:

1. Now the sun will rise so brightly as though no disaster struck in the night. Misfortune happened to me alone. The sun shines on all.
2. Now I know why your eyes reflected these dark flames. I did not suspect then that the beam was already directed there, where all light is born.
3. When your mother enters the door, I turn my head, not toward her, but toward the place near the threshold where I used to see your dear little face when you joyfully came in, O, my little daughter.
4. Often I think they have merely gone out. Soon they will be back in the house. The day is bright! O do not be anxious! They merely took a longer walk.
5. In such a storm, I would never let the children out of the house! Yet they have been taken away, and I did not dare to say a word.

Mahler's musical settings of Rückert's poems reveal a rare affinity of feeling between poet and musician. The chromatic and diatonic steps in the melody are used with literal correspondence to pervading anguish or imagined hope, and the instrumental accompaniment often picks up the singing line in the middle of a phrase, as if to express the speechlessness of words. The last song ends with an otherworldly lullaby: "They rest there, in storm, as in a mother's house." Mahler makes this notation in the published edition of the songs: "These five songs are intended as one inseparable unit, and in performance their continuity should not be broken by applause at the close of any of the songs, or by any other interference."

Kindertotenlieder
Songs of the Deaths of Children

1 Nun will die Sonn' so hell aufgeh'n!

The Song of the Earth (Das Lied von der Erde) *(1907–1909)*

Bruno Walter, Mahler's friend and interpreter, tells a strange story that could have come from Edgar Allan Poe:

> While at work in his cottage in Toblach, [Mahler] was suddenly frightened by an indefinable noise. All at once something terribly dark came rushing in by the window, and when he jumped up in horror, he saw that he was in the presence of an eagle which filled the little room with its violence. The fearsome meeting was quickly over, and the eagle disappeared as stormily as it had come. When Mahler sat down, exhausted by his fright, a crow came fluttering from under the sofa and flew out.

Bruno Walter thinks that this episode happened at the time Mahler was composing *The Song of the Earth*, and that Mahler referred to the work as a symphony in songs: "It was to have been his Ninth. Subsequently, however, he changed his mind. He thought of Beethoven and Bruckner, whose Ninth had marked the ultimate of their creation and life, and did not care to challenge fate. He turned to the Abschied [Farewell—the last movement] and said: What do you think of it? Will not people do away with themselves when they hear it?"

But Mahler did write a Ninth Symphony, and even started on a Tenth. As to *The Song of the Earth*, it is not numbered among Mahler's symphonies at all. It must therefore be considered, as Mahler said to Bruno Walter, a symphony of songs, separate from his purely symphonic works.

The selection of texts to these songs is also characteristic for the spirit of pre-war Europe. It was a set of Chinese poems, translated into German. Chinese poetry and Japanese art were extremely popular among European intellectuals who believed there was in the Orient an immediacy of feeling, a spirit of communion with the eternal that no Westerner could approach. The selection of poetry cannot, therefore, be accidental, and must be regarded as part of the design. All songs of *The Song of the Earth* are united by a single motto, a descending progression of three tones, A—G—E. These three tones may be regarded as a part of the Chinese pentatonic scale, but there is no evidence that Mahler made this connection. The motive was not used explicitly; rather it was Mahler's private magic formula, which he employed in various forms, in augmentation (that is, played twice as slowly) or diminution (twice as fast). It also appears in the retrograde motion, and in ascending intervals, through inversion. All three notes appear together in the concluding chord of the entire work, signifying unity. The symbolic quality of *The Song of the Earth* is thus plainly indicated; yet the movements are greatly diversified, from deep pantheistic contemplation to simple earthly joys.

There are six songs. The first is a "Drinking Song of the Misery of the Earth." The horns give the opening theme, which is built on the three notes of the leading motive. The violins present the leading motive in still another transformation. Tonality is clearly maintained throughout the first movement, but the modulations are frequent and sudden. The pessimistic refrain of the song "Dark is life, and so is death," is heard in a lugubrious phrase in G minor.

The second movement, or the second song, is entitled "The Lonely One in Autumn." It opens in D minor, and the characteristic indication in lieu of the tempo mark is "Somewhat dragging. Tired out." Against the background of muted violins, the oboe intones sadly the three notes of the leading motive. The contralto sings the song of loneliness and soul fatigue. The minor keys are remarkably prevalent.

The third song, "Of Youth," is one of the most optimistic utterances in symphonic literature, the scherzo of this symphony of songs. The orchestration abounds in woodwind color, and the impression of childish delight is heightened by the high register of the entire piece. Also, the Chinese pentatonic scale is used in this movement explicitly, imparting to the piece a definite local color.

The fourth movement is entitled "Of Beauty." The text of the song describes young maidens at play, and once more the pentatonic scale is explicitly employed. There are rhythmic figures that suggest a light dance. This and the third movement constitute the two spots of sunshine in Mahler's pessimistic symphony in songs.

The fifth movement is called "Drunkard in Spring." But the drinking is not gay, it is an escape from life's trouble. The theme is gay but wry, with melodic intervals distorted to express bitterness in artificial gaiety.

The sixth movement is "The Farewell." This is the movement that Mahler thought would inspire suicidal thoughts. The song describes the death of the day, when the sun sets, and the world falls asleep. The oboe, to which Mahler is wont to give his saddest tunes, plays solo against a subdued orchestra. The rhythm grows less distinct, and the feeling of farewell is achieved by a gradual fading away of all music. *The Song of the Earth* closes on a C-major chord with an added sixth. This added sixth is, of course, the high note of the leading motive, A—G—E.

The Song of the Earth was performed posthumously in Munich, on November 20, 1911, six months and two days after Mahler's death; Bruno Walter conducted. The reception of the work and the estimate of its place among Mahler's works varied considerably. Ernest Newman, reviewing Walter's recording in the *Sunday Times of London* of November 27, 1939, places this music very high:

> *Das Lied von der Erde* is not only Mahler's greatest work, but one of the supreme creations of German music. In its special sphere—that of the mutual interpenetration of the two worlds of musical beauty and philosophic contemplation—it is without a rival since *Parsifal*. Not even *Parsifal*, indeed, moves us more profoundly than the long final section of *Das Lied von der Erde*, the concluding pages of which are without a doubt the saddest of all music.

On the other side of the balance is Philip Hale, who summed up Mahler's status in a review in the *Boston Herald* of October 17, 1931: "A strange figure in the symphonic field; a man of great moments but, as Rossini said of Wagner, of dreadful half-hours." "He was looked upon as a great artist, and possibly he was one," commented the *New York Tribune* after Mahler's death, "but he failed to convince the people of New York of the fact, and therefore his American career was not a success. We cannot see how any of his music can long survive him." The *New York Sun* said cryptically: "If he had gone to afternoon teas, he would have been more popular, and would be alive today."

CLAUDE DEBUSSY
(1862–1918)
Poet of Musical Impressions

The French poet Stéphane Mallarmé (1842–1898) wrote: "To name an object is to suppress three quarters of the enjoyment of a poem; this enjoyment consists of the happiness of divining the meaning little by little. To suggest—that is the dream." The music of Claude Debussy responds to these sentiments. Its melodies are ethereal; its suggestions are dreamlike. Music historians call him an Impressionist by analogy with the art of painting in small brush strokes. In his musical impressions, Debussy is attracted by the lesser manifestations of nature; the waves rather than the ocean; the gentle wind rather than the tempest; half-awakened human sensations rather than grand passions; the moon rather than the sun.

The titles of Debussy's works reflect this charm of the minuscule and elusive: "Footsteps in the Snow," "Mists," "The Shadows of the Trees," "Sounds and Perfumes," and "The Goldfish." In his most celebrated piece, "Clair de lune," Debussy paints the silvery moonbeams in delicate tones. The initial musical phrase seems motionless; its serenity is not disturbed when arpeggios begin to roll underneath like a mirrored image of the immobile moon in the sky. In that exquisite creation *Prélude à l'après-midi d'un faune* (*Prelude to "The Afternoon of a Faun"*), inspired by Mallarmé's poem, it is the pastoral flute that sets the mood of poetic dalliance; from that phrase, Debussy develops a charming miniature "in nostalgia and in light, with finesse, with yearning, with richness," as Mallarmé described the music in a letter to Debussy after hearing it for the first time.

In Debussy's symphonic sketch *La Mer*, the dialogue of the wind and the sea is at times turbulent, but the dynamic surgings are of brief duration, pulsating rhythmically without drowning the listener in a heaving tide of water music. The opening movement, "From Dawn to Noon on the Sea," draws a tonal picture of infinite delicacy, and yet the impression is precise. In his opera *Pelléas et Mélisande*, he depicted Maeterlinck's tragedy of love by indirection, in subdued colors, but the magic of this tonal understatement makes the music all the more impressive, and the emotions more penetrating than in conventional operatic writing.

This subtlety of impressions required the formation of a new musical language. Debussy developed his own melody, in poetical musical phrases, in free rhythm, in shimmering tonalities. He moved his harmonies in parallel motion, which was a radical departure from conventional practice. He emancipated discords and abolished the resolutions of dissonant chords prescribed by academic rules.

In search of fluid tonality, Debussy turned to a scale of whole tones, proceeding in uniform steps outside of either major or minor keys. From the Orient, he adopted the pentatonic scale, such as can be played on the black keys of the piano. One of his piano pieces is written in the whole-tone scale, with the middle section in the pentatonic scale on black keys. When he wished to evoke the archaic past, Debussy used the ancient modes, such as can be represented by scales played on white keys starting on other notes than C. In his harmony he applied the consecutive fifths, which were common in the simple music of the remote past, forbidden in classical harmony.

Debussy's orchestration was similarly unconventional; he favored unusual combinations of instruments. He gave most of his telling melodies to the gentle flute; his violins often hovered in high treble. He divided instrumental groups into several sections, so that each player had an individual part to perform. He was not building in large sonorities; rumbling basses and sounding brass had little attraction for him. He muted his horns to change their tone color; he relished the pizzicato strings and the plucked harp. In his orchestral tone paintings, each note had an individual importance; there was no filling out for external effect.

Such innovations, and such recessions to the old, came as a shock to Debussy's contemporaries. He was called an anarchist of music. He was accused of renouncing melody and of converting harmony into perpetual discord. Alarmed by the growing influence of Debussy's music on a new generation of composers, a group of French music theorists published a symposium of opinions under the pointed title *Le Cas Debussy* (*The Debussy Case*), in which Debussy was denounced as a false prophet. Numerous academic musicians expressed the conviction that Debussy's music was nothing but a symptom of decadence, and that it would never exercise lasting influence. Now that Debussy has become a classic of modern music, this little book makes strange reading.

Debussy excels in tonal miniatures and in half-spoken emotions. But he was also capable of great gaiety and of picturesque evocation of festive moods. There is nothing in contemporary orchestral writing that can rival the excitement and the beauty of Debussy's symphonic picture, "Iberia" (from *Images*). This music has more Spanish verve than many scores by the Spanish composers themselves. Debussy makes the violins sound like guitars; the players are instructed to take their instruments from under the chin, put them in their arms, and imitate the guitar by strumming the strings.

Exotic faraway lands fascinated Debussy. When he visited the Paris Exposition in 1889, it was not the Eiffel Tower (which was then inaugurated) that attracted him, but the Burmese dancers with their chimelike gamelans. He had never traveled to the Orient, but his imagination was stirred by its life and manners. For the cover of the published score of *La Mer,* he selected a Japanese print representing a breaking wave.

Debussy possessed a keen sense of humor. In his piano suite, *Children's Corner* (the original title is in English), he parodies the piano exercises of good old Clementi in a movement entitled "Doctor Gradus ad Parnassum." And in the last movement, "Golliwog's Cakewalk," written in the style of early American ragtime, he pokes fun at Wagner by introducing a motive from *Tristan and Isolde*, followed by musical laughter in the treble.

Debussy's art and his new technique are inseparable. His musical impressions could not be set within the framework of nineteenth-century ideas. He revolutionized music without in any way destroying the values of the old. No composer in the new century was unaffected by the profound change that Debussy brought about on the musical scene.

Prélude à l'après-midi d'un faune *(1892-94)*

In the annals of modern music, Debussy occupies an exalted niche as the founder of the French Impressionist movement. Debussy himself deprecated the term; he insisted that he was a composer in the classical tradition of French music. In his later years he liked to add to his name the simple words "musicien français."

The word "impressionism" originated as a derisive neologism describing the manner of painting in Monet's picture *Sunrise, an Impression*, exhibited in 1863 in the Salon des Refusés, after it was rejected by the Paris Salon of acceptable art. Monet's innovation in his "impression" consisted in the subjective treatment of a landscape, in which the image is intentionally thrown out of focus and the lines are blurred so as to bring out the psychological aspects of the scene as perceived by the painter's eye and mind. Impressionism thus challenged the cardinal principles of classical and Romantic art—realism of representation and naturalism in detail.

Rather than be offended by the sarcastic designation, Monet and his group accepted it as an effective slogan, and openly declared themselves Impressionists. This was not the first time that contemptuous sobriquets had been adopted as honorific by their targets. *Sans-culottes*, literally "without knee-breeches," was a demeaning appellation used by French aristocrats for the poor of Paris, but it was picked up as a fighting cry by the disenfranchised populace. The Ashcan School, as a group of realistic American painters of the first decade of the twentieth century was collectively described by the critics, became the title of an honorable chapter in the history of American art. For that matter, "baroque," originally meaning "bizarre," "ungainly," or "tasteless," has been glorified in its application to the sublime art of Bach and Handel.

Is the analogy between French Impressionist art and the music of Debussy at all valid? Analytically, yes. In Debussy's works, as in the paintings of Monet, Manet, Degas, and Cézanne, subjective impressions of objective sounds and lights are recorded with free strokes of the brush; melodic and rhythmic lines are drawn in evanescent curves; the colors themselves are attenuated, often coalescing into a neutrality of complementary hues.

Paul Verlaine describes the essence of impressionism with penetrating intuition in his *Art poétique,* counterposing to the classical precept "est modus in rebus" (Horace's *Ars Poetica*) a refined concept of "la chanson grise où l'indécis au précis se joint" ("the gray song where the indistinct merges with the precise"). And, in a single expressive line, he sums up the aesthetic code of Symbolist poetry and Impressionist art alike: "Pas la couleur, rien que la nuance!" (No color, nothing but shades!) The formula fits Debussy's music to perfection: in it, the indecisiveness of the design is joined by the precision of execution. The gross colors are abandoned, and the fine nuance is installed as a chief artistic aim. Just as the eye is trained to differentiate between light and shadow in Impressionist art, so the ear is disciplined to register and absorb the measured quanta of sonic impulses in Impressionist music. Yet Debussy's melodic curves are nowhere discontinuous, and the melorhythmic particles are integrated in a musical wave in uninterrupted emanation.

Debussy was a master of subdued sonorities, emulating Verlaine's "chanson grise" in the gray but luminous radiation of his instrumental writing. Even his most disagreeable critic, Camille Bellaigue (who was Debussy's classmate at the Paris Conservatory), had to admit grudgingly that Debussy's music "fait peu de bruit" ("makes little noise"), but, he added malevolently, the small noise it makes is "un vilain petit bruit" ("mean little noise").

The technique of musical impressionism comprises many novel procedures: parallel progressions of triads, dominant-seventh chords and dominant-ninth chords; whole-tone scales, causing a temporary suspension of the sense of tonality; free application of unresolved dissonances; individualized instrumentation with unusual combinations of instruments; and, finally, abolition of academic conventions such as the development and recapitulation, in favor of a more supple associative process of composition.

In no other work of Debussy is the spirit of impressionism revealed more poetically than in his *Prélude à l'après-midi d'un faune,* a symphonic eclogue inspired by the poem of Stéphane Mallarmé. Mallarmé, a Symbolist poet par excellence, paints a faun not as a familiar wood sprite of Greek mythology, but as a psychologically disturbed spirit of modern times, beset by anxieties and uncertain of his emotions. The faun reflects on the events of the afternoon of the previous day, reminiscing about his dalliance with sensuous nymphs. He tries desperately to perpetuate these elusive images before they vanish with the substance of his dreams. But were the ravishing creatures present in the reality of that afternoon, or were they the feverish figments of his superexcited imagination? Unable to resolve his doubts, the faun fashions a syrinx from reeds growing by the lake, and he plays upon it a hymn to love.

The *Prélude à l'après-midi d'un faune* was first performed at a concert of the Société Nationale de Musique in Paris on December 23, 1894. A curious notice appeared in a theatrical annual for that year: "The poem of Mallarmé, which inspired Debussy, is so sadistic that the management decided not to print it in the program book, because young girls attend these concerts."

Mallarmé was profoundly impressed by Debussy's music. "It extends the emotion of my poem," he said, "and it recreates the scene much more vividly than color could have done in painting." He inscribed his book of poems to Debussy with the following quatrain:

Sylvain d'haleine première
Si ta flûte a réussi
Ouïs toute la lumière
Qu'y soufflera Debussy!

It is interesting that in this inscription Mallarmé equates light with sound: "Sylvan of primal breath,/leven if your flute has been successful,/llisten to all the light/lthat Debussy will breathe into it."

The instrumentation of the *Prélude à l'après-midi d'un faune* is remarkable. There are no trumpets, no trombones, and no drums. The only instrument to mark the rhythmic caesura is a pair of antique cymbals. The flute is the faun, accompanied by other flutes, oboes, an English horn, clarinets, bassoons, four horns, two harps, and strings. The opening flute solo evokes the sound of a panpipe in undulating convolutions. Despite its fluctuating chromatics, the tonality, E major, is clearly outlined at cadential points. A contrasting theme arises in the violins; it is a spacious diatonic melody, limning the elusive and distant nymphs. Again the melancholy faun intones his dolent air, evoking Mallarmé's lines: "Ne murmure point d'eau que ne verse ma flûte au bosquet arrosé d'accords" ("No water murmurs except that which pours from my flute and sprinkles the plants with its harmony").

The ending is remarkable. Two horns join a solo violin in three-part harmony, forming a series of four mutually exclusive triads comprising all twelve notes of the chromatic scale. This is an intriguing anticipation of the dodecaphonic future of the new century.

Pelléas et Mélisande *(1893, 1898, 1901–2)*

This work was Debussy's masterpiece, a lyric drama in five acts and twelve tableaux, which portrays with translucent penetration the peripeteia of Maurice Maeterlinck's poignantly symbolic play.

Debussy began the work in August 1893, completing the original score two years later. However, he then revised the score, completing a second version in 1898. He reorchestrated the second version in December 1901, and then finally composed some further symphonic interludes shortly before the first performance of the work on April 28, 1902.

Debussy's musical setting is of startling originality and concentrated power of latent expressiveness. The voices sing the poetic lines according to the inflections of natural speech, following every nuance of sentiment in a continuously diversified declamation. The melodic curves tend toward their harmonic asymptotes in tangential proximity and form chords of quasi-bitonal consistency, the modal intervalic progressions with their concomitant cadential plagalities imparting a nostalgically archaic sound to the music. The frequent parallel motion of triadic units, seventh chords and ninth chords provide instant modulatory shifts, extensive vertical edifices in fourths and fifths reposing on deeply anchored pedal points, giving stability in fluidity, while the attenuated orchestra becomes a multicellular organism in which the instrumental solos are projected with pellucid distinction echoing the text in allusive symbolism (when light is mentioned, the strings are luminously tremulous; for water, harps respond). The psychologically adumbrative motives reflect the appearances of dramatic characters in graphically imprecise identifications.

Two weeks before the dress rehearsal of the production, the Paris daily *Le Figaro* published an open letter from Maeterlinck sharply denouncing both Michel Carré's libretto and Debussy's setting and expressing a wish that the production should result in a "prompt and resounding failure." His wrath was aroused because Debussy preferred Mary Garden in the title role to Georgette Leblanc, Maeterlinck's common-law wife.

After the public dress rehearsal on April 28, many critics reacted favorably to the production. Still, there were some who were less-than-impressed, including Arthur Pougin writing in *Le Ménestrel*:

> The public is tired of hearing music which is not music; it is weary of this heavy, continuous declamation, without air and light; it is sated with this unsupportable abuse of chromatics, thanks to which all sense of tonality disappears along with the melodic sense.... Rhythm, melody, tonality— these are three things that are unknown to M. Debussy. His music is vague, without color or nunace; without motion, without life.... What a collection of dissonances, sevenths and ninths, ascending even by disjunct intervals!... Very pretty! No. I will never have anything to do with these musical anarchists!

Nocturnes *(1892–99)*

Debussy composed his orchestral suite *Nocturnes* between 1892 and 1899. In a program note, he or someone speaking on his behalf pointed out that the title had nothing to do with the conventional form of nocturne as glorified by Chopin, but seeks to reflect the gradually diminished light of day before its nocturnal darkening. The first movement, *Nuages*, suggests such a twilight mood with clouds moving slowly in gentle two-part counterpoint, the kind of intervallic construction that suggested to some overeducated commentators a similar procedure in some of Mussorgsky's music; there is a justification for this parallel, for Debussy spent several months in Russia in his youth as a house pianist in the employ of Madame von Meck, the benefactor of Tchaikovsky, and was exposed to Russian music. Madame von Meck made him play a lot of her beloved Tchaikovsky, but later he picked up some Mussorgsky scores which produced a more lasting impression on him.

If *Nuages* is properly affiliated with twilight moods, the second part of the suite, *Fêtes*, is anything but nocturnal. Debussy's program note describes it as a festival of rhythm, dancing in the air, with bursts of sudden light. A procession passes through the festival and becomes a part of it; a luminous dust pervades the scene.

The third movement, *Sirènes*, is even more remote from nocturnal inspiration. It is scored for a women's chorus and orchestra. The chorus is wordless; the sirens did not have to lure Ulysses with articulate verbal exhortations. They sing in a curious undulation of major seconds, a manner calculated to produce a mesmerizing effect, which fits perfectly into the notion of what sirens must have sounded to the imagination of a French musician of the fin de siècle.

So distinct is the final movement of *Nocturnes* in its manner and instrumentation that it was not put on the program together with the two other movements at the first performance of the suite by the Lamoureux Orchestra, conducted by Camille Chevillard in Paris on December 9, 1900. The complete work, including *Sirènes*, was first produced by the same orchestra in Paris on October 27, 1901.

String Quartet, Op. 10 *(1893)*

During the desperate days of the German offensive in the First World War, Debussy proclaimed his national faith by signing, after his name, "Musicien français." Indeed, Debussy was a French musician to the core. To understand Debussy and his music, it is necessary to reconstruct the peculiar ambiance of literary and artistic France at the end of the century, the Paris of Baudelaire, Verlaine, and Mallarmé. The dictum of Mallarmé, whose poetry inspired Debussy's *Prélude à l'après-midi d'un faune*, might well be applied to the music of Debussy: "To name an object is to suppress three-quarters of the enjoyment of the poem, the pleasure of guessing step by step; to suggest is our aim."

But suggestion must also be imbued with logic, like the method of induction in mathematics: departing from a proved relationship between two initial members of a series, to establish this relationship for the entire series. Robert Jardillier, an ardent Debussyist, quotes this line of Verlaine, "cette fantaisie et cette raison," in discussing Debussy's Quartet:

> Reason? It is symbolized by the adoption of a cyclical theme, which pervades the entire Quartet, a close relative of the cantus firmus which unified the medieval Mass. Fantasy? This theme undergoes so many modifications that it is hardly recognizable. It engenders, in the second movement, a sort of furtive Andalousian dance. It gives birth, an instant later, to an infinitely melancholy Andante. All this is bathed in vibrant harmony. This harmony was deemed revolutionary, but that was not its essence. Whether he invoked the pre-Raphaelite virgin, the night of Baudelaire, the park of Verlaine, or the fawn of Mallarmé, whether he gave free rein to his imagination in a string quartet, Debussy showed himself capable of offering, better than anyone else, a key to the life of dreams.

Indeed, the transfigurations of the theme of the quartet are audacious in the extreme. Here the danger of monotony is no less great than the opposite danger, of variegation to the point of the loss of identity. Debussy combats both dangers by deploying an extraordinary range of harmonic and rhythmic variety, still keeping the intervallic integrity of the theme. This theme is stated explicitly at the very opening and recurs, with almost no changes of outline, in all four instruments in the first movement of the quartet, against the varied counterpoint of the rest of the voices, or in the splendid isolation of a solo figure against a shimmering foil of accompanying harmonies. Because the theme of the quartet is based on the interval of the tritone, the feeling of tonality is fluid. But tonality is never abandoned; indeed, a key signature is given in every movement, and the quartet itself is marked as being in the key of G minor. The whole-tone scale, which became so important in Debussy's later works, and which, by its very nature, is tonally neutral, for no dominant and no common triad can be built in it, appears in the quartet but incidentally.

The String Quartet is the only work of its kind Debussy ever wrote. The medium of chamber music, and particularly that of an ensemble of homogeneous instruments, held little attraction for Debussy, whose imagination craved the palette of an orchestra, or an Impressionist poem for a vocal setting. The quartet was performed for the first time by the Ysaÿe Quartet, to which it was dedicated, on December 29, 1893, at a concert of the Société Nationale in Paris. The reception was a mixed one, but there were no cries of outrage such as greeted, several years later, the production of *Pelléas*.

Paul Dukas, Debussy's fellow Impressionist, gave a fine appreciation of Debussy's Quartet:

All is clear and neatly outlined, despite the great freedom of form. The melodic essence of the work is concentrated, but possesses a rich flavor. It impregnates the harmonic tissue with penetrating and original poesy. The harmony itself, despite its great audacity, never shocks. Debussy delights in the succession of full, harmonies, in dissonances without crudity, more harmonious indeed, in their complexity, than the concords themselves. Debussy's melody treads as though on a sumptuous, cunningly ornamented carpet, full of exotic colors, but devoid of gaudiness and discord.

At the first performance of the quartet in Boston, Edward Burlingame Hill, an early champion of French music in America and himself an eminent composer in an idiom that may be called American Impressionism, wrote in the *Boston Evening Transcript* of March 11, 1902:

It is not difficult to appreciate the enthusiasm of the few for Debussy. This Quartet, while decidedly, even audaciously, ultra-modern, is coherent and logical: it shows originality of form without departing too rhapsodically from convention. It is wonderfully subtle poetic music, and seems almost totally new in quartet idiom. Without degenerating into so-called orchestra style, there are many new and startlingly beautiful color effects.

Symphonic Suite: La Mer (1903–5)

When Debussy asked the composer Erik Satie (1866–1925) which part of *La Mer* he liked best, Satie replied: "The first movement, 'From dawn until noon,' particularly about a quarter of eleven." Assuming that the dawn broke in Paris at six o'clock, the spot in the music at a quarter of eleven in the first movement of *La Mer* would come at one of the loveliest passages of the work, when the divided cellos play the motive of the sea. Satie had made a good choice.

In a letter written at the time of the composition of *La Mer*, Debussy said that he had always loved the sea and was destined to be a sailor. Yet he never made a prolonged sea voyage, and his cross-Channel trips to England were infrequent. *La Mer*, a symphonic suite of three movements, is a series of fleeting images of the sea in Debussy's mind.

He revealed some hesitancy about the titles of the three movements. His first idea was to name them as follows: "Mer belle aux îles sanguinaires" "Jeux de vagues," and "Le vent fait danser la mer." The title of the second movement remained, but the first movement was renamed "De l'aube a midi sur la mer" and the third, "Dialogue du vent et de la mer." Debussy completed the score on March 5, 1905, and the first performance took place on October 15, 1905, at the Lamoureux Concerts in Paris, under the direction of Camille Chevillard.

Debussy disliked the word "impressionism," with which his music was tagged, even though the term was accepted as honorable by French painters, to whom it was first applied. His musical language is Impressionist only in the sense that it does not derive from the formal elements of classical music. It is revolutionary in content. Disregarding sacrosanct conservatory rules, Debussy employs parallel progressions of unresolved dissonances, consecutive fifths, and that intriguing exotic scale of whole tones. He dispenses with the classical development of principal subjects, and the subjects themselves are reduced to essentials. A fleeting wave of sound, rushing forward with passionate vehemence, replaces the carefully fashioned type of Baroque melodies; a languorous recession of the melodic line signals the conclusion of the musical phrase. And since dissonances are emancipated, the demarcation between formal sections becomes indistinct, and the flow of music acquires a sense of perpetual transition. Because of the unstable equilibrium of structure, subtle details and dynamic gradations assume great importance in Debussy's music. This is the world in which, as the poet said, "le précis et l'imprécis se rencontrent."

In the first movement, "From Dawn until Noon on the Sea," the panorama of Debussy's ocean unrolls with gentle waves breaking at the shore. The hours from dawn to noon are compressed into a few minutes of music in the score with uncanny hydrological accuracy; the ocean grows lyrical as the day advances, and the melody of the divided cellos sings the enchantment of the sun approaching the meridian. The orchestra regains its undivided strength, without ever attaining the grossness of fortissimo.

The second movement, "Play of the Waves," is the Impressionist equivalent of a scherzo. The orchestra is split into sparkling sections; luminous motives break into prismatic fragments. The continuity of the coruscating interplay remains unbroken to the end.

The last movement, "Dialogue of the Wind and the Sea," starts with a powerful gust of wind in the bass register. The sea is portrayed by a tense chromatic motion underneath the tonal surface, which remains unruffled. But as the kinetic energy of the wind increases, the music becomes turbulent. There is an interesting transformation of the melody of the sea into a progression of whole tones. The waves of sound increase in amplitude, in constant affirmation of tonal grandeur. The work ends triumphantly in a sonorous apotheosis of major tonality.

Why did this magnificent work arouse so much indignation on the part of otherwise enlightened critics on both sides of the Atlantic? In Paris, in a collection of violent dissenting opinions published under the title *Le Cas Debussy*, Debussy was called a "déformateur musical." When *La Mer* reached the United States, the revulsion toward the music was universal among professional music critics. Louis Elson, a respectable American pedagogue and music critic, wrote with a degree of misplaced wit:

> It may be possible that in the transit to America the title of this work has been changed. It is possible that Debussy did not intend to call it *La Mer,* but *Le Mal de mer,* which would at once make the music as clear as day. It is a series of symphonic pictures of seasickness. The first movement is *Headache.* The second is *Doubt,* picturing moments of dread suspense, whether or no! The third movement, with its explosions and rumbling has now a self-evident purpose. The hero is endeavoring to throw up his bootheels.

The *New York Post* wrote: "Debussy's music is the dreariest kind of rubbish. Does anybody for a moment doubt that Debussy would not write such chaotic, meaningless, cacophonous, ungrammatical stuff, as in *The Sea,* if he could invent a melody?" The *New York World* shrugged its Atlas shoulders: "New York heard a new composition called *The Sea,* and New York is probably still wondering why. The work is by the most modern of modern Frenchmen, Debussy. Compared with this, the most abstruse compositions of Richard Strauss are as primer stories to hear and to comprehend."

Two Dances for Harp and String Orchestra: Danse sacrée, Danse profane *(1904)*

During the first decade of the twentieth century, Debussy was the most controversial figure in Paris. He attracted fanatic supporters and he found equally fanatic opponents. The viewpoint of admirers was clear: they welcomed the creation of a new art, and the innovation of music by sonorous suggestion rather than formal composition. The opponents were equally strong in their convictions. They accused Debussy of spreading a musical anemia through the destruction of formal ties that hold a musical composition together. Camille Saint-Saëns (1835–1921) could not reconcile himself to Debussy's music even after Debussy was dead. He wrote in 1920 that Debussy's works resemble music no more than the palette used by an artist in his work resembles a painting. Even the composer and pianist Ferruccio Busoni (1866–1924), who was anything but a musical Tory, said that Debussy's music is like the picture of a beautiful sunset; it fades when one looks at it too closely. The judgment of posterity upon Debussy's music is neither enthusiastic acceptance nor a definite rejection. Debussy has assumed his role as a historic figure. Contemporary musicians rarely imitate his style, but without Debussy behind them, even neoclassical composers of today would not be able to write music effectively.

The great Debussy is represented by *Pelléas et Mélisande*, *La Mer*, some of the *Préludes*, and most of his songs. The Two Dances for Harp and String Orchestra, composed in 1904, are lesser known. These dances were written especially for the chromatic harp, which was new at the time. The first dance is called *Danse sacrée*; the second is *Danse profane*. This antimony of moods is expressed in Debussy's music not by an exaggerated piety of sentiment for the sacred dance, or the savagery of movement in the second, but impressionistically, by suggestion. The harmonic and melodic idiom is interesting because it represents a complete catalogue of characteristic devices employed in French Impressionist music. The *Danse sacrée* employs neomodal progressions in block chords, with a sprinkling of whole-tone scales in the middle section. The *Danse profane* is couched in the Lydian mode, obviously with reference to the ethos of ancient Greek music in which the Lydian mode was regarded as effeminate and lascivious. It is followed by passages in the pentatonic scale. The harmonic idiom includes dominant-ninth chords and progressions of diminished-seventh chords; there are successions of parallel triads. The sonority of both pieces is reduced by the limitations of the harp.

The critical reception of the dances after their first performance at the Cologne concerts in Paris on November 6, 1904, was mixed. The critic of *Le Ménestrel* found "des jolis effets, des recherches amusantes" but complained about the overdose of whole-tone scales. But another critic commented on "an ultrarefined art, idealistic and sensual, absolutely new and of unique gracefulness." From the camp of irreconcilable anti-Debussyists came a growl:

> In M. Debussy's music, dissonance has become the rule and consonance the exception. Consequently those who admire the former style applauded his Deux Danses for chromatic harp and orchestra; whilst the devotees of the latter type of music made grimaces.... His musical plan has no architectural quality; it is vague, hazy, disturbing, almost morbid. Its counterpart in Impressionist painting is to be found in... canvases where the subjects are so submerged in a misty atmosphere as to be barely visible, and where suffering seems to be the dominant note.

Jeux *(1912)*

Debussy was a thorough Parisian who took great interest in all things passing on the Paris scene, from Symbolist poetry to Art Nouveau, from exotic Oriental music, which he heard at the Paris Exposition, to popular American dances at the vaudeville. He himself was an *homme nouveau,* eager to take part in the artistic events of the new century.

One of the most spectacular cultural manifestations in the Paris of Debussy was Serge Diaghilev's Ballets Russes. It gave the French a look into the artistic soul of "la Russie mystérieuse," at the time when the two nations were politically united in an *entente cordiale.* When Diaghilev approached Debussy with a request to write a ballet score for his enterprise, Debussy readily agreed. The product was *Jeux,* described by Debussy as a "poème dansé."

The "jeux" of the title were tennis games. The scene opens on an empty garden at dusk, with dim electric streetlights providing illumination. Suddenly a tennis ball flies across the stage. A young man in a tennis jacket runs after it. Two girls appear and begin to dance. The young man asks one of the girls to dance with him, and the other watches them with some envy. He then dances with the second girl; this time it is the first girl who is jealous. Finally, all three engage in a round. But another tennis ball flies onto the stage. Like frightened children, all three scurry off in different directions.

The novelty in *Jeux* was its scenario, taken from contemporary life rather than from mythology or fairy tales, which were the main sources of the classical French ballet. The ballet was produced by Diaghilev's troupe at the Théâtre des Champs-Elysées in Paris on May 15, 1913. The choreography was by Diaghilev's star dancer, Vaclav Nijinsky (1890–1950), who also mimed the part of the tennis player. Tamara Karsavina and Ludmila Schollar were the two girls. Pierre Monteux conducted the orchestra. The production was successful, but it was completely overshadowed by the sensational première of Stravinsky's *Le Sacre du printemps,* which took place two weeks later at the same theater.

The score of *Jeux* is a typical Debussyan creation. Its kinetic energy, like that of a tennis ball, is instantly spent in a resilient impact, and just as quickly renewed in another burst of musical saltation. Its dynamic scheme is an expertly recorded oscillograph, marked by a series of brief inflations and deflations of well-calibrated sonorous matter, with moments of equipoise between swiftly changing scenes of action.

The ballet opens with an atmospheric prelude (*très lent*), in $\frac{3}{4}$ time, on a landscape of static emptiness. Woodwinds intone soft whole-tone harmonies (*doux et rêveur*), imparting an air of dreamy sweetness. The horns give out *sons d'écho,* hovering over immobile muted strings. The tranquillity of the scene is suddenly invaded by palpitating Spanish rhythms in rapid $\frac{3}{8}$ time, sending off flights of chromatic *étincelles* and scintillations of major seconds in the muted violins. It is the initiation into a dance, with lambent glissandos in the harps and avian trills in the flutes. Evanescent solos appear in the woodwind section, with recurrent implosions generating asymmetric sparks of rhythmic energy. In an episode (*ironique et léger*), a babbling bassoon indulges in a garrulous solo, leading to a climax (*joyeux*).

The music becomes emotionally charged (*toujours plus passionné*), harps splashing, trumpets chanting, and trombones rumbling underneath, with the metal clang of the triangle, tambourine, and cymbals conjuring up the sound of a distant festival. Agitation mounts, reaching a climax (*violent*). But a détente supervenes, with divided violins sliding downward. There is a brief pause, followed by a choreographic envoi with a murmuration of strings (*très doux*) and a susurration of piccolos (*le plus doux possible*), with horns and trumpets (*lointain,* "distant") and the timpani (*très lointain*). A shimmering motion is suddenly suspended, and the orchestra, supplemented by the xylophone and celesta, converges on a unison A in a luminous sonic spark.

JEUX

Six épigraphes antiques *(1914)*

Antiquity attracted the modern composers at the turn of the twentieth century as strongly as the mystery of exotic life in the Orient. Remoteness in space or time supplied the psychological impetus in the search for new means of expression and new techniques of composition. This state of mind was particularly pronounced in France, and most especially in Paris. In this fascination with spatial and temporal distance, the French musicians of the Impressionist group were encouraged by symbolism in poetry and similar trends in painting.

The invocation of exotic antiquity was never literal among French poets and musicians. Rather, in a true Impressionist manner, they conjured up a vision of music in dreamlike memories of something never seen. The pentatonic scale served both for the pipes of Pan and the doll-like dances of the Orient. The whole-tone scale was an artificial creation, but it was for this very reason suitable for poetic visions. Formations of consecutive triads or major ninth-chords, favored by Debussy and his contemporaries, were suggestive of the luxuriance of primitive dalliance. Thus modern devices helped to recreate a picture of graceful antiquity. French Symbolist poetry, which inspired Debussy, was saturated with the essence of eroticism; the imagined freedom of love in remote times and remote lands exercised its own powerful attraction.

The poet Pierre Louÿs asked Debussy in 1899 to write a score of background music for his Grecian poems *Chansons de Bilitis*. The poems were to be recited and mimed. Debussy obliged and wrote a suitably fugacious score for two harps, two flutes, and celesta. The first reading of the poems took place in Paris on June 7, 1901. Much later, Debussy set the same cycle of poems to music for voice and piano, without making use of musical materials of the incidental music of 1901.

In 1914, Debussy extracted six of the ten pieces of incidental music for *Chansons de Bilitis* and arranged them for piano four hands. They were published under the title *Six épigraphes antiques*. Debussy himself wrote the descriptive subtitles for these pieces. He performed them for the first time, with the composer Jean Roger-Ducasse, in this four-hands version in Paris on March 15, 1917. In a letter to his publisher Durand, Debussy said that he had intended to arrange the suite for orchestra. He was too ill to carry out his intention. The symphonic version was eventually produced by the Swiss conductor Ernest Ansermet, who had an intimate understanding of Debussy's orchestral style. Ansermet's score bears this dedication: "To the memory of Claude Debussy I dedicate this work in which I have tried to fulfill a wish that had been his."

The first "epigraph" is entitled "Pour invoquer Pan, dieu du vent d'été." Here Debussy makes Pan play the panpipe in the pentatonic scale; the music is evanescent in its attenuated sonorities. The second piece, "Pour un tombeau sans nom," is unquiet, as behooves an evocation of a nameless tombstone. Hyperchromatic melismas color the music, and there are frequent passages in whole-tone scales. The ending is caducous, transitory, and volatile in its dissonant substance. The whole-tone scale is again in evidence in the third piece, "Pour que la nuit soit propice." The prayer for a propitious night is accentuated by distant drumbeats and chromatic arabesques.

Quite different in mood is the fourth piece, "Pour la danseuse aux crotales." The dancer with castanets of the title is Cybèle, the nature goddess of the Greeks, attended by armed female Corybantes raging through the forest in orgiastic abandon. Debussy sees Cybèle through the mist of legend and the music is almost tranquil in its Grecian modalities. But there are furious, though brief, explosions of passion; chromatic tones intrude, forming jarring dissonances. The ending is on a thirdless seventh-chord.

The fifth epigraph, "Pour l'Egyptienne," is Orientalistically flavored. The melody is sinuous in its wistful arabesques. The rhythm is nervously dotted; the harmonies are austere in their open fifths. The ending is a static aureole. The last piece is titled "Pour remercier la pluie au matin." The gratitude for rain in the morning is expressed by alliteration. Rapid streamlets descend in chromatic passages; then the raindrops are more widely spaced, presently assuming pentatonic configurations. The ending is a reminiscence of the pipes of Pan of the opening. Thus Debussy unifies the six disparate epigraphs by the invocation to the patron of shepherds and hunters, the lover of nymphs, the player upon the syrinx, the god of nature's music.

RICHARD STRAUSS
(1864–1949)
Richard the Second

In his early career, Richard Strauss was often described by journalists and critics, half facetiously, half admiringly, as Richard the Second, the first Richard being, of course, Wagner. As in most such sobriquets, this nomination has a particle of allegorical and historical truth. Wagner had created a new stage genre of music drama, in which characters and ideas were identified by individual themes, the leitmotivs ("leading" motives) of the Wagnerian lexicon. Strauss transplanted Wagner's musical identification tags to the domain of symphonic music, primarily as tone poems. Each was a complex of leading motives, intertwining, overlapping, expanded, contracted, fragmentized, melodically and rhythmically altered, moving in a fantastic counterpoint of instrumental entries. A fanatical coterie of musicians and litterateurs assembled around Strauss and saluted him as a prophet of new German music. Special manuals were issued for first performances of his tone poems, profusely illustrated with musical examples, to guide the listener, like musical Baedekers, through the labyrinth of Straussian thematic polyphony. Strauss, with a robust Bavarian sense of humor, treated these efforts lightly. He was undoubtedly aware of his great role as a musical innovator, but he never regarded himself as a messiah, and had little need for self-appointed exegetes. He once calmed the distress of an erudite listener who found himself without a printed guide at a concert by saying that listening could be done by ears alone.

In these works Strauss established himself as a master of program music and the most important representative of the nascent era of musical modernism; as such, he was praised extravagantly by earnest believers in musical progress and damned savagely by entrenched traditionalists in the press.

In 1894, Strauss conducted the premiere of his first opera, *Guntram*, for which he also composed the text. The leading soprano role was performed by Pauline de Ahna; she was married to Strauss a few months later, and remained with him all his life. While engaged in active work as a composer, Strauss did not neglect his conducting career. In 1894, he succeeded Hans von Bülow as conductor of the Berlin Philharmonic, leading it for a season, and in 1896 became chief conductor of the Munich Court Opera.

Strauss's works of the period included the sparkling *Till Eulenspiegel's Merry Pranks (Till Eulenspiegels lustige Streiche)*; *Thus Spake Zarathustra (Also sprach Zarathustra)*, a philosophical symphonic poem after Nietzsche; *Don Quixote*, variations with a cello solo after Cervantes. He conducted the first performance of his extraordinary autobiographical symphonic poem *A Hero's Life (Ein Heldenleben*, 1899), in which the hero of the title was Strauss himself, while his critics were represented in the score by a cacophonous charivari. For this exhibition of musical self-aggrandizement, he was severely chastised in the press.

For his first visit to the United States, he presented the premiere performance of his *Symphonia Domestica* at Carnegie Hall (1904). The score represents a day in the Strauss household, including an interlude describing, quite literally, the feeding of the newly born baby. The reviews in the press reflected aversion to such musical self-exposure. His opera *Salome*, to the German translation of Oscar Wilde's play, had its American premiere at the Metropolitan Opera in 1907. The ghastly subject, involving intended incest, seven-fold nudity, decapitation followed by a labial necrophilia, administered such a shock to the public and the press that the Metropolitan Opera took it off the repertoire after only two performances. Scarcely less forceful was Strauss's next opera, *Elektra*, to a libretto by the Austrian poet and dramatist Hugo von Hofmannsthal, in which the horrors of matricide were depicted with extraordinary force in unabashedly dissonant harmonies.

Strauss then decided to prove to his admirers that he was quite able to write melodious operas to charm the musical ear. This he accomplished in his next production, also to a text of Hofmannsthal, *The Cavalier of the Rose (Der Rosenkavalier)*, a delightful opéra bouffe in an endearing popular manner. Turning once more to Greek mythology, Strauss wrote, with Hofmannsthal again as librettist, a short opera, *Ariadne on Naxos (Ariadne auf Naxos)*, which he conducted for the first time in 1912 and later expanded into a full-length work (1916).

His next work was the formidable and quite realistic score *An Alpine Symphony (Eine Alpensinfonie*, 1915), depicting an ascent of the Alps, and employing a wind machine and a thunder machine in the orchestra to illustrate an alpine storm. With Hofmannsthal, he wrote *The Woman Without a Shadow (Die Frau ohne Schatten*, 1919), using a complex plot heavily endowed with symbolism. Subsequent works included *Intermezzo* (1924), *The Egyptian Helen (Die ägyptische Helena*, 1928), and *Arabella* (1933), his last collaboration with von Hofmannsthal.

When Hitler came to power in 1933, the Nazis were eager to persuade Strauss to join the official policies of the Third Reich. Hitler even sent him a signed picture of himself with a flattering inscription, "To the great composer Richard Strauss, with sincere admiration." Strauss kept clear of formal association with the Führer and his cohorts, however. He agreed to serve as president of the newly organized Reichsmusikkammer in 1933, but resigned from it in 1935, ostensibly for reasons of poor health. He entered into open conflict with the Nazis by asking Stefan Zweig, an Austrian Jew, to provide the libretto for his opera *The Silent Woman* (*Die schweigsame Frau*, after Jonson). It was produced in 1935, but taken off the boards after a few performances. His political difficulties grew even more disturbing when the Nazis found out that his daughter-in-law was Jewish.

During the last weeks of the war, Strauss devoted himself to the composition of *Metamorphosen*, a work for string orchestra mourning the disintegration of Germany. It contained a symbolic quotation from the Funeral March of Beethoven's *Eroica* Symphony; in 1945 he moved to Switzerland. Although official suspicion continued to linger after the war regarding his relationship with the Nazi regime, he was officially exonerated. A last flame of creative inspiration brought forth the deeply moving Four Last Songs (1948), for soprano and orchestra, inspired by poems of Herman Hesse and Joseph von Eichendorff. With this farewell, Strauss returned to his home in Germany, where he died at the age of eighty-five.

Undeniably one of the finest master composers of modern times, Strauss never espoused extreme chromatic techniques, remaining a Romanticist at heart. His genius is unquestioned as regards such early symphonic poems as *Don Juan* and *Thus Spake Zarathustra*; many of his operas have attained a permanent place in the repertoire, while his Four Last Songs stand as a noble achievement of his Romantic inspiration.

Symphonic Poem: Don Juan, *Op. 20 (1888–89)*

In the dictionary of musical invectives, Strauss occupies many pages. Every symphonic poem he wrote was a signal for the critics of the two hemispheres to make use of their choicest vocabulary of abuse. Strauss stood up well under this bombardment, but suffered most damaging blows from his admiring commentators who published catalogues of themes and fragments of themes used by Strauss, together with the meaning of each of these motives. It is fashionable among contemporary composers to deny literary implications in their music, but Strauss could hardly do that, for the very titles of his tone poems—*Don Juan*, *Death and Transfiguration*, *Till Eulenspiegel*, *Thus Spake Zarathustra*, *Don Quixote*, and *A Hero's Life*—are literary.

Don Juan is the first of Strauss's tone poems, if we disregard the earlier orchestral work, *Macbeth*, which has not been retained in the active repertoire. Strauss wrote *Don Juan* when he was twenty-four years old, and conducted its first performance at Weimar on November 11, 1889. The program carried a quotation from the poem "Don Juan" written by the morbid Austrian poet, Nicolaus Lenau. The portion of Lenau's poem published in Strauss's score pictures a romantic Don Juan, insatiable in his conquests. He expresses the desire to die from a kiss on the lips of the last of his women. He elevates the plurality of his affections to a dogma and poeticizes the manifold charms of beautiful womanhood. He cries, "Out and away to new and new conquests." But he is reconciled to death, a lightning from above that finally strikes a deadly blow to his love power.

Don Juan.
Tondichtung von Rich. Strauss, Op. 20.

This poem, representing the hero as a tragic figure frustrated by his easy triumphs, is the only program that Strauss ever acknowledged, which did not prevent Wilhelm Mauke from expanding the action of Strauss's symphonic poem into a detailed catalogue of places and people, following the text of Lenau in its entirety. According to Mauke, Don Juan makes three conquests in Strauss's symphonic poem, which lasts altogether eighteen minutes in performance. The first conquest is easy, and takes only seventy bars in allegro molto con brio. The opening theme is termed a "storm of delight." The second theme represents the philosophical concept of the multiplicity of womanly essence. Then comes the upsurging Don Juan theme, followed by the theme of the first victim, whom Mauke identifies as Zerlina or, as he affectionately calls her, Zerlinchen. But this conquest leaves a feeling of disgust and lassitude expressed in dreary chromatics. The second conquest starts on the ninth chord in pianissimo. The intended victim is a blonde countess, who lives in a villa one hour's ride from Seville, but there is no Spanish atmosphere in the music. There is a theme of "nameless delight" in the uppermost regions of the violin range. The affair with the countess takes eighty-nine bars, ending in an E-minor crash. The third and tragic love is Anna. She is a G-major creature, but the chromatics of disgust are contrapuntally projected against her theme at the very outset. A new Don Juan theme is introduced—a call to new conquests—but it is caricatured by diminution in the tinkling glockenspiel. He goes to a masked ball (cachinnating chromatics in the woodwinds). Then comes death by the sword of Don Pedro. Don Juan's blood flows slowly down the tremolos of the violins. He expires in E minor.

Don Juan reached America on October 31, 1891, when Arthur Nikisch conducted it at the concert of the Boston Symphony Orchestra. Philip Hale wrote with his usual caustic wit in the *Boston Post*:

> He uses music as the vehicle of expressing everything but music; for he has little invention, and his musical thoughts are of little worth. This symphonic poem is supposed to portray in music the recollections and regrets of a jaded voluptuary. Now, granting that music is capable of doing this, what do we find in this composition? There are recollections, not of Don Juan, but of Liszt and of Wagner. There are also regrets, but the regrets come from the hearers. There is plenty of fuss and fuming; but is there any genuine passion or any real terror from the beginning to the end? Besides, Don Juan was more direct in his methods. His wooing was as sudden and as violent as his descent to the lower regions. According to Strauss, he was verbose, fond of turning corners, something of a metaphysician, and a good deal of a bore. When he made love he beat upon a triangle, and when he was dyspeptic he confided his woes to instruments that moaned in sympathy.

Eleven years later, *Don Juan* was played again by the Boston Symphony Orchestra. This time, Hale, who had a prodigious memory for other people's writings but not for his own, wrote enthusiastically in the *Boston Journal* of November 2, 1902: "A daring, brilliant composition: one that paints the hero as might a master's brush on canvas. How expressive the themes! How daring the treatment of them! What fascinating irresistible insolence, glowing passion, and then the taste of Dead-Sea fruit!"

Symphonic Poem: Till Eulenspiegel's Merry Pranks, *Op. 28* (1894–95)

An early biographer of Richard Strauss, writing in the *Musikalisches Wochenblatt* of April 1897, when Strauss was in his thirties and just beginning to amaze the world, relates an interesting episode of Strauss's apprentice years. His father, Franz, was an excellent player on the French horn, and knew other orchestral instruments well. He taught Strauss never to force an instrument to play beyond its natural capacities. Once, looking over an orchestral score written by his son, he suddenly turned toward him and gave him a slap on the face. "Lausbub," he exclaimed, "so you are writing a high B flat for the flute! Mozart and Beethoven never used it; neither should you." Strauss had great respect for his father as educator and musician, and he remembered his lessons well. When he needed wider range of tone color, he had a new instrument made. Thus, in *An Alpine Symphony*, Strauss wanted a low instrument of the tone color of the oboe. The English horn would not do, for it was associated with pastoral scenes, as in the famous solo in the *William Tell* Overture. Strauss then asked Heckel, the instrument maker in Berlin, to construct a special instrument, which he called the heckelphone.

Strauss imagined all horn players to be as good as his father. He wrote a concerto for horn and orchestra, under his father's inspiration. In *Till Eulenspiegel*, he entrusted to the horn one of the most difficult solo passages ever written for the instrument. It is said that Strauss got the idea of this solo from listening to the first horn player of the Weimar Orchestra practice before each rehearsal. When at the first rehearsal of *Till Eulenspiegel* the horn player complained about the difficulty of the passage, Strauss replied, "Nonsense! I heard you practice it every morning."

Strauss completed the composition of *Till Eulenspiegel's Merry Pranks* (*Till Eulenspiegels lustige Streiche*) on May 6, 1895, and the first performance took place in Cologne on November 5 of the same year. The composition is defined by Strauss himself as an escape, but in the low regions of the double bassoon and the double basses, Till's fate is already sealed. The fateful rhythm, dash and dot, is pounded by the entire orchestra. The kettledrums strike, and the bass drum. Till's motive is in all the flutes, and all the clarinets, helped out by a trumpet and the violins, but each time it is answered by the sepulchral chords of the brasses.

As a last resort, Till decides to joke his way out. There is a merry dance tune, but it is of short duration, and soon gives way to a plaintive cry of the oboe. A lyrical reminiscence follows: Till's whole life passes in his mind. The horn plays its difficult passage, and there is an interlude of pastoral serenity. But grim reality interrupts these dreams. Till is on the march to his destiny. His theme is sounded in the entire orchestra; the march becomes a gallop, a gallop to the gallows. The tumult ceases. There are lugubrious lifeless fifths in the low wind instruments. They are marked *drohend*, "menacing," and they are then filled with equally lugubrious minor thirds. The execution drum beats a roll. There is a stifled outcry of the small clarinet, but only funereal fifths answer it. The small clarinet shrieks out in the last agony, and all is over. There are drops of muted strings. The epilogue commemorates the gentleness of Till, and a tribute is paid to his soul by the reiteration in full orchestra of his motive.

Symphonic Poem: Thus Spake Zarathustra, *Op. 30 (1895–96)*

Also sprach Zarathustra is the first example of an orchestral composition purporting to expound a system of religious philosophy. The full title reads: *Also sprach Zarathustra, Tondichtung, frei nach Friedrich Nietzsche* (*Thus Spake Zarathustra, tone poem, based loosely on Friedrich Nietzsche*). Nietzsche's book, *Also sprach Zarathustra*, bore the subtitle, *A Book for All and None*. It was published in 1892, post-mentally, so to speak, for by that time Nietzsche was completely insane.

Strauss was fascinated with Nietzsche's book, and set to work on his tone poem a few years after its publication. He conducted the first performance of *Also sprach Zarathustra* in Frankfurt on November 27, 1896. He had this to say to an inquiring writer regarding the score: "I did not propose to write philosophical music or to portray Nietzsche's great book in tones. I merely intended to convey by musical means an idea of the development of the human race through its various stages, religious and scientific, culminating in Nietzsche's vision of the superman."

It must be noted that in Nietzsche's book, Zarathustra is not the legendary Persian religious teacher, but merely a convenient spokesman for Nietzsche's own philosophy. The image of Zarathustra came to him, or so it was said, during a walk in the woods near the Silvaplana Lake in the Engadine, when he came in sight of a towering crag. It impressed him as a symbol of the overwhelming grandeur of man's spirit, the footprint of the superman, which was to transcend man in the course of Nietzschean mystical evolution.

A lengthy passage from Nietzsche's book is quoted in the score:

At the age of thirty, Zarathustra left his home at the lake and went into the mountains. His solitude raised his spirit and sustained him for ten years without weariness. But one morning he awoke at dawn and addressed the sun in these words: "Great Star! You would never be happy except for the satisfaction of knowing that people benefit from your light. For ten years you rose to shine in my cave dwelling. You would have wearied of your light and of your journey were it not for me, for my falcon, and for my serpent. We waited for the sunrise each morning and blessed you for your bounty. And now I am weary of my own wisdom, like the bee that has gathered too much honey. I would gladly give away the fruits of my knowledge to other men of wisdom so that they could indulge once more in their follies, and to the poor so that they could profit from their riches. To accomplish this duty I must descend into the depths of the earth, as the sun does when setting behind the ocean, to shed its light upon the nether regions. Oh resplendent star! I must follow you, and go down to men beyond the sunset. Bless me therefore, oh impassive orb, for you can look without envy even on the greatest happiness. Bless the overflowing cup, so that the water shining with golden light may carry everywhere the reflection of your splendor. But the cup is empty again, and Zarathustra must once more become a man." Thus it was that Zarathustra's journey into the depths began.

The music describes Zarathustra's journey. A brief outline is inserted in the score:

First movement: Sunrise. Man feels the power of God (Andante religioso). But man retains his yearning. Second movement: Man plunges into passion, but finds no peace. Third movement: Man turns toward science, and tries in vain to solve life's riddle in a fugue. Pleasant dance melodies are heard, and man becomes his individual self again. His soul soars aloft, letting the world sink beneath him.

German mystical philosophy is often impenetrable. Nietzsche atones for the nebulousness of his own ideas by his linguistic inventiveness (he introduced the word "Übermensch"—"superman"—into international vocabulary), his imaginative metaphors, the power of his aphoristic style, and the stimulating effect of his surprising oxymoronic appositions.

The orchestration of *Also sprach Zarathustra* is on a grand scale, containing, in addition to the ample contingent of strings and wind instruments, a bell, two harps, and an organ. The dominating tonality is C major, mystically associated with purity of thought, because of the all-white, accident-free visual appearance of C major on the musical staff.

The opening of the tone poem is marked by a mysterious rumble in the nethermost regions of the orchestra anchored on C, with the bass drum supplying an ominous roll of thunder. The trumpet announces the cardinal theme of the work, the motive of nature's riddle, consisting of the ascending notes C—G—C. The organ enters with the ponderous resonance of declarative power. The kettledrums pound out the tonic and the dominant. The music portends a weighty development.

These introductory measures mark the beginning of Zarathustra's journey as retailed in Nietzsche's vade mecum. The first stage of the journey is reached in "Von den Hinterweltlern," treating of those who live behind the world of human reality in constant search for ontological permanence. Since this quest is tortuous, the music acquires the patina of modal uncertainty, moving through minor harmonies which color also the motive of nature's riddle, which recurs here. And since rational speculation fails under such chaotic conditions, religion steps in, with a quotation of a Gregorian melody, "Credo in unum deum."

The qualification in the title of the work, *"freely after Friedrich Nietzsche,"* gives Strauss the freedom to select passages from Nietzsche's book suitable for musical representation. The Wagneromantic flow of triadic melodies, saturated with mellifluous harmonies in a sea of chromatic abundance, characteristic of all tone poems of Strauss, makes *Zarathustra* sound more like the all-too-human Straussian personages Don Juan, Don Quixote, or Strauss himself in *Ein Heldenleben*, rather than the Nietzschean superman.

After the eerie mysticism of the music, there is a return to terrestrial emotions in the sections entitled "Von der grossen Sehnsucht" ("Of Great Yearning") and "Von den Freuden und Leidenschaften" ("Of Joys and Passions"). No sooner does the human element expand into self-enjoyment than the plaintive voice of the oboe makes itself heard in "Grablied" ("Song of the Grave"), a lugubrious reminder of ultimate dissolution, when even memories vanish. To illustrate this passing of the cherished scenes of youth and love, themes of previous movements are recalled in pale brilliance.

If life ends in dissolution and memories are obliterated in the grave, there is solidity in the secular blandishments of scientific thought, portrayed in the next section, "Von der Wissenschaft" ("Of Science"). Quite appropriately, science is expounded by means of a scholastic fugue. The subject of the fugue is remarkable. It opens with the motive of nature's riddle, C—G—C, rising in the solemnity of the bass. Beginning with the third note, the theme traverses all twelve different notes of the chromatic scale in a formation of four mutually exclusive triads, two major and two minor. This anticipation of the Schoenbergian method of composition is of historical interest, but it is rudimentary and incomplete, since the essential Schoenbergian ramifications of inversion, retrograde motion, and inverted retrograde are lacking.

The following optimistic episode, "Der Genesence" ("The Convalescent"), leads to a hedonistic "Tanzlied" ("Dance Song"). The song of the dance is a Dionysian waltz, illustrating Nietzsche's humanistic vision: "Now at last the lover's songs are awakened. And my soul, too, is a lover's song."

The concluding section of *Also sprach Zarathustra* is a darksome epitaph, "Nachtwanderlied" ("Song of the Night Wanderer"). The midnight bell counts off its foreboding twelve strokes. The night is quiet, and the wanderer marches slowly toward the daybreak in the "world behind the world." He reaches the empyrean heights in the chord of B major in the upper woodwinds, but far beneath it, in the Stygian depths of the basses, there is sounded the motive of nature's riddle, C—G—C. This superimposition, barely broken off by rests, of two unrelated tonalities is the earliest example of the use of bitonal harmony. Its symbolism, in Nietzschean terms, has moved many a Straussian eschatologist to magnificent verbosity. Strauss himself, prudently, stood aloof from these propaedeutical exercises, preferring to leave the final judgment to the listeners—and the critics.

This judgment proved severe. At its first appearance, *Also sprach Zarathustra* shocked the innocents, offended the purists, and fired the faithful with enthusiasm. Alas and lackaday! In the last third of the twentieth century the work no longer produces any of these strong emotions, and—the ultimate indignity—is even pronounced a bore. Harold C. Schoenberg, reviewing a performance of the work in the *New York Times*, in March 1968, called it, unfeelingly, an "overscored monstrosity," adding, "It used to be an effective vehicle for orchestra. But this vehicle has long since run out of gas."

For unregenerate Straussians, it is easier to bear the contumely and the spittle of spite showered on *Also sprach Zarathustra* when it was a novelty, for such reactions could be attributed to the Victorian obtuseness of the critics. After its first English performance, the *Times of London* described the work as "a hopeless failure, whatever its value as a philosophical treatise," in which "the possibilities of cacophony seem to be exhausted." The *Boston Herald* painted a Boschlike landscape in the guise of a critical review:

> If the interpretation given by Strauss is in any way reliable, Zarathustra was possessed of pulmonic powers of a rhinoceros, and shouted his "Thus Spake" through a megaphone of brobdingnagian proportions. The work is unhealthy; it suffers severely from basstubaculosis and its utterances are too often basstubathetic. The score is at its worst in the Dance Song, a species of symbolic waltz, ushered in with unheard-of caterwauling with a gruesomeness of execrably ugly dissonance—a realistic tone-picture of a sufferer from the worst pangs of sea-sickness.

The *Boston Gazette* was similarly picturesque:

> In *Also Sprach Zarathustra* the genius of Strauss is merciless; it possesses huge lungs and stands close to one's ear. When a man is awakened by an entire city tumbling about his ears, the blowing up of a single building by nitroglycerine passes unnoticed. The composer plays the part of the howling dervish; he whirls madly about until he becomes hysterical, and then he bellows.

Finally, this nosegay from the *New York Evening Post*:

> Nietzsche, though he lives in a lunatic asylum, is one of Germany's favorite philosophers, and his crazy, rambling works have even been translated into English. Strauss, like Nietzsche, is impotent to create anything new, but as you cannot abuse people in music, he abuses the divine art itself. His mind seems to be an absolute desert as regards tangible musical thoughts. What he does invent is new cacophonies.

Fantastic Variations: Don Quixote, *Op. 35 (1896–97)*

Strauss brought the Wagnerian system of leitmotivs to such a degree of complexity that it became a veritable catalogue of musical identification marks, and he elevated the genre of tone poem to the highest point of artistry. The greatest among these tone poems–*Don Juan, Death and Transfiguration, Till Eulenspiegel, Thus Spake Zarathustra, Don Quixote, A Hero's Life*—were all written by Strauss between the ages of twenty-four and thirty-four, a remarkable achievement. All received their inspiration from literary sources.

Perhaps the boldest in conception and in execution is *Don Quixote.* Its subtitle, *Fantastic Variations on a Theme of Knightly Character,* has an ironic ring, but no greater tribute has ever been given in an art form to the immortal Knight of the Sorrowful Countenance. Don Quixote himself is incarnated in the solo violoncello, a curious selection, but superlatively fitting at the hands of a master like Strauss. The character of Sancho Panza, Don Quixote's clumsy but faithful henchman, is confided to a solo viola. Don Quixote may therefore be described as a double concerto for cello and viola with orchestra. Strauss completed the score of Don Quixote on December 29, 1897. The work was performed for the first time in Cologne, from manuscript, with Friedrich Grützmacher as solo violoncellist and Franz Wüllner conducting, on March 8, 1898. Strauss himself conducted it ten days later in Frankfurt, when Hugo Becker was the violoncellist.

The intricacy of contrapuntal involvements in the score among a multitude of thematic elements is staggering. An exegesis of twenty-seven pages was compiled by Arthur Hahn to guide the listener. So literal were the literary allusions in this brochure that the compiler even perceived in the dissonant harmonics of the introduction "an admirable characterization of Don Quixote's notorious tendency to draw wrong conclusions." The main divisions of the score are formed by a lengthy Introduction, a Theme with variations, and the Finale. The variations faithfully represent the most important incidents in the famous Cervantes romance.

In the Introduction, marked "chivalrously and gallantly," a typically Straussian soaring motive introduces the hero. There are dreams in the woodwinds, but there are also evil forces arrayed against Don Quixote by chromatically scheming magicians. The instruments are muted, even the bass tuba, creating a phantasmagoria of blending sonorities. Madness and chivalry collide in discordant harmonies. But Don Quixote is now determined to devote himself to the rescue of the helpless and the innocent.

The theme portrays Don Quixote idealistically. The solo violoncello intones the identifying motive of the hero in a minor key. It is followed by the mundane appearance of Sancho Panza, set grossly in outspoken major. A set of variations follows. The first introduces Don Quixote's ideal lady, the ineffably beautiful Dulcinea. She is in danger from rotating windmills, and Don Quixote rushes to her defense. He is knocked down by the sails, represented by the harp glissando and the drums. The second variation portrays another battle. But the enemy army turns out to be a flock of sheep. There are ingenious effects of muted brass representing a chorus of bleating sheep. The harmonic cloud of dust is panchromatic.

The third variation is a philosophical discussion between the master and the henchman. The cello is idealistic in its calm proclamation of the aims of chivalry; the viola expresses doubts, and soon becomes so insistent in its demands for peaceful life that the cello is forced to summon the entire orchestra to silence the impertinent henchman. In the fourth variation Don Quixote confronts a procession of

Don Quixote.

Fantastische Variationen
über ein Thema ritterlichen Characters.

penitents. Although they sing sacred chants, he believes they are robbers, and lunges at them. He is thrown off his horse. Exhausted, he falls asleep. A dream of sweet Dulcinea descends on Don Quixote in the fifth variation. The tremolos of the woodwinds and muted strings accompany his vision.

Don Quixote finally meets his Dulcinea in the sixth variation. But she is not the ideal woman of his dreams: Sancho Panza cruelly deceived him by passing a common country girl for his beloved. Don Quixote is sure that her transformation was effected by the black arts of his enemies, and he is ready to fight them. The seventh variation carries Don Quixote and Sancho Panza through the air on a wooden horse, in their imagination, of course. Here Strauss introduces the wind machine into the orchestra, which reinforces the blowing chromatics in the flutes, and the whistling glissandos in the harp. In the eighth variation they take a ride in a boat, to the strains of a barcarole.

Don Quixote finally confronts, in the ninth variation, the Two Magicians, his greatest enemies. In reality they are itinerant monks, harmlessly conversing in a duet of bassoons. He attacks them and puts them to rout. The tenth variation sets the end to Don Quixote's adventures. In his last battle, he is defeated by the Knight of the White Moon and returns home to die. The Finale is without strife. The tremolos in the muted strings mark the last feverish excitement; one more idealistic sigh in the cello and Don Quixote de la Mancha is dead. His epitaph is brief; the final chords of the cadence speak of eternal peace.

Symphonic Poem: A Hero's Life, *Op. 40 (1897–98)*

Ein Heldenleben (*A Hero's Life*) was the last of the great series of symphonic poems of Richard Strauss, all of which were composed still in the nineteenth century, each one a masterpiece in its own right: *Don Juan, Death and Transfiguration, Till Eulenspiegel, Thus Spake Zarathustra,* and *A Hero's Life.* The first of these Strauss wrote as a mere youth of twenty-three; the last, when he was thirty-four. The very title, *Ein Heldenleben,* with its obvious autobiographical connotations, shocked the contemporary public. Its post-Wagnerian idiom, with free use of unresolved dissonances, revolted respectable music critics. The appearance of *A Hero's Life* was greeted with an outpouring of righteous indignation.

> Richard Strauss indulges in a self-glorification of the most bare-faced kind. The hero's antagonists are described by him with the utmost scorn as a lot of pigmies and snarling and yelping bowwowing nincompoops. The composer's progressing impotence, however, is most plainly perceivable in the section devoted to his wife. She is represented by a solo violin, which is not a bad insinuation, as much as to say that she plays first fiddle in his life. But the climax of everything that is ugly, cacophonous, blatant and erratic, the most perverse music I ever heard in all my life is reached in the section "The Hero's Battlefield." The man who wrote this outrageously hideous noise is either a lunatic, or rapidly approaching idiocy.

Thus spake the *Musical Courier* of New York in 1899.

Concerning the harmony employed in *Ein Heldenleben*, a Boston music critic opined that "the attempt to play in two different keys at the same time is as disastrous as the attempt of two railroad trains to pass each other on the same track." Even the urbane Philip Hale expressed shock at the self-appreciation expressed by Strauss in *Ein Heldenleben*. "This tone poem," he wrote, "might be justly entitled 'A Poseur's Life,' and a blustering poseur at that."

And finally, here is a bouquet of florid invective from the pen of Richard Aldrich of the *New York Times* in 1905: "In no other work has Strauss so deliberately affronted the ear with long-continued din and discord or... so consciously used ugliness in music to represent conceptions of ugliness, as in *Ein Heldenleben*."

Richard Strauss began the composition of *Ein Heldenleben* in Munich on August 2, 1898, and completed it on December 27, 1898, in Charlottenburg. Strauss conducted the first performance of the work from manuscript in Frankfurt on March 3, 1899. The subtitle is *Tondichtung (Tone Poem)*, an appellation popularized by Strauss. By definition, a tone poem is a narrative in poetic language. Examined impartially at this point of time, *Ein Heldenleben* appears almost traditional in its structure. It begins and ends in the key of E flat major. Its harmonic, melodic, rhythmic, and orchestral elements are entirely within the rational confines of late-nineteenth-century music. The orchestra is huge, but no more so than the orchestra of Wagner or Bruckner.

Ein Heldenleben has a definite story to tell, and it is told with imagination and wit. It may be argued, in fact, that, far from being an outrageous exhibition of self-inflation, *Ein Heldenleben* may be a subtle parody on a composer in the role of a self-made personage from the *Eroica.*

An admirable custom existed in nineteenth-century Germany: whenever a new musical composition of importance was performed, a detailed guide profusely illustrated with musical examples was published for distribution among the listeners. For *Ein Heldenleben,* an impressively voluminous guide was compiled by Friedrich Rösch; it contained seventy thematic illustrations, in addition to a descriptive poem by a volunteer admirer. Yet Strauss told Romain Rolland: "No program of any kind is needed. It is sufficient to know that in this tone poem the hero is fighting off his adversaries."

Ein Heldenleben consists of six distinct sections. The first represents the hero. His theme breathes the eloquence of nobility. According to the exegesis by Rösch, the theme itself comprises four motives illustrating the various attractive sides of the hero. The theme soars ever higher until its heroic character is well established. Then there is a pause on an unresolved dominant seventh chord. It serves as a prelude to a section dealing with the hero's antagonists. They are jabbering enviously, not to say cacophonously, on the piccolo, the flute, the oboes, the English horn, and the tubas. They try to demean the hero by the device of thematic diminution, that is, by halving the note values of the hero's theme. He is dismayed by this impertinence, but soon regains his composure and repels the chromatic assaults of his enemies. He is now free to return to the serenity of his private life. He turns the full power of his affection to his feminine companion, represented by a solo violin. She does not seem to appreciate the hero's attention. The expression marks over the violin part vary from "somewhat sentimental" to "coquettish," "nagging," and "angry." But soon the solo violin becomes tender and loving. Clamorous voices are still heard in the background, but the love duet has now reached the point of appassionato, and the defeated antagonists can no longer disturb the hero's contentment.

Still, like Don Quixote in the preceding tone poem of Strauss, the hero must challenge his new enemies. There are flourishes of trumpets backstage announcing the battle. The hero's theme soars aloft, in augmentation, to avenge the former attempt of his enemies at the diminution of his glory; they now wilt in chromatic impotence. The battle rages on with drums accentuating its ferocity. But the hero's theme is now triumphantly sounded in the potent brass. His victory is total.

The time has now come for the hero's mission of peace. He recalls his earlier musical conquests. Self-quotations appear successively from his previous tone poems, from *Macbeth, Don Juan, Thus Spake Zarathustra, Death and Transfiguration, Don Quixote, Till Eulenspiegel,* and his early opera *Guntram.* Industrious calculators accounted for twenty-three of such self-quotations in all. Did Richard Strauss, at the young age of thirty-four, deliberately try to glorify himself by such means? Or was he indulging in a ponderous jeu d'esprit? He was a complex personality, capable of taking a skeptical view of himself as well as of the world. The indignation of the critics against his outrageous presumption in picturing himself as a hero posted in the center of the musical universe may have been the demonstration of their own lack of humor.

Symphonia Domestica, *Op. 53 (1902–3)*

Richard Strauss had a genius for a creating a musical sensation. He was also the product of an era in which egotism was elevated to the plane of mystical solipsism. The individual was placed above society. God was abolished, and the superman assumed the vacated deistic functions. With a fine mixture of self-aggrandizement and irony, Strauss painted a self-portrait as a hero in his tone poem *A Hero's Life*, and watched with amusement the outraged reaction to his effrontery. After all, he had anticipated it when he depicted his detractors by the cackling cacophony of uneuphonious brass in that work.

In the *Symphonia Domestica* (*Domestic Symphony*) Strauss raised the curtain of his family life, and dedicated the score "to my beloved wife and our young one." He conducted the world premiere of *Symphonia Domestica* at a concert of his works in New York on March 21, 1904. An analytical study, provided by devout Straussians, lists sixty-seven distinct motives identifying various aspects of the characters that pass the scene during twenty-four hours in the life of the Strauss family. Since it was a matter of common gossip in knowledgeable circles that Frau Pauline de Ahna Strauss ruled the household with a whim of iron, there were amused whispers concerning the idyllic musical phrases that Strauss assigned to his imperious spouse. A Boston music critic put the rumors into print when he wrote: "If *Symphonia Domestica* were a true biographical sketch, we fancy that the wife would be portrayed on trombones and tubas while the husband would be pictured on the second violins."

The work is an immense revolving musicorama, subdivided into four sections, which correspond to four symphonic movements. After a sonatomorphic opening, there is a development, a reprise, a Scherzo, an Adagio, and a finale. The paterfamilias is sympathetically introduced by a genial motive in the cellos. But there are more sides to his nature. Strauss magnanimously admits in specific markings in the score that he may be absent-minded, unsocially introspective and at times even temperamental. Frau Strauss is depicted with uxorious deference by a gentle phrase in the violins, grazioso. But there are other sides to her nature, too, which are not grazioso, for she may be capricious, moody, and self-willed, as Strauss dutifully points out in his interlinear comments. The most affectionate musical characterization is reserved for the baby, whose sweet lallation is sounded by the oboe d'amore. Aunts and uncles come to visit the Strauss family and to admire the baby's looks and intelligence. "Ganz der Papa!"—Just like Daddy!—exclaim the aunts through the medium of muted trumpets. "Ganz die Mama!"—Just like Mommy!—opine the uncles on muted trombones, horns, and woodwinds. (The words of these breathless interjections are noted in the score.) The loving relatives depart, and the parents take advantage of the lull to have a moment of play with the child in a vivacious scherzo. But it is late in the day, a lullaby is sung, and the baby is put to bed, wrapped up in warm clothes and covered with blankets and shawls, according to the barbarous precepts of Victorian pediatricians.

It is now seven o'clock, signalized by seven silvery bell strokes on the glockenspiel. The child is asleep and the parents are alone. An expressive adagio introduces a "Liebesszene" ("Love Scene"), with the motives of the married couple intertwining in a blissful marital counterpoint. An emotional upsurge illustrates the growth of mutual passion, culminating in a soaring fortissimo. The flutes out of breath, the whispering harps and the moan of stifled violins sul ponticello draw a veil on the scene of love. The night passes quickly, and in minutes of symphonic time, the clock strikes seven again. The baby wakes up and emits a demanding cry in the woodwinds and muted trumpets. Father, annoyed by this vocal intrusion, makes a grumbling remark, eliciting a counterremark from Mother. A "lively quarrel" ensues in the form of a double fugue, with the baby furnishing a treble in dissonant counterpoint. But lo! Here is the milkman. A bottle of warm milk pacifies the child, the fugal contretemps subsides, and all is well. Strauss makes amends to Frau Strauss with a cello offering. Then they go to the window to greet the morning sun.

"I see no reason why I should not write a symphony about myself. I find the subject as interesting as Napoleon, or Alexander the Great," Strauss said to Romain Rolland in reply to a baffled inquiry. Some critics were unconvinced by his argument. Henry T. Finck, of the *New York Evening Post*, an inveterate old fogey who viewed modern trends in music with constant alarm, voiced the suspicion that *Symphonia Domestica* was nothing more than "a clever method of courting publicity." He denied even the illustrative validity of the music, claiming that the child's motive suggested "a megalosaurian monster rather than a Bavarian baby." "The whole thing," he concluded, "might be called as appropriately *A Trip to Constantinople*, or *A Day at Vladivostok*."

Salome *(1903–5)*

Strauss wrote his one-act opera Salome to the text of a play by Oscar Wilde of that name. The subject was extremely daring for the period, dealing with the apocryphal story of the beautiful dancer Salome who tries to lure John the Baptist into intimacy. The saint curses her in repulsing her unspeakable advances. Herod, who is infatuated with Salome, asks her to dance for him. She consents on condition that he would grant her a wish. She then performs her Dance of the Seven Veils. Having thrown off the last veil, she demands from Herod the gratification of her desire, namely the head of John the Baptist. Horrified, Herod nevertheless carries out his promise. John is beheaded, and his head is brought to Salome on a platter.

Then follows one of the most shocking scenes ever enacted in the theater. Salome speaks to the inanimate head, taunts the saint and kisses his lips. Herod is appalled by this exhibition and orders his soldiers to slay her. The curtain falls.

For this play, Strauss wrote an amazing score, abounding in unresolved dissonances and orchestrated in the most extraordinary manner. The vocal parts, too, were written without regard for traditional operatic singing. The singers were required to master a totally new technique of melodramatic narrative with an angular melodic line and palpitating asymmetrical rhythms.

No wonder, then, that after the first performance of *Salome* by the Dresden Court Opera on December 9, 1905, there was an outcry against the opera. In 1907 the Metropolitan Opera produced *Salome* in New York, arousing such a hullabaloo that the management was forced to take the opera off the boards. The *New York Times* published a letter to the editor by a doctor of medicine which contained the following passage: "I am a man of middle life who has devoted twenty years to the practice of the profession that necessitates a daily intimacy with degenerates. I say that *Salome* is a detailed and explicit exposition of the most horrible, disgusting, revolting and unmentionable features of degeneracy that I have ever heard, or imagined." New York music critics assailed *Salome* for its unresolved dissonances.

"Strauss has a mania for writing ugly music," said the *New York Sun*.

What more natural than that he should cast about for a subject which imperatively demands hideous din to correspond with and justify his concatenated discords? And what more natural than that the noisome Salome should seem an ideal companion for his noisy music? The presentation of such a story is ethically a crime; Richard Strauss's music is aesthetically criminal or at least extremely coarse and ill-mannered. There is one consolation. Thanks to the prevailing dissonance nobody knows whether the singers sing the right notes, that is, the notes assigned to them, or not.

And he concludes the review with this proclamation: "If this be art, then let the music of the future find her mission in the sewer, pesthouse and brothel."

Der Rosenkavalier *(1909–10)*

Hugo von Hofmannsthal was Strauss's most imaginative collaborator and he wrote the libretto of *Der Rosenkavalier*, which was produced in 1911. The intricacy of the plot, with its manifold entanglements, amatory cross-currents, disguises, and contrived mistaken identities, is in the most extravagant manner of eighteenth-century farce. The action takes place in Vienna in Mozart's time. The personages embroiled in the comedy are the Feldmarschallin (the wife of the field marshal), a young count whom she takes as a sporadic lover, an aging Baron, and a nubile lady whom the ineffable baron proposes to marry.

According to the quaint custom of the time, the prospective bridegroom must send to his betrothed a young messenger carrying a rose: this is the Rose Cavalier of the title. The Feldmarschallin selects her young lover for this role. What neither she nor the baron could foresee was the instant explosion of youthful love between the Rosenkavalier and the young lady. The situation becomes further confused when the Feldmarschallin orders the young Cavalier of the Rose to put on a servant girl's dress to conceal his presence in her bedroom. Dressed as a girl, the Rosenkavalier attracts the attention of the foraging aging Baron and, to save the situation, agrees to a tryst with him. As if this were not enough to bemuse the spectator beyond all rational tolerance, the part of the Rosenkavalier is entrusted to a mezzosoprano, so that when he (in actual appearance and physiological gender, she) changes his/her dress, the actress singing the role of the Rosenkavalier reverts, in this process of double transvestitude, to her original god-given gender.

The finale of the opera unravels the numerous strands of the plot when the police arrive as a proverbial deus ex machina. The Feldmarschallin shames the Baron into a behavior befitting his age and status, and she herself gives up the Cavalier of the Rose, who is awarded the welcome prize in the person of the Baron's intended bride. The music redeems the nonsense of the plots of Strauss's comic operas. The Viennese waltzes that enliven the score of *Der Rosenkavalier*, albeit anachronistically for a play that takes place in the eighteenth century, are gorgeous. After the morbid and somber scores of *Salome* and *Elektra*, Strauss proved to his critics that he could produce an opera full of brilliance, wit, and novel musical invention.

The first performance of *Der Rosenkavalier* took place in Dresden on January 26, 1911. A thematic guide was issued for the production, tabulating 118 leading motives employed in the score. The opera won an immediate acclaim; a symphonic suite extracted from the score became a favorite on concert programs.

ARNOLD SCHOENBERG
(1874–1951)
A Musical Prophet

On his seventy-fifth birthday, Arnold Schoenberg sent a circular letter to his friends and admirers, opening with the anguished words, "To be recognized only after death!" The letter is a bitter summary of the life of a star-crossed genius. Schoenberg recalls in it the question he was asked when he was in the Austrian Army in World War I: "Are you the famous composer Arnold Schoenberg?" and his reply: "Somebody had to be, and nobody wanted to, so I took it on, myself." In the same letter, he quotes a prediction he made in 1912: that the second half of the century would make amends by excessive praise for the lack of understanding that his work received in the first half of the century. The biblical flavor of these declarations is in harmony with Schoenberg's messianic complex. For he truly regarded himself as both a martyr crucified by his professional enemies and music critics and the savior of music as formulated in his new dodecaphonic testament. The miracle of Schoenberg's phenomenon was that his lofty prophecy was completely vindicated.

All his life, Schoenberg was acutely conscious of his destiny as a musical reformer. But being a realist, he knew that the struggle for a new language of composition would be cruel, and that he would suffer greatly for his daring. Performances of his works were occasions of wild disturbances. The critics called him a musical anarchist, fabricator of cacophonic antimusic, a de-composer. Like other reformers of genius, Schoenberg had devoted disciples and ardent friends. Two of his pupils, Alban Berg and Anton Webern, achieved great fame on their own merits. But even composers from an entirely different world of music showed curiosity regarding Schoenberg's revolutionary theories. The great Puccini once made a special trip to Florence to hear Schoenberg's song cycle *Pierrot lunaire*, in which the lines are recited in a singsong fashion, half spoken, half sung, to the accompaniment of a strange-sounding little group of instruments. Schoenberg was profoundly moved by this sign of interest on Puccini's part.

Schoenberg was a philosopher in his attitude toward life, but he was also a fighter. In his early days in Vienna, to ensure fair play for modern music, he organized a Society of Private Musical Performances, from which the critics were excluded, and applause was not allowed. At the concerts of Schoenberg's society, all kinds of modern music was presented, not only works by ultramodernists, but also by less radical composers. But Schoenberg soon left Vienna for Berlin.

As the twentieth century advanced, seeking subtler means of musical expression, Schoenberg abandoned the convention of tonality. He wrote melodies that were strangely angular; they leaped and skipped, dangled in deliberate hesitation, hovered with calculated uncertainty over a dissonant chord, broke in a zigzag, or fell precipitously after a sudden ascent. His harmonies arranged themselves into unusual tonal groups, with a distinct preference for dissonance. The key signature disappeared, for there was no longer any key in Schoenberg's music, which was atonal; even transitional occurrences of triads, particularly the assertively strong major triads, became infrequent. Rhythm was free, but the division into measures separated by bar lines to designate meter was preserved even in his most advanced works.

It is interesting to observe that, before the twentieth century, every piece of music ended on a chord containing no more than three different notes, and forming a perfect concord, either a major or a minor triad. No such restriction existed for Schoenberg and his modern contemporaries. Any chord, no matter how dissonant, could mark the end of a composition. Emancipation of dissonance was Schoenberg's slogan, immeasurably widening the range of expression in his music.

Parallels with modern art, and even with modern mathematics, suggested themselves. If Schoenberg's melodies are no longer rectilinear in a classical way, neither, in geodesics, is a straight line the shortest distance between two points. If space is curved, forming an unthinkable hyphenated entity with time, then Schoenberg's dissonant harmonies and free rhythm correspond more closely to the musical reality of modern life.

In Expressionistic paintings, realism gives way to subjective image building, in which optically distorted shapes of familiar objects or human figures seem to reach deeper than conventional art. Schoenberg was also a painter of singular power; his self-portrait, with the keen eyes fixed at infinity, is a remarkable example of psychological expressionism, depicting a face both anguished and aggressive, ironic and firm. Schoenberg also painted a savage caricature in oil, portraying a surrealistic monster with bloated features, bulbous nose, and purple blotches on the cheeks. It bore the title, *The Critic*. His paintings, cognate with Blake and Goya, but perhaps more directly influenced by Impressionists of the prewar era, are subjective visions.

With the gradual dissolution of formal principles of old music, Schoenberg faced the necessity of creating a new musical organization, for his mind demanded order. He described this new organization as "composition with twelve tones related only to one another." Each musical work must be based on a theme containing all twelve different notes. This theme, or tone row, appears in four guises—in its original form, in an inversion (in which the direction of the melodic line is reversed), in retrograde motion (played backward), and in retrograde inversion (the inverted melody played backward). Since each of these four forms can be transposed to any note of the chromatic scale, the grand total of possible derivatives is forty-eight.

The twelve-tone row determines not only the melody, but also counterpoint and harmony. Twelve is a very divisible number, so that the twelve notes of the basic theme or any of its derivatives can be conveniently arranged in two, three, four, or six parts. In florid counterpoint, the notes may skip diagonally from one voice to another. In vertical structures, full chords are formed from the basic thematic materials. Thus the tone row unifies all three aspects of composition—melody, counterpoint, and harmony.

There are 479,001,600 possible permutations of twelve different chromatic notes, and a twelve-tone composer—or, to use the more highfalutin term, a dodecaphonic composer—has a rich selection of tone rows at his disposal. Some of these tone rows are beautiful, dodecaphonically speaking; some are not. Aesthetic standards of beauty in this new musical language may be different from the classical ideals, but they are nonetheless valid.

Schoenberg was extremely sensitive in safeguarding the rights to his method of composition. He reacted vehemently to the claims of Josef Matthias Hauer, an Austrian musician who went so far as to have a rubber stamp made with the words, "the sole inventor and despite all pretensions by untalented imitators the true initiator of twelve-tone music," which he appended to his signature in correspondence. Schoenberg objected violently to Thomas Mann's attribution, in his novel *Doktor Faustus*, of Schoenberg's method to the mythical syphilitic German composer Adrian Leverkühn. In a lengthy letter to the *Saturday Review of Literature* he excoriated Mann for this impropriety. "Leverkühn is depicted from beginning to end as a lunatic," Schoenberg fulminated. "I am seventy-four and I am not yet insane, and I have never acquired the disease from which this insanity stems." Schoenberg also raised the specter of an encyclopedia published in the year 2060 crediting the discovery of the twelve-tone method to Leverkühn or to Thomas Mann himself. Mann tried to assuage Schoenberg's wrath by adding a note of acknowledgment of Schoenberg's dodecaphonic priority in a new edition of *Doktor Faustus*, but he made an egregious faux pas in referring to Schoenberg as "a contemporary composer." This only added fire to Schoenberg's fury. "I wanted to be noble to a man who was awarded a Nobel Prize," Schoenberg wrote, glorying in the pun, and added acidly: "In two or three decades one will know which of the two was the other's contemporary."

Schoenberg was attacked as a cerebral composer who reduced music to a soulless game of numbers, and yet he always insisted on the paramount importance of talent, even in twelve-tone composition. When this writer submitted to Schoenberg a musical treatise purporting to exhaust all workable melodic patterns, dodecaphonic and otherwise, Schoenberg answered in a friendly postcard, but added significantly: "You have in all probability organized every possible succession of tones. This is an admirable feat of mental gymnastics, but as a composer I must believe in inspiration rather than in mechanics."

Schoenberg was a philosopher-musician. He argued from the particular to the general. Even in his purely didactic works, such as his *Harmonielehre* (*Theory of Harmony*), he formulated the rules as inductive steps into universal concepts. He was not, however, an intellectual hermit. He did not remove himself from the world around him. He was a participant in life and had an interest in people. He was an excellent tennis player. He also had some quaint ideas for practical inventions. A list of his projects included a musical typewriter, a proposal for equitable transfer fares on Berlin streetcars, and a recipe for pumpernickel bread.

Much has been said and written about Schoenberg's presentiment of a personal and general catastrophe, as evidenced by his paintings, his writings, and his music. Subsequent events must have strengthened this morbid faith, for no sooner had Schoenberg, in 1925, settled down in Berlin as a professor at the Prussian Academy of Arts than the Hitlerian cataclysm burst over his non-Aryan and modernistic head. Under the stress of a double stigma, he had to leave Germany for France. The shock of a new discrimination led him, probably in the spirit of an emphatic demonstration, to return to the religion of his youth, which he had relinquished thirty-five years earlier. Momentarily in Paris, he responded to a call from America, the last country offering refuge to European undesirables regardless of creed.

There is something biblical in Schoenberg's spectacular martyrdom. In his early life, shuttling between Vienna and Berlin, revered by disciples, derided by scurrilous critics, he was the very picture of a prophet of the faith. Not content with music, he pursued literature and poetry, in the most esoteric form of expression. His poetry, such as the book to *Die Jakobsleiter* (*Jacob's Ladder*), an oratorio begun during the war days (but left unfinished), is abstruse and, to the uninitiated, irritatingly tangential. His choice of words for his monodramas, operas, songs, and song cycles is of the same tantalizing sort, when you seem to grasp the meaning at one moment, only to see it fade into distressing nonsense at another. Often, coarse matter succeeds evanescent symbolism—thus, an early song of Schoenberg's, as yet not out of Wagnerian indentures, ends with the words, "I think of my dog." In one song, Schoenberg "feels the air of other planets," yet in his monodramas he is earthly. A metaphysical woman with child, a strangely unjealous "lover to be," these visions of his operas are as difficult to grasp as a stranger's dream. They were certainly excellent material for easy burlesque, as newspaper critics of both hemispheres discovered to their advantage.

It is fantastic that a mind as relentlessly logical as Schoenberg's was also prone to common superstition. He regarded it as an ill omen that he was born on the thirteenth of the month of September, 1874, and the consciousness of this numerical accident developed into acute triskaidekaphobia. To be sure, he rationalized it as a numerological set of probable concomitances, but the seriousness with which he proceeded to eliminate number thirteen from his references, even to the point of skipping the thirteenth measure from the numbering of bars, is extraordinary. When he noticed that the number of letters in the title of his opera *Moses and Aaron* added up to thirteen, he deleted the second *a* in Aaron, despite the fact that the spelling with two *a*'s was standard in German from the time of Luther. When he reached the age of seventy-six, a friend jocularly pointed out to him that the sum of the digits of seventy-six was thirteen. Schoenberg became quite disturbed at this, and remarked that he might not live through the year. His premonition was only too true. On July 13, 1951, during his last illness, he suffered a collapse, but his mind was clear. He observed to his wife that all would be well if only he would survive the fateful thirteenth, but he died—thirteen minutes before midnight.

Verklärte Nacht (Transfigured Night), *Op. 4 (1899)*

"I personally hate to be called a revolutionist…. I possessed from my very first start a thoroughly developed sense of form. There was no falling into order because there was never disorder. There is no falling at all, but on the contrary, there is an ascending to higher and better order." So wrote Arnold Schoenberg to the author from Hollywood, California, on June 3, 1937, in reply to an inquiry regarding his style of composition. A study of Schoenberg's works confirms his self-estimate. His evolution was logical in the Hegelian sense. Proceeding from Wagnerian and Brahmsian roots, Schoenberg's musical language developed into the method of composition with twelve tones related "only to one another" (Schoenberg's own definition of his epoch-making dodecaphonic system).

Schoenberg began his career as a composer with a work of utmost serenity, a String Quartet in D major, which was performed in his native Vienna in 1897. The formidable Eduard Hanslick wrote a remarkably benevolent review of the piece in which he said half facetiously, "It seems that a new Mozart is growing up in Vienna." It was fortunate for Hanslick that he did not live to hear the new Mozart's later music.

Schoenberg was twenty-five years old when he wrote his first important score, *Transfigured Night* (*Verklärte Nacht*) for string sextet. It was first performed in Vienna on March 18, 1902. In 1917 Schoenberg arranged it for string orchestra; he made another revision of the score in 1943. Ironically, this early work remained Schoenberg's most frequently performed composition. His atonal and dodecaphonic works written during the subsequent fifty years exercised a tremendous influence on composers of all lands, but audiences at large did not give them emotional acceptance.

Transfigured Night is a rare example of a chamber music work with definite literary connotations. It is inspired by a poem of Richard Dehmel, on a subject that was rather bold for its time. A man and a woman walk through a darkening forest. The key is that of D minor, often associated in Romantic music with woods and fields. The opening measures, in their measured tread, vividly suggest people walking. There is an interruption of the mood, a *Luftpause* (pause for breathing), which Schoenberg indicates by a V sign in the score.

So close is the music to the letter of the poem that many melodic passages follow precisely the syllables of the verse. The woman confesses to her lover: "Ich trag' ein Kind und nicht von dir" ("I carry a child, but not from you"), and the melodic rhythm follows the words as in a *Lied*. Her lover urges her not to give way to the consciousness of guilt. The passage is marked "soft, tender, warm." The music soars, the tension rises in chromatic entanglements. After an episode in melancholy F minor, there is a modulation into sunny E major, with a strong pedal point supporting the new tonality. The mood varies between *etwas ruhiger* and *etwas unruhiger*, from "somewhat quiet" to "somewhat unquiet." Wagneromantic gruppetti are catapulted to higher notes. The music grows more agitated, with modulations into remote keys. With tremendous emphasis, the string instruments reach fortissimo in long, protracted metrical divisions. From these emotional heights, there is a tonal descent to the major tonic in D, dissolving in pianissississimo. There is a return to the primordial phrase. The strings are muted in tremolo passages, moving in the direction of the darkly bright key of F-sharp major. Here the violins sing a motive in rhythmic concordance with the prosody of the corresponding words in the poem, "Das Kind das Du empfangen hast sei deiner Seele keine Last" ("The child that you have conceived should on your soul not be a burden").

The measured beats of the pedal point on the tonic D reflect the renewed steps of the lovers. As the moon follows them on their walk, the radiance of their love makes the unborn child one that belongs to both. The "transfigured night" of the title vibrates with the white splendor of D major. The tonal harmony is enhanced by rolling arpeggios supported by deep-seated pedal points, and the paroxysm of luminous emotion recedes into inaudible euphony.

When Richard Dehmel heard *Transfigured Night*, he was moved to write to Schoenberg: "I expected to recall the motives of my poem in your wonderful sextet, but I soon forgot about my words, so bewitched was I by your music. Oh the most beautiful sound! Oh, the reverberation of the maker of words! . . ."

Gurre-Lieder *(1900–1903; 1910–1911)*

Schoenberg's early life in Vienna was hard. At various times he served as a bank clerk and conductor of workers' choruses. He eked out his meager income by orchestrating the operettas of his more fortunate fellow composers. In 1902 he moved to Berlin, where he enjoyed better living conditions. The evolution of his style took him to the borders of tonality, until the sacrosanct foundations of tonal harmony began to crumble and the sturdy tonic-dominant ganglion became atrophied. It was in Berlin that he had his first taste of critical abuse. His innocuous early symphonic poem *Pelléas and Mélisande* (inspired by the same drama by Maurice Maeterlinck as Debussy's great opera) was described in a respectable music journal as a long protracted wrong note. His Chamber Symphony No. 1 provoked the same journal to remark that it should be renamed the "Chamber-of-Horrors Symphony."

As Schoenberg's style grew in complexity, the critical chorus became increasingly shrill in its invective. In 1928, a Berlin writer demanded that Schoenberg be relieved of his teaching position as a protective measure against the musical corruption of the young. Terms like "cacophony," "musical anarchy," "lunacy," "charlatanism," and similes like "cat music" and "a bomb in a poultry yard," became habitual critical expressions whenever Schoenberg's works were performed. Riots erupted at Schoenberg's concerts. On one occasion a critic so completely lost his self-control that he began swinging his cane violently, and broke a window. Charged with disturbing the peace, he claimed intolerable musical provocation in his defense, and was released.

During the years of his struggle for subsistence in Vienna, Schoenberg undertook the composition of his most grandiose score thus far, *Gurre-Lieder* (*Songs of Gurre*), scored for an immense ensemble comprising five soloists, three men's choruses, mixed chorus, and a huge orchestra consisting of twenty-five woodwind instruments, twenty-five brass instruments, four harps, celesta, and a rich assortment of percussion instruments including a set of iron chains, as well as a large contingent of strings. In order to accommodate all these parts Schoenberg had to order special manuscript paper with forty-eight staves. He completed virtually the entire score in an amazingly short time between March 1900 and April 1901. But owing to the pressure of the daily routine of working for a living, Schoenberg put off the completion of the orchestration, and it was not until 1911 that the entire score was finally ready for publication and performance. The first performance of *Gurre-Lieder* took place in Vienna on February 23, 1913, under the direction of the greatly esteemed opera composer Franz Schreker, and it was received enthusiastically.

But the occasion had the character of an almost retrospective event, stylistically speaking, for in the meantime Schoenberg had written such innovative scores as *Pierrot lunaire* and had moved toward the emancipation of dissonance with his atonal piano pieces.

Gurre-Lieder is an oratorio in three parts. The text is by the Danish poet Jens Peter Jacobsen, who wrote the Gurre poems in 1868 at the age of twenty-one. Schoenberg used the German translation by Robert F. Arnold. The story, derived from Scandinavian sagas, is preoccupied with the tragic, symbolic, and supernatural occurrences in the castle of Gurre, on the Esrom Sea in North Zealand, the seat of the Danish King Waldemar, who reigned in the fourteenth century. He fell in love with Tove, a commoner. When the queen discovered his infatuation, she had the girl murdered. The entire action of the poem represents the dream of the dead by the dead. Waldemar rides at night toward Gurre, where Tove waits for him. The dove of the forest announces Tove's death. The King is also dead, but his heart beats wildly in his lifeless body. The dove describes the scene at Tove's sepulchre, with the Queen standing by in repentance for her deed and the King staring at Tove's mute lips. In the second part of *Gurre-Lieder* Waldemar hurls bitter imprecations at God for robbing him of his dearest creature. The third and last part represents the wild hunt in the forest. Waldemar summons the bones of his slaughtered armies, but his men urge him to let them return to the peaceful dreams of their graves. The speaker reads the epilogue, calling on nature to restore life after the spectacle of death.

The shadow of Wagner hangs mightily over Schoenberg's score. As in Wagner's operas, the principal motives possess a deceptive folklike simplicity in their unambiguous triadic structure, but the harmonies are effluent and full of multiple suspensions. At climactic points, these tonal edifices acquire a measure of dissonance that Schoenberg described as "an excursion into the harmony of the future." Also Wagnerian are the resonant cadential ⁶₄ chords marking the moments of eschatological revelation. But in the method of application of these Wagneromorphic elements, Schoenberg forms an original style presaging the ultimate dodecaphonic developments. Specifically Schoenbergian is the utilization of the old polyphonic devices of thematic augmentation, diminution, and motivic fragmentation in the plexus of dissonant counterpoint.

The orchestration is hyper-Wagnerian. The score includes Wagner tubas and such rare instrumental subspecies as the bass trumpet and the double-bass trombone. A historical innovation occurs in the third part of *Gurre-Lieder*, where the trombone glissando is introduced for the first time. When, in America, Schoenberg heard a jazz trombonist execute a glissando, he remarked to a friend, "I invented this sound in *Gurre-Lieder*."

The harmonic motto of the entire work consists of a major triad with an added sixth. This chord, in E-flat major, is outlined in the opening measures of the orchestral introduction. The thematic significance of the harmony is strikingly confirmed by the fact that the same chord, in C major, concludes the entire work. It is interesting to note that the C major triad with an added sixth is also the final chord in Mahler's *The Song of the Earth*. Debussy used the same cadential ending much earlier, as did the untutored ragtime piano players. The expansion of triadic harmony was in the air, and it is idle to attempt to establish the priority of its usage or to trace mutual influences.

After the orchestral prelude comes the first song of Waldemar. It is shaped in a simple, melodic style, but there is a premonition of the later Schoenbergian developments in the bold intervallic leaps of the solo part. In Tove's song, there is an intercalation of the whole-tone scale, a progression much in favor early in the century, which was also a harbinger of atonality. The next poem depicts Waldemar's dramatic ride to the castle of Gurre, culminating in the cry, "Waldemar has seen Tove!" Here Schoenberg lets the entire orchestra swell with luscious harmonies and heave with emotionally charged melodies, until a ringing climax is reached in a Wagneromorphic apotheosis of love. The dialogue between Waldemar and Tove continues, now dramatic in its concentrated chromaticism, now lyrical and tender in its diatonic simplicity. Waldemar's impassioned exclamation, "Du wunderliche Tove!" is perhaps the most eloquent Wagnerophilic passage in the entire score.

A symphonic interlude follows the love-death dialogue between Waldemar and Tove. It is a true tone poem, bearing strong affinity with the music of Richard Strauss, without following specific Straussian procedures. Schoenberg's excursion into the harmony of the future takes place here in a coloristic episode, with muted violins bowing near the bridge in a massive convergence of secundally related inversions of major triads. The effect epitomizes Schoenberg's concept of *Klangfarbe*: "tone color." The symphonic interlude serves as a transition to the fateful poem of the forest dove reciting the course of the tragic events.

The second part of *Gurre-Lieder* comprises Waldemar's song, notable for its systematic exploitation of the minor-seventh chords on the supertonic, mediant, and submediant degrees of the major scale. These usages are also Wagnerian in origin, traceable particularly to *Lohengrin*. Similar harmonies permeate the third part of the work, opening with a section entitled "Wild Hunt." It is in this division, in the orchestral accompaniment to the "Song of the Peasant," that the famous trombone glissando appears in the score.

One of the most striking numbers in the finale is the "Melodrama" (a German term applied to inflected vocal recitation accompanied by instruments), in which the Speaker delivers his exhortation on the rebirth of nature. In a letter to Alban Berg, who prepared an extensive analytic guide for the first performance of *Gurre-Lieder*, Schoenberg emphasizes the difference between this inflected *Sprechstimme* (speech-voice), which outlines the rhythm and stress, and the full-fledged Sprechmelodie ("speech melody," or intonation), in which intervallic proportions are indicated with precision, as exemplified by *Pierrot lunaire*.

Gurre-Lieder concludes with a solemn chorale for full chorus, "See the Sun," set in the radiant key of C major, a tonality that has so often been used by composers as a symbol of purity of soul and redemption from sin. It must be left to students of musical semasiology to account for the psychological association that exists between the spiritual concept of goodness and saintliness and the notational accident of the absence of sharps and flats in the key signature, which results in the visual "whiteness" of the music. This association must have been very strong even to Schoenberg, if he was moved to end *Gurre-Lieder* in that key. It is all the more striking that when he arrived at the formulation of his logically hermetic method of composition with twelve tones related only to one another, he imposed the first and strongest taboo on the C major triad.

Chamber Symphony No. 1, Op. 9 (1906)

No other composer shook the world of music as violently as Arnold Schoenberg. Performances of his works invariably provoked an outburst of anguished indignation on the part of the music critics. Sample quotations are "Schoenberg's opus is not merely filled with wrong notes, but is itself a fifty-minute-long protracted wrong note"; "Schoenberg's music is the reproduction of the sounds of nature in their crudest form"; "The endless discords, the constant succession of unnatural sounds, baffle description"; "Schoenberg's music is the last word in cacophony and musical anarchy, the most earsplitting combination of tones that ever desecrated the walls of a music hall"; "The Schoenberg piece combines the best sound effects of a hen yard at feeding time, a brisk morning in Chinatown, and practice hour at a busy conservatory"; "New exquisitely horrible sounds... the very ecstasy of the hideous.... The aura of Arnold Schoenberg is the aura of original depravity, of subtle ugliness, of basest egoism, of hatred and contempt, of cruelty and of the mystic grandiose."

Schoenberg never flinched from the barrage of malice and invective, which went on for nearly fifty years. In his letter of acceptance of the 1947 Award of Merit for Distinguished Achievement, bestowed upon him by the National Institute of Arts and Letters, he went so far as to credit his critics with encouraging him to continue his struggle. He writes:

> I never understood what I had done to make them as malicious, as furious, as cursing, as aggressive—I am certain that I had never taken away from them something they owned: I had never interfered with their rights.... Maybe I myself failed to understand their viewpoints. But I have one excuse: I had fallen into an ocean, into an ocean of overheated water, and it burned not only my skin, it burned also internally. And I could not swim. At least I could not swim with the tide. All I could do was to swim against the tide—whether it saved me or not.... When you call this an achievement, I do not understand of what it might consist. That I never gave up? I could not—I would have liked to.... Maybe something has been achieved, but it was not I who deserves the credit for that. The credit must be given to my opponents. They were the ones who really helped me.

Schoenberg's role is historic, for he established a new rational system of composition. It is the technique of twelve tones, in which a complete musical work is derived from a unique tone row of twelve different chromatic notes. He arrived at the formulation of the twelve-tone technique by a series of logical steps. His early music was the product of post-Wagnerian chromaticism; it led to the abandonment of all preconceived tonality. The last step was the organization of the atonal fabric into a rational system of monothematic composition based on a twelve-tone row.

Schoenberg's Chamber Symphony No. 1 belongs to the period of transition from fluid tonality to atonality, with chordal harmonies built on fourths rather than on classical thirds. The basic tonality is retained; the form is clearly traceable to the classical sonata and the orchestration adheres to the established practices of early modernism. Even the dissonances are sparingly used, and ultimately resolved. The conclusion of the work is in the same key as the beginning, E major.

But even this mild music aroused a storm of criticism after its first performance in Vienna on March 31, 1913. The Berlin music weekly, *Signale*, reported as follows: "Fifteen brave musicians gave us an opportunity to hear Schoenberg's Chamber Symphony. It would be more suitable to call it the 'Schreckenkammersymphonie.'" The *Musical Courier* in its Berlin dispatch echoed these sentiments:

> Schoenberg has once more baffled the critics and public, this time with his Chamber Symphony for fifteen solo instruments. In order to give the lis-

teners an opportunity to become accustomed to and to find the meaning in the unintelligible mixture of sounds, the whole work was gone through twice, but its interest did not seem to be increased even by this stringent measure. The audience sat perfectly silent as if stunned.

One Berlin critic compared the harmonic structure of the work to a field of weeds and turnips mixed together, and the general opinion was that the composition was a most unaccountable jumbling together of abnormalities.

It is interesting to note that when the Chamber Symphony was performed for the first time in New York on November 14, 1915, at a concert of the Friends of Music conducted by Stokowski, the newspaper comment was surprisingly restrained. One headline even proclaimed: "Schoenberg's Music Is Received Kindly."

Pierrot lunaire, *Op. 21 (1912)*

In the history of the arts there are works of curious destiny. They are creations of small dimensions, often esoteric, and romantically vague. Their purpose is circumscribed. Yet, by some imponderable quality, they inspire more than a small circle of initiates, and become a center of attention and discussion. Often they exercise a subtle but lasting influence. In literature such a work was Baudelaire's collection of poems, *Les Fleurs du Mal,* which, in Victor Hugo's words, created a "frisson nouveau," a new thrill. In painting, there was Manet's picture *Le Dejeuner sur l'herbe,* which became a storm center in the Paris "Salon of the Rejected."

In music, such a work is Schoenberg's *Pierrot lunaire.* It is a set of "thrice seven" melodramas, short poems by Albert Giraud, translated into German by Erich Hartleben. The scoring is extremely tenuous, employing the piano, flute (interchangeable with piccolo), clarinet (interchangeable with bass clarinet), violin (interchangeable with viola), and cello. The poems are not sung, but spoken along a given melodic line. The music is not necessarily a reflection or illustration of the text. At times it deliberately deflects from the meaning of the words in the poems. Thus in "Serenade," Pierrot is pictured as playing on the viola, but the setting is for cello, and when the word "pizzicato" occurs in the text, the cello continues to play arco (i.e., with the bow).

The idiom of *Pierrot lunaire* is expressionistic. The subjective world of the moonstruck Pierrot is here made into a private reality, which a breath of oxygen would instantly destroy. Expressionism in poetry is reflected by integral chromaticism in music, with chromatic tones now crowding narrowly, then dispersing widely through several octaves, creating the feeling of tenseness or spaciousness, according to the design of each piece. This is the language of atonality: there is no determinable key, and the acoustically sharp intervals, major sevenths and minor ninths, prevail over milder dissonances. But this chromatic idiom does not yet constitute the logical system in which the twelve tones of the chromatic scale are arranged in a fundamental series. This twelve-tone technique was not elaborated by Schoenberg until twelve years later.

The twenty-one pieces of *Pierrot lunaire* were written between March 30 and September 9, 1912. It took forty rehearsals to bring the work to performance, which took place in Berlin on October 16, 1912. *Pierrot lunaire,* like every epoch-making work, met with derision on the part of the music critics. The American correspondent for the *Musical Courier* described the music as "the most ear-splitting combination of tones that ever desecrated the walls of a Berlin music hall," and the critic of the *Börsencourier* in Berlin exclaimed in mock horror: "If this is the music of the future, I pray my Creator not to let me live to hear it again."

DER ERSTEN INTERPRETIN
FRAU ALBERTINE ZEHME
IN HERZLICHER FREUNDSCHAFT

DREIMAL SIEBEN GEDICHTE

AUS ALBERT GIRAUDS

PIERROT LUNAIRE

(DEUTSCH VON OTTO ERICH HARTLEBEN)

Für eine Sprechstimme
Klavier, Flöte (auch Piccolo), Klarinette (auch Baß-
Klarinette), Geige (auch Bratsche) und Violoncell

(MELODRAMEN)

von

ARNOLD SCHÖNBERG

Op. 21

PARTITUR

U. E. 5334

Aufführungsrecht vorbehalten — Droits d'exécution réservés

UNIVERSAL-EDITION A.-G.

WIEN Copyright 1914 by Universal-Edition LEIPZIG

I. Teil.

1. Mondestrunken.

Arnold Schönberg, Op. 21.

Universal-Edition Nr. 5334. 5336.

Stich und Druck von Breitkopf & Härtel in Leipzig.

1. "Mondestrunken" ("Moonstruck") speaks poetically of the wine that the moon pours nightly on the waves of the sea, the wine that we drink with our eyes (piano, flute, viola, and cello).

2. "Colombine." The poem extols the "pale blossoms of the moonlight, the white wonder roses" (piano, flute, clarinet, and viola).

3. "Der Dandy" ("Dandy"). The poem treats the figure of Pierrot, the "silent dandy of Bergamo," standing by the fountain in moonlight (piano, piccolo, clarinet).

4. "Eine blasse Wäscherin" ("A Pale Washerwoman"). The poem describes the whiteness of the washerwoman's arms, and of the linen she washes at night (flute, clarinet, and violin, marked "without any expression," and in pianissimo throughout).

5. "Valse de Chopin." An atonal melodic pattern with a Chopinesque élan. The poem dwells on the melancholy charm of a waltz that is like a pale drop of blood coloring the lips of an ailing man (piano, flute, and clarinet/bass clarinet).

6. "Madonna." A poet's appeal to the mother of all sorrows (flute, bass clarinet, and cello, with piano accompaniment in the last measures).

7. "Der kranke Mond" ("The Sick Moon"). Speaking voice with flute, in a nostalgic, but not tragic, poem of the desperately sick moon.

8. "Nacht" ("Night"). Subtitled "passacaglia," which implies the constancy of the thematic pattern, the song is an invocation to the black night. The voice is assigned, by exception, three singing tones in the deep register (piano, bass clarinet, and cello).

9. "Gebet an Pierrot" ("Prayer to Pierrot"). The prayer to restore the gaiety of life to one who has forgotten how to laugh (clarinet and piano).

10. "Raub" ("Theft"). Tale of Pierrot's nightly thieving after the ducal rubies, the bloody drops of bygone fame (flute, clarinet, violin, and cello).

11. "Rote Messe" ("The Red Mass"). Pierrot's blasphemous Mass at eventide (piccolo, bass clarinet, viola, cello, and piano).

12. "Galgenlied" ("The Song of the Gallows"). The condemned man's vision of his last mistress, the withered hussy with a long neck, about to strangle him (piccolo, viola, cello, and piano).

13. "Enthauptung" ("Decapitation"). Pierrot looking in deathly anguish at the unsheathed Turkish sword of the crescent moon, imagining himself being decapitated by it (bass clarinet, viola, cello, and piano).

14. "Die Kreuze" ("The Crosses"). The poet's verses are the crosses on which he is bled (speaking voice with piano, later joined by flute, clarinet, violin, and cello).

15. "Heimweh" ("Homesickness"). In nostalgic mood, Pierrot utters plaintive cries, like the sighs from an old Italian pantomime (clarinet, violin, and piano).

16. "Gemeinheit" ("Outrage"). Pierrot bores a hole in Cassander's skull, while his cries rend the air, stuffs his "authentic Turkish tobacco" into the hole, sticks a reed at the base of the skull, and puffs contentedly (piccolo, clarinet, violin, cello, and piano).

17. "Parodie" ("Parody"). A matron in love with Pierrot is cruelly exposed to light by the playful moon, aping her shining hairpins with its beams (piccolo, clarinet, viola, and piano).
18. "Der Mondfleck" ("Moonspot"). Pierrot takes an evening walk in search of adventure, and the moon puts a white spot on his jacket, which will not come off even though Pierrot tries to scrub it off till early morning (piccolo, clarinet, violin, cello, and piano).
19. "Serenade." Pierrot saws away on his viola with a grotesquely long bow. When Cassander, enraged by this noise at night, bids him stop, he grabs him by the collar and fiddles on his bald pate (cello and piano).
20. "Heimfahrt" ("Journey Home"). Subtitled "Barcarolla," the poem describes Pierrot's homeward journey southward to Bergamo, with the moonbeam for a rudder and a water lily for a boat (flute, clarinet, violin, cello, and piano).
21. "O alter Duft ("O Olden Fragrance). The poem recites the charm of old tales, which enchant the senses, and dispel gloomy moods (flute, clarinet, violin, cello, and piano).

Arnold Schoenberg describes the recording of the work as follows:

The ensemble which recorded *Pierrot lunaire* has been chosen with great care because of the high quality of preceding ensembles that played this piece. Eduard Steuermann, whose performance seems to be unsurpassable, was the first to play the piano part in 1912. He participated in almost all subsequent performances in Italy and France. He also belonged to the ensemble of the Verein für musikalische Privataufführungen (Society for Private Performances in Vienna), which, under the direction of Erwin Stein and my direction, played about one hundred performances in the last twenty years. Erika Wagner-Stiedry has performed the vocal part since that time (with a few exceptions, of which I want to mention particularly the great Marie Gutheil-Schoder), and this proves the great satisfaction her performance has always given me.

It may be interesting to mention that Hans Kindler, now conductor in Washington, D.C., was the first cellist who mastered the enormous difficulties of the cello part in an unforgettable manner. Other cellists who subsequently achieved world fame: Emmanuel Feuermann (with Klemperer conducting), Gregor Piatigorsky (with Arthur Schnabel at the piano, and Fritz Stiedry conducting), Benar Heifetz, the former cellist of the Kolisch Quartet, have played the cello part. I must not forget also the clarinet of Victor Polatschek, now of the Boston Symphony Orchestra.

But a special word must be said about Rudolf Kolisch. I have to discount the fact that he is my brother-in-law; what counts is that he was my pupil; what counts still more is that he has played the violin and viola part in *Pierrot lunaire* since 1921, together with Erika Stiedry and Eduard Steuermann; and what counts most is that he participated in every one of the two hundred rehearsals from the very beginning to the very end, although after the first five rehearsals he had no need for them for himself. He knows this music better than I myself know it, and I was indeed happy that he was the one who prepared the new ensemble for this recording.

I, personally, may admit that my humble contribution to this recording is, perhaps, the spirit in which I composed the work, which is, of course, within the competence of the author. Among conductors who directed performances of *Pierrot lunaire* are two composers, Darius Milhaud, Louis Gruenberg, the well-known German conductor Hermann Scherchen, and two American orchestra leaders, Frederick Stock of Chicago and the great pioneer, Leopold Stokowski.

Mr. Posella (flute), Mr. Kalman Bloch (clarinet) and Mr. Stefan Auber (cellist) have helped to keep the performance on a level satisfying to the most refined and critical connoisseur.

Orchestration of Two Chorale Preludes by Bach (1922)

Schoenberg regarded his own music as a logical stage in the historical development of composition. Accordingly, he believed that classics must be viewed from a modern point of view. In a letter to Fritz Stiedry dated July 31, 1930, he explained: "Our present musical concepts necessitate clarity of the motivic procedures in both the horizontal and the vertical dimensions. We need this transparency in order to examine the musical structure. Taking into consideration these circumstances, the transcriptions I made of Bach's works was not only my right but my duty."

Schoenberg selected two of the best-known Bach chorale preludes—"Schmücke dich, O liebe Seele" ("Deck thyself, my soul, with gladness") and "Komm, Gott, Schöpfer, heiliger Geist," ("Come, God, Creator, Holy Ghost)—both based on Eucharistic Lutheran hymns dating back to the early years of the Reformation. The spiritual power of the former moved Schumann to write to Mendelssohn when he heard him play it in the St. Thomas Church in Leipzig (where Bach was organist a century before): "The melody seems interlaced with garlands of gold, and breathed forth such happiness that were life deprived of all faith, this simple chorale would restore it to us."

In his orchestration of this chorale prelude Schoenberg was extremely faithful to Bach's original. There are no gratuitous alterations or additions in Schoenberg's score. He retained the key of E-flat major used by Bach. The chorale melody is given to cello solo, an instrument Schoenberg knew because he played it, as an amateur. The cello presents the five strains of the chorale in a finely balanced dialogue with the orchestra. The score contains a rich assortment of instruments Bach never used, among them glockenspiel, triangle, and celesta, but they serve as decorative embellishments to emphasize the rhythmic pattern and do not conflict with the harmonic structure of the work.

The second chorale prelude, "Komm, Gott, Schöpfer, heiliger Geist," is orchestrated by Schoenberg with greater boldness than the first in the application of instrumental colors. The melody is given to the oboe and the high clarinet in E flat. The pentachordal cadence descending from the dominant to the tonic of C major is played by four horns in fortissimo. The theme subsequently is given to the trombones, tuba, and bassoons in unison, while the rest of the orchestra provides the ornamentation. The chorale prelude ends in full sonorities.

A Survivor from Warsaw, *Op. 46 (1947)*

Like Mahler, whom he admired so greatly, Schoenberg was born in the Jewish faith, but was converted to Protestantism. The anti-Semitic horrors unleashed by Hitler moved Schoenberg to return to the religion of his forebears. In a ceremony held in a Paris synagogue on July 24, 1933, Schoenberg once more became a Jew. *A Survivor from Warsaw* is an anguished expression of Schoenberg's newly found Jewish consciousness. The work was commissioned by the Koussevitzky Foundation. He completed the composition in twelve days, between August 11 and August 23, 1947. However, its first performance was given not by Koussevitzky with the Boston Symphony Orchestra, but by the Albuquerque Civic Symphony Orchestra under the direction of Kurt Frederick, on November 4, 1948.

Schoenberg was singularly proud of his proficiency in English and frequently engaged in argument with American-born friends about the proper usage of words and idioms. The title *A Survivor from Warsaw* was his own. His publishers felt that the preposition "from" was an unidiomatic rendering of the German "von," and suggested changing it to "of." Schoenberg did put "of" in the manuscript, but inserted a derisive exclamation point in parentheses after it to indicate his disagreement. Eventually he prevailed, and the score was published with the Germanic "from" in the title.

Schoenberg wrote his own English text for the work, and its curious syntax intensifies the sense of unreality, terror, and hopelessness of the situation. The narrative is based on reports Schoenberg received from actual survivors of the hideous hell in the Warsaw sewers where the Jews were hiding. It tells a moving story of the persecuted people who, at the point of death, summon their last courage and together intone the Hebrew prayer Shema Yisroel.

The scoring is for narrator, men's chorus, and orchestra. The narrator's part is written in *Sprechgesang*, inflected speech which Schoenberg introduced in *Gurre-Lieder* and developed in *Pierrot lunaire*. Its notation is unusual. The relative pitch of the syllables of the text is indicated by varying positions above and below a single central line, but sharps and flats are placed in front of these indeterminate notes, giving the visual impression of a musical staff. The final Hebrew prayer, however, is in regular five-line notation.

The work is written according to Schoenberg's method of composition with twelve tones. No more fitting medium can be imagined for this agonizing subject, with "squeezed octaves" resulting in the thematic supremacy of the atonal major sevenths, and with the classical tonic-dominant relationship of a perfect fifth replaced by the tritone, the "diabolus in musica" of the medieval theorists. The chromatic dispersal inherent in the dodecaphonic technique may well have assumed in Schoenberg's mind the symbolic significance of the diaspora of Israel. The illustrative power of the music is further enhanced by the use of a large section of percussion instruments in the score. It is significant, however, that Schoenberg shuns the obvious dramatics of the military drum. When the Nazi Feldwebel (sergeant) shouts, "In a minute I will know how many I am going to deliver to the gas chamber!" the accompaniment is ominously subdued, limited only to strings.

Schoenberg's text of *A Survivor from Warsaw,* with German sentences interpolated in the original, is as follows:

I cannot remember everything. I must have been unconscious most of the time; I remember only the grandiose moment when they all started to sing, as if prearranged, the old prayer they had neglected for so many years— the forgotten creed!

But I have no recollection how I got underground to live in the sewers of Warsaw so long a time.

The day began as usual. Reveille when it still was dark—get out whether you slept or whether worries kept you awake the whole night: you had been separated from your children, from your wife, from your parents, you don't know what happened to them; how could you sleep?

They shouted again: "Get out! The sergeant will be furious!" They came out; some very slow, the old ones, the sick men, some with nervous agility. They fear the sergeant. They hurry as much as they can. In vain! Much too much noise, much too much commotion and not fast enough!

The Feldwebel shouts: "Achtung! Still gestanden! Na wird's mal, oder soll ich mit dem Gewehrkolben nachhelfen? Na jut; wenn lhr's durchaus haben wollt!" ["Attention! Stand still! How about it, or should I help you along with a rifle butt? All right, if you want."]

The sergeant and his subordinates hit everyone: Young or old, strong or sick, guilty or innocent—It was painful to hear the groaning and moaning.

I heard it though I had been hit very hard, so hard that I could not help falling down. We all on the ground who could not stand up were then beaten over the head.

I must have been unconscious. The next thing I knew was a soldier saying, "They are all dead!" Whereupon the sergeant ordered to do away with us.

There I lay aside half conscious. It had become very still—fear and pain. Then I heard the sergeant shouting: "Abzählen!" ["Count off!"]

They started slowly, and irregularly: One, two, three, four. "Achtung." The sergeant shouted again: "Rascher! Nochmals von vorn anfangen! In einer Minute will ich wissen wieviele ich zur Gaskammer abliefere! Abzählen!" ["Faster! Once more, start from the beginning. In a minute I will know how many I am going to deliver to the gas chamber! Count off!"]

They began again, first slowly: One, two, three, four, became faster and faster, so fast that it finally sounded like a stampede of wild horses, and all of a sudden, in the middle of it, they began singing the Shema Yisroel.

MAURICE RAVEL
(1875–1937)
Poet of Simplicity

Maurice ravel's father was a Swiss engineer, and his mother was of Basque origin. The family moved to Paris from the Lower Pyrenees when he was an infant. He began to study piano at the age of seven and attended the Paris Conservatory until 1895, when he left at the age of twenty. That same year, he completed work on his song "Un Grand Sommeil noir," the *Menuet antique* for piano, and the *Habanera* for two pianos (later included in the *Rapsodie espagnole* for orchestra). These pieces already revealed great originality in the treatment of old modes and of Spanish motives, but Ravel continued to study, returning in 1897 to the Conservatory to study with Gabriel Fauré (composition) and André Gédalge (counterpoint and orchestration). Ravel's well-known *Pavane pour une infante défunte* for piano was written during that time (1899).

By 1905, Ravel had written a number of his most famous compositions and was regarded by most French critics as a talented disciple of Debussy. No doubt, Ravel's method of poetic association of musical ideas paralleled that of Debussy; his employment of unresolved dissonances and the enhancement of the diatonic style into pandiatonicism were techniques common to Debussy and his followers. But there were important differences: whereas Debussy adopted the scale of whole tones as an integral part of his musical vocabulary, Ravel resorted to it only occasionally. Similarly, augmented triads appear much less frequently in Ravel's music than in Debussy's. In his writing for piano, Ravel actually anticipated some of Debussy's usages.

Where Debussy's progress was uneventful through the years of his academic study, Ravel had to fight against the conservatism of academic circles. Four times he applied for and was denied the Grand Prix de Rome, a coveted prize not only because of the attendant honors, but because it gave the opportunity to a young composer to write in financial comfort in a villa in Rome. His rejection stirred a scandal, particularly when the six candidates were announced, and they all turned out to be pupils of one professor at the Paris conservatory who was influential in Academy circles.

The "Ravel case" soon became a cause célèbre: far from being pushed back by the decision, Ravel gained tremendously in popularity. Even his former critics rallied to his cause. Ravel was a very modest man, but under certain circumstances he showed great pride. He revealed this pride during a discussion in the musical columns of the Paris newspapers of his dependence on Debussy. Ravel wrote to the influential critic of *Le Temps*, pointing out that his *Jeux d'eau* established a new pianistic technique of his own, quite independent from Debussy, and gave chronological data to support his statement.

In Paris, elsewhere in France, and soon in England and other European countries, Ravel's name became well known. For many years, he was regarded as an ultramodernist. But inspired evocation of the past was another aspect of Ravel's creative genius: in this style are his *Pavane pour une infante défunte*, *Le Tombeau de Couperin*, and *La Valse*. Luxuriance of exotic colors marks his ballet *Daphnis et Chloé*, his opera *L'Heure espagnole*, the song cycles *Shéhérazade* and *Chansons madécasses*, and his virtuoso pieces for piano, *Miroirs* and *Gaspard de la nuit*. Other works are deliberately austere, even ascetic, in their pointed classicism: the piano concertos, the Sonatine for piano, and some of his songs with piano accompaniment. For Diaghilev's Ballets Russes he wrote one of his masterpieces, *Daphnis et Chloé*; another ballet, *Boléro*, commissioned by Ida Rubinstein and performed at her dance recital at the Paris Opéra on November 22, 1928, became Ravel's most spectacular success as an orchestral piece.

Ravel never married, and lived a life of semiretirement, devoting most of his time to composition. He accepted virtually no pupils, although he gave friendly advice to Vaughan Williams and to others, but he was never on the faculty of any school. Not a brilliant performer, he appeared as a pianist only to play his own works, often accompanying singers in programs of his songs. Although he accepted engagements as a conductor, his technique was barely sufficient to secure a perfunctory performance of his music. When World War I broke out in 1914, he was rejected for military service because of his frail physique, but he was anxious to serve; his application for air service was denied, but he was received in the ambulance corps at the front. His health gave way and, in the autumn of 1916, he was compelled to enter a hospital for recuperation. In 1922 he visited Amsterdam and Venice, conducting his music, and in 1923 he appeared in London. In 1926 he went to Sweden, England, and Scotland, and he made an American tour as a conductor and pianist in 1928, returning to Paris to complete the commission for a dance piece, *Boléro*.

Following his American tour, an honorary degree of doctor of music was conferred upon Ravel by Oxford University. (In the Latin text of the diploma he was described as "Musarum interpretes modorum Daedalus Mauritius Ravelius.") This year of *Boléro* marked the peak of Ravel's worldly success. It was also the year during which he felt the ominous signs of an incipient cerebro-vascular disturbance. His mind was alert, but he was beset by what he called "une tristesse affreuse." He suffered from amnesia. Once, he could not remember his own name. His doctors spoke alarmingly of "apraxia" and "dysphasia." He began to lose the ability to write notes or words. He knew the individual letters that made up each word he wanted to write, but he could not remember the order in which they occurred. His speech became disarticulate. A friend described his state as a procession with muted fifes and muffled drums, on a mental journey into the night.

In a desperate effort to save Ravel, brain surgery was performed. No tumor was found; Ravel's condition was due to arteriosclerotic degeneration of a main cerebral blood vessel. The operation was futile; Ravel sank into a coma and died a few days later. At his funeral, the writer Colette said, "He was deprived of memory, lost the power of speech and ability to write. He died stifled, while there still surged within him so many harmonies, so many memories of bird songs and guitars, of dancing and melodious nights."

An ironic postscript to Ravel's life was the posthumous fate of his royalties, which grew to considerable sums of money owing particularly to the success of his fascinating tour de force, *Boléro*, based on a single theme and never, except in the last measure of the coda, diverging from the basic key of C major. Ravel left his estate to his brother, who in turn bequeathed it to his housekeeper; she married a peasant from central France who survived her and received millions of francs of revenue from music he could not understand. There was a litigation on the part of Ravel's distant cousins, but the French law of inheritance of property by a lawful spouse prevailed.

ORCHESTRAL MUSIC
Alborada del gracioso *(1908);* Rapsodie espagnole *(1919)*

It has been said that the best Spanish music has been composed by Frenchmen. The Spanish pieces of Bizet, Chabrier, and Debussy seem to sustain this paradoxical notion; the music of Isaac Albéniz, Eduardo Granados, and Manuel de Falla may be more authentically Spanish, but French works in the Spanish vein seem to possess an impetuous élan that has an immediate appeal to the listener. Ravel felt very close to Spain; he was born on its border at Ciboure, in the Basses-Pyrénées, on March 7, 1875. His mother was of Basque descent; as a child Ravel could actually speak the unspeakable Basque language. His father was a mechanical engineer from Switzerland who played a role in the manufacture of early motor cars. Marveling at Ravel's precise technique in instrumental writing, someone remarked that he wrote music with the lapidary care of a Swiss watchmaker. Ravel never attained perfection, or even competence, as a performer; he played piano poorly, and had to use the notes and a page turner even when accompanying a singer in his own songs. He was even more inept as a conductor, and his sense of pitch was defective. But with myriad pianists and conductors to perform Ravel's music, the lack of his own capacities at the keyboard or on the podium was not of any consequence.

Among Ravel's works in the Spanish vein, *Alborada del gracioso* is one of the most succulent. *Alborada* is an early-morning song, as contrasted with *serenade*, which is an evening song. *Gracioso* is the Spanish word for a graceful jester.

Alborada del gracioso is therefore a jester's salute at dawn. The piece is gracefully symmetric, with evocative, melodious sections contrasted with exciting dance rhythms. It was originally a part of Ravel's piano suite *Miroirs*; Ravel orchestrated it at a later time in his inimitable colorful manner. The orchestral version of the *Alborada del gracioso* was performed for the first time in Boston on February 16, 1921.

Rapsodie espagnole is another work of Ravel's rooted in Spanish melodies and rhythms. It is an orchestral suite in four movements: "Prélude à la nuit," "Malagueña," "Habanera," "Feria." The "Prélude" opens with a wistful descending tetrachord on muted strings, establishing the mood of the entire piece. It is echoed by wind instruments, all in muted colors, concluding with an improvisation on the English horn.

There follows a brilliant *malagueña*, a dance from southern Spain suggesting the rhythms of a fandango. It progresses gradually from subdued sonorities to explosions of rhythmic energy. The next movement is a *habanera*, set in a characteristic Cuban rhythm evoking the time when Spain dominated the Caribbean islands. The last movement, "Feria," is a spectacular Spanish fiesta set in a dual meter, $\frac{6}{8}$ and $\frac{3}{4}$ time, with conflicting stresses made more beguiling by coloristic instrumental devices, including such effects as glissandos on natural harmonics in the viola and the cello. The work was performed for the first time in Paris on March 15, 1908, at a concert conducted by Edouard Colonne.

Ravel is often paired with Debussy as an initiator of a new harmonic and instrumental style of composition, but he is rarely described as an Impressionist composer. His music does not employ the luxuriant sonorities typical of Debussy's orchestral palette; on the contrary, Ravel is very careful in assigning his effects with a minimum of purely pictorial displays. Unlike Debussy, who favored parallel harmonic progressions and cultivated the whole-tone scale, Ravel retained the classical tonalities, combining melodies and chords in pandiatonic superstructures.

Valses nobles et sentimentales *(1912)*

In May 1911, the Société Musicale Indépendante in Paris decided to test the critical capacity of the audience and professional music critics by giving a "concert without the names of the composer." Several works of the modern school were accordingly presented anonymously, among them, and for the first time, Ravel's *Valses nobles et sentimentales*. Emile Vuillermoz, one of the initiators of the concert, described the event in the memorial publication *Maurice Ravel par quelques-uns de ses familiers*, issued in Paris in 1939:

> Ravel was in a loge in the midst of a group of society dilettantes who habitually swooned when they heard even two bars of Ravel's music. Heroically faithful to his oath as a conspirator, the composer of *Valses nobles et sentimentales* had not forewarned them that his unpublished work was included in the program. When they heard this composition played with an imperturbably serious mien by Louis Aubert, the composer's sycophantic companions began to jeer, hoping to give Ravel pleasure by assailing ferociously these "ridiculous pages." Stoically, but no doubt somewhat bitterly, Ravel accepted these remarks in silence, but I am not sure whether he ever forgave me for unwittingly placing him in so awkward a situation that night.
>
> Machiavellian to the end, we distributed among the listeners little slips

of paper, with the request to name the composers of the pieces played. The results of this referendum were terrifying. The professional critics cautiously abstained from voting, and the next day they failed to publish a single word about this evening that must have been so disconcerting to them. As to the rest, they naively ascribed works, in which the personality of our extreme modernists was clearly reflected, to Mozart, Schumann, Chopin, Gounod, Wagner, or Mendelssohn. No one perceived the hand of Ravel in this succession of waltzes, which bear so clearly Ravel's distinctive imprint.

An American writer heard Ravel play the *Valses* in Paris a year later and recorded his impressions of the man and the artist in the pages of the *Musical Courier*: "He is a very boyish-looking little man, and you wonder to look at him, at his tremendous force and passion as a composer.... There seems to be a strangely fascinating discordant note added to nearly every harmony. You wonder constantly how he does it, and why it is so delightful." The "fascinating discordant note" is the added sixth, which Ravel particularly favors in the *Valses*. And Ravel liked to use a parallel row of six-five chords over a pedal tone, a procedure that, to an untutored ear, gives an impression of a recurring discordant note. The rhythms of several of the *Valses nobles et sentimentales* anticipate *La Valse*, written seven years later. Some of the harmonies and dynamic effects of the earlier work have also found application in *La Valse*, but the similarity is that of allusion rather than of identity.

Ravel orchestrated the work for the Russian dancer Trouhanova, who gave a dance recital in Paris on April 22, 1912, with Ravel's *Valses*, under the new title of *Adélaïde, ou Le Langage des fleurs*. The scenario, written by Ravel himself, was an imaginative tale from the early nineteenth century, and dealt with the young courtesan Adélaïde, the old Duke, and the young lover, Lorédan. The lovers exchange flowers, each of which has a meaning. The score bears an epigraph from Ravel's favorite poet, Henri de Régnier: "le plaisir délicieux et toujours nouveau d'une occupation inutile" ("the delicious and always new pleasure of a useless occupation"). There is a fine point of irony in this quotation, which supplements the irony of the title.

Daphnis and Chloé: *Suite No. 2 (1913)*

The sobriquet "Swiss watchmaker of music" refers to Ravel's exquisite equilibration of instrumental sonorities and close attention to the minuscule nuances of dynamics. Another relevant detail in this definition is to Ravel's Swiss family origin, for his father was a Swiss engineer who invented a steam automobile.

His name is commonly bracketed with that of Debussy as initiators of the Impressionist idiom in composition. The term may be applied to Debussy's music by analogy with French Impressionist paintings, but Ravel's art tends toward neoclassicism. His harmony is more precise than the fluid modulatory language of Debussy, and he rarely makes use of the elusive whole-tone scale, with its tonal instability. Rather, he stylizes archaic modes, never abandoning the implicit tonality.

In *La Valse*, Ravel invokes the scene of waltzing couples in Vienna; in *Boléro*, he distills and integrates the rhythms of Spain. His scores are choreographic par excellence. His ballet *Daphnis and Chloé* was produced by Diaghilev's Ballets Russes in Paris on June 8, 1912. Ravel extracted two symphonic suites from this ballet, of which the second is by far the more popular. The scenario is derived from a bucolic love story. Daphnis, the shepherd, is asleep in front of the grotto of the nymphs. Other shepherds appear seeking Daphnis and Chloé, who also tends a flock of sheep. They need the sanction of Pan for the consummation of their love. In pantomime, they reproduce the magic story of Pan's love for the nymph Syrinx and, by doing so, they become lovers themselves.

DAPHNIS ET CHLOÉ

Une prairie à la lisière d'un bois sacré. Au fond, des collines. A droite, une grotte, à l'entrée de laquelle, taillées à même le roc, sont figurées trois Nymphes, d'une sculpture archaïque. Un peu vers le fond, à gauche, un grand rocher affecte vaguement la forme du dieu Pân. Au second plan, des brebis paissent. Une après-midi claire de printemps. Au lever du rideau, la scène est vide.

Introduction et Danse religieuse

(+) *La clarinette basse doit avoir un mi♭. Sinon prendre le ton de La.*
The bass clarinet should have an E♭. Otherwise use the instrument in A.

The second symphonic suite of *Daphnis and Chloé* comprises three scenes; Dawn, Pantomime, and General Dance. Dawn is portrayed by a delicate murmuration of flutes and clarinets supported by two harps glissando. The annotation in the score reads: "Not a sound but the murmur of brooks of dew that flows from the rocks." The birds are heard, illustrated by three solo violins and the trills of the piccolo. In the meantime, the melody of the dawn after its inception in the divided double basses spreads into the upper strings and the lower woodwind instruments. The roulades of the piccolo represent the shepherd's pipe, soon answered by the high clarinet representing another shepherd. The tide of assembled sonorities rises as Daphnis and Chloé fall into each others' arms.

The rivulets of fluid sonorities in the woodwinds and the harps, and the silvery cataracts of the celesta subside, and the Pantomime begins, with Daphnis representing the god Pan and Chloé playing the part of the lost nymph Syrinx. The nymph escapes from Pan, who tries to reach her. As she vanishes, Pan plucks some tall flowers and fashions a panpipe from the stems. His melancholy song is intoned by the flute, accompanied with the utmost gentleness by muted strings. The nymph yields to the fascination of Pan's languorous plaint and appears before him. A General Dance follows to celebrate the imagined reunion of Pan and Syrinx. The lovers swear their undying fidelity with two sheep as witnesses. The bacchantes enter the scene and start a dance, shaking tambourines, striking cymbals, and drumming insistent rhythms. The sonorous wizardry of the General Dance is achieved by the constant ebb and flow of dynamic strength, vanishing to the threshold of audibility and then mounting to plangent fortissimo.

Le Tombeau de Couperin *(1920)*

There are two equally important directions in modern French music: innovation and restylization. Ravel, equipped with an exquisite sense of values and a precise science of musical equilibration, was as expert in reviving the French past as he was in building its musical future.

Le Tombeau de Couperin is Ravel's tribute to France's greatest Impressionist—for, indeed, Couperin was a precursor of impressionism. Long before Virgil Thomson began painting symphonic portraits at musical sittings with live subjects, Couperin wrote a series of pieces for clavecin in which he subtly pictured the girlish characters of the Timid One, the Indiscreet One, and even the Irritating One. In the midst of the aesthetic fight for the acceptance of French impressionism, Jean Cocteau recalled Couperin in defense of Erik Satie; the public is shocked by the titles of Satie's pieces, he declared, but accepts "the most cockeyed" titles of Couperin: *Le tic-toc choc, Les culbutes Ixcxbxnxs, Les Coucous bénévoles,* and *Les Trésorières surannées.*

Ravel's tribute to Couperin is more of a handshake of two kindred spirits across 207 years of time than an offering on Couperin's glorified tomb. The music of Ravel is a twentieth-century counterpart of Couperin's. The manner and the attitudes are the same; the idiom is tonal, touched up with a pandiatonic brush, and seasoned with droplets of chromatic harmony. Ravel wrote this suite as a set of six piano pieces in 1914–17; he later orchestrated four of them, and they were performed for the first time by the Pasdeloup Orchestra in Paris on February 28, 1920.

Le Tombeau de Couperin, as an orchestral suite, contains four movements: Prélude, Forlane, Menuet, and Rigaudon. The Prélude begins in a murmuring hurly-burly of the woodwinds, punctuated by plucked strings. A chromatic descending line helps to sustain the even motion, in which the strings soon join. A feeling of stability comes from the pedal points in the transition; the hollow fifths in parallel progressions suggest an archaic detachment. The dynamics are subdued, and then a sudden crescendo wells up to a climactic chord of the thirteenth. After a few scattered figurations and a protracted trill, the Prélude comes to an end.

The Forlane is a stylization of an old dance of Italian origin that is close to a gigue in rhythm. It is a gay dance, and Ravel keeps its original gaiety in soft instrumental colors as a nostalgic reminiscence of another era. The Menuet has a characteristic recessive bass, leading to a cadential construction every fourth bar. The tonic-dominant pedal point is the ground for the middle section, following the classical formula. The *rigaudon* is a seventeenth-century dance of southern France; it was often adopted in the classical suite. Ravel modernizes it in a spirited manner. The harmonic texture is pandiatonic, so that not a single accidental mars the initial eight bars of the score. The middle section approaches the rhythm of a polka. The Rigaudon ends with a decisive flourish in clear C major.

La Valse *(1920)*

The original title of *La Valse* was simply *Wien*, German for Vienna. It is a pity that this title was not allowed to stand. "Wien" evokes in the mind a definite picture of the carefree, amorous atmosphere of the imperial city that the indefinite title *La Valse* fails to convey. When the title was changed, it was necessary to add an explanatory note, in which the locale of the scene was marked with deliberate latitude: an imperial court circa 1855. The score is subtitled choreographic poem, which shows that Ravel had in mind a ballet interpretation of the music. He marks the places in the score in which the waltzing crowd appears through the rifts in the clouds, and the fortissimo passage where the light of the chandeliers suddenly illuminates the scene.

La Valse was performed for the first time at the Concerts in Paris on December 12, 1920. Ravel was often late in completing his scores for a previously arranged performance, and this explains the mistakes in Ravel's chronology, which are unfortunately found in the monographs by Ravel's Boswell, Roland-Manuel, who also gives a premature date for *La Valse*, January 8, 1920.

The misdating of the first performance was the more unnecessary since Roland-Manuel was in close touch with the progress of Ravel's work on *La Valse*. On January 17, 1920, Ravel was unexpectedly nominated chevalier of the Legion of Honor. He refused to accept the nomination. "Quelle histoire ridicule," he wrote to Roland-Manuel, "Who could have played this trick on me? And *Wien* must be completed by the end of the month. Have you noticed that the Legionnaires are similar to morphine addicts, eager to force others to share their passion, perhaps to justify it in their own eyes?" "The end of the month" referred to in Ravel's letter was January 1920, and so *La Valse* could not conceivably have been performed on January 8.

The elimination of "Wien" from the title of *La Valse* has misled the critics. In one of those vague reviews with more literary allusions than relevant analysis, the critic of *Le Ménestrel* gives this description: "To the grace and languor of a Carpeaux is here opposed the anguish of Prud'homme: 'We are dancing on a volcano.' This bacchanal has in its joy something foreboding, like drunkenness betraying a debility, perhaps by the dissonances and shocks of orchestral colors...."

Henry Prunières is much more scholarly and much more literary. Writing in La Revue musicale, he gives a specific program of *La Valse*.

A classical Viennese Waltz, or rather a phantom of a waltz in a dream. Crushed with fatigue after the ball, one falls asleep, and the rhythms just heard haunt him. Indistinct at first, they gradually take shape. Shreds of phrases emerge, the melody is organized, and the waltz appears, quite simple, a bit caricatured, a waltz of Johann Strauss and Offenbach. It sweeps the couples, it hurries along, pressed, out of breath, hesitating for a moment, but never stopping.... The dancers whirl, the heads are dizzy, the walls, the floors vibrate. The gyrating hallucination reaches a paroxysm. Suddenly, awakening comes, or perhaps a plunge into unconsciousness, and all disappears. Never has Ravel's art been more perfect. This is a tour de force, this waltz that lasts twelve minutes without an episode, without a stop. Inexhaustible verve animates this whole piece, written with a dizzy virtuosity, and visibly to the great enjoyment of the author himself.

Alfredo Casella, who was closely associated with Ravel, describes *La Valse* as "a masque of human life, with its pomp and glory, its luxury of sight and sound, its hours of golden youth, one generation treading upon the receding footsteps of another."

Eight years after the composition of *La Valse*, Ravel wrote his famous *Boléro*, which he himself described as an "orchestral crescendo lasting seventeen minutes." *La Valse* is also a continuous movement, but it seethes in constant dynamic oscillation, never approaching the constancy of the key and rhythmic pulse that characterize *Boléro*. Ravel varied his technique, but whatever technique he used, his art of precision and immediate effectiveness never failed him.

Orchestration of Pictures at an Exhibition, *by Modest Mussorgsky (1922)*

Modest Mussorgsky wrote his suite for piano, *Pictures at an Exhibition,* in 1874 as a tribute to the memory of his friend, the Russian painter Victor Hartmann. Each number of the suite illustrates one of Hartmann's drawings or water colors. The very name of Hartmann has vanished into oblivion, and is preserved for posterity only through the glory of Mussorgsky's music.

Pictures at an Exhibition was brilliantly arranged for orchestra by Ravel in 1922, on a commission from Serge Koussevitzky, for a fee of 10,000 francs. Koussevitzky performed it for the first time in Paris on October 19, 1922.

Mussorgsky's suite is a leisurely musical promenade through a gallery of Hartmann's pictures. Brief interludes between each pair of pictures represent a walk from one to the next. A thematic musical promenade opens the gallery. The first painting is *Gnomus*, a dwarf-shaped nutcracker. In Ravel's orchestration, the music is punctuated by the sounds of rattles and whiplashes, as nut fragments fly apart under the impact of the gnomus. After a promenade, the viewer is conducted to Hartmann's Italian drawing *Il Vecchio Castello*. The image of an old Italian castle is depicted in the music by a melody in a minor mode. In Ravel's orchestration, the theme is played by the alto saxophone.

After another promenade, the scene shifts to the Garden of the Tuileries in Paris, with children playing happily in the sunlight. The next picture presents a striking contrast. A clumsy Polish oxcart, *Bydlo*, hobbles on the cobblestones of a village road. It rumbles by with uncouth noise, and then disappears in a cloud of musical dust. Ravel assigns the theme of the rough-wheeled vehicle to the bass tuba, a most fitting instrument for such an object.

Another promenade introduces the "Ballet of Unhatched Chickens in Their Eggshells." There is a lot of scratching inside and a lot of cracking sounds as the eggshells break up and let the chicks emerge into the world of light. Ravel's orchestration makes the most of the amusing "ballet," with expert use of the celesta, harp, and high woodwinds.

We next are confronted with a painting of sociological significance, a grotesque sketch entitled *Samuel Goldenberg and Schmuyle*. These personages are Polish Jews, one rich, the other poor. The rich Jew is appropriately pompous, sermonizing his unfortunate companion in an orientalized mode with its rich proliferation of augmented seconds in a minor mode. In Ravel's orchestration, the rich Jew orates in imposing unisons in the lower register, while the poor Jew pipes dejectedly on a muted trumpet.

From Poland we cross to a market scene in Limoges, France, with French housewives bickering and haggling, chattering and jabbering in perpetual commotion. There follows a solemn tableau, *Catacombae*. In sepulchral tones, Mussorgsky invokes Hartmann's spirit to guide him through the ancient Roman catacombs. In an ensuing chorale, "Cum mortuis in lingua mortua," Mussorgsky communes "with the dead in a dead language." Bidding farewell to the land of the dead, Mussorgsky plunges into a revelry of Russian folklore in *A Hut on a Hen's Legs*, where dwells the hideous Russian witch Baba Yaga. The music is full of demoniacal tritones and sharply dissonant major sevenths. Baba Yaga rides the broomstick through the stormy skies on an avalanche of scales.

Then, without a break, the music leads to the grand finale, *The Great Gate of Kiev*. This is an apotheosis of Holy Russia, with church bells pealing and religious chants intoned with devotional fervor. The motive of the opening promenade returns, dressed up in opulent harmonies. Ravel's orchestration is resplendent in depicting the golden glory of Mussorgsky's Russia.

Pictorially, *The Great Gate of Kiev* was a sketch drawn by Hartmann for an arch to be erected in Kiev to commemorate the escape of Czar Alexander II from an assassination attempt engineered by Russian nihilists. But the second attempt, in 1881, succeeded, and the great gate of Kiev was never built. Mussorgsky died in the same year, at the age of forty-two, a victim of acute alcoholism.

Boléro *(1928)*

In 1928, Ravel made a grand tour of the United States as conductor in programs of his own works. He wrote to a friend from Los Angeles in February:

> The sun shines in full splendor; it is a wonderful city decked in flowers, and I hate to think that it will be cold again when I come back to Paris. But the triumphs are fatiguing. In Los Angeles, I actually avoided seeing people; besides, I was dying of hunger. I made a trip to Hollywood, the city of the cinema, and met various stars, among them Douglas Fairbanks, who fortunately speaks French.

During his entire American tour, Ravel's mind was preoccupied with a commission he had accepted from the danseuse Ida Rubinstein, who wanted him to write a Spanish-colored symphonic movement for her modern dance recital. Ravel decided on a bold idea: to build the entire work on a single theme in the single tonality of C major, without any change in the rhythm of the underlying accompaniment. The theme assumed a bilateral form, the first section progressing along the C-major scale, the second beginning on B-flat and descending slowly toward the dominant G in a flatted Phrygian cadence. Despite these tonal alterations, the fundamental harmony remains firmly anchored on C, with the remarkable exception of eight bars before the coda, when a sudden modulation into E major is effected.

Ravel called the piece *Boléro*, even though some of his Spanish friends grumbled that it was more like a fandango or a *seguidilla* in character and rhythm. Ravel himself described the *Boléro* as "a rather slow dance, uniform in its melody, harmony and rhythm," the latter being tapped out continuously on the drum. The only element of variety is supplied by the orchestral crescendo. Asked for his own opinion about the value of *Boléro*, Ravel replied, ruefully: "Malheureusement, il est vide de musique." Devoid of music or not, *Boléro* became Ravel's most celebrated work, spreading his name and fame across the five continents.

The first performance of *Boléro* took place at the Opéra in Paris, on November 22, 1928, produced by Ida Rubinstein, who was also the dance soloist. The scene was set in a realistic Barcelona café, with a voluptuous dancer surrounded by a group of men, shouting encouragement and voicing their delight.

Formally, *Boléro* is a veritable tour de force. It consists of eighteen variations, each employing either the first or the second part of the bilateral subject, and each in a different orchestration. The first eight variations are given largely to eight solo instruments: flute, clarinet, bassoon, small clarinet, oboe d'amore, muted trumpet, tenor saxophone, and soprano saxophone. In the subsequent variations, the "orchestral crescendo" is created by the doubling of instruments and the accretion in sonority of the accompanying rhythmic figures. The ninth variation is remarkable from the acoustic standpoint. In it, a French horn solo, supported by the celesta, is accompanied in the high treble by two piccolos, forming the sixth and the tenth overtone of the melody. Ravel specifically indicates that the high notes are to be played pianissimo, as actual overtones, which are weaker the higher they are. Visually, the passage looks like a progression of consecutive parallel triads in open harmony, but acoustically, in proper performance, the overtones should not be heard as harmonic ingredients, but are calculated to produce a magical alteration in the tone color of the solo instrument, converting it into a sort of hyperhorn.

The tenth variation combines the oboe, the oboe d'amore, the English horn, and the clarinet in its melodic projection. The eleventh is a trombone solo; the remaining variations increase the contingent of the participating instruments. In the last variation, the piccolos, trumpets, saxophone, and violins intone the second section of the subject in mighty vociferation. It is this last variation, before the coda, that contains the extraordinary modulation into E major. C major returns for an abrupt ending on a Phrygian cadence.

WORKS FOR SOLO INSTRUMENT AND ORCHESTRA
Tzigane *(1924)*

The musical greatness of Ravel is twofold. He conjures up images of sensuous subtlety, or else he stylizes the artifacts of yesterday, recreating the musical past as though seen through a memory-dimming refractor. To some aestheticians, stylization is an inferior art. Others argue that it is a prerequisite of artistic self-renewal, that without constant adaptation of the past to the present there is no continuity in art.

In appreciation of his mastery, Ravel has been called the "Swiss watchmaker of music." But he was also attacked as an artificer out of touch with the real world. The *Manchester Guardian* wrote about Ravel in April 1924:

> Never was an artist more fastidious, more afraid of all that is crass and gross, and never a composer so precious, so remote from nature, so anxious to avoid all plain-speaking human sympathy. If ever a man was born at the wrong time, that man is Ravel. He belongs spiritually to the artificial eighteenth century. To him, trimmed hedges and glittering waterworks are nature, while fragile Sèvres shepherdesses come as near humanity as he wishes to get.

Ravel was conversant with porcelain shepherdesses, but also with waltzing bon-vivants and warm-blooded Gypsies, as shown in *La Valse* and the famous *Boléro*. His *Tzigane* (the title means a Gypsy, with specific reference to Gypsy musicians), a *rapsodie de concert* written for the Hungarian violinist Yelly d'Aranyi, is the stylization of a type of music reputed for its reckless spirit and orgiastic abandon. No fragile Sèvres shepherdess is the Gypsy songstress of Ravel's *Tzigane*!

When Ravel played the piano part of *Tzigane* for the first time, with d'Aranyi, at a London concert of his works 1924, the critics were frankly perplexed. "One is puzzled to understand what Ravel is at," wrote the *London Times*. "Either the work is a parody of all the Liszt-Hubay-Brahms-Joachim school of Hungarian violin music, or it is an attempt to get away from the limited sphere of his previous compositions, to infuse into his work a little of that warm blood it needs." The *Manchester Guardian* was unqualifiedly enthusiastic: "*Tzigane* is an astounding bravura piece, full of the most wonderfully telling effect. Ravel has once again proved his unique gift of exploiting instrumental resources and finding new and entrancing sound-values. But there is more in this work, which toys delightfully with some Hungarian conventions and remolds them into something new and fascinating."

In 1925, Ravel orchestrated the piece and it was performed in Amsterdam by Samuel Dushkin with the Concertgebouw Orchestra conducted by Willem Mengelberg. After its Boston performance, H. T. Parker, the critic of the *Boston Evening Transcript*, wrote: "It is difficult to believe that Ravel would mock, much less parody, with Gallic adroitness, the rhapsodies of technique and tone, the extravagance of feeling, common enough in these Gypsy violinists. Rather, he would outdo them at their own game, with a variety of invention, a subtlety of exaction, beyond their less cerebral powers." Every critic commented upon the extraordinary difficulty of the solo part. "If it is a joke," observed Philip Hale, "not many violinists can play it on the audience."

Tzigane opens with a long cadenza for violin alone. It is intervallically constructed upon the so-called Gypsy scale. From the outset, there is an abundant display of modern virtuoso technique, with difficult progressions, harmonics, and double, triple, and quadruple stops. After the violin has come to an end of its exertions, there is a cadenza for the harp, projected against the "Parisian" bitonality of C and F-sharp major. These two cadenzas serve as preliminaries to the principal section, Moderato. The violin has a dancing Gypsy tune. Then the clarinet comes in with another Gypsy melody, accompanied by the violin solo in ethereal harmonics. Later, the violin picks up the clarinet's tune and, after some intensive reiteration of its Gypsy intervals, arrives at a cascading cadenza. There is a brief pause, and once more the Gypsy dance is resumed, this time with the oboe playing the original violin tune. The orchestra has a dancing interlude; the violin plays difficult harmonics, and then, as though for relief, glides in fifths over the open strings, fortissimo. Now the harp plays sonorous glissandos, while the violin is trilling its Gypsy refrain. Then comes the section marked grandioso, in which the violin plays an imposing singing air. Finally, the soloist starts on its last dash, with 488 sixteenth notes in changing velocities, coming abruptly to a stop, and ending the vertiginous dance.

Concerto for the Left Hand (1931)

Amputation of an arm is a most distressing event, but by a quirk of fate, it contributed to the creation of several excellent piano concertos for the left hand alone. The amputee in the case was Paul Wittgenstein, the Austrian pianist who lost his right arm on the Russian front in the First World War. He was taken prisoner and spent some unpleasant time in Omsk, Siberia, before being repatriated in 1916. Nothing daunted, he developed an extraordinary virtuosity for the left hand alone. Being a member of a rich family, and having been reared in a philosophical milieu (his brother was the famous logician Ludwig Wittgenstein), he decided to convert a misfortune into an artistic fortune. Accordingly, he commissioned several contemporary composers, among them Richard Strauss, Ravel, and Prokofiev, to write one-arm piano concertos.

Such works are not unknown in the piano repertory. Scriabin wrote a couple of charming pieces for left hand alone when his right hand was disabled as a result of excessive practice. And there was a Hungarian composer named Géza Zichy who lost his right arm in an hunting accident and proceeded to write left-hand piano pieces; he played his three-hand arrangement of Liszt's Rákóczy March with Liszt himself providing his own functional two hands.

It so happened that Ravel was already at work on a two-arm piano concerto when he accepted Wittgenstein's commission. The left-hand concerto is a single movement, symmetrically segmented into three sections: lento, allegro, lento. Ravel was at the time very much impressed by (then novel) jazz music, which he heard during his American trip in 1928; the allegro in the left-hand concerto is alive with jazz and blues rhythms. Ravel points out that the work is actually monothematic, and that a keen ear can easily perceive the intervallic and rhythmic turns common to both the fast middle section and the outer slow sections. The concerto was performed by Wittgenstein in Vienna on November 27, 1931; later, Ravel coached a two-armed French pianist, Jacques Février, to play the work, and he performed it in Paris on January 17, 1933.

Concerto for Piano and Orchestra in G Major (1932)

Ravel was working on two piano concertos in 1930, and they could be no more distinct in style if two different men had written them. One was really half a concerto, commissioned by the Austrian pianist Paul Wittgenstein, who had lost his right arm on the Russian front during World War I. The one-armed concerto was, despite its limitation, filled with opulent impressionistic harmonies. The second concerto, for both hands, was Ravelesian in a surprising sense. It breathed the air full of invigorating ozone, as though refreshed by the peals of a rhythmic thunderstorm. The electric sparks exploding throughout the pages of the concerto are those of American jazz, which Ravel absorbed during his American tour in 1928. Listening to this music, one might be tempted to say that the great Ravel became infatuated with the sound of Gershwin's *Rhapsody in Blue*. But jazz was not entirely a novelty to French musicians at the time; a Negro jazz band played an engagement at the Casino de Paris as early as 1918.

The Concerto in G Major was first performed by Marguerite Long in Paris on January 14, 1933, with Ravel himself conducting the orchestra. It is in three movements. The first, Allegretto, leaps into action at once in a state of hyperthyroid euphoria, with the piano playing bitonal arpeggios, the right hand on white keys, and the left on black keys. The mood changes suddenly; the piano projects a meditative solo, leading to an episode reminiscent of Ravel's early *Pavane pour une infante défunte*, with its archaic modalities and a sense of timeless serenity. Syncopation erupts again; there is an expansive ascent of chordal harmonies along the pentatonic scale, Gershwinian in its unabashed songfulness. Then the musical landscape is shifted once more in a virtuoso display of pianistic technique, with trills and thrills painted with a lush brush on an Impressionistic palette of tones.

The second movement, Adagio assai, is, by contrast, highly restrained. Ravel told Marguerite Long that it took him many days to find the proper mold for this movement. The piano plays unaccompanied for thirty-three bars; the gemmation of the austere melody and its florification are remarkable. The orchestra picks up the tonal thread, while the piano indulges in scale runs. The antiphony between the soloists and the orchestra is maintained in perfect balance to the end.

The third and last movement, Presto, is a glorified fanfaronade, interrupted by shrill outcries in the high register of the woodwinds. The bustle continues without letup; the percussion section, which includes wood blocks and slapstick, is busy. Jazzy bits of color are splashed in glissando trombones. There is a tremendous buildup of tempo and sonority in the coda, and the concerto ends with declarative concision.

CHAMBER MUSIC
String Quartet in F Major (1903)

When the Kneisel Quartet gave the first American performance of Ravel's String Quartet in F Major in New York on December 11, 1906, the music aroused wonderment among New York music critics. History repeats itself with monotonous regularity. Going over a stack of clippings from the time of Berlioz down to the time of Arnold Schoenberg, one finds the same sort of incomprehension, dubious brand of humor, and polysyllabic invective. These critical outbursts have a semblance of humanity in them when they are directed against revolutionary works like Stravinsky's *Le Sacre du printemps*. But the innocent music of Ravel's String Quartet lacks revolutionary elements, and it is baffling that the New York music critics of 1906 should have been perturbed by it. Yet the adverse judgment was unanimous. Wrote the *New York Tribune*:

> M. Ravel is content with one theme which has the emotional potency of one of those tunes which the curious may hear in a Chinese theatre, shrieked out by an ear-splitting clarinet. This theme serves him for four movements during which there is about as much emotional nuance as warms a problem in algebra. In the second movement, which stands for the old-fashioned scherzo, the four viols essay the noble language of the banjo effectively. This, we suppose, is the cerebral music, and the psychical music that we read about in the dithyrambs sung by the young men of France.

The reviewer added, with sesquipedalian humor, that Ravel's music was "a drastic dose of wormwood and assafoetida," which caused a "horripilation of nerves," and he complimented the audience on its tolerance: "The audiences of the Kneisel Quartet are a gentle and well-bred folk. Even when music revolts them they do not utter catcalls or throw missiles at the performers. Instead, they give a respectful hand to the musicians, evidently crediting them with good intentions."

The New York critics were not alone in being nonplussed by Ravel's simple music. The *London Times* wrote on December 7, 1907, after the first performance of Ravel's String Quartet in England: "There is no recognizable principle of construction, and the only wonder is how the thing is kept going so long without a principle." In the same review, Ravel's piano pieces are dismissed in the following words: "The *Jeux d'eau* is another piece of the descriptive order of no kind of musical interest, but *Pavane* [*pour une infante défunte*] has some faint suggestions of the antique." In according some merit to *Pavane*, the London reviewer must have anticipated the time when the piece was to be converted into a popular song.

Ravel's String Quartet was performed for the first time in Paris, on March 5, 1904, at a concert of the Société Nationale, under the auspices of the famous Schola Cantorum. The Société Nationale was not devoted exclusively to the cause of modern music. In fact, its organizers fought shy of extreme examples of modernity so that eventually the more modern members bolted, and formed a new organization definitely modernistic in its aspirations, under the name Société Musicale Indépendante.

Charles Koechlin writes in a letter to the author of *Music Since 1900*:

> The Société Nationale had been very useful to French art, but since about 1900 it found itself under the influence of Vincent D'Indy. While pieces of mediocre students of the Schola Cantorum were performed at the Society's concerts, works of real value were often rejected. Even Ravel was accepted with suspicion, and at the first performance the whole clan of the Schola was hostile to the point of impoliteness.

Still, the quartet was performed, and D'Indy praised the music in a public statement.

Ravel's String Quartet is in the orthodox four movements. The first movement is Allegro moderato, marked *très doux*. It is in alla breve time. The melodic idiom is strictly diatonic, but the modulatory plan is very free, with parallel progressions typical of the French school. The second movement is in double time, § and §, which results in cross-accents. This is a characteristic rhythm of Iberian and Ibero-American national dances. The third movement is slow, in changing meters. The fourth and last movement is quick and agitated. It opens in the rhythm of §, and subsequently alternates with § and §. The concluding harmonic progression is an ascending series of major chords on a root progression of minor thirds. This progression became a cliché of modernism, and was used to good effect in Hollywood movie music.

Sonatine (1905)

Written in 1905, Ravel's Sonatine for piano is of simpler texture than his *Jeux d'eau*, written several years earlier. The first movement, in a modal style imparting pastoral serenity, is designed in miniature. Both hands operate in the high register (G clefs in both staves is a typical Ravel imprint); dynamics are subdued; the movement is very short, but it includes the formal elements of a sonata, with the three sections—exposition, development, and recapitulation—clearly recognizable. The second movement, a modified Minuet, maintains the poetic air of miniature writing: it is a stylization of the old dance, rather than its literal reproduction. The third and last movement is an animated Rondo, and is the longest movement of the Sonatine. The left hand is again placed in the treble, which, as in the first movement and partly in the second, creates and sustains the air of poetic miniature.

Introduction and Allegro (1906)

The Introduction and Allegro is, in essence and form, a concertino, or little concerto, for harp, accompanied by flute, clarinet, and string quartet. Ravel wrote it in

1906, when he was thirty-one years old. Jules Renard, the French writer, noted in his diary on November 19, 1906, in reference to Ravel: "a musician of the advance-guard, for whom Debussy is already an old beard." This is, of course, a literal translation: the French *vieille barbe* means a back number, a has-been, and the fact that Debussy wore a beard and Ravel was always close-shaven has no bearing on the case. Jules Renard's remark is interesting in that many critics accused Ravel of imitating Debussy, who, consequently, could not be just an old beard for him. Ravel, a man of great modesty, was moved to protest the allegations in a letter to the music critic of *Le Temps*, pointing out that he had used a style of writing usually associated with Debussy before Debussy did so, and gave dates in support of his claim. At the same time, he reiterated his profound respect for the elder master.

In the light of history, Ravel is bracketed with Debussy as representative of French impressionism. The term impressionism itself originated in 1874, when Claude Monet exhibited his picture *Impressions*, and the critic Louis Leroy, in the French publication *Charivari*, called Monet and his followers "impressionists" in derision. The name stuck, and was later applied to Debussy and the modern school of French music. The Impressionist school developed a musical style, characterized by subtly changing moods, languorous melodies, and highly individualized instrumentation.

The Introduction opens with a duet between the flute and clarinet. The strings enter in expressive pianissimo, and the harp is heard in brilliant arpeggio. The word "arpeggio" itself comes from *arpa*, which is Italian for "harp." The cello introduces a broad melody against the shimmering pianissimo of the violins, flute, and clarinet. The movement grows in tempo and sonority, only to subside again, marking the transition to the principal part, Allegro.

Allegro opens with a harp solo. The flute picks up the melody, to the accompaniment of plucked strings (pizzicato) in the violins. The melody is passed from one instrument to another; there is a gradual increase in sonority until a climax is reached.

The flute and clarinet play, accompanied by strings pizzicato. The principal theme makes a brief appearance, and is reduced to a seesaw figure of two notes. There is an interplay of instrumental colors. The movement grows more animated. The harp resumes, accompanied by plucked strings and fluid arpeggios in the flute and clarinet. The vestigial two-note figure is heard again, then the clarinet plays the melody in full against the strings pizzicato. The bell-like harmonics of the harp are heard; the movement grows in force, reaching a sonorous climax. The violins, having climbed to the high register, descend chromatically.

Webster's Dictionary defines the word "cadenza" as "parenthetic flourish, or flight of ornament." This definition has a fine literary sound, but it fails to mention that a cadenza should contain material drawn from the principal themes of the composition. This harp cadenza does. There are reminiscences from the opening duet of the woodwinds, and the cello tune from the Introduction. The bell-like sounds are the harmonics. After a full quota of "parenthetic flourishes," the harp plays the Allegro theme, accompanied by the trills of the entire ensemble. The melody is passed to various instruments, the movement recedes, then flares up again, and there are short interludes for the harp solo. The final reiteration of the principal melody in variation form in the harp, accompanied by pizzicato strings, leads to a brilliant conclusion.

BÉLA BARTÓK
(1881–1945)
Modern Janus

The career of Béla Bartók is a striking illustration of modern society's willful neglect of a great composer. We are all familiar with the tales of poverty of men of genius in bygone times, but it is peculiar that lessons of history could not be learned in the twentieth century.

Béla Bartók was a renowned figure in modern music when he made his way to the United States from his native Hungary. World War II was already raging; friends provided Bartók and his wife with enough funds to reach neutral Portugal. Mrs. Elizabeth Sprague Coolidge, the munificent American patroness of music, paid his transatlantic boat fare and an honorarium for an appearance at the Coolidge Festival in Washington. But other concert engagements were rare and difficult to obtain, and critical reviews in the American press were curiously hostile. Thanks to the efforts of members of the music department at Columbia University, Bartók obtained an appointment to classify a collection of Serbo-Croatian folk songs, at an annual salary of $2,500. But soon the special funds ran out and Bartók lost his job. He declined an offer to teach a summer course in composition at a midwestern college, on account of the rudimentary state of his English. He proposed to teach piano instead, but no one was interested in engaging a famous modern composer in such a capacity. "Never in my life," he complained in a pathetic letter to a friend in 1942, "since I have been on my own, earning my living from the age of nineteen, have I been in such a horrible financial situation. Where can I find pupils or a teaching job?"

A Hungarian compatriot in New York, who ran a small phonograph company, arranged for Bartók to record some of his piano music. To help Bartók out, he deliberately inflated the royalty statement and sent Bartók a substantial check. The following year, Bartók made recordings for the Columbia Phonograph Company, and was outraged when he received a modest check corresponding to the actual number of records sold. He promptly decided to sue, arguing that if a small outfit, owned by a Hungarian refugee, could do so advantageously with his records, it was obvious that the wealthy Columbia Phonograph Company was out to cheat him of his rightful income. It was with some difficulty that the conspirators who had engineered the unrealistic royalties in the first place dissuaded Bartók from filing the suit.

The story of Bartók's financial predicament finally reached the press. The *New York Times* published an article, "The Strange Case of Béla Bartók," which raised the question as to why a master of such stature could not be assured a subsistence minimum in the richest country in the world.

In the meantime, Bartók's health deteriorated. He suffered from a variety of ailments—asthma, arthritis, stomach ulcers, periodic fever, acne. To these was added dread leukemia. The little great man weighed only eighty-seven pounds before he died in a New York hospital on September 25, 1945. The funeral expenses were paid by the American Society of Composers and Publishers, but for several years there was not enough money to erect a tombstone on his grave.

Despite his disheartening experiences, Bartók was well aware of his position in music history. He even anticipated posthumous honors that might come his way. In his will he inserted a stern injunction not to have a Budapest street named after him as long as there were places bearing the names of Hitler and Mussolini. The injunction proved to be unnecessary. The Nazi and Fascist street signs were swept away by the course of events, and a street was named after Béla Bartók. The Hungarian post office honored Bartók's memory by issuing a series of airmail stamps with his portraits.

The great Hungarian composer began playing the piano in public at the age of eleven. At the Royal Academy of Music in Budapest, he studied piano with Istvan Thoman and composition with Hans Koessler, graduating in 1903. His earliest compositions revealed the combined influence of Liszt, Brahms, and Richard Strauss, but he soon became interested in exploring the resources of national folk music, which included not only Hungarian melorhythms but also elements of other ethnic strains in his native Transylvania, including Romanian and Slovak. He formed a cultural friendship with Zoltán Kodály, and together they traveled through the land collecting folk songs; then his interest in folk-song research led him to tour North Africa in 1913.

Bartók toured the United States as a pianist from December 1927 to February 1928 and gave concerts in the Soviet Union in 1929. He resigned his position at the Budapest Royal Academy of Music in 1934, but continued his research work in ethnomusicology as a member of the Hungarian Academy of Sciences, where he was engaged in the preparation of the monumental *Corpus Musicae Popularis Hungaricae.*

In his own compositions he soon began to feel the fascination of tonal colors and impressionistic harmonies as cultivated by Debussy and other modern French composers. The basic texture of his music remained true to tonality, which he expanded to chromatic polymodal structures and unremittingly dissonant chordal combinations; in his piano works he exploited the extreme registers of the keyboard, often in the form of tone clusters to simulate pitchless drumbeats. He made use of strong asymmetrical rhythmic figures suggesting the modalities of Slavic folk music, a usage that imparted a somewhat acrid coloring to his music. The melodic line of his works sometimes veered toward atonality in its chromatic involutions; in some instances he employed melodic figures comprising the twelve different notes of the chromatic scale; however, he never adopted the integral techniques of the twelve-tone method.

Bartók was not a prolific composer. He never wrote a symphony, and his other works are of moderate dimensions. But he was a fervent experimenter in novel sonorities. He gave particular prominence in his scores to instruments of percussion and indeed the piano itself became a percussion instrument in his technique. His renunciation of the pianistic luxuriance of Chopin, Liszt, and Debussy in favor of an austere, almost ascetic mode of expression required compensation in the subtlety of nuances. Dynamic contrasts assume in Bartók's piano writing a special significance. The frequent utilization of the extreme registers, high and low, imparts a drumlike timbre to the sound; chords grow by accretion of dissonance rather than by expansion of harmonies. The asymmetrical rhythms in rapid successions of even time units build up nervous tension. But despite the percussive character of Bartók's piano writing, in slow movements, there is a genuine lyrical quality achieved by unadorned melodic modalities, with folklike inflections.

Far from being a cerebral purveyor of abstract musical designs, Bartók was an ardent student of folkways, seeking the roots of meters, rhythms, and modalities in the spontaneous songs and dances of the people. Indeed, he regarded his analytical studies of popular melodies as his most important contribution to music. Even during the last years of his life, already weakened by illness, he applied himself assiduously to the arrangement of Serbo-Croatian folk melodies of Yugoslavia from recordings placed in his possession.

He was similarly interested in the natural musical expression of children; he firmly believed that children are capable of absorbing modalities and asymmetrical rhythmic structures with greater ease than adults trained in the rigid disciplines of established music schools. They can learn new accents, intervals, and harmonies as easily as they learn a new language. His collection of 153 piano pieces—entitled, significantly, *Mikrokosmos*—was intended as a method to initiate beginners into the world of unfamiliar tonal and rhythmic combinations, a parallel means of instruction to the Kodály method of schooling. In this remarkable collection, a modern child—and a modern teacher—will find a comprehensive exposition of the entire wealth of modern musical resources, an anthology of little masterpieces demonstrating the use of pentatonic, diatonic, and chromatic scales arranged in asymmetric rhythms and dissonant counterpoint.

Literally, *Mikrokosmos* means "the little world," but it may also, in Bartók's sense, mean the world of the little ones. The first four books of *Mikrokosmos* contain mostly pieces and exercises for beginners. But even in the simplest pieces, Béla Bartók follows a method of his own. There is no insistence on C major as the fundamental tonality, which is characteristic of most piano courses, so that the student develops a C major complex and measures all other modes and scale patterns against this chosen key. Instead, the modal feeling is established from the very first steps. There is no raising of the seventh in the minor mode, and the semicadences fall freely on different degrees of the modal scale. The rhythm, too, is freed from the symmetric rigidity of the common collections of piano exercises, and is composed of note values in changing patterns.

Melodic statements in Bartók's music are short, often abrupt, and they are developed not by baroque exfoliation but by spatial juxtaposition and temporal compression and extension. They are derived from the basic patterns of popular songs and dances of the Hungarian, Bulgarian, Romanian, and Turkish ethnic groups which make up the musical melting pot of Bartók's native Transylvania. They are modal and usually confined within the first four or five notes of the scale. Bartók's polyphony is rough-hewn; canonic and fugal progressions in his music are motivic rather than germinal. These cellular thematic proteins are constantly activated by the powerful enzymes of Bartók's rhythms, which are also of Balkan origin. They are asymmetrical, compounded of unequal groups of equal note values.

The insistent pounding on a single tone with unperiodic stresses is an inherent idiomatic trait of Balkan folk music, and Bartók uses the cumulative energy of such reiterated beats as an aesthetic sledgehammer to enthrall and subjugate even the most antagonistic listener. His harmonic usages are wide-ranging, including simple triadic constructions and congested globules of dissonant sounds employed functionally as single units. Acoustically harsh minor seconds and major sevenths often replace the classical thirds and octaves in Bartók's counterpoint, while the ambiguous tritone becomes the cornerstone of both his melody and his harmony, superseding the tonic-dominant fifth.

Duke Bluebeard's Castle *(1911; revised 1912, 1918)*

Bartók was thirty years old when he wrote his only opera, *Duke Bluebeard's Castle*. It was first performed in Budapest seven years later, on May 24, 1918. The legend of Bluebeard was immortalized by Charles Perrault in his celebrated *Mother Goose Tales* (*Les Contes de la mère l'Oye*), published in 1697. Besides Bluebeard, the collection contains such famous nursery stories as "Cinderella," "The Sleeping Beauty," and "Little Red Riding Hood." Perrault's version of the Bluebeard story takes the familiar form of a rescue tale. When Bluebeard's latest wife, driven by curiosity, disobeys his stern order, and opens a secret door, she finds behind it the heads of Bluebeard's slain wives. Her own life is saved by the opportune arrival of her brothers. The Bluebeard tale has been elaborated by numerous writers, and made the subject of several operas. The most notable modern interpretation is found in Maurice Maeterlinck's play, in which Bluebeard appears as a victim of his own fears whose wives, except the last, eventually come to his aid in a mystical reincarnation.

Bartók's librettist, Béla Balázs, treats the tale of the sextuple murderer as a neomedieval mystery play wherein Bluebeard's last wife, who is called Judith, induces him to open all the doors voluntarily. The action is focused on the castle itself rather than its inhabitants. Judith follows Bluebeard of her own volition, impelled by the desire to let the light of day shine into the segregated chambers. Blood pervades the scene, and is illustrated in the score by a motive based on the narrow intervals of the minor second. The first chamber contains instruments of torture; the second is an armory; the third yields a treasure trove of jewels; the fourth is a flower garden; the fifth reveals a magnificent landscape; the sixth is a lake of tears. The last door hides three of Bluebeard's wives, who are still alive. But

Judith must follow them into darkness. Bluebeard remains alone. The conclusion admits of diverse interpretations; perhaps the wives are only memories in Bluebeard's mind awakened by Judith, who becomes a memory herself in the end.

5

HERZOG BLAUBARTS BURG

A kékszakállú herceg vára

Béla Bartók, Op. 11.

Prolog des Barden

Sinnender Sage
Verborgene Klage,
Verwesender Worte unsterblicher Sinn
Ist heute das Spiel, dessen Künder ich bin,
Ihr Herren und Damen.

Alte Geschichten
Ergötzen und richten.
Wen?_ Euch und mich, heut' Auge in Auge,
Wer von uns fehlte, wer von uns tauge,
Ihr Herren und Damen.

Was Sehnsucht streute,
Dess bleiben wir Beute.
Nicht unser Meinen, nicht unser Toben
Entscheidet die Lose_ob unten, ob oben,_
Ihr Herren und Damen.

Drum: was wir heut spielen,
Gilt uns und noch vielen.
Wo ist die Bühne? Wer sieht Euch zu?
Was treibt Euch hasten, was gibt Euch Ruh,
Ihr Herren und Damen?

(Der Vorhang hebt sich)

Regös prologusa

*Haj regö rejtem
Hová, hová rejtsem
Hol volt, hol nem: kint-e vagy bent?
Régi rege, haj mit jelent,
Urak, asszonyságok?*

*Im, szólal az ének.
Ti néztek, én nézlek.
Szemünk pillás függönye fent:
Hol a szinpad: kint-e vagy bent,
Urak, asszonyságok?*

*Keserves és boldog
Nevezetes dolgok,
Az világ kint haddal tele,
De nem abba halunk bele,
Urak, asszonyságok.*

*Nézzük egymást, nézzük,
Regénket regéljük.
Ki tudhatja honnan hozzuk?
Hallgatjuk és csodálkozzuk,
Urak, asszonyságok.*

(A függöny szétválik a háta mögött)

Der Barde: Geigen beginnen, lasset das Sinnen.
A regös: Zene szól, a láng ég, Kezdödjön a játék.

Hört nun und seht; und geht es zu Ende, und hat es gefallen, so reget die Hände, Ihr Herren und Damen. | Ein Schloß,_ muß ich's nennen? Ihr solltet es kennen! Noch seht Ihr es kaum, doch bald sollt Ihr's hören....
Szemem pillás függönye fent, Tapsoljatok asszonyságok. | Régi vár, régi már Az mese, ki róla jár, Tik is hallgassátok.

Mächtige, runde, gotische Halle. Links führt eine steile Treppe zu einer kleinen eisernen Türe. Rechts der Stiege befinden sich in der Mauer sieben große Türen: vier noch gegenüber der Rampe, zwei bereits ganz rechts. Sonst weder Fenster, noch Dekoration. Die Halle gleicht einer finstern, düstern, leeren Felsenhöhle. Beim Heben des Vorhanges ist die Szene finster, der Barde verschwindet in ihr.
Hatalmas kerek gotikus csarnok. Balra meredek lépcső vezet fel egy kis vasajtóhoz. A lépcsőtől jobbra hét nagy ajtó van a falban; négy még szemben, kettő már egész jobboldalt. Különben sem ablak, se disz. A csarnok üres sötét, rideg, sziklabarlanghoz hasonlatos. Mikor a függöny szétválik, teljes sötétség van a szinpadon, melyben a regös eltünik.

Universal-Edition Nr. 7026

Bartók's opera breaks away completely from both the Baroque Italian genre and the Wagneromorphic music drama, but it retains the principle of leading motives, or leitmotiv. The blood motive in jarring minor seconds is omnipresent. Other motives are responsive to the situations depicted on the stage. A fanfare is sounded when the armory door is opened; the glitter of the jewels is reflected in the shimmering tremolos in the strings, as are also the flowers in the garden. The murder motive is represented by the giant strides of vacuous fifths moving in chromatic ascension, with resulting differential semitones that recall once more the blood motive. At a climax, the fifths overlap to form chords of major sevenths arrayed in parallel motion.

It is interesting to note that although Bartók wrote the opera in 1911, when Debussian impressionism was the dominant influence among modern composers, he was reluctant to adopt any of the favorite devices of the French modern school: whole-tone scales, the luscious dominant-ninth chords, the voluptuous unresolved suspensions over diminished-seventh chords. The orchestration, too, is devoid of coloristic scoring characteristic of the Impressionist palette. The music of Bartók's opera is austere, almost ascetic in its economic choice of musical resources. The only extrinsic effect is the use of a pentatonic motto at the opening and at the close of the opera. The pentatonic scale is of course an ancient Magyar modality, and is also a ubiquitous tonal matrix of ancient civilizations. In this reference, Bartók may have intentionally emphasized the national and the universal meaning of his work.

The Miraculous Mandarin: *Suite (1918–19)*

Béla Bartók possessed an instinctive feeling for the diversity and the richness of folk music, but as a composer shaped by twentieth-century ideas, he sought new methods of musical self-expression. After an inevitable period of academic romanticism, he felt the fascination of French impressionism. The idea of painting nature in subjective terms, the new techniques that emancipated dissonance and allowed free interchange of tonalities, modalities, and rhythms, took possession of him. He wrote symphonic music marked by the delicacy of Impressionistic half colors.

But the brutal impact of the First World War dispersed the mists of the Impressionistic palette. In its stead came the psychologically tortured Germanic art, which became known as expressionism, and which split the scale into its common denominators in an atonal penumbra. On the opposite side of the aesthetic ledger, musicians experienced the assault of fauvism, a sophisticated savagery that affected primitivistic postures. The euphony of impressionism, the tense chromaticism of expressionism cohabitated, but never blended, with powerful earthy dissonant harmonies and grotesque asymmetrical rhythms of neoprimitivism; musical folklore provided physical material for this primitivistic explosion.

The music of Bartók combined these twentieth-century techniques, and the spontaneity of his folkloric inspiration imparted a sensation of natural vitality and concrete strength. Wit and warmth were the attributes of his style, while intervallic angularity became part of his modernistic lyricism. Above all, his music radiated deep conviction and individualistic self-assurance. The score of Bartók's pantomime *The Miraculous Mandarin* belongs to his Expressionistic period. Its subject is both surrealistic and symbolic: the supremacy of sensual passion and its triumph over death itself. When lust is assuaged, the body dies. He wrote the score of The Miraculous Mandarin between October 1918 and May 1919, during the worst phases of the Hungarian Civil War.

The story of *The Miraculous Mandarin* deals with a prostitute and a company of pimps, who lure susceptible men, then rob them. The first customer, an impecunious gentleman, is bounced out. He is followed by a young student who is also short of money. But he is handsome and the girl dances with him free of charge. Then the Mandarin appears, obviously prosperous and obviously passionate. He dances with the girl, but she is horrified by his hideous embraces. Her confederates leap upon him, rob him of his money, and attempt to murder him. They try to suffocate him under a pillow, they stab him repeatedly, but he still refuses to succumb. They hang him from a chandelier, but it collapses. The girl, affected by the Mandarin's will to survive, decides to submit to him. At last his desire is gratified; his wounds begin to bleed, and he dies.

The first performance of *The Miraculous Mandarin* was given in Cologne on November 27, 1926, but the police prevented a second performance. An attempt was made to produce the pantomime in Budapest for Bartók's fiftieth birthday in 1931, but after the final rehearsal, the production was banned. Even after the libretto was revised to eliminate the more lurid situations, no theater would risk announcing a performance.

Bartók extracted an orchestral suite from the music of the pantomime, and it was played by the Philharmonic Society in Budapest on October 15, 1928, under the direction of the eminent conservative composer Ernst von Dohnányi. Then the war came and Bartók fled to America. The permissive postwar era removed all moralistic objections to the story of *The Miraculous Mandarin*, and the pantomime had numerous posthumous performances in Europe, and some in America.

The musical idiom of the score of *The Miraculous Mandarin* is starkly dissonant, but at the same time extremely economical. There is no gratuitous agglomeration of discords. The melodies are free of academic key relationship but they retain the sense of modality, often joining groups of notes from different modes. As a result there is a sense of tonal obliquity, ideally suited for a grotesque subject. Expected octaves are squeezed to major sevenths or expanded to augmented octaves, and perfect fifths are reduced to tritones, the cornerstones of the modern idiom, harmonically in bitonal conjunctions and atonally in melodic writing. The Mandarin himself is introduced by a scale of the augmented octave.

Most interestingly, Bartók assigns a pentatonic subject to the Mandarin when he meets the prostitute, as an ethnic allusion to his Chinese ancestry. But this pentatonic melody is harmonized by two rows of noncoinciding tritones, forming excruciatingly dissonant combinations. There are also lyric passages, but the lyricism is acidulated. The orchestration is luxuriant in its effective use of instrumental timbres, and its commentaries on the stage action are most eloquent; some passages suggest lust in a strikingly naturalistic manner. The score of *The Miraculous Mandarin* is a classical example of the modern musical usage.

Concerto for Piano and Orchestra No. 1 (1926)

Béla Bartók's genius was twofold. As an ardent collector of folk songs among the diversified ethnic groups in his native Transylvania, he acquired a profound understanding of popular melodies and rhythms that form the foundation of all musical developments. As a composer whose imagination was stimulated by a modern environment, he evolved a musical language in which dissonances are treated on equal terms with consonances. To listeners brought up on the obsolescent notion that music must be euphonious, Bartók was incomprehensible. "If the reader were so rash as to purchase any of Béla Bartók's compositions," wrote Frederick Corder, a British musician, in an article entitled "On the Cult of Wrong Notes" and published in *The Musical Quarterly* of 1915, "he would find that they each and all consist of unmeaning bunches of notes, apparently representing the composer promenading the keyboard in his boots."

In historical perspective, it is clear that Bartók had revolutionized the art of piano playing. A professional pianist himself, he knew the resources of the instrument. But instead of emulating the refined nuances of the French masters of Impressionistic techniques or contributing to the emasculation of the piano by epicene neo-Baroque practices, Bartók restored the primary function of the keyboard as a medium of percussive sonorities. His piano music, in which the rhythmic impulse determines its course, is concise, terse, and curt.

Bartók wrote three piano concertos, of which the first is technically the most complex. Bartók gave its first performance as soloist in Frankfurt on July 1, 1927, with Wilhelm Furtwängler conducting the orchestra. The concerto is in three movements: Allegro moderato, Andante, and Allegro molto. Bartók described the tonality of the work as E minor, but it is E minor only in the Bartókian sense, for the crucial mediant is missing in the tonic chords, with the noncommittal supertonic placed in its stead. Although the harmonic fluctuation and the prevalence of dissonances make the key signature gratuitous, Bartók occasionally makes use of it in the score, perhaps to indicate that he does not exclude tonality on principle.

The first movement, Allegro moderato, introduces its principal theme by the process of gradual assembly of prefabricated segments. Diatonic and chromatic passages form contrasting episodes in the development section, with triadic progressions in parallel motion sustaining the sense of basic tonality. Meters and rhythms are in a constant flux of asymmetrical patterns, with the eighth note serving as the least common denominator. The recapitulation echoes the relationship of the tonic and the dominant of the exposition, but metrical alterations give it a novel aspect. The movement comes to a natural close when all viable melodic, harmonic, and rhythmic elements of the original thematic material are exploited to their full potential.

The second movement of the concerto, Andante, is a study in percussion sonorities, in which the piano is antiphonically counterposed to an ensemble of drums and other instruments. Bartók gives detailed instructions in the score for the proper method of obtaining the required sound effects: the manner of striking a suspended cymbal on the rim from below, centrifugal and centripetal glissandos on the drumheads, etc. The piano itself becomes an instrument of percussion, with an emphasis on clarity and dynamic variety. As for harmonies, Bartók builds them by gradual encrustation and deposition of additional tonal elements. In this movement, dominated as it is by hard and clearly demarcated rhythmic units, the harsh major sevenths and the impinging minor seconds become the vertebrae of the harmonic skeleton.

The finale, Allegro molto, is an impetuous toccata, in which the initial motoric impulse generates a relentless rhythmic ostinato. Motivic fragments appear and disappear, congregate and segregate, integrate into large sonic columns and disintegrate in a rhythmic collapse. Each additional note in a chord, each alteration in the rhythmic pattern, each dynamic differentiation, each intercalation of rests, is of thematic import. In Bartók's music even silences are singularly eloquent.

Concerto for Piano and Orchestra No. 2 (1930–31)

Bartók wrote three piano concertos; the third was his last completed work. The Second Piano Concerto represents a syncretism of many elements: the ethnic musical folkways of southeastern Europe, classical polyphonic devices, dissonant counterpoint, polytonality and polyrhythmy. The concerto is in three movements: Allegro, Adagio—Presto, and Allegro molto. There are no key signatures.

The first movement, Allegro in ⅜ time, opens with a trumpet solo playing a folklike tune. This tune later appears in the forms of inversion and retrograde inversion. In the inverted form the direction of intervals is reversed without changing the rhythmic formula. The visual design of retrograde inversion (which is identical with inverted retrogression) can be obtained by turning the original theme upside down, or by looking at the inverted form in the mirror without turning the page upside down, the reflection supplying the retrograde image. The rhythmic pulse is firm, the dominating metrical unit being a quarter note. Canonic imitation is rampant. The piano is exercised in bland scale passages, but harmonically the idiom is increasingly dissonant. In the recapitulation the subject is inverted. There follows a long cadenza for piano solo, in which the subject appears in the horns in retrograde inversion, imitated by trumpets and trombones, and leading to a sonorous coda.

The second movement begins in Adagio, with a perpendicular structure of naked Gregorian fifths. The upper levels then diverge from the lower, leaving a gap in the middle. The scheme is further developed in chorale-like tones. This serves as an introduction to Presto, with the solo piano occupying the forefront, playing scales bitonally in minor sixths—a favorite device of Bartók—and in seconds. There are strettos and fugatos; parallel progressions reach greater consistence through harmonic inspissation, eventually expanding into tone clusters, with the right hand striking fistfuls of black keys, and the left of white keys. (Tone clusters were invented by the American composer Henry Cowell; Bartók, respecting Cowell's priority, wrote him for permission to use this device in the Second Concerto.) The movement ends cyclically with an epilogue of fifths.

The third and last movement, Allegro molto, is set into motion by a big boom on the bass drum. The piano solo resumes its customary scale playing. Bartók makes a virtue of repetitive use of unadorned percussive figures; the kettledrums beat a primitivistic tattoo of two notes, C and E flat, and the piano responds in the kettledrum register with a syncopated figure on E flat and G flat. It takes a long time before the piano rises to higher reaches of the keyboard; on its way it plays a brusque duet with the bass drum. The soloist atones for this dalliance by plunging into parallel scales in major thirteenths. A churchly interlude breaks up the motion for a brief moment, but with celerity and alacrity the piano and the orchestra make their final run toward the ending in fortissimo, in the clearest G-major key.

Music for String Instruments, Percussion, and Celesta (1936)

Written for the Chamber Orchestra of Basel, Switzerland, and first performed there on January 21, 1937 under the direction of its founder Paul Sacher, Music for Strings, Percussion, and Celesta is in four movements: Andante tranquillo, Allegro, Adagio, and Allegro molto. The Andante tranquillo opens with a minuscule fugue in muted strings; its subject is serpentine in its chromatic involution. A brief but still very slow stretto follows. The subject is combined with its own inversion, accompanied by a shimmering display of celesta colors. The second movement, Allegro, is, by contrast, full of driving energy. The momentum never slackens. The melodic structure is polymodal, but centripetally directed towards C, which is the final note of the movement.

The Adagio begins with a xylophone solo in a rhythmically varied reiteration on a single high note. The strings command the melodic ground, with numerous trills, glissandos and flutelike effects, while the piano, the harp, and the celesta provide a floating accompaniment. The movement ends as it began, with the xylophone solo on the same high F. The last movement, Allegro molto, is an exposition of alternating sonorities and intervallic groupings. It concludes energetically on an A-major chord.

Concerto for Violin No. 2 (1937–1938)

The greatness of Bartók lies in the innovative quality of his instrumental works. He was fascinated by the asymmetric rhythms of the Magyar, Romanian, and Slavic folk songs of Transylvania, where he was born, and his works reflect many of these materials. Bartók was a brilliant pianist, but he also had profound knowledge of other instruments. He wrote his First Violin Concerto at the age of twenty-six, but did not take steps toward its publication or performance. A movement from this early concerto was incorporated into another work.

In 1937, the Hungarian violinist Zoltán Székely commissioned Bartók to write a violin concerto for him. Bartók set to work with enthusiasm, and completed the concerto on December 31, 1938. Székely played its first performance on April 23, 1939, with the Concertgebouw Orchestra of Amsterdam, Willem Mengelberg conducting. Although no identifying number was attached to the concerto in the published score, it was subsequently listed as No. 2, to take cognizance of Bartók's earlier violin concerto.

The score bears no key signature, but the opening and the ending are centripetally directed toward B major. It is in three movements: Allegro non troppo, Andante tranquillo, and Allegro molto. The form is classical, but the language is modern. In the violin part, Bartók applies the principle of polymodality, largely developed by himself. By shifting the basic modality, he is able to effect instant modulation; by interpolating chromatic tones he creates coloristic images. His harmonies are translucid despite their dissonant texture. Surprisingly, he incorporates, early in the first movement, a twelve-tone motive. It is not worked out according to the Schoenbergian dodecaphonic method, but it is not an accidental insertion, for it reappears in the third movement, with some of the notes of the series in simple permutation. Most important of all, in his Second Violin Concerto, Bartók succeeds in creating a new type of modern virtuoso piece, brilliant in technique and highly effective in performance.

Contrasts for Violin, Clarinet, and Piano (1938)

Béla Bartók's music has a percussive quality, for percussion is the essence of rhythm; but instead of applying actual percussion instruments, Bartók used special effects: the high treble, or the lowest bass register of the piano keyboard; pizzicato of the violin, asymmetric syncopation. Against this background, his melodies appear unhindered by accompaniment, thus securing the optimum of expressive power.

Contrasts, his suite of three pieces for violin, clarinet, and piano, was written especially for Joseph Szigeti and Benny Goodman. The manuscript bears the date: Budapest, September 24, 1938. These are studies in contrast. The first movement is the Hungarian counterpart of American blues. The violin and piano provide the steady accompanying figure for the flourishes of the clarinet, and then the violin takes up the theme, while the clarinet plays arpeggios in quickly changing tonalities. After a slower interlude, the movement is resumed in syncopated rhythm against the booming glissandos of the piano. There is a passage in which the theme is played canonically against its own inversion—a favorite device of Bartók's. A brilliant and difficult clarinet cadenza leads to a conclusion.

The second movement is a short and slow chorale in the two solo instruments, punctuated by darksome trills in the bass. The third piece is a fast dance, opening with the fifths of a mistuned violin, with the E string lowered a semitone and the G string raised to G sharp. However, there is another violin in reserve, which the player is instructed to pick up when normal tuning is required, much as the clarinet player changes from an instrument in A to one in B-flat.

The clarinet, and then the piano, introduce a dancing rhythm in even notes, punctuated by cross-accents. The interval of the diminished fifth, the tritone, produced by the special tuning of the violin, dominates the melodic texture of the movement. There is the characteristic canon between a fragment of the theme and its inversion. The movement then comes to a short stop, and resumes in an uneven meter of thirteen eighths in a bar. There are convergent and divergent progressions in the Lydian mode, which is the only mode that has the tonic interval of the tritone. Once more there is a pause, and the rhythmical interplay between the violin and the clarinet, and the right hand with the left hand of the piano, presents a double canon with the thematic fragments in direct and inverted forms. The violin (the one normally tuned) has a long cadenza. The movement ends brilliantly with an abrupt chord.

Concerto for Two Pianos and Orchestra (1940)

The Concerto for Two Pianos and Orchestra is a transcription of Bartók's Sonata for Two Pianos and Percussion, composed in the summer of 1937 in Budapest, and first performed by Bartók and his second wife, Ditta, in Basel on January 16, 1938. In December of 1940 he transcribed it for two pianos and orchestra; this version of the work was first performed by the Royal Philharmonic Orchestra in London on October 14, 1942. Sir Adrian Boult conducted; the soloists were Louis Kentner and Llona Kabos. The *Musical Times* of London commented briefly: "This may be the music of tomorrow; it is difficult to see how it can ever be the music of any considerable public." The first American performance followed on January 21, 1943, by the New York Philharmonic conducted by Fritz Reiner; the piano parts were performed by Bartók and his wife.

The Concerto for Two Pianos represents the culmination of Bartók's techniques in writing for the piano treated as a percussion instrument, with a percussion ensemble regarded as an integral part of the orchestra. The concerto is in three movements: Assai lento, Lento ma non troppo, and Allegro non troppo. There is no key signature, but in the spiraling modalities formed by asymmetrical intervallic structures, shifting tonal foci are clearly present. In the opening movement, the principal motive is a convoluted figure filling in the chromatic tones within the compass of a tritone. The music acquires momentum by intervallic accretion, inversion, and canonic imitation. The agitation grows until the tempo reaches the Allegro molto. Amid polytonal collisions, clear major triads are flashed. A grandiose declaration, un poco maestoso, is made. A rolling motion leads to a fugue charged with static electricity. Kinetic energy accumulates; the pianists cross the keyboards in opposite directions. Sonorous harmonic blocks are hewn out of thematic materials. A powerful coda brings the movement to a conclusion.

The second movement, Lento ma non troppo, is an elegy. The initial melody oscillates slowly along shifting modal modes. Then a nervous quintuplet appears, pulsating rapidly, increasing in strength and speed, and soon reaching the uppermost register of the keyboard in fortissimo. A series of dissonant chords is set in motion in the piano parts, while the thematic quintuplets maintain their rhythmic pulse in the orchestra. The nostalgic melody returns; the quintuplet motto echoes it. The ending is very slow and very soft.

The third movement, Allegro non troppo, is a brilliant rondo. It embodies most of Bartók's favorite pianistic devices: rapid polymodal passages traversing the entire keyboard, triadic parallelisms, multiple dissonant trills, crisp arpeggiated chords. The coda is remarkable: limpid major triads diverge in the twin pianos, ending in an unadulterated C major.

Concerto for Orchestra (1943)

Béla Bartók found a haven in America from devastated Europe at the outbreak of World War II and spent his American years, until his death in New York in 1945, in difficult financial circumstances. He was a master pianist, but not the possessor of the fashionable abilities of a romantic virtuoso. He was a teacher of great stature, but did not fit into the easygoing curriculum of American music schools. His compositions, difficult to perform, were not commercially lucrative. His reputation among musicians and music scholars was high—but not his income. When he fell ill, his personal circumstances became even more distressing, and his predicament was openly discussed in the press. Serge Koussevitzky commissioned him to write a symphonic work and offered a modest down payment, but Béla Bartók was reluctant to accept the money, afraid that because of his illness he would be unable to complete the work. Koussevitzky was persuasive and solicitous, and Béla Bartók accepted the commission, completed the score in October 1943, and named it the Concerto for Orchestra. Koussevitzky conducted the first performance of the Concerto for Orchestra with the Boston Symphony on December 1, 1944. In his program annotations, Bartók explained that the title referred to the virtuoso treatment of the instrument, so that there is always a temporary soloist playing a miniature concerto with orchestral accompaniment. The Concerto for Orchestra was destined to become his most popular work.

The Concerto for Orchestra is in five movements: Introduzione, Giuoco delle coppie, Elegia, Intermezzo interrotto, and Finale. The first movement opens with sylvan murmurs in the strings and flutes; a gently swaying motion leads to a scherzo in rondo form the ending is abrupt and tonally clear. The second movement, "a game of pairs," begins and ends with a side-drum solo. The title gives the clue to the structure of the music, which is a series of duos of wind instruments paired at different intervals, the bassoons in sixths, the oboes in thirds, the clarinets in sevenths, the flutes in fifths, the muted trumpets in major seconds. The time signature is $\frac{2}{4}$, another pair. The third movement, an elegy, is marked by an effusion of melismatic arabesques and canonic imitations.

The fourth movement, an "interrupted intermezzo," is a burlesque with the thematic interval of the tritone imparting wry humor to the music. The "interruption" occurs with the sudden intrusion of a rather insipid tune, which turns out to be the military German theme from Shostakovich's "Leningrad" Symphony. This tune ruled the radio waves at the time Bartók was composing his Concerto for Orchestra, and annoyed him. He disguised it somewhat, and made it sound even closer to the original source, the song "Dann geh' ich zu Maxim" from Lehár's operetta *The Merry Widow*. The quotation is introduced by a mocking glissando in the trombones and followed by a chromatic cascade of the woodwinds.

The Finale opens like a glorified military march with a deliberate atonal twist. The main part of the movement is a rapid rondo, which includes a vigorous fugue going through ingenious telescopic contractions and expansions of the subject. The concluding section of the Finale mobilizes all the resources of the orchestra. It is also the most varied movement rhythmically, but it is maintained within the metrical framework of ²⁄₈. Bartók also provided an alternative and more emphatic ending in which the descending figure of the original version is replaced by an ascending run of three and a half octaves, along the Lydian mode, reinforced by a vesuviating glissando in the horns and trombones.

IGOR STRAVINSKY
(1882–1971)
Perennial Revolutionary

Igor Stravinsky! This name has a metallic ring to it that has long outgrown purely musical associations. It has become a symbol of the urbanistic, geometric, lapidary modern age. Poets rather than musicians find the most expressive words to define the music of Igor Stravinsky; despite its complexity it speaks a direct language to the uninitiated. Musicians whose formative period belongs in the nineteenth century cannot accept Stravinsky wholeheartedly, for Stravinsky's every note negates the heritage of the immediate past.

Stravinsky starts his musical career with an academic symphony, and he enters the peak of maturity (which is reached at fifty-four, if we are to believe Aristotle) in the academy of classical knowledge. *Apollon Musagète*, *Oedipus Rex*, *Perséphone*—in these subjects Stravinsky finds the greatest freedom of abstraction, the static beauty that is germane to absolute music. Between these two academic solstices, there has passed a season of greatest storms, luxuriant growths, and spectacular upheavals. *The Firebird*, a sumptuous panorama of Russian fairy tales on a direct line from Rimsky-Korsakov's tradition, marks the ascent of Stravinsky's star in Paris, where it was performed at the Diaghilev ballet on June 25, 1910.

Nine years later Stravinsky revised this score and chastened it. It is interesting to compare the two orchestrations, the first abundant with harps, celestas, woodwinds; the second stripped to the essentials, the celesta replaced by a percussive pianoforte, the woodwinds reduced, the development and transitional passages cut. It is a bowdlerized edition of a great work, and yet, under Stravinsky's knife, the overorchestration of the first version is convincingly shown. In *The Firebird*, behind the Russianizing orientalism of the idiom, there is the true Stravinskian color: the tritone plays a greater role in melodic constructions than with any of Stravinsky's precursors, but as yet is not extended onto the harmonic plane, and so stops short of bitonality.

May, 1911. In Rome Stravinsky finishes *Petrushka*. The bitonality comes to fruition, the C major is combined with F-sharp major. The syncopating rhythm, which had appeared in *The Firebird* in the "Infernal Dance of Kashchei," is here carried to its ultimate potentiality—the destruction of the main beat, leaning, so to speak, on a vacuum. Some tunes used in *Petrushka* are from Russian folk music; there is also a French chansonette and a Viennese waltz.

March 8, 1913. Stravinsky marks the date at the end of the score of *The Rite of Spring* (*Le Sacre du printemps*). The simple bitonality of *Petrushka* is submerged under more inclusive harmonies. Two clarinets play at the interval of the major seventh instead of the octave. The distinction between the major and the minor key is obliterated. A new "frictional" tonality contains both the major and minor triads. The rhythm and meter merge in the "Danse sacrale," and the main beat is relegated into a fiction by being deprived of any substance. The drums themselves are syncopating. The peak of effective complexity has been reached.

Thursday, May 29, 1913. The first performance of *The Rite of Spring*. It is accompanied by a scandal, about which too many legends have been formed. It is said, for instance, that Saint-Saëns, perplexed by the sound of the opening solo of the bassoon, in its highest register, mockingly inquired: "What instrument was that?" and, told it was a bassoon, rose and went home.

The war. Stravinsky is in Switzerland. He finishes *The Nightingale* (*Le Rossignol*), an opera on a pseudo-Chinese tale by Hans Christian Andersen. But already a change is apparent—the time of large orchestral works has passed. The war requires wartime music, reduced, stripped to an economical minimum. Stravinsky meets Charles-Ferdinand Ramuz, the Swiss novelist, who suggests a half-mystical story about a soldier, the devil and the fiddle. Stravinsky dreams a dream: a Gypsy woman gives breast to a child, and at the same time plays the violin with the entire length of the bow. Stravinsky uses the melody of the dream—and the manner of playing with the entire bow—for his *Soldier's Story* (*L'Histoire du soldat*), scored for only seven instruments.

The armistice approaches. From America the first sounds of jazz are heard. Stravinsky composes the chamber work *Ragtime*. The main beat is reinstalled. It is almost a recantation of his prewar syncopation. Ramuz, in his informal way, notes down his impressions of Stravinsky at that period: his professorial punctiliousness, his pointed neatness, his calligraphic writing, his table with multicolored inks and freshly sharpened pencils on it. Ramuz credits Stravinsky with an invention: that of a roulette that traces the five-line staff on paper... a convenient gadget.

June 13, 1923. Ernest Ansermet, the Swiss mathematician-conductor, directs the first performance of *The Wedding* (*Les Noces*). Four pianos, thirteen percussion instruments, voices, choruses. Every singing note, spoken word, and percussive sound are here scientifically placed in position, so as to contribute to the maximum efficiency of the whole. Impressionism here suffers its last defeat. The rhythms and meters are crossed, the bar lines overridden. Here, as in *The Soldier's Story*, a written meter means nothing but an arithmetical fiction. In fact, there is no common meter for the entire ensemble. The conductor should here conduct one rhythm with one hand, and another rhythm with the other hand; or, better still, robot conductors should be installed, beating the smallest unit, and marking the true downbeat for each group.

Small operas, *Renard* and *Mavra*, continue the tradition of *The Soldier's Story* and *The Wedding*. Harmonically speaking, the idiom is tonal. The superposition of the tonic upon the dominant and the free use of all degrees of the diatonic scale only emphasize the feeling of tonality. This feeling of tonality grows more and more definite.

Finally, Stravinsky's mind turns to the fountainhead of tonality; his Octet for Wind Instruments recreates the idiom before Bach. With the Piano Concerto (1924) Stravinsky launches the movement in modern music that has been so erroneously designated as a movement "back to Bach." No, Stravinsky goes back much further than Bach. His works, in which a religious note is beginning to sound not only in the titles but in the dedications themselves, indicate his growing fascination with theological music of the Middle Ages. Already in *The Wedding* there is a feeling of the medieval Organum, as in the successive fourths of the prayer. The reversion to the Latin language in *Oedipus Rex* is also significant. Medieval Latin exercised a great influence on the musical line. In fact, hymnal melos was often a mere function of the vocables of the text, so that there were even special neumes adaptable to certain classes of sounds. Stravinsky's request to Jean Cocteau to have a Latin text written to *Oedipus Rex* clearly indicated his predilection for certain forms of a very definite historical and ideological moment. *Oedipus Rex* is thus a modern Passion play, to a pagan subject, in the holy language of Christian Rome.

The *Symphony of Psalms* bears an inscription, "ad majorem Dei gloriam," which is also indicative of a tendency. Stravinsky works to restore music to its former position as an accessory to a loftier purpose—*theologiae ancilla*. In form, this music may be classical, or even Romantic. In each case it will recreate the theological spirit as reflected in this or that century. That it is a renaissance of a renaissance does not mean that it has to be inferior. Great music has been written in the spirit of a revival of a preceding period. Those that bemoan Stravinsky's present trend underrate his power of rising above commonly insurmountable barriers.

The Nightingale (Le Rossignol) *(1908–1914)*

The Chinese emperor is dying and his life is supported by the singing of the nightingale. But when the Japanese ambassador thoughtlessly presents the emperor with a mechanical nightingale, the real bird flies away, and the emperor's health declines dangerously. As a discordant funeral march is played, the real nightingale is brought in, and the emperor regains his strength. The moral seems to be that things natural cure all ills. The opera, produced in Paris in 1914, is extremely dissonant, with harmonies built on the tritone and the major seventh. The element of atonality is employed with grotesque effectiveness.

The Firebird: *Suite (1910; revised 1919, 1945)*

For his 1910 season of the Ballets Russes, a remarkable enterprise that played Russian music with a cast of Russian dancers all over the world except Russia itself, its great impresario Serge Diaghilev needed a ballet score with a Russian folk flavor. In St. Petersburg, he approached Anatol Liadov, composer of delectable symphonic miniatures that figuratively smelled of the Russian soil, but Liadov was notoriously indolent, and nothing came of the project. The name of young Igor Stravinsky was then brought out as a possible substitute. Stravinsky was a student of Rimsky-Korsakov's during the last years of the master's life, and had absorbed the inimitable coloring of Rimsky-Korsakov's orchestra that suited the Russian folk tales so well. For Stravinsky's ballet Diaghilev suggested the subject of the Russian folk hero Ivan Tsarevich, the monster Kashchei and the magical Firebird. The final title, in French, was *L'Oiseau de feu*, described as a "conte dansé."

Introduction to Stravinsky's *Firebird*

Stravinsky describes the circumstances attending the composition of *The Firebird* in his autobiography:

> Towards the end of the summer of the year 1909, I received a telegram which upset all my previous plans. Diaghilev, who had just arrived in St. Petersburg, asked me to write the music to *The Firebird* for the season of The Ballets Russes at the Paris Opéra in the Spring of 1910. The offer was flattering. I was chosen among musicians of my generation to collaborate in an important enterprise.... I worked on the score with frenzy, and when I finished it, I felt the necessity of rest in the country before going to Paris.

Stravinsky completed the score in St. Petersburg on May 18, 1910, a month before his twenty-eighth birthday, and dedicated it to Rimsky-Korsakov's son Andrey (1878–1940). It was his last work written in Russia. *Petrushka* and *The Rite of Spring* were composed abroad.

The Firebird was produced by Diaghilev and the Ballets Russes in Paris on June 25, 1910. The French composer Gabriel Pierné conducted the orchestra. Stravinsky writes in his *Chroniques de ma vie*: "The spectacle was warmly applauded by the Paris public. Of course, I do not attribute this success entirely to my music: it was equally due to the sumptuous scenery of the painter Golovin, the brilliant interpretation of Diaghilev's dancers, and the talent of the ballet master." The ballet captivated the Parisians by the exotic exuberance of its rhythm and the splendor of its instrumentation. Among the innovations in the score was a glissando on the harmonics in the strings covering the range of the first twelve overtones of the natural series.

In 1919 Stravinsky revised the score, eliminating much of its panache, reducing the opulent orchestral apparatus to a practical minimum, scuttling the supernumerary instruments, excising ornamental passages, eliding cadenzas, deleting paraphernalia, in sum, plucking the flaming plumage of the Firebird and divesting Kashchei of some of his brassy terrors. But the loss in flamboyance is compensated in this revised version by greater compactness and functional solidity.

That was the time when Stravinsky, watching the economic disruption of the European world from his refuge in Switzerland, thought that the era of huge orchestral conceptions was past, that it was imperative to limit the medium to a practical level. In that new orchestration he, so to speak, returned the luminous feather to *The Firebird*. With the deleted passages for the harps, the celesta, and the bells went also the light that "shone like an untold number of candles." And that is why the early version of the score is still by far the more popular among conductors and orchestras.

The story of *The Firebird* follows the classical Russian folk tale in essential details. Ivan Tsarevich captures the Firebird as she picks the golden apples in the enchanted garden of the fearsome Kashchei the Immortal. She begs him to release her in exchange for one of her magic feathers. Thirteen royal princesses, captives of Kashchei, appear and dance around. Ivan falls in love with one of them and follows her into Kashchei's castle, but is seized by the guards. He waves the magic feather and the Firebird appears at his summons. She reveals to him the secret of Kashchei's immortality, which is hidden in an egg kept in a casket. Ivan smashes the egg; Kashchei perishes, his captives are set free, and Ivan marries his beloved princess.

Stravinsky handles his musical materials in this score with a mastery that still astounds. The Introduction, depicting Kashchei's garden, imparts an air of mystery;

its principal melody is embanked within the interval of the tritone, so beloved by Russian musical story tellers because of the demonic associations inherited from the medieval symbolism of the tritone as *diabolus in musica*. The Dance of the Firebird is a tableau vivant in gorgeous chromatic harmonies. By contrast, the Round of the Princesses enchants by the diatonic purity of its music. The Infernal Dance of Kashchei and his subjects is charged with syncopated energy. The Berceuse is a poetic vignette. The Finale unleashes the entire wealth of orchestral resources bearing forth an oriflamme of triumphant sonorities.

Igor Glebov, the Russian critic, said of the score of *The Firebird*: "Stravinsky has indeed caught the luminous golden feather in this fairy tale. The entire score of *The Firebird* sparkles with the rainbow colors of precious stones and orchestral timbres." This luminous quality places *The Firebird* on the borderline of impressionism, with its tonal *chatouillement* ("tickling") and coloristic pointillism.

Petrushka *(1911)*

Stravinsky tells in his autobiography that one of the most important dates in his life was the Siloti concert in St. Petersburg, at which Diaghilev, the great Russian impresario, was present, and heard an early Stravinsky piece for orchestra. It was on February 6, 1909 and as a result of this hearing, Diaghilev decided to commission Stravinsky to do some orchestrations of Chopin for his Paris season. For the following season, Diaghilev asked Stravinsky to write an original ballet, based on the Russian fairy tale "The Firebird." Stravinsky wrote for this ballet a music gorgeously Russian. When it was produced by Diaghilev in Paris on June 25, 1910, Stravinsky was only twenty-eight years old, and it was a beginning of a long association with Diaghilev, which determined Stravinsky's career up to the very time of Diaghilev's death in 1929. Stravinsky left Russia to write Russian music in France, Switzerland, and Italy, and eventually became a French citizen.

Petrushka was Stravinsky's second ballet written for Diaghilev. It did not assume the shape of a ballet at once. For a time, Stravinsky toyed with the idea of composing a short piece for piano and orchestra, in the manner of Weber's Konzertstück (Concert Piece) for piano. It was to be a compressed piano concerto, and the piano part was largely ready, when Stravinsky decided to put a new meaning into the piece. Stravinsky describes the genesis of the score in his autobiography:

> In composing *Petrouchka* I wanted to experiment with a work for orchestra, in which the piano would play the predominant part, a sort of Konzertstück. I conceived a clear vision of a puppet turned loose with a cascade of demoniacal arpeggios to which the orchestra responds by menacing fanfares. There follows a terrible brawl resulting in a pitiful defeat of the poor puppet. After completing my burlesque piece, I took long walks by the shores of the lake of Geneva, thinking of a title that would express in a single word the character of my music. And then, all of a sudden, I was seized with joy: Petrouchka! The eternal unlucky hero of puppet shows. I had found my title!

"Petrushka" is a diminutive for Peter, used by Russian peasants, but specifically it is the name of a puppet popular at Russian fairs after Lent. Thus, Petrushka is the counterpart of a character in the English Punch and Judy show. He is usually the pathetic lover who gets beaten up by the villain, and is thwarted in all his enterprises. He is quarrelsome without cunning, and aggressive without caution. However, it was not Stravinsky's intention to write a musical biography of Petrushka, in the manner of Strauss's *Till Eulenspiegel*. Stravinsky's score is a panorama of the Russian pre-Lent festival *Maslenitza* (literally, "butter time"). There are many sideshows in Stravinsky's ballet: the organ grinder, the magician with his flute, a dancing bear. Among the crowds there are two categories of typical visitors: children's nurses and coachmen. Petrushka's tragedy is a part of the show. He quarrels with the Moor over the love of a ballerina, and gets his skull cracked.

Stravinsky completed the composition of *Petrushka* in Rome, on May 26, 1911. The ballet was produced by Diaghilev in Paris on June 13, 1911, and its success was instantaneous, but quite lacking in the riotous quality that accompanied the production of *The Rite of Spring*. The three scores, *The Firebird*, *Petrushka*, and *The Rite of Spring* constitute the "Russian" period in Stravinsky's evolution. In all three, the subjects are intensely Russian, and in *Petrushka* Stravinsky actually uses the themes of popular Russian songs in the score, the only work in which he does so openly. There are Russian melodies in *The Wedding*, which he wrote during the years of the world war and after the armistice, but these melodies are original. *The Soldier's Story*, composed in 1918, employs Russian rhythms but makes no direct use of actual melodies. The Russian period of Stravinsky comprises the years from 1910 to 1924, after which he changed his style to a special type of classical writing.

The expressly Russian style of *Petrushka* did not deter composers of many nations—French, Spanish, Americans—from imitating its harmonic and even rhythmic idiom. The impact of *The Rite of Spring* on creative musicians was even greater, affecting young talents as well as composers of established reputation. When Stravinsky abandoned the Russian style and adopted a classicism bordering on academicism, musical opinion followed him in that change. However, it may be that Stravinsky himself followed the changes necessitated by the economic and political reorganization after the First World War, and in one case, that of *The Soldier's Story*, he declared his intention to reduce the apparatus of modern orchestra to an efficient minimum so as to make frequent performances possible without great expenditure of money.

The subtitle of *Petrushka* reads: *Burlesque Scenes in Four Tableaux,* which establishes the character of the score as stage music. Yet, the orchestral suite from *Petrushka* has proved extremely effective without the visual theater, although early critics of the score, in Europe and America, wrote that ballet action was essential to illustrate the music. Similarly, *The Rite of Spring* and *The Firebird* stand by themselves as effective orchestral suites. Historically, Stravinsky was right in acknowledging Diaghilev as the animator of his creative work, but the ballet was to Stravinsky merely a medium of expression, and his music, divorced from action, remains undiminished in its artistic power.

Alexandre Benois, the coauthor with Stravinsky of the libretto of *Petrushka*, called it "a street ballet," because its action reflects the street life of old Russia. The first and last scenes take place at the Admiralty Square in St. Petersburg during the reign of Czar Nicholas I in the 1830s. The season is the Shrovetide, or Mardi Gras, when Russians of all classes gorged themselves on food in anticipation of a long Lent. (Regular contests in gluttony used to be held at that time for the greatest consumption of bliny, buttered pancakes; one story had it that a merchant held a record of 120 bliny in one day, but he died the next morning.) The second scene is in Petrushka's room, and the third is in the apartment of the Blackamoor, Petrushka's successful rival in love. He enters the Blackamoor's room in the middle of a love scene with the ballerina, and is ignominiously thrown out. In the final scene, the puppets engage in an open fight. Petrushka is struck down by the Blackamoor with his scimitar and falls piteously to the ground. The spectators are horrified, but the puppeteer reassures them that Petrushka is merely a creature of wood and sawdust. He carries Petrushka's broken remains off the stage as darkness descends on the scene. Then comes an unexpected climax. Petrushka's ghost suddenly appears on the top of the theatrical booth and thumbs his nose at the public. There is a mystical exchange of roles; Petrushka becomes the master of the show, and the puppeteer his servant.

Stravinsky wrote his very Russian score in Switzerland, completing the manuscript in May 1911, when he was only twenty-eight years old. The first performance took place at Diaghilev's Ballets Russes in Paris, on June 13, 1911. Pierre Monteux was the conductor. The choreography was by Mikhail Fokine. The part of Petrushka was interpreted by the most celebrated of all Russian dancers, Vaclav Nijinsky (1889–1950). Shortly after the Paris production of *Petrushka*, Alexandre Benois wrote an impassioned account in a daily St. Petersburg newspaper of the history of the ballet, and of his own part in it:

> In my unbounded admiration for the unquestionable genius of Stravinsky's music, I was quite willing to minimize my own part in the creation of *Petrouchka*. The subject of the ballet was entirely Stravinsky's idea, and I only helped him to organize it in a concrete dramatic form. But the libretto, the cast of characters, the plot and the dénouement of the action, as well as a number of other details, were almost wholly mine. My share in the production, however, seems trivial in comparison with Stravinsky's music. When at a rehearsal Stravinsky asked me who should be listed as the author of *Petrouchka*, I replied without a moment's hesitation, "You, of course." Stravinsky objected to this verdict and insisted that I should be named as the actual author of the libretto. Our combat de générosité was resolved by putting both our names on the program as co-authors, but I succeeded in having Stravinsky's name placed first, despite my alphabetical precedence. Still, my name appears twice in the score, because Stravinsky decided to dedicate *Petrouchka* to me, which touched me infinitely.... From my earliest childhood I carried the vivid memories of the riotous turmoil and merrymaking of the "plain people" of St. Petersburg at the Shrovetide, the peepshows and the excitement of the street fair, where my friends used to come "to learn what Russia really is like." These unforgettable scenes of a vanishing world remain dear and near to me in many ways. Some will say that these memories are colored by the remoteness of my childhood, and that in reality it was just dirt, brawling, and lust. Naturally, these street fairs were not idyllic events conforming with the bittersweet ideals of virtue so dear to our temperance societies. But no matter how much drunkenness, how much crudity there was in these scenes, the street life had its own rights, and set its own rules of conduct and its own code of decency.

The perception of *Petrushka* by the Parisians was a far cry from the scandal that greeted the production of Stravinsky's *The Rite of Spring* two years later. "*Petrushka* is a marvel," reported the critic of the Paris journal *Comœdia*.

It is simply astonishing. Apart from an abundance of musical themes, original and classical, and a profusion of fantastic rhythms, Stravinsky's orchestration is extraordinary. Instrumental timbres flow in a stream in a most uncommon way, creating among the audience a sense of inexpressible exhilaration. Not a single measure is wasted. And what boldness in handling of the instruments! What eloquence! What life! What youthfulness!

Among musicians who were enthralled by Stravinsky's youthful exuberance was Debussy, but he sounded a note of caution to posterity. In a letter to a friend he wrote:

> I saw Stravinsky the other day. He is a spoiled child who sometimes sticks his fingers into the nose of music. He is also a young savage who sports extravagant cravats, kisses women's hands while stepping on their toes. In his old age he will be insufferable, that is to say that he will not tolerate any other kind of music than his own. But at the moment, he is incredible!

Petrushka was not only an amazing spectacle and an extraordinary ballet. It also set a landmark of modern music from the purely technical standpoint. The score contains the first consistent use of bitonality, the "*Petrushka* chord," as it came to be known, which combines the polarized keys of C major and F-sharp major, the two tonalities standing at the opposite ends of the vertical axis in the cycle of scales. This bitonal combination had a pianistic origin, for *Petrushka* was originally conceived by Stravinsky as a Konzertstück for piano and orchestra. Stravinsky experimented at the keyboard, playing on the white keys with his right hand and on the black keys with his left, resulting in a series of bitonal arpeggios.

The melancholy theme of "Petrushka's Cry" also contains elements of C major and F-sharp major. Besides these original inventions, Stravinsky freely borrowed melodic and rhythmic materials from Russian folk songs, mostly from collections published by Tchaikovsky, Rimsky-Korsakov, and others, fashioning them with ingenious alterations to suit his purposes. There are also in the score of *Petrushka* a couple of dance tunes borrowed from Joseph Lanner. One such borrowing ended up in an embarrassment. Stravinsky picked up a popular song which he heard played on a barrel organ. It turned out to be a music-hall chansonette fully protected by copyright. As a result, Stravinsky was obliged to pay a royalty to the publishers of the song each time *Petrushka* was performed.

The Rite of Spring (Le Sacre du printemps) *(1911–1913)*

Stravinsky completed the manuscript of the piano version of *The Rite of Spring* in Clarens, Switzerland, and wrote in the score, in blue and red pencil: "Today, Sunday, on the 17th November, 1912, suffering from an unbearable toothache, I finished the music of *The Rite of Spring.*" This was the most fruitful toothache in music history. No composition written since 1900 produced a comparable impact on the evolution of modern musical thought than *The Rite of Spring*. Even though it is a typically Russian product (its subtitle is *Scenes from Pagan Russia*), composers of all lands have, in one way or another, been deeply moved and inspired by its music.

The first performance of the work took place at the Théâtre des Champs-Elysées in Paris on May 29, 1913, produced in its original conception as a ballet commissioned to Stravinsky by Serge Diaghilev, the impresario of the famous Ballets Russes. The original Russian title is, in literal translation, *The Sacred Spring*. The French title, under which it was produced, is *Le Sacre du Printemps*, and the English most commonly used, *The Rite of Spring*.

ЧАСТЬ ПЕРВАЯ
ПОЦЕЛУЙ ЗЕМЛИ
Вступление

FIRST PART
A KISS OF THE EARTH
Introduction

Introduction to Stravinsky's *Rite of Spring*

The Paris production gave rise to a riot without precedent in the annals of music. Just what happened exactly has been reported in numerous contradictory accounts, most of them unverifiable. Jean Cocteau, not a very reliable witness, reported that the old Comtesse de Pourtalès stood up in her loge and, brandishing her fan, exclaimed, "This is the first time in my sixty years that I was taken for a fool." In his postcard sent to Maximilian Steinberg, Rimsky-Korsakov's son-in-law, from Neuilly, a suburb of Paris, and dated 3 July 1913, Stravinsky presents a more sanguine report of the occasion:

I was very much satisfied with the way *The Rite of Spring* sounded in the orchestra; I was happy, really happy to hear this long awaited symphonic setting. Nijinsky's choreography was unsurpassable. But there was plenty of trouble at the performance, at times reaching the point of actual fist fights. We will have to wait a long time for the public to be accustomed to our language, but I am absolutely convinced that what we have accomplished was right, and this gives me strength for further work.

On the picture side of the postcard Stravinsky, who was then recovering from an attack of typhoid fever, wrote: "This is my room where I spent many desperate hours in dreadful agony."

The reaction to *The Rite of Spring* in the press was that of a catatonic shock. "Never was the cult of the wrong note practiced with so much industry, zeal and fury," wrote Pierre Lalo (nephew of the composer Édouard Lalo), in *Le Temps* of June 3, 1913. American music critics joined the chorus of condemnation after *The Rite of Spring* was performed in the United States. W. J. Henderson, in the *New York Sun*, called Stravinsky "a cave man of music." A writer in the *Boston Herald* of January 27, 1924, burst into verse:

> Who wrote this fiendish *Rite of Spring*,
> What right had he to write the thing,
> Against our helpless ears to fling
> Its crash, clash, cling, clang, bing, bang, bing?
> And then to call it *Rite of Spring*,
> The season when on joyous wing
> The birds melodious carols sing
> And harmony's in everything!
> He who could write *the Rite of Spring*,
> If I be right, by right should swing!

Saint-Saëns, the grand *seigneur* of French music, who attended the performance, was reportedly stunned by the opening bassoon solo. "What instrument is this?" he whispered to a friend. "Why, the bassoon, of course," the other answered, "If this is a bassoon, then I am a baboon," Saint-Saëns remarked, and haughtily left the theater. This introductory bassoon solo is indeed a marvel. Set in the highest register of the instrument it makes the player feel like a puffer fish about to explode from inner pressure when pulled out of the water. But the melody itself is simple; it was in fact taken by Stravinsky from an old collection of Lithuanian folk songs.

The ballet is in two parts: "The Kiss of the Earth" (usually translated "Adoration of the Earth," which changes the subject into the object) and "The Great Sacrifice." In the introduction, the music is made predominantly by wind instruments entering canonically in varied and sometimes dissimilar thematic configurations. The opening scene proper, "Spring Fortune-telling" (thus the Russian title, variously rendered as "Spring Auguries" or "Harbingers of Spring"), marked by stomping dissonant chords in the string with cross-accents punctuated by blurting and burning French horns, while gentler figures are given out by the English horn and the bassoons. Soon the high winds join the proceedings, the flutes and clarinets tonguing a series of fluttering chromatics.

The fortune-telling leads to "Dances of Smartly Dressed Girls" (usually, and misleadingly, translated "Dance of Adolescents"), redolent of Russian folk-song refrains. Another change of scene, and we are witnessing a brutal "Abduction Game," with its truncated meters, pullulating rhythms and asymmetric chordal ejaculations. It is followed by a serene interlude as a preface to "Spring Rounds." The tunes are stunted and slow in starting off, but when the point of saturation is reached, an eruption of myriad coruscating tonal particles ensues. The serene entr'acte returns as a transition to yet another game, "Contest Between Two Camps," in which two groups contend in a millennial Russian bowling match in which gnarled logs, stood on end in a row, are toppled over by whittled bats. The themes are made up of three or four notes of the diatonic scale, evoking the melodic patterns of the oldest known Russian songs.

Another shift of scene, and there begins a "Procession of the Oldest and Wisest Chief." His hoary wisdom is introduced by hollow-sounding brasses against a constant unaltering drumbeat. The procession stops abruptly. After an intermediate soft discord in the strings, the earth itself is stirred to a dancing measure. The Russian title is untranslatable; it can be paraphrased as "The Stepping Out of the Dancing Earth." The terrestrial solo is solid: the main beat is relentlessly driven into the ground. But above the quaking bass there is a proliferation of secondary seismic activities throwing up enormous boulders of blunt sonorities. With the dance of the earth the first part of the ballet comes to an end.

The second part, "The Great Sacrifice," opens with a reedy murmuration in the wind instruments; the strings, too, affect a similar sound, expressly marked flautando. This introduction leads to the scene entitled, in Russian, "Maidens' Secret Rites and Walking in Rounds" (usually translated as "Mysterious Circles of the Adolescents," although this translation leaves out the crucial reference to the feminine gender unavailable in English adjectives). A girl is elected to be honored by the multitudes, and a festive dance follows, "Glorification of the Chosen Maiden" (in Russian the suffix indicates the gender). The conventional prettiness and harmonious shapeliness that such a subject might suggest are of course totally absent from this scene of pagan ritual; the meters are apocopated, the strong beats are asymmetrically distributed, and the themes are outcries of elemental vital forces.

The scene ends as abruptly as it began. The next tableau is "Appeal to the Forefathers" (a more accurate translation than the usual "Evocation of the Ancestors"). The music conjures up the visions of Russian pagan idols, the stolid stony statues that once lined the banks of the Dnieper River at Kiev before they were hurled down about A.D. 1000, when Russia became nominally a Christian nation. The next scene depicts the "Ritual Action of the Human Ancient Ancestors." The musical action is limited to the low instrumental register of the orchestra; the melodic resources are reduced to a few notes; but before the terminal petrifaction sets in there is an explosion of latent energy in the high reaches of the wind instruments.

The Rite of Spring concludes with an overwhelming "Danse sacrale" ("Sacred Dance"). The choreography indicates the sacrifice of the chosen maiden, but the Russian title reads simply "The Great Sacred Dance," with the subtitle "The Chosen One." The "Danse sacrale" interrupts its ruthless drive to allow a rhythmically relaxed and metrically steady section. Then its savage progress is resumed and, after a fertilizing scratch on the Cuban gourd, the *guiro*, *The Rite of Spring* comes to a shattering close on a multiple discord anchored in the lower depths of the brasses and strings and nailed down by a blow on the bass drum. The finale is the most complex section of the entire score.

For 1913, when *The Rite of Spring* was first presented to the public, this cataract of unrelieved discords within a network of fantastically entangled rhythms was an overwhelming experience, beyond the powers of most musicians to grasp. For many years, only Pierre Monteux, who led the first performance of the ballet and its first performance as a purely symphonic score, was able to cope with the formidable difficulties of this finale. Much later, Stravinsky himself rewrote the finale, smoothing down the thorny rhythms and rearranging the instrumentation. But in the meantime a whole generation of young conductors arose to whom the difficulties under which Koussevitzky and his contemporaries labored and faltered were elementary. Most conductors perform *The Rite of Spring* from memory.

Is it any wonder that *The Rite of Spring* outraged the world of 1913 still basking in pristine innocence before the wars? The crashing assault of the orchestral dissonances coupled with the exotic Russian choreography, in which the great Nijinsky was the star, administered a shock that was too much to bear. For several decades *The Rite of Spring* was unacceptable in Stravinsky's native land, not because he was an émigré (so was Rachmaninoff, whose popularity never waned in Russia despite his outspoken hostility to the Revolution), but because of the nature of its musical language. In 1959, Leonard Bernstein conducted *The Rite of Spring* in Moscow, nearly forty years after its previous Russian performance, and another performance was given in Russia during Stravinsky's visit there in 1962. It was only in 1965 that the Soviet State Publishing House finally issued the full orchestral score of *The Rite of Spring*.

The Wedding (Les Noces) *(1921–1923)*

Stravinsky described this work, called *Svadelka* (*Little Wedding*) in Russian, as "choreographic scenes with singing and music." Since it is performed on the stage, it occupies an intermediate position between cantata and opera. First produced for Diaghilev's Ballets Russes in Paris in 1923, it is scored for chorus, soloists, four pianos, and seventeen percussion instruments. The music is rooted in Russian folk song, but the harmonic and contrapuntal realization is propulsive and acrid, while always keeping within the diatonic framework of tonality. The libretto consists of four scenes tracing the rituals of a peasant betrothal and wedding.

Octet for Wind Instruments (1923)

Throughout his extraordinary career Stravinsky anticipated the spirit of the musical times, and by so doing became the leader of generations of composers. He then legislated the new aesthetic development and by force of his conviction made it inevitable. No sooner had the music world accepted the shattering innovations of *The Rite of Spring* than Stravinsky reversed his course and turned back to Bach, or even further into the past. This past was also the future, the plus and minus signs of the temporal function intersecting in the present.

The portents of the new departure from the luxuriant style of Stravinsky's early ballets appeared at the time of the First World War. The war, Stravinsky believed, made the huge modern orchestra obsolete for economic reasons; besides, the lavish productions of the velvet era of the young century became aesthetically unacceptable. It seemed to be purposeless to dispense musical sonorities with an extravagant disregard for their utility, when the same artistic message could be conveyed more cogently with less expenditure of instrumental means. Finally, and most important, there was a challenge. Large panoramas of sound are notoriously easier to design than compact drawings in the Gothic or Baroque manner. For a master of the musical craft, the task was to create *multum in parvo*, not *parvum in multo*.

Highly significant of this period was Stravinsky's revision of his sparkling ballet score *The Firebird*. He plucked the score of its flaming feathers, dimmed the rainbow colors of the orchestra, eliminating decorative passages and other luscious delights. The new score may possess superior consistency and organization, but unregenerate music lovers kept faith with the incandescent virgin version, leaving the revision to the watchers of trends.

Stravinsky's new aesthetic code found its perfect realization in his Octet for Wind Instruments. Stravinsky reveals that the composition of the work was inspired by a dream in which he found himself surrounded by a group of instrumentalists playing some attractive music. The only thing he could remember upon awakening was that there were eight instruments in the ensemble. The very next morning he began the composition of the Dream Octet for flute, clarinet, two bassoons, two trumpets and two trombones. He completed the score in Paris on May 20, 1923, and conducted its first performance at the Koussevitzky concerts at the Opéra in Paris on October 18, 1923. Jean Cocteau described Stravinsky's appearance on the podium as that of an "astronomer preoccupied with the solution of a magnificent instrumental calculation made with the aid of silver numbers."

The Octet is a study of musical self-sufficiency. Every note counts; each Baroque trill performs a necessary function. The form is exquisitely balanced; the melodies arch their intervallic components with calculated precision. Yet within this circumscribed art there is room for a variety of expressive means. As in Baroque music, the mood changes readily from lyricism to drama, from elegiac contemplation to propulsive virility. The instrumentation, from bassoon to flute, from bass trombone to trumpet, provides a complete range of useful registers in wood and brass. Artful coupling of homonymous or heteronymous instruments contributes contrapuntal richness to the texture.

The work is in three movements: Sinfonia, Tema con variazioni, and Finale. In the Sinfonia, the least common denominator of the metrical division is a sixteenth note. The meters vary; a frequent grouping is the alternation of bars of $\frac{3}{8}$ and $\frac{2}{16}$. The idiom is strongly tonal, and modulations are effected by carefully prepared shifts of inner voices. Equivocal mediants (third scale-steps), typical of Stravinsky's harmonic writing, provide the link between homonymous major and minor triads. Canonic imitations become increasingly frequent. Acrid chromatics create somber interludes, but the texture is never opaque.

The second movement, Tema con variazioni, is remarkable in its syllogistic development. There are five distinct variations, of which the first returns twice. The theme itself is formed of permutations of four notes within a major third, leaving out the middle note to avoid a suggestion of chromatic filling. The theme is subjected to melodic and rhythmic translocations, giving rise to dancing measures—a conventionalized polka, a fast waltz, as well as a lyrical romance.

The Finale is centered on C major, with the principal measure of $\frac{2}{4}$. The pulse is often asymmetrical; a dancing chorale combines austerity with Baroque hedonism. Tonal elaborations result in the formation of a pandiatonic web. The work comes to a close on a tonic $\frac{6}{4}$, which traditionally serves as the antepenultimate chord in an authentic cadence. Stravinsky leaves it unresolved; in his neo-Baroque domain, it is more consummate, more expressive, more challenging in its finality.

Stravinsky deemed it advisable to give to his public, stunned and embarrassed by his recession, the reasons for the revaluation of his former values. "My Octet is a musical object," he wrote in 1924.

> This object has a form and that form is influenced by the musical matter with which it is composed. The differences of matter determine the differences of form. One does not do the same with marble that one does with stone. My Octet is made for an ensemble of wind instruments. Wind instruments seem to me to be more apt to render a certain rigidity of the form I had in mind than other instruments—the string instruments, for example, which are less cold and more vague.

Oedipus Rex *(1927; revised 1948)*

Igor Stravinsky has been many things to many people. He was the magnificent conjurer of symphonic fairy tales; the shatterer of the earth in his prodigious ballet scores; a disciplined scholar who initiated his private renaissance of classical forms; the enlightened technician of twentieth-century methods, and a musical philosopher who succeeds in uniting, with Aristotelian logic, the disparate elements that enter the art of composition.

At Stravinsky's hands, the oldest forms become new, and the newest forms become traditional. His "Russian" stage works—*Petrushka*, *The Rite of Spring*, *The Wedding*—were first produced outside Russia. Their impact affected the evolutionary course of modern music in national cultures of many lands. Neoclassical trends observable for several decades of European and American music were in part the consequence of Stravinsky's revival of ancient forms. It was not inconsistent with these developments that Stravinsky should have eventually adopted the strong discipline of the method of composition with twelve tones related only to one another. Yet through all these avatars, the essential Stravinsky persevered. There are rhythms, there are melodies, there are harmonies, there are orchestral and vocal devices in Stravinsky that are common to all his works. His stylistic departures, digressions, and detours seem to be the converging roads to the essential Stravinsky.

Perhaps the most formalized, and thus the purest, work of Stravinsky is *Oedipus Rex*, an opera-oratorio in two acts, after Sophocles. *Oedipus Rex* is written to the text by Jean Cocteau—the Jean Cocteau of 1927, Catholic and mythologist. He had run the gamut of human infatuations, embracing a faith which, to the overcynical, may have appeared as his latest perversity. Cocteau was anxious to narrate to the world a story well known; of things dead, he would speak in a dead language. Latin is the Esperanto of the true Catholic—but Cocteau's proselytism is of recent date and his schooldays remote. Therefore a Monsieur J. Danielou is entrusted with the task of translation. Mindful of the audiences that may be shy of classical learning, Cocteau retranslates Danielou's ecclesiastical Latin into telegraphic French. The Latin diction is carefully supervised; the performers are advised against minor mousetraps and admonished to harden the consonants, replace the dental *c* by the guttural *k*, sound a broad *u*.

The production, as originally intended, was to combine aspects of both opera and oratorio. Singers were to be placed in fixed positions, except the incidental characters of Soothsayer, Shepherd and the Messenger. Stylized costumes and scenery were to be employed, but entrances and exits were symbolically signalized by drawing, or withdrawing, curtains behind which the principal characters were placed. The cast included Oedipus (tenor), Jocasta, his mother (mezzo- soprano), Creon, her brother (bass-baritone), Tiresias, the Soothsayer (bass), the Shepherd (tenor), and the Messenger (bass-baritone). A speaker was also included to give a running account and interpretation of the events. The first performance of *Oedipus Rex* took place in Paris on May 30, 1927, as oratorio; the first stage production was given in Vienna on February 23, 1928.

Concerto in D for Violin and Orchestra (1931)

Stravinsky's classical period began with his Piano Concerto of 1924, which he himself played during his first American tour. There followed *Oedipus Rex*, the *Symphony of Psalms*, the *Capriccio*, and the Violin Concerto, all in various ways works of classical caliber. Stravinsky undertook the composition of the Violin Concerto as a commission from the Russian violinist Samuel Dushkin, who also advised him on technical matters. One day, at a lunch with Dushkin in a Paris restaurant, Stravinsky wrote a chord of three widely separated notes, D below the G-clef staff, E a ninth higher, and a high A an eleventh above the E, and asked Dushkin if it could be played on the violin. Dushkin looked at it in dismay and said, "No." "Quel dommage," remarked Stravinsky. What a shame. Returning home, Dushkin tried the chord on his instrument, and found that it was quite playable. He telephoned Stravinsky at once; the chord became a motto of the concerto, its "passport," as Stravinsky described it, opening each of the concerto's four movements.

In the Violin Concerto, the orchestration is "normal." The clarinet is the only supernumerary instrument in the score of the concerto; there is an English horn, which would stand in opposition to the practice of the nineteenth-century symphony, but not necessarily of the early eighteenth. The key of the concerto is that of D, major or minor, the most common (because the easiest for the strings) for all symphonies, concertos, and overtures up to about 1800. In this instance, Stravinsky is once more a conservative.

The mixture of styles that is immediately evident in the Concerto in D is really of no consequence. Some influences (we would call it deliberate admixtures) are quite unexpected, that of César Franck, for instance (the latter was a pioneer of remotely related suspensions and resolutions). Others are the familiar ghosts—Handel, Bach. Tchaikovsky is conspicuously absent, unless we attribute the episodic subject of the orchestra in the Toccata to his psychic voice. The very opening of the Toccata is in the general style of the early eighteenth century with corrections of the neoclassical movement. Again, the obvious dissonances, the wrong notes in the right place, are not the result of any newfangled systems of polytonal writing, but proceed from a higher sense of tonality.

The form of the concerto is that of an instrumental suite, austere, almost ascetic in its rejection of "brio." There is an element of virtuosity, but of a Baroque type devoid of any flourishes. The titles of the movements are descriptive of the formal structure: Toccata, Aria I, Aria II, and Capriccio; Presto. The Toccata, as the title suggests, presents a rapid current of even notes; the harmony is touched with nontoxic dissonances; the concluding chord contains the first five degrees of the D-major scale in spacious distribution.

The second and the third movement of the concerto bear the titles Aria I and Aria II. Here we have Stravinsky the Serene, revealed to us in Apollo. But we cannot pass by one technical device largely employed by Stravinsky that, for want of appropriate terminology, may be described as "unfinished resolution," a sort of driving into a blind alley, making a dead stop when confluence is expected. Thus, in Aria I, the violin stops one degree short of the expected conclusion, in its scale-like passages, while the orchestral accompaniment, in a web of pure tonality, furnishes the implied resolution. This method is not new: in the Octet, Stravinsky showed several examples of similar "dead stops," and always against a background of perfect tonality.

Perhaps the most noble use of the "suspensions" of higher orders is made in the middle section of Aria II. The musical tension is ideally calculated to bring a perfect catharsis in the final resolution. It is in a movement like this that one begins to understand why it took Stravinsky a day to complete a measure. Every note seems to possess a directional force that likens it to a mathematical vector.

Aria I, after the presentation of the chordal "passport," turns to D minor; the melody is almost operatic in its bel canto expansiveness. Aria II, by contrast, abounds in trills, ornaments, and arabesques. The Capriccio reveals the persistence of eternal Stravinsky, with its splitting syncopations and tiny detonations of rhythmic energy at asymmetric time intervals; the concluding Presto brings up memories of the "Danse sacrale" in *The Rite of Spring*.

As far as the writing for the solo instrument is concerned, there is nothing particularly excruciating for a seasoned performer. The violin part of *The Soldier's Story* is without question the more complicated. Rhythmically, only the Violin Concerto's final Presto presents any serious difficulty. It took all the uncanny ingenuity of Stravinsky to graft it on to the Capriccio, to prepare it, as he did, with the dark gaps and falls of the immediately preceding music.

In another place and under other auspices it would not be difficult to prove a thesis that Stravinsky's melodies are always built within the walls of a tonic and its dominant, sometimes atonally (in "Petrushka's Cry" in the second scene of the ballet, in the mother's complaint in Scene 2 of *The Wedding*, etc.), sometimes tonally (as in the passage referred to above). In the Capriccio, there is a glimpse of the former Stravinsky in the ominous rests on the stronger parts of the measure. Finally, the crowning Presto bristles, as of old, with contrary rhythms set against the measured steps of the bass tones. What are these advancing and retreating chromatic tones of the cellos if not the familiar "bubbles" in "The "Kiss of the Earth" of *The Rite of Spring*? The relationship is much more than a more coincidence, or identity of procedure. In it is the spirit of *The Rite of Spring* that is with us again.

Every one of the four movements of the Violin Concerto opens with the identical chord of the violin, the D of the open string, the E, a ninth above it, and the high A, at two and a half octaves above the fundamental tone. Thus does Stravinsky establish the classical unity with an emphasis. In *The Wedding*, composed in 1917, the mysterious effect of a bell's clank at the end of the work is obtained by a similarly positioned chord, with the interval of a ninth at the root. This collation of harmonic textures alone will show how consistent Stravinsky's present idiom is with his past. In the first movement (the Toccata) we find a violin passage in double stops with the characteristic seesaw movement, in iambic prosody, which instantly recalls the parallel movements in *Petrushka*. Besides, in this passage Stravinsky's melody is characteristically confined within the interval of a fifth.

What then was the ultimate purpose underlying the composition of this concerto? The answer may be simple: it was to write a Violin Concerto for Samuel Dushkin, the virtuoso. The work was commissioned and done according to the requirements of the commissioner. This honorable practice was responsible for many a masterpiece from Mozart and Beethoven; why should not Stravinsky do the like? In this he is only following a great tradition. A "notary's contract" here assumes a nonallegorical significance. What was the result of this contract? A masterpiece, which, in addition to its inherent qualities, is rich in demonstration of how a transient problem of style may be subordinated to a higher synthesis.

In the Violin Concerto, as in no other composition, Stravinsky fused his various styles, and also the styles of various other composers, so solidly that the mixture appears monolithic. This may be a tribute to the composer's technical mastery, but it also may be a revelation of unity in seemingly disparate elements, a revelation of Stravinsky in the true Platonic sense, as one face of many facets.

Perséphone *for Narrator, Tenor, Chorus, and Orchestra (1933; revised 1949)*

Stravinsky conducted the first performance of his ballet-melodrama *Perséphone* in Paris on April 30, 1934. The work is scored for tenor, chorus, and orchestra with a narrator, to the text by André Gide. Ida Rubinstein appeared in the title role as dancer and speaker. The myth of Persephone (in Roman usage, Proserpina) tells of the beautiful daughter of Zeus and Demeter abducted by Hades, or Pluto, the ruler of the netherworld, while gathering flowers in the fields of Sicily. Her mother's search for her is the subject of many legends and poems. She lit her torches by night from the fires of the volcano of Etna. When Zeus himself intervened, the lower world was forced to release Persephone for six months every year, a sojourn symbolic of the burying of the seed in the ground and the growth of the corn. After a period of barrenness, Demeter returns to her duties as the patroness of agriculture, and the fields are once more covered with corn. (The word "cereal" is derived from Ceres, the Roman form of Demeter.)

Stravinsky's language in *Perséphone* is marked by austerity of harmonic idiom and severe economy of sonorous means. In 1934, Stravinsky published a lengthy article in the Paris daily *Excelsior* on the eve of the performance of *Perséphone*, in which he resolutely renounced the practices that he had applied with such success in the ballet scores of his Russian period. "I abhor instrumental effects used solely for the sake of color," he wrote.

> In *Perséphone* the listener should not expect to be dazzled by seductive sonorities, for I have long ago abandoned the futility of brio. I abhor the necessity of wooing the public. It embarrasses me. Let those who make a profession of this honorable practice, in composing as well as in conducting, enjoy it to the point of complete satiety. The public expects the artist to disembowel himself and to exhibit his entrails. This action is regarded as the noblest expression of art, and is termed variously as Personality, Individuality, or Temperament. Things that are felt and things that are true are susceptible to projections on an enormous scale. I follow a very definite path. It cannot be the subject of a debate or criticism. One does not criticize somebody, or something, that functions. The nose is not manufactured. The nose is. So is my art.

Stravinsky's stern admonition to critics to watch their step aroused some consternation in the musical press. *Le Monde Musical* felt constrained to respond:

> M. Stravinsky warns us that his way in art is not to be debated or criticized. Such self-assurance is probably without precedent in music history. Bach, Mozart, Beethoven, Wagner, Debussy, Fauré, were all conscious of the validity of their art, but none of them presumed to guarantee the vitality and the durability of their works. Curiously, it is not as the composer

of such works as *Petrushka*, *The Firebird*, *The Nightingale*, or *The Rite of Spring*, which have earned him world renown, that Stravinsky aspires to enter the Pantheon. No, it is his works which even his most fervent admirers fail to acclaim, works written during the period of his "return to Bach," that he regards as "enormous projections.".... At its first performance, *Perséphone* received scant appreciation from the audience. During the last scene, in which Persephone descends into Hell for the second time, someone was heard to whisper: "Let's hope she stays there."

Jeu de cartes: *Ballet in Three Deals (1935–37)*

Igor Stravinsky began his career as a ballet composer, and throughout his spectacular stylistic avatars, his first love for musical choreography never diminished. Despite the extraordinary harmonic and rhythmic complexity of his early masterpieces, such as *Petrushka* and *The Rite of Spring*, the sense of classical form is ever present in Stravinsky's ballet scores, so that the choreographer has a clearly drawn blueprint to follow. Owing to this classical structure, Stravinsky's ballets lend themselves naturally to concert performances in the form of a symphonic suite without stage action.

The genesis of *Jeu de cartes* (*Card Game*) was this: In 1935 Edward Warburg and Lincoln Kirstein asked Stravinsky to write a work for the recently organized American Ballet Company. George Balanchine, the Russian ballet master, long associated with Stravinsky, was to design the choreography. After consultation among all persons concerned, the choice was made, and the ballet was named *Jeu de cartes*, variously translated as *Card Game*, *A Game of Cards*, or *The Card Party*, the game itself being poker, of which Stravinsky was an aficionado.

Dramatically, the scenario unfolds as a morality play that might be entitled *Malice Punished*. The malefactor is the Joker, ideally suited for the role of a villain because of its chameleonic cunning in assuming the character of any other card in the pack and thus fitting into a winning hand. The scenario is in three deals. The cards are shuffled before each deal; accordingly, the introductory measures illustrating the shuffling are identical in all three movements.

A moralistic motto is attached to the score, from La Fontaine's fable "The Wolves and the Sheep":

> Il faut faire aux méchants guerre continuelle.
> La paix est fort bonne de soi,
> J'en conviens; mais de quoi sert-elle
> Avec des ennemis sans foi?

> Continual war must be waged on evil men.
> Peace in itself is good, we know.
> I agree; but what will happen then
> If we deal with a faithless foe?

Stravinsky completed the score on December 6, 1936. He conducted its first performance presented by the American Ballet Company at the Metropolitan Opera House in New York on April 27, 1937. It had a cordial reception in the press.

The first deal opens in vigorous marchlike measures. A delicate *pas d'action* follows, introduced by a poetic flute solo, seconded by a grumpy bassoon. The duet undergoes metric contractions, creating a momentary nervous twitch. Then the

Joker makes its arrogant entrance. "The Dance of the Joker" is marked by aggressive accents, terminating abruptly on an ascending scale of five notes, forming a straight, a promisingly strong hand. Then it stands pat. One of the players quits, but another remains to challenge the Joker. A waltz follows in tranquil motion.

The second deal, like the first, opens with a shuffling of the pack. The game proceeds with a march in hearts and spades, embellished with elegant roulades and interrupted by implosions of concentrated gambling energy. The Queens enter and coquettishly exhibit themselves in four handsome variations. The Queen of Hearts, making her pointes with matronly grace in allegretto, seems to have stepped out of the second movement of Beethoven's Eighth Symphony, Allegretto scherzando. The tonality, B-flat major, is the same, and the melody revolves around the same notes of the tonic triad. The coincidence is not unintentional. In one of his Delphic utterances, Stravinsky declared his right to delve into the treasury of old music for raw materials: "After studying many pages of a certain composer, I sense his musical personality and, like a detective, reconstruct his musical experience."

The second variation is a swift flight on gossamer wings, a dance in the finest tradition of the French Rococo. Its coruscating brilliance is peculiarly fitted to the suit of diamonds, which it represents in the scenario. There follows a stately variation for the Queen of Clubs, showing a fine panache. The fourth variation is a dance of the forbidding Queen of Spades, but a smile is painted on her face in gaudy colors. There is a resemblance in the violin countersubject in this variation to a theme from *Die Fledermaus* by Johann Strauss. The fifth variation is a *pas de quatre*, confident in the invincibility of the high hand of four of a kind. But its self-assurance soon vanishes in a precipitous coda in which the Joker joins the rival player and overwhelms the four Queens with four Aces. A triumphant march, with the victorious Joker strutting in the lead, concludes the second deal.

The cards are shuffled again in the introduction to the third deal, the most tense of the entire card game. All three players hold flushes, and they eye each other in a deceptively courteous waltz, in which an inquisitive listener may perceive echoes of Ravel's *La Valse*. Then a fierce contest between Spades and Hearts erupts in a presto. Here occurs one of the most direct quotations, from Rossini's *Barber of Seville*. The rhythms are identical; there are minor divergences in the degrees of the scale in the melody.

The Stravinsky-ized Rossini tune assumes a primary thematic significance in the Finale. The Joker, holding a straight in Spades, parades his megalomania in brass. He ignores the diffident Hearts, not realizing that they are preparing a colossal bluff, concealing an all-conquering Royal Flush. The Joker is foiled, his malice punished, virtue triumphs, and the poker game ends with a diatonic ascent into the climactic chord of the minor seventh on the ground tone of E.

Symphony in Three Movements (1942–45)

Stravinsky entered the Pantheon as composer of immortal masterpieces of modern music, but his significance is enhanced by his extraordinary ability to anticipate, foresee and presage the vital changes in the nascent style of the time, and then to lead younger composers in the new directions by writing works that serve as models. This exercise in stylistic prolepsis has at various stages of his career confused and bewildered some of his admirers. The most drastic change occurred at the dawn of the neoclassical era, when Stravinsky gave up the luxuriance of fairy-tale music as revealed in dazzling color on the pages of *The Firebird, Petrushka*, and *The Rite of Spring*, and proclaimed the supremacy of music as fact, self-sufficient, economic, and unencumbered by illustrative representation. He made a declaration of principles in an article published in 1924: "I consider that music is only able to solve musical problems; and nothing else, neither the literary nor the picturesque can be in music of any real interest. The play of the musical elements is the thing." These views, it may be observed parenthetically, are similar in a remarkable degree to the postulates of musical aesthetics in Hanslick's famous book *Vom Musikalisch-Schönen (On the Beautiful in Music)* published in 1854.

Stravinsky's Symphony in Three Movements belongs to the period of "music as fact." It was written for and dedicated to the New York Philharmonic Society, which Stravinsky conducted in the work's first performance on January 24, 1946. In his program note he warns once more against speculative interpretation of the meaning of the work: "The Symphony has no program, nor is it a specific expression of any given occasion; it would be futile to seek these in my work." Then he retreats slightly, leaving the door ajar for intrusive seekers of hidden meanings: "During the process of creation in this our arduous time, of sharp and shifting events, of despair and hope, of continual torments, of tension and, at last, cessation and relief, it may be that all those repercussions have left traces in this symphony. It is not I [*sic*] to judge."

In a detailed and interesting analysis of the Symphony in Three Movements, published in the program book of the New York Philharmonic, Ingolf Dahl—himself a composer of eminence and knowledge, and an authoritative (and authorized) spokesman for Stravinsky for many years—emphasizes the "great seriousness" of the work and outlines its principal structural factors: additive construction of themes outside the framework of conventional sonata form, progress measured by succession of blocks, "unified by a steadily and logically evolved organic force." Dahl makes a prediction: "One day it will be universally recognized that the white house in the Hollywood Hills, in which this Symphony was written and which was regarded by some as an ivory tower, was just as close to the core of a world at war as the place where Picasso painted Guernica."

The revelation comes then that Stravinsky, an avid cinema buff, was inspired in the composition of the first movement of the Symphony by a documentary film of the scorched-earth policy in China during its desperate defense against Japanese invasion. Some sections, it appears from Stravinsky's own admission, actually represent in the form of an instrumental conversation the Chinese peasants digging the earth. The second movement also had its genesis in a film, its materials being part of the unrealized score for a motion picture of Franz Werfel's *Song of Bernadette*. As for the third movement, Stravinsky states that it was a musical reaction to watching the goose-stepping Nazis in a newsreel, the final fugue reflecting the rise of the Allied powers, leading to victory. But these associations have, of course, nothing to do with the music of the symphony, which is to be judged by its intrinsic value. (Hanslick, who was as inimical to fanciful interpretations of music as Stravinsky, states plainly in his essay that it is a matter of utter indifference, aesthetically speaking, whether a composer did or did not associate his works with certain ideas, images or events.)

The three movements of the symphony are played without pause. In the New York Philharmonic program book, the first movement is entitled Symphony-Overture, but in the published edition there is no title, only a metronome mark, corresponding to a rapid tempo, of 160 beats to a minute, in $\frac{4}{4}$ time. The opening is fortissimo, with a soaring motto rising powerfully. The regulated pulse of the rhythmic scheme suggests a toccata, an impression reinforced by the employment of the piano as a concertizing instrument in the orchestra. Baroque sequences and pandi-atonically enriched triadic harmonies establish a classical mood. The common denominator of a quarter note is maintained rigorously, but there are subterranean eruptions of massive chords, causing the metrical bars to collapse asymmetrically.

This Stravinskian antinomy, in which absolute steadiness of the basic beat generates equally steady interference, may best be described by a term from rhetoric, *aposiopesis*, as if Stravinsky, with Virgil's Neptune, disciplines the rapid notes *Quos ego!* There is a remarkable episode for piano in terse counterpoint of single notes in the right and in the left hand, in multiple dialogues with other groups of the orchestra. The coda recalls the thematic materials of the opening; large chords of superincumbent harmonies herald the end, while the bass clarinet is left alone, alone, fluttering with instinctive wing motion. The concluding chord is a pandia-tonic extension of the C-major triad, with the flute on the fifteenth overtone, B.

The second movement, Andante, opens with a tremor in the violins on the tonic of latent D major. It slides upward through a *Schleifer* ("slide") to the mediant of the key, but Stravinsky puts a noneuphonious F-natural against it. The ambivalence of the triadic third is of course Stravinsky's trademark, found in virtually all his works, beginning with the early cantata *Zvezdoliky* (*King of the Stars*) and used thematically in *The Rite of Spring*.

The bucolic dalliance of distilled tonality and the tantalizingly Rossinian melorhythmic devices are soon disrupted by the insertion of bars in asymmetrical time signatures, recalling the ambiance of *The Rite of Spring*. The resulting melodic accretion and apocopation create great tension, which is allowed to resolve in a moment of tranquilization in the form of a brief interlude.

Then, attacca! The last movement is a Rondo: Con moto, with the piano assuming the dominant role, in the double tonality of C major and C minor. The bassoons start a commotion underneath; there is considerable agitation elsewhere, but it subsides into a series of convulsive silences, with only a few pointed arrows shooting from a quick quiver of trombones in a dark exchange with sharp notes on the piano. Explosions—and implosions—follow. After a magistral figure, the symphony ends in fortississimo, on a pandiatonic chord of D-flat major, with an added sixth and an added ninth.

Circus Polka *(1942; arranged for orchestra, 1944)*

Composers of all times and all ages liked to indulge in innocuous whimsicalities. Somehow, some of these light pastimes resulted in interesting musical discoveries. Mozart wrote a piece intended to make fun of village musicians, but in it he prophetically included passages in whole-tone scales and polytonal harmonies. Saint-Saëns classified pianists as animals in his suite *Carnival of the Animals*. Schoenberg inserted the song "Ach du lieber Augustin" in one of his string quartets. Erik Satie deliberately used nonsensical titles that somehow made sense.

As the well-known adage has it, humor is a very serious business. Stravinsky's humor invariably contains a grain of serious intent. For all the dashing nonchalance of his *Circus Polka*, the piece contains interesting contrapuntal and harmonic devices, stylistically related to Stravinsky's early ballets. Still, the music remains entirely functional, the kind that is commonly played by provincial bands. Stravinsky wrote his *Circus Polka* (for a young elephant) in Hollywood on February 15, 1942, on a commission from the Barnum & Bailey Circus, to be played at its regular shows. On January 14, 1944, Stravinsky conducted the piece in a fuller orchestral version with the Boston Symphony Orchestra.

The polka rhythm is but occasionally broken up by asymmetrical insertions of alien rhythms. Otherwise the piece proceeds without any pseudo-sophisticated notions. For the ending, Stravinsky regales his public with a magnificently cacophonous rendition of Schubert's Military March.

Coda

Long, long ago, I was hired by Serge Koussevitzky in Paris to play for him on the piano the scores he had to conduct. That was before the availability of long-playing records or any other mechanical aids to conducting, and Koussevitzky was accustomed to having a pianist hammer out his scores, while he practiced beating time. The immediate task for him was to master the changing meters in *The Rite of Spring*. We spent practically the entire summer in Biarritz in 1922 on *The Rite of Spring*, using the piano four-hand arrangement made by Stravinsky and published a few years before. I did my best to combine the main melodic and harmonic ingredients of the score, trying to get at least the meters and rhythms right. To me it was a great experience, a dream come true, with musical and other celebrities dropping in now and then—including Stravinsky, with whom we used to spend evenings playing poker at nominal stakes. (When Koussevitzky would raise the ante, Stravinsky would say "Into the bushes," a Russian phrase meaning "No contest," and would throw his cards on the table, even when he had a winning hand.)

It was not long before I realized that Koussevitzky was apt to add what he used to call a *Luftpause* (pause for breathing) to prime-number meters, such as 5 or 7, inevitably converting them to the more comfortable time signatures of 6 or 8. The crisis came in the final "Danse sacrale," which required a human metronome to get the minimal beats grouped into proper bar lines. Such sudden metrical changes as $\frac{3}{8}$, $\frac{2}{8}$ and $\frac{3}{16}$ in rapid tempo simply did not work out, and Koussevitzky was becoming annoyed with himself and, by ricochet, with me. Having reached a rhythmic cul-de-sac, I experienced a sudden moment of plenary inspiration: I proposed to Koussevitzky to recombine the pesky bars so as to reduce them to the common denominator of an eighth note, with only an occasional intrusion of an intractable bar of $\frac{5}{16}$ (e.g., $\frac{1}{8} + \frac{2}{8} + \frac{2}{16} + \frac{3}{16} + \frac{2}{16} + \frac{3}{16} = \frac{16}{16} = \frac{4}{4}$, common march time). Koussevitzky rejected my plan out of hand on the ground that it would be tampering with Stravinsky's rhythmic structure. I assured him that the only change would be visual, in Koussevitzky's own beat, and that the original rhythmic sequences would remain unaltered, but he would not listen. We returned to Paris in the fall, and Koussevitzky had his first orchestral rehearsal of *The Rite of Spring*. It was a disaster. On his way back from the rehearsal he told me to try out my idea of rebarring the "Danse sacrale." I gladly complied. My version worked without a hitch. Koussevitzky was delighted, and told everybody that I was a great mathematician (he liked to boast about the excellence of his serfs). The mathematics involved in my arrangement required the knowledge of addition of simple fractions. The score with my realigned bars in blue pencil is still kept in the library at Symphony Hall, Boston, which was Koussevitzky's final preserve. In 1943, Stravinsky himself rearranged the meters of the "Danse sacrale" to facilitate performance; it was not in any way connected with my arrangement, but was motivated by Stravinsky's desire to simplify the notation.

SERGEI PROKOFIEV
(1891–1953)
His Signature—SRG PRKFV

Sergei Sergeievich Prokofiev did not believe in vowels: they were to him unstable, subject to slurring, broadening, or clipping. He signed his name in consonants only: PRKFV. There was in this signature something of the man himself, a certain petulance, impatience, and a businesslike attitude of economy. There was also a spirit of independence, a refusal to conform, and perhaps a boyish defiance.

Prokofiev's imagination conjured up attractive monsters and humorous witches. He was nine years old when he completed an opera called *The Giant*, and it was duly performed at his uncle's estate in the country. The score was actually written out by Prokofiev himself, in piano arrangement, of course, in lieu of the orchestra. His cousin took the part of the orchestra at an upright piano; Prokofiev sang the role of the hero who overwhelms the giant with a toy pistol. A tall aunt was the giant. It was a costume performance, and every actor was attired in a most impressive garb.

After such a revelation of youthful ability, Prokofiev was taken to Moscow, where he was introduced to the greatest Russian contrapuntist, Sergei Taneyev, who treated him to a piece of chocolate and then listened to his playing of the overture to his second opera, called *Desert Islands*. After that, Taneyev told the boy's mother to take him to a conservatory student for harmony lessons. But even as a child, Prokofiev was full of his own notions about harmony, and was not happy to study with a student. Fortunately the famous Russian composer Reinhold Glière happened to be visiting Prokofiev's family and captivated the boy's imagination by explaining to him in simple, and yet learned, words the mysteries of sonata form and orchestration. Then the master and the pupil would play a game of croquet, and also chess, for Prokofiev was a prodigy not only in music but also in that intellectual game so beloved by Russians. He soon rose to the rank of first category, just a notch below that of chess master.

Even when Prokofiev became a famous composer, he still spent hours at the chessboard, in long arduous games with his musical colleagues. He played a public match with the violinist David Oistrakh. The terms were most curious: the winner was to receive a prize of the Club of the Masters of Art; the loser was to give a concert especially for professional musicians who were also chess players. For some reason, only seven out of the scheduled ten games were played, and no winner was announced. But both Prokofiev and Oistrakh gave their concerts as losers, and of course Oistrakh played Prokofiev's works, of which he was an ardent admirer.

Young Prokofiev knew so much about music when he entered the St. Petersburg Conservatory that he experienced difficulties in slowing himself down, even in the class of the great Rimsky-Korsakov himself. Besides, he was risking his academic reputation by performing his utterly unorthodox piano pieces at concerts of modernistic societies in St. Petersburg. With great self-assurance, Prokofiev decided to play his own piano concerto for the commencement exercises at the conservatory. His pianism was of the highest caliber, and even though his concerto was dissonant, the conservatory jury felt compelled to give him the first prize, which was a grand piano.

Satire and grotesque are characteristic of Prokofiev's early music, but are not essential in his creative temperament, which is lyrical and poetic. Prokofiev, the composer of the piano suite *Sarcasms*, is also the author of the moving poem for voice and piano, "The Ugly Duckling," after the tale by Hans Christian Andersen, in which the beautiful cygnet is shunned and snubbed by the ducklings, whose idea of bird beauty is the opposite to swans. Maxim Gorky, the great Russian novelist, remarked, when he heard Prokofiev's "Ugly Duckling": "You know, he must have written this about himself." Indeed, Prokofiev was an ugly duckling of Russian music in the academic surroundings of the St. Petersburg Conservatory, where he was educated. At a time when dissonances were allowed in composition only when they were safely resolved into perfect concords, Prokofiev amused himself by writing piano pieces in which the right hand played in one key and the left in another. And he brought perturbation into the comfortable world of 1912 by composing a Scherzo for a quartet of bassoons. When the four players filed on the stage, armed with these forbidding-looking instruments, a sarcastic concertgoer observed to his companion: "Let's leave before they start shooting."

The secret of Prokofiev's strength is his directness of musical utterance. His style may be defined as romantic realism. As a realist, Prokofiev writes dynamic music full of motion, and strong contrasts of rhythm and accent. As a romanticist, he favors fantastic tales for subject matter, seasoned with fine humor or sharp grotesque.

Chronologically Prokofiev's creative biography falls into three periods. The first, from childhood (Prokofiev began to compose very early) to his trip abroad in

1918, is characterized by abundant and aggressive energy. In 1914, he played his First Piano Concerto as a graduation piece at the St. Petersburg Conservatory. He was already known at that time as the author of piano pieces of semihumorous or fanciful inspiration. His first orchestral composition of importance was the *Scythian Suite*, composed in 1914–15. It was also his first work in the national Russian style. Like Stravinsky's *The Rite of Spring*, with which it has otherwise no points of contact, Prokofiev's *Scythian Suite* is inspired by the pagan era (Scythians were early inhabitants of the plain that is now European Russia). During the turbulent days of the Revolution, he wrote his most uncompromisingly dissonant score, the demoniac incantation, *Seven, They Are Seven*. And only shortly before that, he wrote the *Classical* Symphony (Symphony No. 1, Op. 25) ingeniously contrived in the style of a twentieth-century Mozart. The sketches of the First Violin Concerto were made at the same period.

Prokofiev's dual nature, stormy and impetuous on the one hand and lyrical and poetic on the other, is revealed in his cantata, *Seven, They Are Seven*, on an ancient Sumerian legend, and the *Classical* Symphony. They were both written in 1917, when Prokofiev was 26, but the contrast between the two could not be greater. The primitive force displayed in the cantata, with its raging dissonances and convulsive rhythms, is the very opposite of the *Classical* Symphony, gentle and easygoing. The witty Gavotte from the *Classical* Symphony is a series of deceptive cadences that lead into unexpected keys. No harmony laws are broken, but the effect of modernistic surprise is achieved with finesse.

Prokofiev began his career as the enfant terrible of Russian music, who shocked the sensibilities of his own professors at the St. Petersburg Conservatory and was the object of indignant reviews in Russian newspapers. When the Revolution came in 1917, Prokofiev was hailed by the artistic vanguard as a natural ally of the new society. But conditions for work in Russia, torn by civil war, were intolerable, and Prokofiev left St. Petersburg, went through Siberia to Japan, and from Japan to America. When he made his first American tour in 1918—he was twenty-seven years old then—his ability to shock was undiminished. "Every rule in the realm of traditional music writing was broken by Prokofiev," the *New York Sun* lamented in pain. "Dissonance followed dissonance in a fashion inconceivable to ears accustomed to melody and harmonic laws upon which their music comprehension has been reared."

His concerts in New York created a sensation. He was regarded as the very personification of Bolshevism in music. The American composer Reginald De Koven, author of the famous song "O Promise Me," could not contain himself in anger. "Mr. Prokofiev strikes me as a ribald Bolshevist innovator and musical agitator," he wrote in his capacity as music critic for the *New York Herald*. The respectable and knowledgeable critic of the *New York Tribune*, H. E. Krehbiel, declared that Prokofiev's compositions "invite their own damnation" and "die the death of abortions." His recital of his piano works prompted an American critic to describe his reaction in tumultuous prose: "Crashing Siberias, volcano hell, Krakatoa, sea-bottom crawlers! Incomprehensible? So is Prokofiev." But at the end of his review, he sounded an ironic note of caution, suggesting that the time might come when Prokofiev would be regarded as "the legitimate successor of Borodin, Mussorgsky and Rimsky-Korsakov." The warning was prophetic. Prokofiev is now acknowledged as a rightful heir of these great Russians, who in their time were also the targets of misguided obloquy. Perhaps the most amazing of these American reactions to Prokofiev was the report in *Musical America*:

Those who do not believe that genius is evident in superabundance of noise looked in vain for a new musical message in Mr. Prokofiev's work. Nor in the *Classical* Symphony, which the composer conducted, was there any cessation from the orgy of discordant sounds. As an exposition of the unhappy state of chaos from which Russia suffers, Mr. Prokofiev's music is interesting, but one hopes fervently that the future may hold better things both for Russia and listeners to Russian music.

It was in New York that Prokofiev produced his whimsical opera, *The Love for Three Oranges*, based on a comedy by the famous Italian eighteenth-century writer Carlo Gozzi. The opera was produced in Chicago on December 30, 1921. It leads with a prince who laughs at a witch, who, in retaliation, puts a curse on him that deprives him of all ability to laugh unless and until he finds three big oranges, which he does. A princess emerges from one of the oranges and asks for water. The prince cuts the second orange to get some orange juice to quench her thirst, but finds another princess there. He cuts the third and last orange, with a similar result. Fortunately, the third princess is not thirsty, and instead is full of romantic sentiments. There is an expected happy ending. Prokofiev's musical score is alive with rollicking melodies and exciting rhythms. The march from *The Love for Three Oranges* has become famous. Prokofiev started work on another opera in New York, *The Fiery Angel*, but completed it later in Europe.

In 1921, Prokofiev settled in Paris, the capital of modern music and modern art. There he found two champions of his music, the ballet impresario Sergei Diaghilev and the celebrated conductor Serge Koussevitzky. Prokofiev's association with Diaghilev was most fruitful, producing the ballets *Buffoon*, *Steel Step*, and *Prodigal Son*, of which the first was particularly popular. He also composed symphonies and concertos for Koussevitzky. This was a magnificent triumvirate of Sergeis. All three Sergeis were émigrés, but political estrangement from Russia was not to the youngest Sergei's liking.

In 1932, Prokofiev accepted an invitation from the Soviet government to give a few concerts of his music. In 1934, he returned permanently to Russia and settled in Moscow. He was received as a prodigal son, given a dacha to live in, an apartment in Moscow, and all the facilities for having his music performed. But in Stalin's Russia he had to tame his musical genius to meet the stipulations of "socialist realism," demanding that art be made accessible to the masses. Still, despite the annoying pressure, Prokofiev wrote some of his most felicitous scores after his return to Russia, notably the symphonic fairy tale *Peter and the Wolf*.

Prokofiev continued to compose tirelessly, for the stage, for the orchestra, for instruments, for voices. His style acquired a new nobility, and his music grew more intensely Russian in character. One of Prokofiev's most important works is the cantata *Alexander Nevsky*, based on his music for the Soviet film of the same name. Alexander Nevsky was the Russian prince who inflicted a decisive defeat on the Teutonic Knights in the battle of Lake Peipus, in Northern Russia, fought on April 5, 1242. The subject had obvious political implications. This rout of seven centuries ago would be repeated if the descendants of the Teutonic Knights would venture to attack Russia. Hitler failed to heed this musical warning, and indeed the Nazi legions suffered one of their greatest defeats near that same Lake Peipus.

Then trouble began. Prokofiev was accused of imitating the decadent ways of the West, of indulging in such cosmopolitan deviations as atonality and polytonality. He made a concession to the dominant Soviet policy of socialist realism by composing a Youth Symphony, quite conventional in its style. He even wrote an overture for Stalin's sixtieth birthday, an inferior work which received perfunctory notices (none from Stalin himself) and was politely forgotten. There was no Russian soul in his music, his Soviet detractors proclaimed. Much more ominous was the attack on Prokofiev, Shostakovich, and other Soviet composers in a resolution of the Central Committee of the Communist Party of the Soviet Union in 1948, containing accusations of "formalism" and genuflection before the West. Prokofiev replied to it with dignity, protesting that he had never questioned the paramount importance of melody and tonality, the two mainstays of traditional music, but he admitted and mildly repented for the temptations he had undergone during his sojourn in Europe and America.

At the end of his resources, and to prove that he could handle a Soviet theme, Prokofiev wrote an opera, *A Tale of a Real Man*, to an emotionally patriotic libretto dealing with a Soviet pilot who, despite the loss of both legs in combat, trained himself to use artificial limbs and was readmitted to active service. The opera was roundly condemned by Soviet officials after a private performance as lacking in melody and Russianism. Despite this rebuke, Prokofiev continued to compose productively. The hapless opera, not the best of Prokofiev's works, was premiered posthumously. The legless pilot, the hero of the opera, attended the production and expressed his admiration for Prokofiev's genius. His last symphony, the Seventh, was hailed as a true Soviet masterpiece. Predictably, it was deplored in the Western press as a sign of Prokofiev's decline.

Prokofiev died suddenly of a massive stroke in Moscow in the afternoon of March 5, 1953. By chronological irony, Stalin died in the same evening, a few hours after Prokofiev. Days passed before the composer's death was announced in the press, which was totally absorbed by the dictator's passing. Then the cult of Stalin was dispelled by his successor, Nikita Khrushchev. With the abrupt change of appreciation, Prokofiev was declared to be a great Russian composer and a postage stamp was issued in his honor, while Stalin's body was ignominiously removed from Lenin's mausoleum.

In large measure, Prokofiev helped to shape and organize the new musical language that is loosely called modern music. He began to speak it as a youth, and his contemporaries thought he was gibbering in an alien tongue. During his productive career, he gradually simplified, rather than complicated, this language, and suddenly the world began to understand it. The dissonance of Prokofiev's music has become the concord of musical children of today. Prokofiev's name has a secure place in the history of music. But to the very young among Prokofievites he is, above all, the author of *Peter and the Wolf*, a symphonic fairy tale for children, which he wrote in two weeks in April 1936 for a performance in the Children's Theater in Moscow. *Peter and the Wolf*, written for children, has enough musical spice in it to delight the professionals as well. And is not *Peter and the Wolf* a significant parable about the Nazi wolf who sets out to attack the peaceful neighbor? The bird's argument in favor of strong wings, capable of flying high, is justified by the untimely end of the unfortunate duck, a bird without air power.

ORCHESTRAL MUSIC
Sinfonietta, Op. 5/46 (1914; revised 1929)

Prokofiev wrote in his autobiography: "The first period of my creative work is classical, whose origin lies in my early childhood when I heard my mother play

Beethoven's sonatas. It assumes a neoclassical aspect in the sonatas and the concertos, or imitates the classical style of the eighteenth century, as in the Gavottes, the *Classical* Symphony, and, in some respects, in the Sinfonietta."

Prokofiev's neoclassicism, however, is vastly different from the neoclassicism of other twentieth-century composers who, having exhausted the resources of modern harmony, retreated into the safe harbors of the past. Prokofiev stylized the old forms with nostalgic irony, adding unexpected flourishes to their symmetrical arabesques, and interrupting the stately flow of quasi-classical melody with rude cadences, as if to say "Shut up!" He was the witty narrator of the old-fashioned tales, rather than a pious worshipper of the imperishable beauty of a venerated art. His best-known and most successful stylization of musical classicism was the *Classical* Symphony, written when he was twenty-six.

His Sinfonietta, composed much earlier, when he was only eighteen, is another example of neoclassicism à la Prokofiev. The original version was never performed and never published. Prokofiev rewrote the work for a performance by Alexander Siloti and his orchestra in St. Petersburg on October 24, 1915. He rewrote it again in Paris in 1929. The original score was marked Op. 5; the revision became Op. 48. The material for the second and the fourth movement was entirely new, and there is an inevitable discrepancy of style between this newly rewritten music and the virtually untouched harmonies of the first and third movements.

Symphony No. 1 in D Major, Op. 25 (Classical) (1916–17)

In wartime Petrograd (the city's name from 1914 to 1924), Prokofiev was the enfant terrible of Russian music. His piano pieces were the delight of the musical radicals, and the desperation of the pedagogues of the Petrograd Conservatory, of which Prokofiev was a product. It was not the ultramodern idiom that shocked the conservatory conservatives. Scriabin, in his last works, was much more destructive of tonality and time signature than Prokofiev ever was. But there was a certain impishness in Prokofiev that was offensive to the academic elders. The time signature, and even the tonality, were there, but the melody leaped from one octave to another, and the harmonies changed unexpectedly, in total disregard for the rules of modulation.

When Prokofiev decided to write a symphony, his first, he chose the classical idiom, partly to prove that he knew his métier, partly to tease his detractors, but mostly out of a desire to renovate, not to imitate, the classical form. Having shocked the Russian academicians with his dissonances, he set out, with exquisite irony, to write a piece of music in an entirely orthodox manner, with well-behaved harmonies, and in strict classical form—a "classical" symphony. Accordingly, he affixed the name *Classical* to his Symphony No. 1, Op. 25. He wrote it in 1916–17, fateful years for Russia, and conducted it for the first time at a concert in Petrograd—at that time a desolate, famine-stricken city—on April 21, 1918. Shortly afterward, he left Petrograd and Russia, arriving in America by the route of the Pacific Ocean, and then going to Europe.

The *Classical* Symphony in D major has an unmistakable something which is the essence of Prokofiev. There was no difficulty for Prokofiev to write in the classical style, if classicism means tonality, definite metrical structure and strong sense of form. Even the waggishness of Prokofiev's humor is classical, in the manner of Mozart and Haydn, rather than romantic à la Schumann. Prokofiev was a believer in architectonic construction, and was strongly anti-Impressionist. It would have been unnatural for Debussy to write a "classical" symphony, but for Prokofiev it was almost inevitable that he should have written one. It seems gratuitous, therefore, to suggest that he consciously tried to imitate Mozart, or any other model. For the *Classical* Symphony is not an imitation, but an augmentation, an enhancement of a style that is flexibly classical rather than stagnantly academic.

The first movement, Allegro, in $\frac{2}{4}$, opens gaily, and follows the appointed course of all classical sonatas and symphonies. The trained ear will catch some very unusual turns and modulations. The contrasting theme, in the dominant key, enters with a plunge of the violins two octaves down from a high note, with the bassoon accompanying in staccato figures. With the two themes having said their say, the official exposition of the classical form closes, and the unofficial part begins—the development section, where the themes are used in any or all keys, in various rhythmical forms. The return of the official business, or the recapitulation, comes without obvious preparation, but both themes are immediately recognizable. The movement ends gaily as it began.

This lyric second movement, Larghetto, in $\frac{3}{4}$ time, is built on the model of a brief rondo. The principal melody begins on a high note of the violin (Prokofiev was fond of this device), and the mood is established forthwith. Episodes are introduced for contrast, and the pulse of the music is accelerated through the use of variations. The principal melody is heard for the third time, and the movement closes gently.

The third movement, Gavotte, is a tour de force of stylization. The form is perfect; the Gavotte starts with a half-bar upbeat, according to the customary formula, and the tonality is clear D major. A musette in G forms the middle section, giving the bagpipe effect, and the Gavotte returns, with slight modifications, ending gracefully without modern pretensions. But every bar brings a modulatory surprise. Prokofiev heads toward one key and lands in another, or so it seems. At strategic moments, however, there is always the expected tonic, and its appearance is timed according to the symmetry of the dance. A Russian poet of olden times used a happy figure for such welcome unexpectedness: "It is like cool lemonade in summertime."

The Finale is in $\frac{2}{4}$, and again in sonata form. The orchestration is deft, and the woodwind instruments are treated with particular felicity. When the principal section returns in the form of a recapitulation, the orchestration is modified, a procedure that avoids the monotony of academic repetition. The ending is brilliant.

Concerto No. 1 in D Major for Violin and Orchestra, Op. 19 (1916–1917)

Prokofiev began his career as an enfant terrible of Russian music. He horrified his professors at the St. Petersburg Conservatory by his musical inventions, including a piece written in two keys simultaneously. But he fascinated the moderns of his day by his intransigence, his daring, and his self-assurance. His percussive piano playing, in programs of his own works, with his strong fingers leaping in all directions at once, electrified sympathetic young audiences. Some called him a "white Negro," alluding to the unbridled syncopation of ragtime as performed by black Americans in vaudeville shows.

Despite his rebellious modernism (which he preferred to call *novatorstvo*, "innovationism"), Prokofiev kept faith with classical form and tonal harmony. His *Classical* Symphony demonstrates his ability to pull the *Zopf* ("pigtail") off the classical scalp, while retaining the viable elements of the old cranial structure. His famous fairy tale for children, *Peter and the Wolf*, written in a manner entirely free from elementary condescension, shows his natural affinity for the imaginative world of the very young.

Prokofiev's First Violin Concerto was written in 1917, when he was twenty-six, shortly before he left Russia for a lengthy sojourn in Western Europe. Its first performance did not take place until October 18, 1923, in Paris, with Marcel Darrieux as the soloist and Serge Koussevitzky conducting the orchestra. The concerto is in three movements, Andantino, Vivacissimo, and Moderato, in the key of D major, a tonality eminently suitable for the instrument. It is written in a virtuoso style, but its bravura is subordinated to the musical content.

The melodic, rhythmic, and harmonic elements of the score represent the four principal characteristics of Prokofiev's music, as he enumerated them himself in his autobiographical notes: classical, innovative, motoric, and lyrical. In the opening movement, a general sense of tranquillity envelops the music. The second movement is a typical scherzo, and here he indulges his whimsy. There are special effects such as glissandos ending in harmonics, pizzicatos with the fingers of the left hand, etc. The finale returns to the contemplative mood of the opening movement, bringing the work to a close in a satisfyingly cyclical form.

Concerto No. 3 in C Major for Piano and Orchestra, Op. 26 (1917–21)

The career of Sergei Prokofiev is a tale of dramatic progress, from his early days as an enfant terrible in Old Russia who exasperated the bourgeoisie by his aggressively discordant music to his posthumous glorification as the true heir to the Russian national school of composition. Soviet musicologists made a convincing case in demonstrating that Prokofiev's most enduring works were written in Russia, and that his talent went into an eclipse during his peregrinations in Europe and America. Indeed, Prokofiev's most popular works—the *Classical* Symphony, *Peter and the Wolf, Romeo and Juliet*—were all composed in Russia. The sole exception seems to be the Third Piano Concerto, which Prokofiev played for the first time with the Chicago Symphony Orchestra on December 16, 1921. However, the concerto was sketched in almost complete detail before Prokofiev left Russia in 1918.

It has been a critical cliché to describe Prokofiev's music as being exclusively the product of rhythmic energy with little lyrical content. Prokofiev dispatched a wrathful letter to the author remonstrating with him for having stated in an article that there is an absolute preponderance of marching rhythms in Prokofiev's music, rebuking him for underestimating its inherent lyrical quality, and pointing out that $\frac{3}{4}$ meters are encountered as frequently in his scores as marching $\frac{4}{4}$ time.

The Third Piano Concerto tends to prove Prokofiev's contention. There is as much lyric sentiment in it as propulsive rhythmic energy. The introductory andante is music with a smile—diatonic, relaxed, humane. But immediately after that, an assault of virile bravura is launched on the white keys of the piano. Not a single sharp, not a flat, mars the whiteness of the precipitant scales and arpeggios in this Allegro for several pages of the score. Such displays of C-major power are hallmarks of Prokofiev's piano writing. The rhythmic momentum never slackens until an abrupt ending on C in unison.

The second movement, Andantino, is a theme with variations. The musical texture is limpid; the piano part is interlaced with the accommodating orchestral accompaniment in an untrammeled contrapuntal web. It is a poetic interlude of singular attractiveness.

The third and last movement, Allegro ma non troppo, in rondo form, opens with an ingratiatingly bland phrase in modally inflected A minor. Prokofiev's familiar tendency toward plagal cadences intensifies the modal impression. There are several extended cadenzas of fresh thematic content. In the coda, the orchestra is drawn into full participation. The concerto concludes pragmatically in a forceful succession of pandiatonically enriched C-major triads.

Divertimento, Op. 43 (1925, 1929)

The Divertimento is only nominally neoclassical. The title goes back to eighteenth-century practice, and so do the markings of the four movements. But the melodic and harmonic language is uncompromisingly modernistic. The Divertimento is compounded of materials from different periods. The first and third movements are taken from the ballet *Trapeze*, which Prokofiev wrote in 1925; the remaining movements were completed in 1929. The opus number was assigned later, and does not represent the exact chronology of his creative catalogue.

The first movement is marked Moderato, molto ritmato. There are harsh-sounding chords that might illustrate a determined action of scrubbing the floor clean, the relentless rhythmic drive that is characteristic of the Russian ballet. But then there is suddenly heard a celestially tender chant, for the entry of gauze-clad ballerinas. The second movement, Larghetto, is not dependent on a ballet scene; it is a simple lyric invocation of the quality that Prokofiev himself regarded as of the greatest importance in his work. "My lyricism has for a long time been unappreciated, and it has for this reason, grown but slowly," he wrote in his autobiography. "But in later works, I devoted more and more attention to lyric expression."

The third movement, Allegro energico, is a spirited dance. In this movement, too, the stage action is vividly suggested by the music. This is a strongly rhythmed dance, with stamping and jumping. The last movement, Allegro non troppo e pesante, is, on the other hand, an exposition of purely musical, nonchoreographic elements. There are characteristic scale runs, beginning in one key and passing without benefit of modulatory transitions into another, a semitone higher as to the tonic. The mood changes from fast milling motion to songful meditation, in sudden contrasts, typical of Prokofiev's music.

Prokofiev conducted the first performance of the Divertimento in Paris on December 22, 1929. The reception was mixed; some critics found it a dazzling score, one of Prokofiev's best; others were not so sure. The critic of *Le Ménestrel* complained that the Divertimento was as little diverting as possible.

Concerto No. 5 in G Major for Piano and Orchestra, Op. 55 (1932)

Prokofiev wrote five piano concertos. The first was his graduation piece at the St. Petersburg Conservatory. The third became a standard work of the modern piano repertory. The Fourth Concerto, for left hand alone, was written for the one-armed Austrian pianist Paul Wittgenstein. The Fifth Piano Concerto, composed in Paris in 1932, represents the Western, neoclassical, and hedonistic period in Prokofiev's career. It originally bore a noncommittal title, Musique pour piano et orchestre, following the fashion of absolute music then prevalent in Europe. This derivation explains the fact that the work is in five movements rather than the usual three, thus assuming the structure of an instrumental suite with piano concertante. Prokofiev gave its first performance in Berlin on October 31, 1932, with Wilhelm Furtwängler conducting the Berlin Philharmonic.

The first movement, Allegro con brio, traverses the basic outline of sonata, in an abbreviated form, approximating that of a sonatina. There are two contrasting subjects, a vigorous fanfarelike projection, and a balladlike lyrical theme. The exposition is characteristically laconic, and the themes follow one another without gratuitous obliquity. Toward the end of the movement there is a lively antiphonal interchange between the soloist and the orchestra.

The second movement, Moderato ben accentuato, is a scherzo-march in rondo form. It is marked by the spirit of grotesquerie, reminiscent of Prokofiev's youthful *Sarcasms*. The third movement is Toccata: Allegro con fuoco. The toccata was always Prokofiev's favorite Baroque form, fitting perfectly into the scheme of his modern pianism. The element of mechanistic constructivism, fashionable at the time, finds its reflection in this toccata. The fourth movement is Larghetto. Here, Prokofiev is a true lyricist. A pastoral quietude breathes in the leisurely flow of this movement, permeated by the bucolic poetry of an eclogue.

The Finale: Vivo, is a study in digital dexterity. The music drives on with ruthless determination to a coda in a pyrotechnical display of G-major chords. It is interesting to note that virtually all the themes and motives in Prokofiev's Fifth Piano Concerto are in major keys, symbolic perhaps of the artificial optimism animating musicians and politicians alike in the era of unstable equilibrium between two world cataclysms.

Concerto No. 2 in G Minor for Violin and Orchestra, Op. 63 (1935)

As a professional pianist, Prokofiev naturally devoted much of his energies to the composition of piano music, but he also made a careful study of other instrumental techniques, and wrote concertos for violin and for the violoncello. His First Violin Concerto was composed in 1917 and presents a fine blend of Prokofiev's rhythmic propulsion and lyric poetry. He wrote his Second Violin Concerto in 1935, specially for the Belgian violinist Robert Soetens, with whom Prokofiev made a concert tour in Spain, Portugal, Morocco, Algeria, and Tunisia. The first performance took place in Madrid on December 1, 1935, with Prokofiev present in the audience. The soloist was Soetens, and the conductor was Fernández Arbós.

Prokofiev's Second Violin Concerto is, like the first, set in three movements, but stylistically the two concertos are different. The later work lacks the grotesquerie typical of young Prokofiev, and it is less cosmopolitan, more national than Prokofiev's previous instrumental compositions. Like the First Concerto, it is firmly tonal, but digressions from the fundamental key of G minor start immediately after the opening of the first movement, Allegro moderato. The form of sonata-allegro is clearly discernible, however. A lyrical second subject appears in fine contrast with the energetic first subject. Russian commentators find national melodic traits in Prokofiev's lyrical expansiveness here. Modulations are multitudinous; at least eight statements in eight different keys, major and minor, of both subjects can be found in the first movement.

The second movement, Andante assai, represents a set of variations, a technique in which Prokofiev was a master. The violin passages approach the Baroque usages in their elaboration, but the texture is light and the solo part is never obstructed.

The Finale: Allegro ben marcato, is full of kinetic energy, a modern bacchanal—brusque, aggressive, impetuous. The violin tosses its accented tones over its entire range. It is a typical display of Prokofiev's spirited manner, which led some friendly critics to describe his productions as "soccer music." And, for the first time in the concerto, there are identifiable modernites, such as polytonality. The rhythmic design is strongly accented, but there are sudden abscissions and apocopes, creating a stimulating asymmetry. There is an extraordinarily long coda, but the ending, with a plagal cadence often favored by Prokofiev, and with acridly dissonant harmonies, is decisive and curt.

Symphonie Concertante *in E Minor for Violoncello and Orchestra, Op. 125 (1952)*

Prokofiev was a pianist of unique powers, capable of maintaining an even percussive beat with his steely long fingers without deviating from a set tempo. It was a technique ideally suited for the performance of his own piano works. But he encountered difficulties in composing for other instruments in a virtuoso style. In technical matters he sought the advice of professionals, much as Brahms and Dvořák consulted with the violinist Joseph Joachim to help them along in the technical details of their violin concertos. In his violin music, Prokofiev had David Oistrakh for his Joachim. For his cello works, he had Mstislav Rostropovich.

Prokofiev's *Symphonie Concertante* is the doppelgänger of his First Concerto for cello and orchestra, written in 1938. He rewrote it radically, leaving intact only the designation of tempo of the movements and the principal tonality, E minor. What was to be a revision of his First Cello Concerto became practically a new piece. During the composition of this nonidentical musical twin, Prokofiev discussed technical details with Rostropovich in numerous sessions. The score was completed in 1952. Rostropovich played it for the first time in Moscow on February 18, 1952, a little more than a year before Prokofiev died.

It must be recalled that Prokofiev's last years of life were darkened by a series of personal and professional disasters. He had divorced his first wife, mother of his two sons, and married a younger woman, which alienated many of his friends. He was beset by circulatory ailments. Most ominous of all, he could not come to terms with the Soviet officialdom. He was made a target of the infamous decree of the Central Committee of the Communist Party of the USSR of February 10, 1948, for his modernistic aberrations and allegedly un-Soviet attitudes toward the official doctrine of socialist realism. He refused to go to Stalin's Canossa, and responded to the charges in a coldly factual letter, free of the expected protestations of loyalty or expressions of penitence.

In his instrumental music, Prokofiev was always a man of the theater, even though he never attached an explicit program to his symphonies and concertos. In his book on Prokofiev's symphonies, the Soviet composer Sergei Slonimsky (nephew of the author) speaks of the "cinematographic character" of Prokofiev's symphonic structures: "Just as in the cinema the artistic power of separate images is subordinated to the general creative concept and is infinitely expanded by its continuous succession, so in Prokofiev's symphonic production the juxtaposition and mutual relationship of numerous concrete episodes and incisive graphic details are parts of the purely symphonic thematic development and form."

The *Symphonie Concertante* justifies its title by its consistent symphonic development. There are three movements. The first, in E minor, in $\frac{2}{4}$ time, is marked Andante. After a stormy but brief exordium in a series of divergent dissonant chords, the cello plays a gentle E-minor solo, built in swaying patterns with impulsive accents. The violins pick up the tune for a while; then the cello resumes its role as soloist. A dramatic change supervenes in a ponderous passage of accented beats, with the cello growling on the low C string. Rhythmic density increases; the orchestra roars; the cello solo travels from the lowest to the highest region of its range while maintaining a steady metric pace. The tonal fabric remains clear, but there are rapid modulations. The music comes to a boil in a succession of modal-sounding minor-seventh chords. After a lyric episode, followed by a review of the principal thematic materials, the tempo slackens to adagio, and the movement concludes in quiet E minor.

The second movement, Allegro giusto, in ⁴⁄₄ time, in C major, is a kinetic toccata. The form of toccata is a favorite of Prokofiev, for it enables him to maintain a steady motion, creating a reservoir of cumulative energy. The pianistic key of C major holds Prokofiev in thrall even in writing for other instruments. When Prokofiev as a brash young man first assailed the academic ears of Russian audiences early in the century, he was called a soccer player of music. In his *Symphonie Concertante*, and particularly in the second movement, Prokofiev plays the game of soccer without allowing any interference on purely conventional grounds. But after a period of purposeful exertion, there is a dulcet episode in E major marked by a tranquilizing oscillating rhythm. The cello is given a long cadenza, and then the toccata movement resumes its course. The tonality is bland D minor, arrayed in triadic harmonies, but is ornamented by overhanging semitones which form atonal stalactites. Prokofiev's artful game then changes to antiphonal tennis, with softball chords tossed from the orchestra to the cello and back. The melodies, the harmonies, the rhythms are very Russian in the lyric interludes, such as a cantabile passage in the cello. Once more the sonorities swell up, and the cello sweeps the ground in large ambulating intervals. The toccata movement returns, Allegro assai, with an A-major ending.

The third and last movement, Andante con moto, in ³⁄₄, is in the key of E major, in classical correspondence to the initial key of E minor. There is a recitative in the cello part, followed by a harmonious chorale. The tempo changes decisively to vivace in ³⁄₄ time. The rhythmic impetus is unfaltering in its steadfast succession of even eighth notes, and later in even quarter notes. The rondolike progress is free of circumlocution. The ending, on the tonic E, is pert, terse, and curt.

OTHER WORKS
The Fiery Angel *(1919)*

A subject that fascinated Russian composers was the realm of religious superstition magnified by the earnest belief in the power of witches. But rather than select a Russian tale of witchcraft, as did Glinka, Mussorgsky, and Rimsky-Korsakov, Prokofiev became interested in a historical drama after a novel by the Russian writer Valery Bryusov, *The Fiery Angel*, dealing with the tremendous upheaval during the Counter-Reformation in Germany in the sixteenth century.

A young woman, Renata, who suffers from hysteria, is accused of having carnal relations with Satan. She is protected by the heroic knight Ruprecht, who dares to deny the existence of witches. In this opera, Prokofiev adopts the unusual, for him, system of leitmotivs. Among secondary figures in the libretto are the terrifying image of the Grand Inquisitor and the almost comic attendants, Faust (who sings bass) and Mephistopheles (who is given the part of a tenor). *The Fiery Angel* of the title is Renata's treacherous lover, Count Heinrich, who abandons her after a brief encounter. The climax of the opera is Renata's trial as a witch (for she refuses to admit that the Fiery Angel is really the devil) and her immolation at the stake.

The score, composed in 1919, is perhaps the most effective of Prokofiev's stage works. Yet it had to wait many years before its first complete production, at the Venice Festival on September 14, 1955, more than two years after Prokofiev's death. Refusing to wait indefinitely for the production, Prokofiev used some thematic materials from *The Fiery Angel* in his Third Symphony.

String Quartet No. 1, Op. 50 (1931)

The String Quartet Op. 50, was a commissioned work, written for the Library of Congress and first performed by the Brosa Quartet at the Elizabeth Sprague Coolidge Festival in Washington, D.C., on April 25, 1931. It has an unusual construction: there are two slow Andante movements separated by a fast interlude. The material of the last movement of the quartet is used in one of the six piano pieces in Opus 52. Prokofiev frequently transplanted ideas and thematic material from one medium to another. This suggests that his musical thoughts had an absolute character, independent of the particular instrumental combination in which they originally appear. Yet Prokofiev was supremely adept in his use of instrumental techniques and his understanding of the nature of the instruments was complete. There was no idle experimenting, no splashes of impressionistic color, no counterpoint for counterpoint's sake only. Prokofiev used his medium economically and efficiently. His was the technique of classical music even though his harmony and rhythm were products of modern times.

Peter and the Wolf (1936)

There is a quality in all of Prokofiev's music that makes it peculiarly appealing. It is, perhaps, the underlying simplicity of the musical phrase, a strong feeling for a central tonality, the driving rhythmic pulse. Prokofiev's music is always marching on in ¼ time, with dreamy lyrical interludes in ⅜ time for a contrast. In Soviet Russia, where Prokofiev made his home after years abroad, this marching quality was associated with optimism; and the lyrical strain was taken to reflect the universal humanism of emotion. Prokofiev was, therefore, accepted in Russia as a positive artistic force "consonant" with the times.

Prokofiev wrote much music based on fairy tales, but it is only in *Peter and the Wolf* that he succeeded in creating a masterpiece which, like the best in children's literature, appeals to sophisticated adults as well. The primary purpose in writing this "symphonic tale for children," as it is subtitled, was to teach the children to recognize the instruments of the orchestra. Each character is represented by an instrument, or a group of instruments: the bird by the flute, the duck by the oboe, the cat by the clarinet in the low register playing staccato, Grandfather by the bassoon, the wolf by the chord of three French horns, Peter by the strings, the shots of the hunters by the kettledrums and the bass drum.

Each character is also given a special leading motive. These leading motives are supposed to be played on the corresponding instruments before the performance so the children learn to associate them with the characters of the tale. The story, which is Prokofiev's own, is told by the narrator to the accompaniment of the music, or between the episodes, during the pauses. The tale has also an implied political significance, for in it the wolf, who during his career as a ruthless aggressor has gobbled up the defenseless duck and threatened the safety of the cat and the bird, is finally outwitted by the Soviet Boy Scout Peter, is caged by the hunters who come to Peter's aid, and is placed in the zoo for everyone to behold and marvel.

The original production of *Peter and the Wolf* took place at the Children's Theater in Moscow on May 2, 1936. Prokofiev sketched the music during the month of April 1936, and completed the scoring only a week before the performance. The text of the tale, with hints as to the orchestration, follows:

Early one morning Peter opened the gate and went out on a big green meadow. [Strings playing Peter's leading motive.] On a branch of a big tree sat a little bird, Peter's friend. "All is quiet," chirped the bird gaily. [The flute plays the bird's theme, later joined by violins pizzicato and the oboe. Peter's motive appears in the strings, while the flute plays roulades.]

Soon a duck came waddling around. She was glad that Peter had not closed the gate, and decided to take a nice swim in the deep pond in the meadow. [The duck's theme is played by the oboe, accompanied by other woodwinds and strings.] The flute-bird chirps in the high treble.

Seeing the duck, the little bird flew down upon the grass, settled next to the duck, and shrugged her shoulders: "What kind of bird are you if you can't fly?" said she. To this the duck replied: "What kind of bird are you if you can't swim?" and dived into the pond. [This dialogue is pictured in the orchestra by the roulades of the flute and the theme of the duck played by the oboe.]

They argued and argued, the duck swimming in the pond, the little bird hopping along the shore. Suddenly something caught Peter's attention. He noticed a cat crawling through the grass. [The cat's theme appears in the clarinet, playing staccato in the low register, and accompanied by the double-bass.] The cat thought: "The bird is busy arguing. I'll just grab her." Stealthily she crept toward her on her velvet paws. [The cat's theme is played a fourth higher by the clarinet.] "Look out," shouted Peter, and the bird immediately flew up into the tree [fluttering arpeggios in the flute against the pizzicatos of the strings], while the duck quacked angrily at the cat from the middle of the pond. The cat crawled around the tree and thought: "Is it worth climbing up so high? By the time I get there the bird will have flown away." [The cat's theme continues in the clarinet and there are gasping sounds in the flute.]

Grandfather came out. He was angry because Peter had gone to the meadow. It is a dangerous place. If a wolf should come out of the forest, then what would he do? [A grumbling phrase in the low register of the bassoon, against harp beats of the strings.] Peter paid no attention to Grandfather's words and declared that Boy Scouts are not afraid of wolves. [Peter's theme in the strings, doubled by the clarinet.] But grandfather took Peter by the hand, led him home, and locked the gate [Grandfather's theme in the bassoon].

No sooner had Peter gone than a big gray wolf came out of the forest. [Three horns in a sinister theme in a minor key.] The cat quickly scurried up the tree. [The cat's theme rising chromatically in the low register of the clarinet.] The duck quacked, and in her excitement jumped out of the pond. No matter how hard the duck tried to run, she couldn't escape the wolf. He was getting nearer, nearer, catching up with her, and then he's got her, and with one gulp swallowed her. [The muted trumpet trills on a high note. The cello harmonic is the duck's last sound, then the oboe "sadly and expressively" plays the duck's theme in pianissimo.]

And now, this is how things stood: the cat was sitting on one branch, the bird on another, not too close to the cat, and the wolf walked around the tree looking at them with greedy eyes. In the meantime, Peter stood without the slightest fear behind the closed gate watching all that was going on. He ran home, took a strong rope and climbed up the high stone wall. One of the branches of the tree around which the wolf was walking stretched out over the wall. Grabbing hold of the branch, Peter lightly climbed over onto the tree. Peter said to the bird: "Fly down and circle around the wolf's head, only take care that he doesn't catch you." [Each character is followed by his leading motive in the orchestra, but now the flute plays Peter's theme.]

The bird almost touched the wolf's head with her wings while the wolf snapped angrily at her from this side and that. How the bird did worry the wolf! How he wanted to catch her! But the bird was cleverer, and the wolf couldn't do anything about it [repeated chords in the orchestra].

Meanwhile, Peter made a lasso and, carefully letting it down, caught the wolf by the tail and pulled with all his might. [The lasso is represented by swirling passages in the violin.] Feeling himself caught, the wolf began to jump wildly, trying to get loose [muted trumpet with a loud chords in the orchestra]. But Peter tied the other end of the rope to the tree, and the wolf's jumping only made the rope around his tail tighter.

At that moment a group of hunters came out of the woods, following the wolf's trail and shooting as they went [a rollicking march in the orchestra]. Peter, sitting in the tree, shouted: "Don't shoot! Birdie and I have already caught the wolf. Now help us take him to the zoo." [Peter's theme in waltz time.]

And now imagine the triumphant procession: Peter at the head, after him the hunters leading the wolf, and, winding up the procession, Grandfather and the cat. Grandfather tossed his head discontentedly: "Well, and if Peter hadn't caught the wolf? What then?" [The cat's clarinet theme and grandfather's bassoon theme in counterpoint. Then Peter's theme in the brass.] Above them flew the bird, chirping merrily: "My, what fine follows we are, Peter and I! Look, what we have caught!" [Flute playing variations on the hunters' march]. And if one would listen very carefully, he could hear the duck quacking in the wolf's belly, because the wolf in his hurry swallowed her alive. [The oboe plays the duck's theme, then the orchestra leads to a brief finale.]

Cinderella *(1946)*

Russian composers have always favored operas and ballets on the subject of virtue conquering evil; fairy tales are natural scenarios for such bittersweet productions. Prokofiev contributed to this genre in his ballet *Cinderella*; in it the repressed "cinder girl" wins the love of a prince, much to the annoyance of her envious stepsisters. The score is written in the classical manner, emulating the musical choreography of the European Rococo. "I want to make my Cinderella as danceable as possible," Prokofiev wrote in one of his pronouncements. And indeed, the music dances in numerous court entertainments, variations, gavottes, and interludes.

The overall style is typical of Prokofiev; there is a gentle irony in depicting Cinderella's gradual emancipation, and the orchestral sonority is subdued. In fact, Soviet critics complained that Prokofiev's tonal painting was "too tender" for the tradition of grand ballet, and even suggested a more robust and louder orchestration. In the end, Prokofiev's treatment of the fairy tale won out, and *Cinderella*, as a ballet and in the form of orchestral suites, became one of his most popular compositions. It was first produced in Moscow on November 21, 1945.

DMITRI SHOSTAKOVICH
(1906–1975)
Besieged Nationalist

Dmitri Dmitrievich Shostakovich's style and idiom of composition largely defined the nature of new Russian music. He was a member of a cultured Russian family: his father was an engineer employed in the government office of weights and measures, and his mother was a professional pianist. Shostakovich grew up during the most difficult period of Russian Revolutionary history, when famine and disease decimated the population of Petrograd (now St. Petersburg). Of frail physique, he suffered from malnutrition. Glazunov, the director of the Petrograd Conservatory, appealed personally to the commissar of education, Lunacharsky, to grant an increased food ration for Shostakovich, essential for his physical survival.

At the age of nine he commenced piano lessons with his mother, and in 1919 he entered the Petrograd Conservatory, where he studied piano with Leonid Nikolayev and composition with Maximilian Steinberg, graduating in piano in 1923, and in composition in 1925. As a graduation piece, he submitted his First Symphony, Op. 10, written at the age of eighteen. It was first performed by the Leningrad Philharmonic on May 12, 1926, under the direction of Nicolas Malko, and subsequently became one of Shostakovich's most popular works. His Second Symphony, Op. 14, composed for the tenth anniversary of the Russian Revolution in 1927, bearing the dedication "To October" and ending with a rousing choral finale, was less successful despite its Revolutionary sentiment. He then wrote a satirical opera, *The Nose*, Op. 15, after Gogol's whimsical story about the sudden disappearance of the nose from the face of a government functionary. Here, Shostakovich revealed his flair for musical satire; the score featured a variety of modernistic devices. *The Nose* was produced in Leningrad on January 12, 1930, to considerable popular acclaim, but was attacked by officious theater critics as a product of "bourgeois decadence," and was quickly withdrawn from the stage.

Somewhat in the same satirical style was the ballet *The Golden Age*, Op. 22 (1930), which included a celebrated dissonant polka, satirizing the current disarmament conference in Geneva. There followed the Symphony No. 3, Op. 20, with a choral finale saluting International Workers' Day. Despite its explicit Revolutionary content, it failed to earn the approbation of Soviet spokesmen, who dismissed the work as nothing more than a formal gesture of proletarian solidarity. Shostakovich's next work was to precipitate a crisis in his career, as well as in Soviet music in general: it was an opera to the libretto drawn from a short story by the nineteenth- century Russian writer Nikolai Leskov, entitled *Lady Macbeth of the District of Mtzensk*. It was produced in Leningrad on January 22, 1934, and was hailed by most Soviet musicians as a significant work comparable to the best productions of Western modern opera. But both the staging and the music ran counter to growing Soviet puritanism. A symphonic interlude portraying a scene of adultery behind the bedroom curtain, orchestrated with suggestive passages on the slide trombones, shocked the Soviet officials present at the performance by its bold naturalism. After the Moscow production of the opera, *Pravda*, the official organ of the Communist party, published an unsigned (and therefore all the more authoritative) article accusing Shostakovich of creating a "bedlam of noise." The brutality of this assault dismayed Shostakovich, who readily admitted his faults in both content and treatment of the subject, and declared his solemn determination to write music according to the then-emerging formula of "socialist realism."

Shostakovich's next stage production was a ballet, *The Limpid Brook*, Op. 39, portraying pastoral scenes on a Soviet collective farm. In this work, he tempered his dissonant idiom, and the subject seemed eminently fitting for the Soviet theater. But it, too, was condemned in *Pravda*, this time for an insufficiently dignified treatment of Soviet life. Having been rebuked twice for two radically different theater works, Shostakovich abandoned all attempts to write for the stage, and returned to purely instrumental composition. But, as though pursued by vengeful fate, he again suffered a painful reverse. His Symphony No. 4, Op. 43 (1935–36), was placed in rehearsal by the Leningrad Philharmonic, but withdrawn before the performance when representatives of musical officialdom and even the orchestra musicians themselves sharply criticized the piece. Shostakovich's rehabilitation finally came with the production of his Symphony No. 5, Op. 47 (first performance, Leningrad, November 21, 1937), a work of rhapsodic grandeur, culminating in a powerful climax. It was hailed, as though by spontaneous consensus, as a model of true Soviet art, classical in formal design, lucid in its harmonic idiom, and optimistic in its philosophical connotations.

The pinnacle of his rise to recognition was achieved in his Symphony No. 7, Op. 60. He began its composition during the siege of Leningrad by the Germans in the autumn of 1941. He served in the fire brigade during the air raids, then flew from Leningrad to the temporary Soviet capital in Kuibishev, on the Volga, where he completed the score, which was performed there on March 1, 1942. Its symphonic development is realistic in the extreme, with the theme of the Nazis, in mechanical march time, rising to monstrous loudness, only to be overcome and reduced to a pathetic drum dribble by a victorious Russian song. The work became a musical symbol of the Russian struggle against the overwhelmingly superior German war machine. It was given the nickname "Leningrad," and was performed during the war by virtually every orchestra in the Allied countries.

After the tremendous emotional appeal of the "Leningrad" Symphony, the Symphony No. 8, written in 1943, had a lesser impact. The Ninth, Tenth, and Eleventh Symphonies followed (1945, 1953, 1957) without attracting much comment; the Twelfth, Op. 112 (1960–61), dedicated to the memory of Lenin, aroused a little more interest. But it was left for his Symphony No. 13, Op. 113, premiered in Leningrad on December 18, 1962, to create a controversy that seemed to be Shostakovich's peculiar destiny. Its vocal first movement for solo bass and male chorus, to words by the Soviet poet Yevgeny Yevtushenko, expressing the horror of the massacre of Jews by the Nazis during their occupation of the city of Kiev and containing a warning against residual anti-Semitism in Soviet Russia, met with unexpected criticism by the chairman of the Communist party, Nikita Khrushchev, who complained about the exclusive attention in Yevtushenko's poem to Jewish victims, and his failure to mention the Ukrainians and other nationals who were also slaughtered. The text of the poem was altered to meet these objections, but the Symphony No. 13 never gained wide acceptance. There followed the remarkable Symphony No. 14, Op. 135 (1969), in eleven sections, scored for voices and orchestra, to words by Federico García Lorca, Apollinaire, Rilke, and the Russian poet Kuchelbecker.

Shostakovich's last symphony, No. 15, Op. 141, performed in Moscow under the direction of his son Maxim on January 8, 1972, demonstrated his undying spirit of innovation. The score is set in the key of C major, but it contains a dodecaphonic passage and literal allusions to motives from Rossini's *William Tell* Overture and the fate motive from Wagner's *The Valkyries*. Shostakovich's adoption, however limited, of themes built on twelve different notes, a procedure that he had himself condemned as antimusical, is interesting both from the psychological and sociological standpoint. He experimented with these techniques in several other works—his first explicit use of a twelve-tone subject occurred in his Twelfth String Quartet (1968). Equally illuminating is the use in some of his scores of a personal monogram DSCH (based on the German spelling of his name), standing for the notes D, Es, C, and H, German nomenclature for D, E-flat, C, and B.

One by one, his early works, originally condemned as unacceptable to Soviet reality, were returned to the stage and the concert hall. The objectionable Fourth and Thirteenth Symphonies were published and recorded. The operas *The Nose* and *Lady Macbeth of the District of Mtzensk* (renamed *Katerina Izmailova*, after the name of the heroine) had several successful revivals.

What is remarkable about Shostakovich is the unfailing consistency of his style of composition. His entire oeuvre, from his first work to the last (147 opus numbers in all), proclaims a personal article of faith. His idiom is unmistakably of the twentieth century, making free use of dissonant harmonies and intricate contrapuntal designs, yet never abandoning inherent tonality. His music is teleological, leading invariably to a tonal climax, often in a triumphal triadic declaration. Most of his works carry key signatures and his metrical structure is governed by a unifying rhythmic pulse. Shostakovich is equally eloquent in dramatic and lyric utterance; he has no fear of prolonging his slow movements in relentless dynamic rise and fall, and the cumulative power of his kinetic drive in rapid movements is overwhelming.

Through all the peripeties of his career, he never changed his musical language in its fundamental modalities. When the flow of his music met obstacles, whether technical or external, he obviated them without changing the main direction. In a special announcement issued after Shostakovich's death, the government of the USSR summarized his work as a "remarkable example of fidelity to the traditions of musical classicism, and above all, to the Russian traditions, finding his inspiration in the reality of Soviet life, reasserting and developing in his creative innovations the art of socialist realism, and in so doing, contributing to universal progressive musical culture."

ORCHESTRAL MUSIC
Symphony No. 1, Op. 10 (1924–25)

Shostakovich's First Symphony, so popular in Russia and abroad, was a graduation piece, composed at the age of nineteen. It was performed by the Leningrad Philharmonic under the direction of Nicolas Malko, on May 12, 1926. There are four movements, and the symphony follows the standard form with this difference: not the third, but the second movement is a scherzo (as in Beethoven's Ninth).

Shostakovich remained faithful to this form in all his symphonies, and in the great majority of his other compositions. But within each movement there are deviations and striking individual touches that make for unmistakable originality. In the recapitulation he usually reverses the order of the first and second subjects of a sonata-allegro. The instrumentation is individualized, and Shostakovich likes to open a symphony with an instrumental solo. From the metric-rhythmic standpoint, there is a remarkable insistence on duple time. The rhythmic figure of an eighth note and two sixteenths is particularly frequent. When, as in the first movement of the First Symphony, there are episodes in $\frac{3}{4}$ time, they often take the form of a caricature of a waltz.

This prevalence of duple time in Shostakovich's music is not peculiar to Shostakovich among Soviet composers, and it has something to do with a general, if unformulated, feeling that the marching duple time expresses healthy optimism, while the languid dactylic $\frac{3}{4}$ time suggests laxity of spirit, out of keeping with the revolutionary times. It is also characteristic that in Shostakovich's music, as in the music of other Soviet composers, passages in $\frac{3}{4}$ time are usually in minor modes. A notable exception to this is the Shostakovich type of rapid scherzo. But such scherzos are invariably *a quattro battute* (in four beats), and are simply masked bars of $\frac{12}{4}$ or $\frac{12}{8}$.

The following characteristics of Shostakovich's technique in the First Symphony became his trademarks, and are found in virtually the entire repertoire o his symphonic and chamber music:

1. A highly rhythmic opening subject, fundamentally diatonic, but embellished with chromatics. This theme is usually given to the clarinet or bassoon.
2. Individualized instrumentation with frequent division of the strings, and special effects, such as violin glissandos.

3. Exploitation of the lowest and highest registers, particularly the low reaches of the brass and high notes in the strings.
4. Independent role of the percussion. There is a kettledrum solo at the end of the First Symphony.
5. Inclusion of the piano in the orchestral score.
6. Inverted pedals in tremolos in the violins. In the second movement of the First Symphony, the high E in the second violins is repeated 576 times at a stretch, for the total duration of one minute and thirty-eight seconds.
7. Extensive scale runs.
8. Sudden modulations, directly into the tonic.

Symphony No. 5, Op. 47 (1937)

On September 25, 1966, on the occasion of his sixtieth birthday, Dmitri Shostakovich was awarded the highest honor of the Soviet Union, the Order of Hero of Socialist Labor. He was the first Soviet musician to be given this distinction. A sentimental tribute was tendered him on the same day by the Union of Soviet Composers, which organized a concert of his works in Moscow with his son Maxim as conductor. Shostakovich received an ovation at the end of the concert.

It was not always that Shostakovich was honored in his native land. He knew bitter disappointments and was repeatedly attacked by the self-appointed legislators of Soviet dogma according to the gospel of socialist realism. Particularly vicious was a 1936 article in *Pravda* entitled "Bedlam Instead of Music," which condemned Shostakovich for the signs of decadence and modernistic aberrations in his opera *Lady Macbeth of the District of Mtzensk*, ominously pointing out that the opera was suspiciously successful in Western Europe and America. This was followed a short time later with a similar blast in *Pravda* for Shostakovich's faulty representation of the life on a Soviet collective farm in one of his ballets.

Discouraged and humiliated, Shostakovich abandoned the musical theater and returned to his first love, symphonic music. Shostakovich had every expectation to recoup his fortunes by writing a new symphony. His First Symphony, which he wrote at the age of eighteen, scored an immediate success, with repeated performances all over the world. His Second and Third Symphonies, each with a choral ending to texts of revolutionary content, failed to strike fire but obtained a succès d'estime. His Fourth Symphony met so much opposition during rehearsals on account of its advanced harmonic idiom that Shostakovich decided to withdraw it from performance. It was not performed until a quarter of a century later.

With grim determination, Shostakovich embarked on yet another symphony, his Fifth. It proved to be his winning piece. Its first performance on November 21, 1937, by the Leningrad Philharmonic Symphony Orchestra, under the direction of the modernistically minded conductor Eugene Mravinsky, earned instant acclaim. As if obeying a common impulse, novelists, aviators, actors, and plain Soviet citizens rushed into print to express their admiration for the new work. Shostakovich himself issued a statement announcing that the inner meaning of the symphony was the dignity of an individual, and that the finale represented the triumph of man over the doubts and the tragedies reflected in the first three movements.

Like most of Shostakovich's symphonies, the Fifth Symphony contains four movements: Moderato, Allegretto, Largo, and Allegro non troppo. The first movement opens with an eloquent exordium in D minor, Beethovenlike in its sweeping power. A lyrical subject is introduced in a brooding episode. The tension mounts; a characteristic rhythmic figure of two rapid beats followed by a note of double value, a motto of many of Shostakovich's scores, imparts an air of dramatic expectation. The initial Beethovenlike theme is brought back in amplified orchestral sonorities in the recapitulation. The movement ends softly.

The Allegretto is an optimistic scherzo. The formal structure is cyclic, with regular recurrences of principal themes. There follows a slow movement, Largo. Here the melodic presentation is spacious and solemn. Climaxes are built by the process of deliberate accumulation of dynamic power, with a détente leading to a quiet coda. The Finale: Allegro non troppo, is charged with kinetic energy. Lyrical interludes provide expressive contrasts. Then the initial theme of the movement reappears in proclamatory fanfares in D major. The peroration is one of the most protracted endings in symphonic literature; tension is built by a relentless reiteration of strategic notes. In the final measures, the strings, reinforced by the piano, play dominant A in multilevel octaves 253 times, with bulging sonorities reaching a bursting point before coming to a stop on the tonic D in unison.

Symphony No. 7, Op. 60 ("Leningrad") (1941)

It was during the epochal siege of Leningrad that Shostakovich composed his Seventh Symphony, commonly known as the "Leningrad" Symphony. The score bears no such title, but it is dedicated to the city of Leningrad. It is cast in the key of C major, associated with simple courage, unambiguous purpose, and victory.

In October 1941 Shostakovich flew out of Leningrad over the enemy lines to the wartime Soviet capital Kuibishev on the Volga River. There, on December 27, 1941, he completed the fourth and last movement of the symphony. By that time, the personnel of the Bolshoi Theater Orchestra of Moscow were also in Kuibishev, and the work was performed there for the first time on March 1, 1942.

It is typical of Shostakovich that he can draw a grand symphonic design, panoramic in its dimensions and admittedly representational in its source of inspiration, and yet preserve classical form in all its purity and orthodoxy. Each of his symphonies has an explicit or implicit program, but all can be interpreted as works of absolute music. In this respect he follows Mahler, who also liked to assign philosophical or psychological connotations to his symphonies. Mahler often repudiated the programmatic subtitles that he had originally sanctioned. Shostakovich, too, insisted that his symphonies should be judged solely on their musical merit and not according to their subject matter.

The "Leningrad" Symphony opens with an energetic Allegretto. The melodic structure of the main subject is wide-spaced, with emphatic rhythmic suspensions. (Some musical analysts see in this broad intervallic scheme a symbolic allusion to the immensity—and therefore invincibility—of Russia.) A contrasting second subject, of a lyric nature, is introduced and in turn generates a pastoral twin melody. The mood is gentle and pacific—a prelude to disaster, and it is not long in coming. The tonality shifts from serene C major to the somber key of E-flat major, which in the color scheme of Rimsky-Korsakov, the teacher of Shostakovich's teachers, is associated with fortified cities and camps. An ominous drumbeat introduces a mechanical march tune, the menacing leitmotiv of the Nazi machine; soon another drum joins the parade, and yet another. The monstrous beat grows by simple accretion and instrumental amplification. The tune is repeated eleven times without alteration, and soon takes possession of the entire orchestra.

Unexpectedly, the Nazi machine runs into obstacles. A new song emerges powerfully from the depths; it is a Russian song, and it begins to undermine the Nazi tune, wrenching it out of shape and breaking it up. A fierce contrapuntal strife ensues; the drums still persevere in their mechanical beat, but the tide has turned. There is a tremendous accumulation of sounds, in which the tonic, the dominant and the subdominant are commingled in a pandiatonic complex. From this almost intolerable tension arises the main subject, but it is in a minor key. It grows and expels the musical enemy; at the end only broken fragments of the Nazi tune are audible among the debris.

Tchaikovsky's Overture "1812" comes to mind, for in that earlier patriotic piece, there was also a conflict between two warring melodies. It was unfortunate, from a musical standpoint, that Tchaikovsky was compelled to let the rather undistinguished czarist anthem conquer the inspiring "Marseillaise." In the Soviet version of the piece, the czarist hymn is replaced by the concluding chorus of Glinka's opera *A Life for the Czar* (which itself has been renamed *Ivan Susanin*, after its peasant hero).

It is interesting to note that the second half of the Nazi tune is nearly identical with the celebrated song "Then Go I to Maxim's," from Lehár's operetta *The Merry Widow*, very popular in Russia, and also beloved by Hitler, despite the non-Aryan extraction of its librettist. Could it be that Shostakovich unconsciously imitated this popular air? Bártok, who was slightly annoyed by the constant playing of Shostakovich's "Leningrad" Symphony on the radio as he lay ill in a New York hospital, incorporated the Lehár-Shostakovich fragment in the fourth movement of his Concerto for Orchestra, which he was composing at the time; he gave it to a cachinnating clarinet, and embellished it with sardonic trills.

The second movement of the "Leningrad" Symphony, Moderato, is an elegiac scherzo. It bears no thematic or dramatic relationship to the war, but serves as a nostalgic reflection of happy youth. The form of a scherzo is a favorite of Shostakovich; it appears in virtually all his instrumental works, as a playful interlude between the dramatic first movement and the ensuing meditative section.

Strange and foreboding inaction pervades the third movement, Adagio. Shostakovich confided to friends that in it he intended to portray his native city, Leningrad, enveloped in misty twilight, when its vistas, its river, its granite embankments are immobile and poetical in their northern stillness. The sound of the flute floats fleetingly over the surfaces of the attenuated orchestral accompaniment. Three strokes of the soft tam-tam announce the end of the nocturnal dream, and the advent of the decisive last movement, Allegro non troppo. Its main subject appears with great force, and almost immediately sprouts new melodies and motives, with sharpened rhythms and restless accents.

In such varied developments Shostakovich is a true symphonist. And since his symphony is a Russian work, the concentration and accumulation of thematic material inevitably assumes the shape of a temperamental Russian dance. Both musical and psychological considerations compel the insertion of a wistful episode; in the "Leningrad" Symphony it becomes a threnody for the fallen. The principal key is that of C minor, and it takes a series of chromatic ascensions before the major tonic is reached. Shostakovich has never been reticent in his proclamatory finales, and the "Leningrad" Symphony, by its very nature, demanded a total mobilization of trumpets, horns, and trombones. Curiously, C minor perseveres almost to the end, alternating and even combining with C major. The dissonant sonorities created by this superposition heighten the dramatic tension and enhance the effect of the victorious C-major apotheosis. The symphony ends in glory.

In the United States, a lively competition developed for its first American performance. Serge Koussevitzky of the Boston Symphony Orchestra, forgetting his long-standing opposition to the Soviet regime, proclaimed that Shostakovich was for the twentieth century what Beethoven was for the nineteenth, a fighter for liberty. As a Russian, he tried hard to play the work first, but was frustrated in his desire because of the exigencies of schedules, and lost out to Arturo Toscanini, who gave the first performance of the "Leningrad" Symphony at one of his summer concerts with the NBC Symphony Orchestra in July 1942. The score was microfilmed in Russia, and the precious capsule was sent by air to Persia, by automobile from Teheran to Cairo, from there to Casablanca, to Brazil, and finally to New York. More than sixty performances of the "Leningrad" Symphony were given in America alone during the season 1942–43. Not all the music critics were enthusiastic, but they unanimously paid their respect to Shostakovich as a patriotic symphonist. *Life* magazine remarked, tongue in cheek, that criticism of the work might endanger the war effort and undermine the crucial Russian alliance.

Shostakovich was thirty-four years old when he wrote the "Leningrad" Symphony. It was his *Eroica*. (Beethoven was not quite thirty-four when he completed the *Eroica*). Historically and aesthetically, the Leningrad Symphony is unique. No composer before Shostakovich had written a musical work depicting a still raging war, and no composer had ever attempted to describe a future victory in music with such power and conviction, at the time when his people were fighting for their very right to exist as a nation. No wonder then that the "Leningrad" Symphony became a symbol of the war effort, acquiring propaganda value in the most exalted sense of the word.

Music generated amid cataclysmic events seldom maintains its original impact. It was inevitable that the "Leningrad" Symphony should lose some of its overwhelming power, not because of the depreciation of its musical substance but because of the passage of historical time. What is remarkable is that it has endured, that it did not become a mere curiosity like Beethoven's *Wellington's Victory* and so many other ancient battle pieces. The "Leningrad" Symphony still remains a formidable accomplishment, a work of power and, to use Shostakovich's own favorite expression, spiritual beauty.

Symphony No. 10, Op. 93 (1953)

The Tenth Symphony follows the general lines of most of its predecessors. Shostakovich completed the score on October 27, 1953, and it had its first performances a few weeks later, on December 17, 1953, in Leningrad, and on December 28, 1953, in Moscow, both under the direction of Eugene Mravinsky.

The first movement, Moderato, establishes a contemplative mood at once in introspective wavelike figures in the lower strings. The tonality centers on E minor, and the principal time signature is $\frac{3}{4}$, which is maintained almost without shifts. The entire movement represents the steady growth of the subject until a fortissimo climax is reached. Then the melodic arch curves on its downward slope. In conformity with Shostakovich's concept of cyclic form, the movement comes to a close, returning to the original E-minor theme.

The second movement, Allegro, in $\frac{2}{4}$, is set in the key of B-flat minor, polar to the initial key of the work. The melodious theme recalls Soviet marching songs as cultivated by youth organizations. The snare drum punctuates the symmetric rhythm. Joyful fanfares are heard, but they are strangely chromatic. Again the cyclic form compels the music to return to its source, after an episode in an alien key.

The third movement, Allegretto, is a scherzo, set in the vicinity of C minor.

True to his musical credo, Shostakovich energetically reiterates the vigorous rhythmic beat. But there is something else in this movement that commands attention. The thematic four notes with which the scherzo begins are regrouped in the development, forming the configuration of the notes D, E-flat, C, B, which represents Shostakovich's monogram using the German spelling. This signature is an extraordinary projection for Shostakovich, whose extreme modesty rarely allowed him to inject personal references into his music.

In the scherzo, Shostakovich's monogram is so inconspicuous that it has to be searched for in order to be discovered. But in the finale, an andante followed by an Allegro, Shostakovich assigns it to the full brass section in fortississimo (*fff*). The Allegro has the familiar quality of the final movements in other symphonies by Shostakovich, a determined vital élan consonant with the Soviet ideas of youth and progress. His signature appears and reappears in the orchestra. In the end it forms a stretto in the kettledrums, a fantastically bold recourse. The coda is in flaming E major, the homonymous major key of the initial movement.

Symphony No. 11, Op. 103 ("The Year 1905") (1957)

The Eleventh Symphony is subtitled "The Year 1905." This was the year of the heroic but unsuccessful revolution against the czarist regime. Shostakovich wrote the symphony for the fortieth anniversary of the Bolshevik Revolution of 1917. It had its first performance in Moscow on October 30, 1957. Like most of his symphonies, the Eleventh Symphony is in four movements. Here, however, each movement is given a specific historical, topical, or symbolic title. The first movement, Adagio, is named "Palace Square." The music conveys the atmosphere of 1905 by interpolating chants from the ritual of the Russian Orthodox Church (Russia was a church state, and prayers were obligatory in schools and at official functions) and military bugle calls. In contrast to these czaristic sounds are heard strains from Revolutionary songs, particularly prison songs.

The second movement, called "January 9," is ominous in its associations. This was the day in 1905 when workers of St. Petersburg, then the capital of Russia, led by an unfrocked priest (who was later exposed as a double agent and executed by his former comrades), petitioned the czar for better living conditions but were met with rifle fire in front of the Winter Palace. The music derives from two contrasting subjects: that of the people, trustful, praying, demanding, and that of the brutal government authorities, unfeeling and automatic, somewhat akin to the Nazi theme in the "Leningrad" Symphony. A precipitous fugato leads to a dramatic denouement with trumpet calls and drumrolls illustrating the shooting down of the demonstrators. The melody of the revolutionary song "Boldly step forward!" appears momentarily, but is soon drowned in the intonations of horror and sorrow.

The third movement, "Eternal Memory," is a revolutionary requiem. It opens with a complete quotation from the song popular in Russia early in the century: "You fell the victims of a fateful struggle, martyrs of unstinted love for the people." The spirit of passive lament exemplified by this song gives way to the proclamation of revolutionary action. Ringing bells arouse the people to take arms against the oppressive power of the autocratic government.

The last movement, "Alarm," contains melodies of many revolutionary songs, among them the old mournful Polish song "Warszawianka," which was very popular in Russian revolutionary circles in 1905. These songs become part of a complex polyphonic web, accompanied by dramatic sounds of distant bells. The Eleventh Symphony pictures the story of a revolutionary defeat in 1905, but it also foretells the triumph in 1917.

Concerto No. 1 for Piano, Trumpet, and Strings, Op. 35 (1933)

The aesthetics of popular appeal is not an exact science, but it is possible to state the reasons for Shostakovich's unquestionable gift of musical communication. It lies in his uncompromising sincerity of expression, his lucidity of musical statement, his adroitness in building powerful climaxes, his natural talent for melody, and his rhythmic drive. With all this, Shostakovich speaks a musical idiom which is his own, readily recognizable, and universally understandable. Shostakovich was a profoundly national composer, yet he never borrowed actual Russian songs for themes of his music. His Russianism lies in the characteristic inflection of his melodic line, in the intervallic turns, and in the pulsating rhythms. Shostakovich adopts large panoramic forms and yet manages to keep the details in sharp relief. His range of dynamics reaches from effective fortissimo to the faintest pianissimo, and he makes a point of utilizing the highest and the lowest instrumental register. He contrasts the slow, drawn-out tempo of his adagios with the rapid-fire movement of his scherzos.

Shostakovich's First Piano Concerto, first performed by the composer with the Leningrad Philharmonic on October 15, 1933, is a characteristic work, embodying the satirical and the lyrical side of his nature. It is scored for piano, trumpet, and string orchestra. The lyrical element is derived from Russian city ballads, while the satiric passages reveal a virtuoso style, which in the piano part assumes at times a Czernylike aspect. The concerto ends in a remarkable succession of C-major chords in the extreme upper register of the piano keyboard, seconded by trumpet flourishes. The extraordinary effect produced by this ending on the audience is almost physiological in its impact. Shostakovich did not contrive such effects as a deliberate bid for applause, but neither did he recoil from applying a musical uppercut that may appear vulgar to the esoterically minded, but that is not alien to one who, like Shostakovich, had a healthy instinct for celebrating at the end of a good day's work.

Concerto for Violin and Orchestra, Op. 77 (1947–48)

In the world of contemporary music, Shostakovich occupied a position somewhat similar to that held by Sibelius at the turn of the century. Basically Shostakovich was a traditionalist. Most of his symphonies are cast in the classical four movements, and the construction of his musical phrases is remarkably uniform in its symmetry. The sense of tonality is strongly felt. What makes Shostakovich a distinctly twentieth-century figure is his freedom of handling these materials. Tonal melodies are apt to be diverted without the benefit of academic modulation. The stridently dissonant harmonies occasionally resulting from such usages seem natural. But Shostakovich does not pursue variety for variety's sake. He does not hesitate to resort to literal repetition when his sense of dramatic power demands it. The rhythmic pattern of an eighth note followed by two sixteenth notes is Shostakovich's musical monogram.

The Violin Concerto was first performed in Leningrad on October 29, 1955, with David Oistrakh, to whom the concerto is dedicated, as soloist. It is in four movements, each bearing a descriptive title: Nocturne, Scherzo, Passacaglia, and Burlesque. The Nocturne preserves the mood of tranquillity throughout. The basic key is A minor, but tonal digressions into neighboring keys, typical of Shostakovich, impart a sense of mobility, enhanced also by increased rhythmic frequency. The ending, in which the solo violin is muted, travels into the highest treble. The Scherzo is in the key of B-flat minor. It is characteristically lively and light in substance. Playful glissandos, favorite with Shostakovich in his writing for strings, further enliven the music.

In the Passacaglia, set in F minor, Shostakovich follows the classical form of thematic variation. What is unique in this movement is a long introduction for orchestra, and an even longer cadenza for unaccompanied violin solo. Without a transition, the Passacaglia merges into the Finale: Burlesque. The rhythmic formula of Shostakovich's favorite pattern in eighth notes and sixteenth notes provides the final impetus. The violin solo repeats the highest available E fifty-six times in rapid movement, leading to an ending in A major, in a classical affirmation of the basic key of the concerto.

VOCAL WORKS
The Nose, *Op. 15 (1927–28)*

The Nose, an opera written in the same period as the Second Symphony, belongs to the constructivist type of composition. Shostakovich had absorbed the lessons of contemporary German opera, and the technique of writing of Arnold Schoenberg, Ernst Krenek, Paul Hindemith, and Alban Berg. Operas and orchestral works by these Western masters were widely performed in Leningrad in the late 1920s, and Shostakovich had the opportunity to study their effect. For his text, he selected Gogol's fantastic tale of the nose that became detached from a customer's face in a barber's chair, and began to live an independent life as a petty government official. Here, Shostakovich revealed his flair for musical satire; all sorts of absurdities occur, interspersed with satirical darts at czarist bureaucracy. In the end, the nose resumes its rightful place, much to its owner's relief.

The score is a brilliant exercise in modernistic grotesquerie. Shostakovich introduced such novel effects as an orchestral sneeze, the imitation of the sound of shaving in double-bass harmonics, hiccups on the harp, and an octet of eight janitors singing eight different advertisements. The orchestra of the opera is small, but the percussion instruments are greatly increased in numbers and are featured in an interlude. The part of the nose itself is to be sung with the nostrils closed, to produce a nasal effect.

When *The Nose* was presented for the first time in Leningrad on January 13, 1930, the direction of the theater thought it prudent to announce it as an "experimental spectacle." It was greeted with great exhilaration among Soviet musicians, but received a chilly blast from the Kremlin; officious theater critics attacked it as a product of "bourgeois decadence," accused Shostakovich of imitating decadent Western models, and silenced the work's advocates, leading to its being quickly withdrawn from the stage.

Lady Macbeth of the District of Mtzensk, *Op. 29 (1930–32)*

Both satirical and dramatic elements find their expression in Shostakovich's opera *Lady Macbeth of the District of Mtzensk*, which he himself described as a "tragic satire." It was written between 1930 and 1932 and first produced in Leningrad on January 22, 1934. The book, taken from a short story by the nineteenth-century Russian writer Nikolai Leskov, portrays a strong-willed woman who, stifled in her ambition and seeking an outlet for her energies, poisons her merchant husband at the instigation of her lover; later, czarist justice leads to a murder-suicide in prison.

In the introduction to the program book of the opera, Shostakovich states his intention to treat the Russian Lady Macbeth as "a positive character, deserving the sympathy of the audience." Concerning the musical idiom of the opera, he writes:

> The musical development is projected on a symphonic plan, and in this respect my opera is not an imitation of old operas, built on separate numbers. The musical interludes between the scenes are continuations and developments of the preceding musical idea, and have an important bearing on the characterization of the events on the stage.

D. SHOSTAKOVICH
OP. 29/114
KATERINA IZMAILOVA

OPERA IN 4 ACTS, 9 SCENES
(REVISED EDITION, 1963)
LIBRETTO
BY A. PREISS AND D SHOSTAKOVICH
BASED ON N. LESKOV'S STORY
" LADY MACBETH
OF THE MTSENSK DISTRICT"
ENGLISH TRANSLATION BY E. DOWNES
SCORE
VOLUME I

ДЕЙСТВИЕ ПЕРВОЕ
Картина первая

ACT ONE
Scene One

Сад в доме Измайловых. В саду Катерина Львовна.
The garden of the Izmailovs' house. In the garden is
Katerina Lvovna.

★ Контрабасы играют без сурдин на протяжении всей оперы
The doublebasses are never muted throughout the whole opera

2162

The opera was extremely successful with audiences and was hailed by the press as the greatest achievement of Soviet operatic art. It was produced in New York at the Metropolitan Opera House on February 5, 1935, by the Cleveland Orchestra, Artur Rodzinski conducting. The spectacle made a sensation, and the audience included ranking members of the capitalistic set of New York City. The production was more realistic than in Russia, and many were scandalized by the symphonic interlude, with suggestive trombone glissandos as the lovers retire behind the curtains of a bedroom on the stage.

But what seemed the peak of Shostakovich's popular achievement nearly proved his artistic undoing. On January 28, 1936, *Pravda*, the organ of the Communist party, published an article condemning the opera and its tendencies and raised the question, fatal to a Soviet composer, as to whether the success of *Lady Macbeth* among bourgeois audiences abroad was not due to its confused and politically neutral ideology, and to the fact that it "tickled the perverted tastes of the bourgeois audience by its jittery, noisy, and neurotic music." The opera was accused of vulgar naturalism and aesthetic snobbism. The writer was outraged by the attempt to "solve all problems on the merchant's bed," and by the author's expressed sympathy with the murderous heroine. The article had a profound effect on Soviet musicians, and opened a series of discussions in which not only Shostakovich himself but also his erstwhile exegetes were attacked.

Song of the Forests, *Oratorio for Children's Choir, Mixed Choir, Soloists, and Orchestra, Op. 81 (1949)*

Throughout his tempestuous career, Shostakovich was repeatedly urged by the Soviet policy makers to write music in the manner of socialist realism. His *Song of the Forests* came very close to that elusive ideal. To some admirers of Shostakovich, it may also represent a rather grim excursion to Canossa. When *Song of the Forests* was performed in Moscow on November 6, 1949, several musicians commented frankly that Shostakovich had betrayed his great gifts by writing this score. The unbelievers were promptly castigated by the critic of *Sovietskaya Musica* as "myopic retrogrades and camouflaged formalists." And the critic commended Shostakovich for his "boldness and honesty in repudiating his former means of self-expression which would obstruct the realistic treatment of a great contemporary subject."

It is characteristic of the duality of Shostakovich's nature that a year after the composition of *Song of the Forests*, he should have written a set of Twenty-four Preludes and Fugues for Piano, Op. 87 (inspired by his visit to Leipzig for the Bach bicentennial), which are totally different in style from the harmonic simplicity and folk-like quality of *Song of the Forests*. Shostakovich was promptly berated by the editorial writer of *Sovietskaya Musica* for this "reversion to a neoclassical stylization which strives to recreate on an elaborate modernistic plane some mournfully subjectivist pages of Bach which are farthest removed from our world outlook."

The text of *Song of the Forests*, by the Soviet poet Eugene Dolmatovsky, illustrates the extraordinary combination of intense nationalism with the glorification of communism, a feature of the Soviet arts in general. Most revealing in this respect are the lines in which the words "the dawn of communism" (*zaria communisma*) rhyme, by an assonance, with "sacred fatherland" (*suyataya otchizna*). The subject of the oratorio is the reforestation campaign undertaken in Russia to repair the devastation of the war. There are seven movements, arranged in a fine contrast of tempo and mood. A motto theme appears in every movement. This theme bears a remarkable similarity to that of "Of Youth" from Mahler's *Song of the Earth*. Whether this is a coincidence or a subconscious tribute to Mahler, of whom Shostakovich was fond, is a matter of conjecture. Of course, after it gets going, the theme branches out into traditional melorhythmic patterns of Russian folk music.

The opening movement, descriptive of the end of the war and the advent of the "victorious spring," is the simplest in its melody and harmony. Yet even in this movement, Shostakovich allows himself a sudden modulation, from C major into E-flat major and back to C major, which smacks of essential modernism. The second movement is very Russian, with the typical melodic cadences effected by an upward leap from the subdominant to the tonic. The third movement, which evokes Old Russia, has an aria for bass solo that might have come from *Boris Godunov.* Despite this obvious derivation, the aria gives an impression of spontaneity and original inspiration. After all, Shostakovich is a talent of the first order, and even when he imitates others, he does honor to the source.

The fourth movement, descriptive of the planting of young trees by Soviet boys and girls, is musically the best of the entire oratorio. The muted trumpet theme, accompanied by a snare drum, that introduces the young planters is a first cousin of the second theme of the opening movement in Shostakovich's Seventh Symphony, even though the connotations of the two themes are diametrically opposite—young Soviet sprouts in *Song of the Forests* and the mechanized Nazi hordes in the Seventh Symphony. In this little fanfare, Shostakovich manages to create a mood of joyful work with remarkably simple means, by twisting the major third of the key into an augmented second. Then follows a gay children's chorus, with some acerbities that add spice to the simple folklike melody.

After this charming interlude, the music of the fifth movement, "Stalingraders Come Forward," relapses shockingly into unsophisticated vulgarity. The tune sounds very much like an incongruous replica of the march from *Aïda.* It is curious that the laudatory review of *Song of the Forests* in *Sovietskaya Musica* described this shabby tune as redolent of "the most characteristic intonations of the Soviet mass song." The sixth movement, "Tomorrow's Promenade," with its fine tenor aria, is lyric in mood. The motto theme reappears here in its original form, sung by the chorus without words. There follows an artful symphonic development.

The finale, in which all the combined musical forces take part, begins with a fugal introduction, and then proceeds according to the time-honored method of securing a rousing effect. Yet the music is not entirely undistinguished. Here and there are touches of the typical Shostakovich. The concluding chorus is a Soviet counterpart of the envoi of the biblical oratorio, "ad majorem Dei gloriam": "Glory be to the Leninist party! Glory to the people forever! To the wise Stalin—glory, glory!"

What is the moral to be drawn from this attempt of Shostakovich's to depart from his natural idiom in order to achieve a compromise with the temporal powers? *Song of the Forests* certainly cannot be dismissed as a worthless pastiche. This music, whatever its self-imposed limitations, is alive, and there are passages that are among the finest written by Shostakovich. Strangely enough, there are reminiscences in this work of such creations of Shostakovich's supposed formalistic past as the Cello Sonata of 1934 and the proscribed opera *Lady Macbeth of the District of Mtzensk.* Even when Shostakovich tries to repress his natural gift, he still comes out many notches higher than his orthodox Soviet contemporaries.

CHAMBER MUSIC
Quintet for Piano and String Quartet, Op. 57 (1940)

Shostakovich played the piano part in the first performance of the Quintet Op. 57 on November 23, 1940, at the Moscow Festival of Soviet Music. The reception was as favorable as that of his Fifth Symphony three years before, *Pravda* published an enthusiastic article:

After the grandiose vistas of the tragically tense Fifth Symphony with its philosophical search, this Quintet, lyrically lucid, human and simple, may be an intermezzo before a new monumental work, in which the great talent of Shostakovich may depict heroic figures of our era. One thing is beyond doubt: Shostakovich's Quintet is not written as a recreation; it is not a step aside; it is music created in full measure of power, it is a work that propels the art of music, opening new broad horizons ahead.... Shostakovich's Quintet is not only the most significant of his attainments; it is undoubtedly the best musical composition of the year 1940.

This is the same *Pravda* that in 1936 had delivered a vitriolic attack on Shostakovich for his opera *Lady Macbeth of the District of Mtzensk* (the charge was erotic naturalism in the stage treatment and leftist aberration in the music) and the ballet *The Limpid Stream* (in which Soviet life was said to have received a frivolous and oversimplified treatment).

In a statement to the Soviet news agency TASS, Shostakovich expressed his gratification at the reception of the Quintet Op. 57 in these words:

The year 1940 was a most significant year for me. In the summer of that year I composed my Quintet for Pianoforte and Strings. This work was very well received by the widest circles of Soviet audiences, and this means that my music is understood by the masses, that it satisfies their requirements. The knowledge of this gives me great joy, for there can be no greater satisfaction than to feel such close kinship with one's own people.

The quintet is in five movements. The first, entitled Prelude, opens with a slow introduction in the Beethoven manner, with a strong modal flavor redolent of the Russian folk song. The piano plays the opening measures, and is later joined by the string instruments. A scherzolike episode intervenes; then the original theme returns, in full sonority, ending on a G-major chord.

The second movement is a Fugue, almost school-like in its regular entries: the first violin, then the second, the cello, and the viola. But the melodic intervals are subtly changed, lending an unexpected modal quality to this most tonal of all musical forms. The movement is very slow, but there is an increase of tension when the theme, in double-quick time, is projected against itself at normal speed. After a short recitative in the piano, repeated in the cello, the themes are telescoped. The ending is peaceful and nostalgic in its aloofness from all motion.

The third movement is a Scherzo, in quick ¾ time, in a new key of B major. It is a typical perpetual motion in Shostakovich's favorite style, akin to a similar movement in the Cello Sonata. The dancing tune of the violin in the middle section has also had many relatives in other compositions of Shostakovich. And the fanfares of the ending remind us of the finale of his First Piano Concerto.

The fourth movement is an Intermezzo. From a slow and expressive beginning, it progresses toward a passionate climax, receding again into the calm of open harmonies in the conclusion. The Finale opens with a piano solo, in pianissimo. The movement is animated with a marchlike rhythm, but lyrical interludes are many. The first violin plays a long passage in staccato, which leads to a poetic coda in G major, pianissimo. There is a hint of the Russian folk song, as in the choral ending of *Lady Macbeth of the District of Mtzensk*, and in a similar conclusion of the Cello Sonata.

The familiar earmarks of Shostakovich's style are all in evidence in this quintet: the boisterous scale passages running off to an alien tonic; the contrasting use of extreme registers with the gaping distances of three octaves in unison writing; the meditative lyricism of slow sections; the stubborn repetition of blocked chords and single notes; the emphatic rhythmic beat. The harmonic structure is a compromise between the sanctified classical models and the modernity of the present century. Shostakovich handles this hybrid idiom in a masterly fashion.

String Quartet No. 4, Op. 83 (1949), and String Quartet No. 8, Op. 110 (1960)

Since string quartets are symphonies in miniature, it is natural that they should reflect Shostakovich's symphonic conceptions. Most of his symphonies and most of his string quartets are in four movements of a classical design; a supernumerary fifth movement is apt to be a cyclic summation. A rondo type of sonata form is a favorite of Shostakovich for the opening and concluding movements. A rapid scherzo is invariably present. What is quite extraordinary is his predilection for long-drawn slow sections. Only a composer supremely confident of his capacity to maintain the inner logic of musical expression can risk the peril of monotony in such extensive prolongations. Sibelius and Mahler knew how to handle the problem of slow movements, but did not escape sharp criticism when they seemed to falter. Shostakovich met similar criticism stoically; he calmly explained that quiet contemplation was an integral part of his musical philosophy, as powerful in its expression as the triumphant spirit of his famous symphonic codas.

Was Shostakovich a true modernist? He was attacked by the conservatives as a purveyor of cacophony, and by the radicals as a masticator of old Russian tunes. By the evidence of his music, neither description is just. Perhaps he was an Unmodernistic Modern, an International Russian. No contradiction in terms is involved here. Shostakovich made use of the modern dissonant idiom within the framework of tonality, but he emphatically rejects modernistic experimentation, including the kind he practiced himself in his youthful works. His music is profoundly Russian, but this Russianism is of an international quality, like the Russianism of Mussorgsky. His music is of the modern age but is rooted in the melodic and harmonic traditions of the immediate past; his appeal is universal but the resources of his inspiration are national.

The Fourth String Quartet, Op. 83, was written in 1949 and belongs to the period of consolidation of Shostakovich's stylistic habits. Like most of his instrumental compositions, it is in four movements: Allegretto, Andantino, Allegretto, and still another Allegretto. All three Allegrettos are predominantly in $\frac{4}{4}$ time, of four quarter notes to a bar; the slower movement, Andantino, is in $\frac{3}{4}$ time. The principal tonality is D major, the most convenient key for string instruments. In the very opening we are confronted with a phenomenon not observed in modern music since Bruckner and Mahler: deliberate and conscious repetition! Such repetition, typical of Shostakovich in its literal application, can be stultifying, but it can also be mesmeric. As in Bruckner, as in Mahler, so in Shostakovich, the mesmeric quality prevails.

The first movement of this quartet is built on a series of pedal points; the tonic D in the bass is sustained for sixty-four bars before it yields to a modulatory development. The main theme is gay and simple, but somber moods supervene; the ending is effected in a gradual dynamic softening. The Andantino is a lyrical waltz in F minor alternating with major keys; as in the first movement, the ending is soft. The third movement displays considerable variety. The principal theme is given out by the muted cello; it is a broad Russian melody sung against the steady rhythms in the other instrumental parts. The opening is in C minor; the ending is in C major; syncopated rhythms in repeated patterns enliven the contrasting middle section of the movement. The final Allegretto opens in C major in a direct link with the preceding movement, but its character is totally different; the motion is swifter, the rhythms are broader, and the pedal points more binding. There are interesting technical effects in the slides toward natural harmonic tones. The pedal point is established on the tonic D, and the ending comes in the gentlest tonal transparencies.

Shostakovich wrote his Eighth String Quartet, Op. 110, in 1960. Although it is in five movements, the concluding Largo is in effect an epilogue and a recapitulation of the opening Largo. The fourth movement is also a Largo; thus we have three very slow movements in a single work. Not even Mahler essayed such a design! The second movement is an Allegro molto, and the third an Allegretto, performing the function of a scherzo. The Eighth Quartet is practically monothematic; what is even more remarkable is that Shostakovich does not attempt to present the main theme in varied forms. Quite to the contrary, it is introduced bleakly and determinedly, like a subject in a Bach fugue; it resembles, in fact, rhythmically and melodically the subject of the fourth fugue of the first volume of the *Well-Tempered Clavier*. It rarely modulates, but is heard time and again through the entire quartet in its original key of C minor. Why? The riddle is easily solved.

The Eighth Quartet is an autobiographical work. Shostakovich's thematic signature D, Es, C, H, which appears here, is found also in the Tenth Symphony, written five years earlier than the quartet. Furthermore, the Eighth Quartet contains incidental melodic quotations from his First Symphony, written at the age of eighteen, and allusions to old Russian Revolutionary songs that he used in his programmatic Eleventh Symphony. The insistent repetition of these fragments, the slow cumulative rise of subsidiary contrapuntal voices, the systematic avoidance of contrasts, ought to create a feeling of musical frustration, even consternation, among the performers and the listeners. Instead, and contrary to all academic rules and admonitions, the total impression of this somber and solemn work is that of tragic consummation. Shostakovich has said that his Eighth Quartet is a personal dedication and a secular requiem for the victims of fascism. This explains the various thematic allusions. But no announced or implied programmatic intent, however noble, can elevate a composition above its intrinsic merit. It is the power of Shostakovich's music in this quartet that makes the listener accept the almost unacceptable persistence of thematic patterns, and only a master can exercise this power with such enormous effect.

Coda

When I met him in Leningrad in August 1935, Shostakovich was already a luminary of the first magnitude on the Russian horizon. The Intourist agency listed him among sightseeing attractions: "Come to the Soviet Union, see the Kremlin and hear Shostakovich." So I was eager to see Shostakovich.

One of the few remaining old-fashioned *izvostchiks* (buggy drivers) took me, for the sum of seven rubles, to Dmitrovsky Pereulok, No. 5, where Shostakovich lived with his widowed mother and his wife. I did not know which was his apartment, and there was no janitor of whom I could inquire. But suddenly I heard someone play the piano. It was an unusual sort of playing, and it was unusual music, rhythmic, simple in outline, but adorned with considerable dissonance. There could be no mistake; it was Shostakovich playing his own music. I ascended the stairs toward the source of that music, and soon found myself in front of a door on the third floor. I rang the bell. The door opened, and there was Shostakovich, a bespectacled young man, looking a little like a picture of Schubert. He led me to the studio, where a grand piano stood, and almost immediately plunged into a discussion of musical affairs in Russia and in America. On the piano I noticed the score of Stravinsky's *Symphony of Psalms*. Shostakovich told me that he admired the structural perfection of the work, and had even arranged it for four hands.

I observed that he was a very accurate sort of person. On the table there was a leather-bound book in which he noted the time of composition of each of his works, the year, month, and day, and sometimes the hour. There was nothing amateurish about the man. He was not given to temperamental outbursts, and was always glad to accept suggestions from his interlocutors, from his colleagues, from his correspondents.

After an hour or so of musical discussion, Shostakovich's mother announced that tea was served. We went to another room, not very spacious, but homelike, with flowerpots on the windowsill and a bird in a cage. Shostakovich introduced me to his wife. As I learned afterward, his mother was a musician, and a graduate of the St. Petersburg Conservatory in the piano department. She eagerly discussed her son's music, and wanted to know in detail what they thought of Shostakovich in America.

We returned to the studio. At the piano, I tried going over some of Shostakovich's preludes, which I was going to play in America. Then we went over the piano part of his Cello Sonata. There is one passage that sounds like exercises in scales, and I wanted to know how Shostakovich plays them, straightforwardly, or with humorous exaggeration. I was surprised to find that he was not a humorist by nature, and that the satirical strain in his music was not meant to be witty, but constructively critical of the subject. For instance, the scene at the police headquarters in *Lady Macbeth of the District of Mtzensk* was not intended to be grotesque, but served the purpose of exposing the rottenness of the regime of Czar Nicholas I. The celebrated polka from *The Golden Age* was originally a satire on the Disarmament Conference in Geneva. Shostakovich always considered himself a practical musician writing functional music, whether in satire or in glorification.

GLOSSARY

Absolute pitch. Ability to name instantly and without fail any note struck on the piano keyboard or played on an instrument. This is a rare, innate faculty, which appears in a musical child at a very early age, distinct from "relative pitch," common among all musicians, in which an interval is named in relation to a previously played note. Also known as "perfect pitch."

Accent. A stress.

Acciaccatura (It.) (ăht-chăh-kăh-toórăh). A note a second above, and struck with, the principal note and instantly released.

Adagio (It.) (ăh-dăh′jŏh). Slow, leisurely; a slow movement.

Ad libitum (Lat.) (ăhd li′bi-tŭm). A direction signifying that the performer's preferred tempo or expression may be employed; that a vocal or instrumental part may be left out.

Alla breve (It.). In modern music, two beats per measure with the half note carrying the beat; also called "cut time."

Allegretto (It.) (ăhl-lĕh-gret′tŏh). Quite lively; moderately fast.

Allegrissimo (It.) (ăhl-lĕh-gris′sē-mŏh). Very rapidly.

Allegro (It.) (ăh-lā′grŏh). Lively, brisk, rapid.

Alleluia. The Latin form of Hallelujah! (Praise the Lord!) as used in the Roman Catholic service.

Allemande (Fr.) (ăhl-l′mahn′d), **allemanda** (It.) (ăhl-lĕh-măhn′dăh). A lively German dance in ⅜ time.

Andante (It.) (ăhn-dăhn′tĕh). Going, moving; moderately slow tempo.

Andantino (It.) (ăhn-dăhn-tē′nŏh). A little slower than andante, but often used as if meaning a little faster.

Antiphonal. Responsive, alternating.

Appoggiatura (It.) (ăhp-pŏhd-jăh-too′răh). "Leaning" note; a grace note that takes the accent and part of the time value of the following principal note.

Arabesque. A type of fanciful pianoforte piece; ornamental passages accompanying or varying a theme.

Arco (It.). Bow. *Arco in giù*, down-bow; *arco in su*, up-bow.

Aria (It.) (ah′rē-ăh). An air, song, tune, melody.

Aria da capo (It.). Three-part form of operatic aria: principal section with main theme; contrasting section with second theme and key change; elaborated repeat of principal section.

Arietta (It.) (ăhrē-et′tăh), **ariette** (Fr.) (ah′rē-et′). A short air or song; a short aria.

Arpeggio (It.) (ar-ped′jŏh). Playing the tones of a chord in rapid, even succession.

Atonality. The absence of tonality; music in which the traditional tonal structures are abandoned and there is no key signature.

Attacca (It.). Begin what follows without pausing, or with a very short pause.

Augmentation. Doubling (or increasing) the time value of the notes of a theme or motive, often in imitative counterpoint.

Barcarole (Ger.). A vocal or instrumental piece imitating the song of the Venetian gondoliers.

Bel canto (It.) (bel kăhn′tŏh). The art of "beautiful song," as exemplified by eighteenth and nineteenth century Italian singers.

Binary. Dual; two-part.

Binary form. Movement founded on two principal themes, or divided into two distinct or contrasted sections.

Bitonality. Harmony in two different tonalities, as *C* major and *F* sharp major played simultaneously.

Bolero (Sp.). A Spanish national dance in ¾ time and lively tempo (*allegretto*), the dancer accompanying his steps with castanets.

Bourrèe (Fr.) (boo-rā′). A dance of French or Spanish origin in rapid tempo in ¾ or ⁴⁄₄ time.

Burlesque. A dramatic extravaganza, or farcical travesty of some serious subject, with more or less music.

Cacophony. A raucous conglomeration of sound.

Cadence. Rhythm; also, the close or ending of a phrase, section, or movement.

Cadenza (It.) (kăh-den′dzăh). An elaborate passage played or improvised by the solo instrument at the end of the first or last movement of a concerto.

Canon. Musical imitation in which two or more parts take up, in succession, the given subject note for note; the strictest form of musical imitation.

Cantabile (It.). "Singable"; in a singing or vocal style.

Cantata (It.) (kähn-tah′tăh). A vocal work with instrumental accompaniment.

Canzonetta (It.), **canzonet.** A solo song or part-song; a brief instrumental piece.

Capriccio (It.). An instrumental piece of free form, distinguished by originality in harmony and rhythm; a caprice.

Castrato (It.) (kăh-strah′tŏh). A castrated adult male singer with soprano or alto voice.

Celesta. Percussion instrument consisting of tuned steel bars connected to a keyboard.

Cembalo (It.) (chĕm′băh-lŏh). Harpsichord, pianoforte; in old times, a dulcimer.

Chaconne (Fr.) (shăh-kŏhn′). A Spanish dance; an instrumental set of variations over a ground bass, not over eight measures long and in slow ¾ time.

Chamber music. Vocal or instrumental music suitable for performance in a room or small hall.

Chansonette (Fr.). A short song of a light nature.

Chorale (kŏh-rahl′). A hymn tune of the German Protestant Church, or one similar in style.

Chorus. A company of singers; a composition sung by several singers; also, the refrain of a song.

Chromatic. Relating to tones foreign to a given key (scale) or chord; opposed to diatonic.

Clavecin (Fr.). A harpsichord.

Coda (It.) (kŏh′dăh). A "tail"; hence, a passage ending a movement.

Con brio (It.). "With noise" and gusto; spiritedly.

Concertante (It.). A concert piece; a composition for two or more solo voices or instruments with accompaniment by orchestra or organ, in which each solo part is in turn brought into prominence; a composition for two or more unaccompanied solo instruments in orchestral music.

Concertino (It.). A small concerto, scored for a small ensemble; the group of soloists in a concerto grosso.

Concerto (It.) (kŏhn-chăr′tŏh). An extended multi-movement composition for a solo instrument, usually with orchestra accompaniment and using (modified) sonata form.

Concerto grosso (It.) (kŏhn-chăr′tŏh grô′sŏh). An instrumental composition employing a small group of solo instruments against a larger group.

Con forza (It.). With force, forcibly.

Consonance. A combination of two or more tones, harmonious and pleasing, requiring no further progression.

Contralto (It.) (kŏhn-trăhl′tŏh). The deeper of the two main divisions of women's or boys' voices, the soprano being the higher; also called alto.

Contrapuntal. Pertaining to the art or practice of counterpoint.

Contrapuntist. One versed in the theory and practice of counterpoint.

Counterpoint. Polyphonic composition; the combination of two or more simultaneous melodies.

Countertenor. A male singer with an alto range.

Courante (Fr.) (koo-răhn′t), **coranto** (It.). An old French dance in ¾ time.

Crescendo (It.) (krĕh-shen′dŏh). Swelling, increasing in loudness.

Da capo (It.). From the beginning.

Development. The working out or evolution (elaboration) of a theme by presenting it in varied melodic, harmonic, or rhythmic treatment.

Diatonic. Employing the tones of the standard major or minor scale.

Diminished-seventh chord. A chord consisting of three conjunct minor thirds, outlining a diminished seventh between the top and bottom notes.

Diminuendo (It.) (dē-mē-noo-en′dŏh). Diminishing in loudness.

Diminution. The repetition or imitation of a theme in notes of smaller time value.

Dissonance. A combination of two or more tones requiring resolution.

Divertimento (It.) (dē-vâr-tē-men′tŏh), **divertissement** (Fr.) (dē-vâr-tēs-mahn′). A light and easy piece of instrumental music.

Dodecaphonic. Using the technique of modern composition in which the basic theme contains twelve different notes.

Dolce (It.). Sweet, soft, suave; a sweet-toned organ stop.

Dolcissimo (It.). Very sweetly, softly.

Dominant. The fifth tone in the major or minor scale; a chord based on that tone.

Double stop. In violin playing, to stop two strings together, thus obtaining two-part harmony.

Duple time. Double time; the number of beats to the measure is divisible by two.

Eighth note. A note equal to one-half of the duration of a quarter note.

Embellishment. Also called a grace; a vocal or instrumental ornament not essential to the melody or harmony of a composition.

Enharmonic. Differing in notation but alike in sound.

Entr'acte (Fr.). A light instrumental composition or short ballet for performance between acts.

Exposition. The opening of a sonata movement, in which the principal themes are presented for the first time.

Falsetto. The highest of the vocal registers.

Fandango (Sp.). A lively dance in triple time, for two dancers of opposite sex, who accompany themselves with castanets or tambourine.

Fantasia (It.) (făhn-tăh-zē′ăh), **Fantasie** (Ger.) (făhn-tä-zē′). An improvisation; an instrumental piece with free imitation in the seventeenth to eighteenth centuries; a piece free in form and more or less fantastic in character.

Finale (It.) (fē-nah′lĕh). The last movement in a sonata or symphony.

Fioritura (It.) (fē-ŏh-re-too′răh). An ornamental turn, flourish, or phrase, introduced into a melody.

Flautando (It.). A direction in violin music to play near the fingerboard so as to produce a somewhat "fluty" tone.

Forlane (Fr.). A lively Italian dance in § or ⅜ time.

Forte (It.) (fôhr′těh). Loud, strong.

Fortissimo (It.) (fôhr-tis′sē-mŏh). Extremely loud.

Fugato (It.) (fŏŏ-gah′tŏh). "In fugue style"; a passage or movement consisting of fugal imitations not worked out as a regular fugue.

Fugue (fewg). Contrapuntal imitation wherein a theme proposed by one part is taken up equally and successively by all participating parts.

Gamelan. A typical Indonesian orchestra, variously comprised of tuned gongs, chimes, drums, flutes, chordophones, xylophones, and small cymbals.

Gavotte (Fr.). A Gavot; an old French dance in strongly marked duple time (*alla breve*), beginning on the upbeat.

Gigue (Fr.) (zhig), **giga** (It.) (je-′găh). A jig.

Glissando (It.). A slide; a rapid scale. On bowed instruments, a flowing, unaccented execution of a passage. On the piano, a rapid scale effect obtained by sliding the thumb, or thumb and one finger, over the keys.

Glockenspiel (Ger.). A set of bells or steel bars, tuned diatonically and struck with a small hammer. Also, an organ stop having bells instead of pipes.

Grace note. A note of embellishment, usually written small.

Grandioso (It.). With grandeur; majestically, pompously, loftily.

Gregorian chant. A system of liturgical plainchant in the Christian Church, revised by Pope Gregory I for the Roman Catholic ritual.

Gruppetto or **gruppo** (It.). Formerly, a trill; now, a turn. Also, any "group" of grace notes.

Habanera (Sp.). A Cuban dance, in duple meter, characterized by dotted or syncopated rhythms.

Half note. A note one-half the value of a whole note.

Harmony. A musical combination of tones or chords; a composition's texture, as two-part or three-part harmony.

Heckelphone. A double-reed instrument somewhat misleadingly called the baritone oboe; gives out a rich, somewhat hollow sound.

Hocket, hoquet. Texture in which one voice stops and another comes in, sometimes in the middle of a word; a hiccup.

Improvisation. Offhand musical performance, extemporizing.

Interlude. An intermezzo; an instrumental strain or passage connecting the lines or stanzas of a hymn, etc.

Intermezzo (It.) (-med′zŏh). A light musical entertainment alternating with the acts of the early Italian tragedies; incidental music; a short movement connecting the main divisions of a symphony.

Interval. The difference in pitch between two tones.

Inversion. The transposition of one of the notes of an interval by an octave; chord position with lowest note other than root.

Key. The series of tones forming any given major or minor scale.

Key signature. The sharps or flats at the head of the staff.

Konzertstück (Ger.). A concert piece, or a short concerto in one movement and free form.

Krebsgang (Ger.) (krĕps′găhng). Literally, "crab walk"; a retrograde motion of a given theme or passage.

Ländler (Ger.). A slow waltz of South Germany and the Tyrol (whence the French name "Tyrolienne") in ¾ or ⅜ time.

Larghetto (It.) (lar-get′tŏh). The diminutive of largo, demanding a somewhat more rapid tempo.

Largo (It.) (lar′gŏh). Large, broad; a slow and stately movement.

Leitmotiv (Ger.) (līt′mŏh-tēf′). Leading motive; any striking musical motive (theme, phrase) characterizing one of the actors in a drama or an idea, emotion, or situation.

Lento (It.) (len′tŏh). Slow; calls for a tempo between andante and largo.

Libretto (It.) (lē-bret′tŏh). A "booklet"; the words of an opera, oratorio, etc.

Lydian mode. The church mode that corresponds to the scale from *F* to *F* on the white keys of the piano.

Madrigal. A vocal setting of a short lyric poem in three to eight parts.

Mediant. The third degree of the scale.

Melisma. A melodic ornament with more than one note to a syllable.

Melos (Gk.). The name bestowed by Wagner on the style of recitative employed in his later music dramas.

Meter, metre. In music, the symmetrical grouping of musical rhythms; in verse, the division into symmetrical lines.

Metronome. A double pendulum moved by clockwork and provided with a slider on a graduated scale marking beats per minute.

Minor. Latin word for "smaller," used in music in three different senses: 1. a *smaller* interval of a kind, as in minor second, minor third, minor sixth, minor seventh; 2. a key, as in *A* minor, or a scale, as in *A* minor scale; 3. a minor triad, consisting of a root, a minor third, and a perfect fifth above the root.

Minor ninth. A small interval between two notes.

Minor third. An interval of three half tones.

Minuetto (It.) (mē-noo-et′tŏh), **minuet.** An early French dance form.

Mode. A generic term applied to ancient Greek melodic progressions and to church scales established in the Middle Ages and codified in the system of Gregorian chant; any scalar pattern of intervals, either traditional to a culture or invented; the distinction between a major key (mode) and a minor key (mode).

Moderato (It.) (mŏh-dĕh-rah-tŏh). At a moderate tempo or rate of speed.

Modulation. Passage from one key into another.

Monodrama. A dramatic or musical presentation with a single performer.

Motive, motif (Fr.). A short phrase or figure used in development or imitation.

Musette (Fr.). A small oboe; a kind of bagpipe; also, a short piece imitating this bagpipe, with a drone bass; a reed stop on the organ.

Music drama. The original description of opera as it evolved in Florence early in the seventeenth century (dramma per musica).

Neoclassicism. A revival, in twentieth-century compositions, of eighteenth-century (or earlier) musical precepts, exemplified by many of the post-WWI works of both Stravinsky and Schoenberg.

Neumes. Signs used in the early Middle Ages to represent tones.

Nocturne (Fr.). A piece of a dreamily romantic or sentimental character, without fixed form.

Notation. The art of representing musical tones, and their modifications, by means of written characters.

Obbligato (It.) (ŏhb-blē-gah′tŏh). A concerted (and therefore essential) instrumental part.

Oboe (Ger.) (oh-boh′ĕ). An orchestral instrument with very reedy and penetrating though mild tone.

Oboe d'amore (It.). Literally, "oboe of love"; an oboe that sounds a minor third below the written notation; used in many old scores, and also in some modern revivals.

Octave. A series of eight consecutive diatonic tones; the interval between the first and the eighth.

Octet. A composition for eight voices or instruments.

Opéra bouffe (Fr.), **opera buffa** (It.). Light comic opera.

Operetta (It.), **opérette** (Fr.). A "little opera"; the poem is in anything but a serious vein; music is light and lively, often interrupted by dialogue.

Oratorio (It.) (ŏh-răh-tô′rē-ŏh). An extended multi-movement composition for vocal solos and chorus accompanied by orchestra or organ.

Orchestration. The art of writing music for performance by an orchestra; the science of combining, in an effective manner, the instruments constituting the orchestra.

Ornament. A grace, embellishment.

Ostinato (It.). Obstinate; in music, the incessant repetition of a theme with a varying contrapuntal accompaniment.

Overtone. Harmonic tone.

Overture. A musical introduction to an opera, oratorio, etc.

Pandiatonicism. A modern term for a system of diatonic harmony making use of all seven degrees of the scale in dissonant combinations.

Partita (It.) (par-tē′tăh). A suite.

Passacaglia (It.) (păhs-săh-cahl′yah). An old Italian dance in stately movement on a ground bass of four measures.

Pastoral. A scenic cantata representing pastoral life; an instrumental piece imitating in style and instrumentation rural and idyllic scenes.

Pedal point. A tone sustained in one part to harmonies executed in the other parts.

Pentatonic scale. A five-tone scale, usually that which avoids semitonic steps by skipping the fourth and seventh degrees in major and the second and sixth in minor.

Phrase. Half of an eight-measure period. Also, any short figure or passage complete in itself and unbroken in continuity.

Phrygian mode. A church mode corresponding to the scale from *E* to *E* on the white keys of the piano.

Pianissimo (It.) (pē-ăh-nēs′sē-mŏh). Very soft.

Piano (It.) (pē-ah′nŏh). Soft, softly.

Pianoforte (It.) (pē-ah′nŏh-fôr′tĕh). A stringed keyboard instrument with tones produced by hammers; a piano.

Pitch. The position of a tone in the musical scale.

Pizzicato (It.) (pit-sē-kah′tŏh). Pinched; plucked with the finger; a direction to play notes by plucking the strings.

Plagal mode. A church mode in which the final keynote is a fourth above the lowest tone of the mode.

Polka (Bohemian, *pulka*). A lively round dance in $\frac{2}{4}$ time, originating about 1830 as a peasant dance in Bohemia.

Polonaise (Fr.) (pŏh-lŏh-näz′). A dance of Polish origin, in $\frac{3}{4}$ time and moderate tempo.

Polyphonic. Consisting of two or more independently treated melodies; contrapuntal; capable of producing two or more tones at the same time, as the piano, harp, violin, xylophone.

Polyrhythm. The simultaneous occurrence of several different rhythms.

Polytonality. Simultaneous use of two or more different tonalities or keys.

Prelude. A musical introduction to a composition or drama.

Prestissimo (It.) (prĕh-stis′sē-mŏh). Very rapidly.

Presto (It.) (prâ′stŏh). Fast, rapid; faster than "allegro."

Program music. A class of instrumental compositions intended to represent distinct moods or phases of emotion, or to depict actual scenes or events; sometimes called "descriptive music," as opposed to "absolute music."

Progression. The advance from one tone to another (melodic) or one chord to another (harmonic).

Quarter note. One quarter of a whole note; equal to one beat in any time signature with a denominator of 4.

Quintet(te). A concerted instrumental composition for five performers; a composition, movement, or number, vocal or instrumental, in five parts; also, the performers as a group.

Range. The scale of all the tones a voice or instrument can produce, from the lowest to the highest; also called "compass."

Recapitulation. A return of the initial section of a movement in sonata form.

Recitative (res′īta-tēv′). Declamatory singing, free in tempo and rhythm.

Reprise (Fr.) (rŭ-prēz). A repeat; reentrance of a part or theme after a rest or pause.

Retrograde. Performing a melody backwards; a crab movement. Also, one of three standard techniques in twelve-note composition (retrograde, inversion, transposition) wherein all notes of a set are played in reverse (i.e., backward).

Retrograde inversion. A standard technique in twelve-note composition wherein all notes of a set are played in a reverse succession, which also mirrors the original set.

Rhapsody, rapsodie (Fr.) (răhp-sŏh-dē′). An instrumental fantasia on folk songs or on motives taken from primitive national music.

Ricercare (It.) (rē-châr-kăh′rĕh). Instrumental composition of the sixteenth and seventeenth centuries generally characterized by imitative treatment of the theme.

Rigaudon (Fr.), **rigadoon.** A lively French dance, generally in $\frac{4}{4}$ time, that consists of three or four reprises.

Ripieno (It.) (rēp′yä′nŏh). A part that reinforces the leading orchestral parts by doubling them or by filling in the harmony.

Ritornello (It.) (rē-tor-nel′lŏh), **ritornelle** (Fr.) (rē-toor-nel′). A repeat; in a concerto, the orchestral refrain.

Romanza (It.). A short romantic song or a solo instrumental piece.

Rondeau. A medieval French song with instrumental accompaniment, consisting of an aria and a choral refrain.

Rondo (It.) (rohn′dŏh′). An instrumental piece in which the leading theme is repeated, alternating with the others.

Roulade (Fr.) (roo-lähd′). A grace consisting of a run from one principal melody tone to another; a vocal or instrumental flourish.

Rubato (It.) (roo-bäh′tŏh). Prolonging prominent melody tones or chords.

Saltarella, -o (It.) (săhl-tăh-rel′hăh,-lŏh). A second division in many sixteenth-century dance tunes, in triple time; an Italian dance in $\frac{3}{4}$ or $\frac{6}{8}$ time.

Salto (It.) (săhl′tŏh). Leap; skip or cut.

Sarabande (Fr. (săh-răh′bahn′d), Ger. (săh-răh-băh-n′dĕ). A dance of Spanish or Oriental origin; the slowest movement in the suite.

Scale. The series of tones that form (a) any major or minor key (diatonic scale) or (b) the chromatic scale of successive semitonic steps. Also, the compass of a voice or instrument.

Scherzando (It.) (sk,r-tsăhn′dŏh). In a playful, sportive, toying manner; lightly, jestingly.

Scherzo (It.) (skâr′tsŏh). A joke, jest; an instrumental piece of a light, piquant, humorous character. Also, a vivacious movement in the symphony, with strongly marked rhythm and sharp and unexpected contrasts in both rhythm and harmony; usually the third movement.

Score. A systematic arrangement of the vocal or instrumental parts of a composition on separate staves one above the other.

Semitone. A half tone; the smallest interval in the Western scale.

Serenade. An instrumental composition imitating in style an "evening song," sung by a lover before his lady's window.

Sforzando, sforzato (It.) (sfŏhr-tsăhn′dŏh, sfŏhr-tsah′tŏh). A direction to perform the tone or chord with special stress, or marked and sudden emphasis.

Sinfonia (It.) (sin-fŏh-nē′ăh). A symphony; an opera overture.

Singspiel (Ger.) (zingk′shpēl). A type of eighteenth century German opera; usually light, and characterized by spoken interludes.

Sonata (It.) (sŏh-nah′tăh). An instrumental composition usually for a solo instrument or chamber ensemble, in three or four movements, contrasted in theme, tempo, meter, and mood.

Sonata form. Usually the procedure used for first movements of classical symphonies, sonatas, and chamber works; may be used for other movements as well.

Sonata-rondo form. A rondo-form movement in at least seven sections, where the central episode functions as a development section.

Sonatina (It.), **Sonatine** (Ger.). A short sonata in two or three (rarely four) movements, the first in the characteristic first-movement, i.e., sonata, form, abbreviated.

Soprano (It.). The highest class of the human voice; the female soprano, or treble, has a normal compass from c^1 to a^2.

Sostenuto (It.) (sŏh-stĕh-noo′tŏh). Sustained, prolonged; may also imply a tenuto, or a uniform rate of decreased speed.

Spinet (spin′et or spī-net′). An obsolete harpsichordlike instrument; a small modern piano.

Staccato (It.). Detached, separated; a style in which the notes played or sung are more or less abruptly disconnected.

Stop. That part of the organ mechanism that admits and "stops" the flow of wind into the pipes; on the violin, etc., the pressure of a finger on a string, to vary the latter's pitch; a *double stop* is when two or more strings are so pressed and sounded simultaneously; on the French horn, the partial closing of the bell by inserting the hand.

Stretto (It.) (stret′-tŏh, tăh). A division of a fugue in which subject and answer follow in such close succession as to overlap; a musical climax when thematic and rhythmic elements reach the saturation point.

String quartet. A composition for four stringed instruments, usually first and second violin, viola, and cello.

Subdominant. The tone below the dominant in a diatonic scale; the fourth degree.

Submediant. The third scale tone below the tonic; the sixth degree.

Suite (Fr.). A set or series of pieces in various (idealized) dance forms. The earlier suites have four chief divisions: the Allemande, Courante, Sarabande, and Gigue.

Supertonic. The second degree of a diatonic scale.

Symphonic poem. An extended orchestral composition which follows in its development the thread of a story or the ideas of a poem, repeating and interweaving its themes appropriately; it has no fixed form, nor has it set divisions like those of a symphony.

Symphony. An orchestral composition in from three to five distinct movements or divisions, each with its own theme(s) and development.

Syncopation. The shifting of accents from strong beat to weak beat or between beats.

Tam-tam. A large Eastern unpitched suspended gong struck with a felt-covered stick.

Tarantella (It.) (tăh-răhn-tel′lăh). A southern Italian dance in 6/8 time, the rate of speed gradually increasing; also, an instrumental piece in a very rapid tempo and bold and brilliant style.

Tema con variazioni (It.). Composition in which the principal theme is clearly and explicitly stated at the beginning and is then followed by a number of variations.

Tempo (It.) (tem′pŏh). Rate of speed, movement; time, measure.

Tempo primo (It.). At the original pace.

Ternary. Composed of, or progressing by, threes.

Ternary form. Rondo form; ABA form, such as the minuet and trio.

Tessitura (It.) (tes-sē-too′răh). The range covered by the main body of the tones of a given part, not including infrequent high or low tones.

Tetrachord. The interval of a perfect fourth; the four scale-tones contained in a perfect fourth.

Timbre (Fr.) (tăn′br). Tone color or quality.

Toccata (It.) (tŏhk-kah′tăh). A composition for organ or harpsichord (piano), free and bold in style.

Tonality. A cumulative concept that embraces all pertinent elements of tonal structure; a basic loyalty to tonal center.

Tone color. Quality of tone; timbre.

Tone poem. Also called "symphonic poem"; an extended orchestral composition that follows the thread of a story or the ideas of a poem.

Tone row. The fundamental subject in a twelve-tone composition.

Tonic. The keynote of a scale; the triad on the keynote (tonic chord).

Treble. Soprano. *Treble clef*: the G clef.

Tremolo (It.) (trâ′mŏh-lŏh). A quivering, fluttering; in singing, an unsteady tone.

Triad. A three-note chord composed of a given tone (the root), with its third and fifth in ascending order in the scale.

Trill. The even and rapid alternation of two tones a major or minor second apart.

Triplet. A group of three equal notes performed in the time of two of like value in the established rhythm.

Tritone. The interval of three whole tones.

Tutti (It.) (too′tē). The indication in a score that the entire orchestra or chorus is to enter.

Upbeat. The raising of the hand in beating time; an unaccented part of a measure.

Variations. Transformations of a theme by means of harmonic, rhythmic, and melodic changes and embellishments.

Violoncello (It.) (vē-ŏh-lŏhn-chel′-lŏh). A four-stringed bowed instrument familiarly called the cello.

Vivace (It.) (vē-vah′chĕh). Lively, animated, brisk.

Vivacissimo (It.). Very lively, *presto*.

Vivo (It.). Lively, spiritedly, briskly.

Voice. The singing voice; used as synonym for "part."

Whole tone. A major second.

Whole-tone scale. Scale consisting only of whole tones, lacking dominant and either major or minor triads; popularized by Debussy.

Woodwind. Wind instruments that use reeds, and the flute.